Coordination and Information

A National Bureau
of Economic Research
Conference Report

Coordination and Information

Historical Perspectives on the Organization of Enterprise

Edited by **Naomi R. Lamoreaux and Daniel M. G. Raff**

The University of Chicago Press

Chicago and London

NAOMI R. LAMOREAUX is professor of history at Brown University and a research associate of the National Bureau of Economic Research. DANIEL M. G. RAFF is associate professor of management at the Wharton School and a faculty research associate of the National Bureau of Economic Research.

The University of Chicago Press, Chicago 60637
The University of Chicago Press, Ltd., London

© 1995 by the National Bureau of Economic Research
All rights reserved. Published 1995
Printed in the United States of America
04 03 02 01 00 99 98 97 96 95   1 2 3 4 5
ISBN: 0-226-46820-8 (cloth)
      0-226-46821-6 (paper)

Library of Congress Cataloging-in-Publication Data

Coordination and information : historical perspectives on the
    organization of enterprise / edited by Naomi R. Lamoreaux and Daniel
    M. G. Raff.
        p.   cm.—(A National Bureau of Economic Research
    Conference report)
    Includes bibliographical references and indexes.
        1. Industrial organization (Economic theory)—Congresses.
    2. Business intelligence—Congresses. 3. Comparative organization—
    Congresses. 4. Industrial organization—History—Congresses.
    5. Industrial organization—United States—History—Congresses.
    I. Lamoreaux, Naomi R.   II. Raff, Daniel M. G.   III. Series:
    Conference report (National Bureau of Economic Research)
    HD2326.C66   1995
    338.7—dc20   94-41674
                                                               CIP

Contents

Introduction: History and Theory in Search of One Another

Naomi R. Lamoreaux and Daniel M. G. Raff

This book continues a project we and our colleague Peter Temin began with *Inside the Business Enterprise,* published in 1991. The title of that volume implicitly posed a question: What actually goes on inside firms? Both common sense and a rudimentary formal education in economics suggest the simple answer "entrepreneurs combine capital, labor, and raw materials." We argued that one cannot understand firms' internal structure and dynamics—and for that matter, firms' competitive dynamics—unless one also studies how firms handle information.

The various articles in *Inside the Business Enterprise* analyzed the ways in which firms collect information about production processes and customers and the problems that their (always imperfect) methods of data collection pose. The focus was the late nineteenth and early twentieth centuries, when firms of great size and organizational complexity first emerged in significant numbers. Daniel Raff and Peter Temin set the stage by providing an overview of the relevant economic theory on imperfect information and the internal organization of firms. The rest of the essays explored specific examples of how firms coped with information problems. Margaret Levenstein traced the development of cost-accounting techniques at a pioneering chemical giant, JoAnne Yates described the methods several large manufacturing firms adopted to handle their increased flow of information, and Naomi Lamoreaux showed how information problems shaped banks' lending policies. Bradford De Long

Naomi R. Lamoreaux is professor of history at Brown University and a research associate of the National Bureau of Economic Research. Daniel M. G. Raff is associate professor of management at the Wharton School and a faculty research fellow of the National Bureau of Economic Research.

The authors thank their collaborator in this series, Peter Temin, and, equally, John Sutton, Michael Enright, and Avner Grief for helpful conversations. Geoffrey Carliner and Martin Feldstein continued to give encouragement and support. The usual disclaimer applies.

argued that monitoring by financiers at J. P. Morgan improved the performance of the turn-of-the-century consolidations Morgan financed, whereas Thomas Johnson claimed that senior managers' misinterpretation and misuse of financial accounting information has in recent years generated serious inefficiencies in physical production and even product-line planning in large-scale enterprises.

The current volume extends the focus of the first by exploring ways in which firms coordinate economic activity in the face of asymmetric information—that is, information not equally available to all parties. In any economic activity more complex than Robinson Crusoe surviving alone on the beach, coordination is a vitally important task. The first fundamental theorem of welfare economics tells us that in an ideal world of complete information and perfect competition, the market provides the optimal coordination mechanism.[1] In our imperfect world of asymmetric information, however, the market does not always perform as well. Some activities are better coordinated within firms or other complex organizations, while other activities are better coordinated by firms cooperating among themselves. The problem is to determine the circumstances under which each form of coordination is likely to be superior.

We think of this second set of inquiries as digging more deeply rather than more broadly than those of the first volume. The first in effect presumed the firm as an institution, taking as given its organizational tasks, boundaries, priorities, and menu of control mechanisms. Here we try to question these explicitly. In so doing, however, we continue the approach of the first volume, exploring our issues and developing our themes in concrete institutional and historical detail. There are good reasons to proceed in such a manner. The abstract accounts favored by economists leave out much of the activity that goes on inside firms, and scholars studying how the economy works should not be ignorant in this area. More important, much of this activity is interesting when viewed from an economic perspective—that is, it has the potential to stimulate insights and productive theoretical questions.

Like its predecessor, the National Bureau of Economic Research conference that yielded this volume brought together both economists and business historians. Our motive in running the conference in this way (and equally in publishing the revised articles) is a feeling that the time is ripe for an exchange of ideas between economists and business historians. In recent years, economists have begun to move beyond black-box conceptions of the firm and to develop an elaborate body of theory that could in principle enhance work in business history. Business history has begun a complementary transit, moving beyond the idiosyncratic studies of individual firms and industries that long characterized the field. Seen from a distance, it seems clear that history and theory are now in search of one another. Our goal is to help the process along by encouraging economists and business historians to see one another as a natural audi-

---

1. For a lucid treatment, see Koopmans 1957.

ence and so, we hope, to stimulate each other to write better and more useful theory and history.

The Coordination of Economic Activity

The business historian most responsible for making this dialogue possible is, of course, Alfred D. Chandler, Jr. (see especially 1962, 1977, 1990). Chandler's key innovation was to place the problem of coordination squarely at the center of the study of business history. His focus was on why the economy came to be dominated by large firms. His method was to survey individual case studies and to analyze the traits of large panels of surviving firms. Chandler argued that managerial coordination was superior to coordination by the market wherever industries were characterized by "economies of speed"— that is, wherever consistently faster throughput reduced unit costs. In such industries, vertical integration (forward as well as backward) enabled firms to avoid supply bottlenecks and dispose smoothly of output if they could coordinate their various units effectively. Investment in the organizational capacity needed to manage vertically linked enterprises was thus the key to competitive success. Firms that did not make such investments lost ground. Those that made them first tended to establish very durable positions of market leadership.

At about the same time as Chandler was developing this argument, Oliver Williamson was beginning work on the transactions-cost view of the firm. Following Ronald Coase's classic but long-ignored work of the 1930s, Williamson asked why some activities were coordinated within firms and why some were coordinated by the market (Coase 1937). Coase had hypothesized that under certain circumstances internalizing transactions within firms reduced the cost of organizing and enforcing them through the market, and Williamson attempted to give this idea more concrete expression. For example, he proposed that firms emerged to manage investments with a great deal of "asset specificity," because otherwise the sunk character of the investments exposed their owners to threats that their profits might be expropriated (Williamson 1975, 1985).

Chandler's account of the evolution of large firms stimulated Williamson to recast it in terms of his own theoretical framework, and the subsequent development of his ideas clearly derived from and, equally important, influenced in turn those of Chandler (Williamson 1981, 1985; Chandler 1990). This was the first fruit of the newly possible collaboration between business history and economic theory. There are reasons to believe, moreover, that the harvests will only grow richer. In the first place, recent developments in economic theory will enable scholars to probe more deeply the coordination problems that Chandler highlighted. Moreover, many related issues remain largely unexplored.

Chandler focused attention on large firms' dependence on managerial coordination, but he actually had surprisingly little to say about how this coordination was achieved throughout the organization. Recent research in economics on principal-agent problems, however, has raised explicitly the question of how managerial hierarchies can be most efficiently structured and run.[2] At the heart of this literature are the observations that managers may have interests that differ from those of the owners of the firm, and that the latter may have only a limited ability to check up on what the former are doing. In theory, stockholders can invest in various monitoring mechanisms. They can also structure compensation systems to create incentives for managers to operate in their interests. The important questions, then, are which combinations of monitoring and incentive systems will function best in specific situations, and what the costs to the economy of relying on managerial coordination within very large firms are likely to be. The leveraged buyout movement of the 1980s certainly raised the possibility that such coordination has potentially substantial costs, and hence the question whether other forms of coordination might actually be superior.[3] There is also a growing body of literature arguing that certain solutions to the principal-agent problem commonly adopted by American firms have had the undesirable consequence of reducing flexibility and inhibiting innovation (see, e.g., Piore and Sabel 1984; Abernathy 1978).

Principal-agent analysis can be extended beyond the problem of stockholders' versus managers' interests to interactions among managers of different ranks and indeed to all employment relations within the firm, a subject to which Chandler devoted little attention despite the great deal of managerial time and energy it absorbs. The subject is important because it links up with larger concerns such as labor relations and the evolution of control systems within firms. Once again, recent history—in this case the competitive challenge posed by new industrial powers like Japan—has raised the possibility that the solutions adopted by large American firms have been less than optimal (Lazonick 1990, 1991).

The principal-agent approach is equally useful in considering firms' relations with those who supply them with capital, another topic given little attention in Chandler's books. Despite the financial reporting requirements mandated for public companies by the Securities and Exchange Commission Act of 1934, arm's-length suppliers of capital know vastly less about the operations and prospects of companies who are seeking their money than do the managers of the companies themselves. This asymmetry naturally affects the contractual terms on which investors are prepared to part with their funds and therefore the structure of the firms obtaining finance. It also has real consequences for the population of firms and ipso facto for the population of organizational institutions, particularly as firms' need for external finance varies over the

2. For a summary of much of this literature, see Milgrom and Roberts 1992.
3. For a polemical but rigorous analysis, see Jensen 1993. For a more colorful treatment, see Burroughs and Helyar 1990.

business cycle (Calomiris and Hubbard 1993). Firms whose organizations and affairs appear less transparent (and so less trust-inspiring) to banks and investors are more likely to be winnowed out during downswings.

Principal-agent theory has its critics, or course. The standard complaint lodged by historians is that it pays no attention to time or context. In part, this criticism is simply a confused reaction to the role of simplifying assumptions in economic theory: although the earliest models were very stripped-down indeed, this was largely a matter of expository style and not necessarily a feature of the insights they generated. Moreover, the historian critics should take heart from the way the economists' literature developed thereafter. Game-theoretic methods quickly gained ascendency, and that brought a new specificity to the analysis. Precisely what each actor knew at the moment of decision mattered. What each could credibly communicate and commit to mattered too. So did who moved when. But there was more. The first game theorists had sought unique equilibrium solutions to their problems. These would inevitably be independent of history. But as research advanced, it became clear that the games frequently possessed multiple possible equilibria.[4] Because only one outcome could actually happen, theorists needed to think about selection principles. Players' expectations came to be recognized as quite important, as did the history of relations between the players.[5] Time and context mattered after all.

The essays in this volume and its predecessor have much more in common with game theory in this later phase than they do with the early models that historians have criticized. But they are still much more oriented to questions of organization than to questions of development. There is, however, an emerging body of theory that focuses attention on developmental issues, particularly on how expectations and organizational routines lead over time to the creation of competences that are difficult for other firms to replicate.[6] Such competences contribute to the long-term sustainability of profits under conditions of product-market competition. The new theory promises a foundation for comparative historical work at the level both of firms and nations. We plan to assess its usefulness in subsequent work.

The Essays

The ideas about imperfect information and its consequences that we described above provided the impetus for the current volume. Although only some of the essays employ them, or even formal economic theory, in a direct or self-conscious way, all are motivated by questions growing out of this literature. They provide much detail on the organization of firms and markets that

---

4. The problem is even worse with repeated games, the most natural setting for formalizing the sort of issues we study.

5. The classic of this idea, though it first appeared well before the literature we are discussing here, is Schelling 1960. For a recent textbook treatment, see Kreps 1990.

6. Its roots lie in Nelson and Winter 1982. See, for example, Teece, Pisano, and Shuen 1994.

should be new to economists and historians. They also contribute collectively to the development of a more sophisticated view of economic coordination under conditions of imperfect information—particularly of the role played by large managerial firms.

Part I focuses on coordination problems within the firm. In the first essay Daniel Raff addresses employment relationships in the early-twentieth-century automobile industry. He shows that as technology changed—as the industry moved from artisanal production to Ford-style mass production—the value of coordinating the efforts of employees also changed and so did the compensation systems manufacturers employed. Under a system of artisanal production, with only minor complementarities between jobs, a decentralized system of task and effort management may well have been a profit-maximizing one. With increasing interdependence between and sometimes within work groups, however, the value of coordination grew. The central idea of the paper is that compensation systems are incentive systems and, as such, are useful to managers as instruments of control. With the new technology, the old instruments were expensive in their information-processing demands. The new compensation systems helped managers achieve their desired level of coordination through economizing on information processing in their task of aligning workers' incentives with managers' goals.

Daniel Nelson's essay offers a contrasting view of the diffusion of new coordination and compensation schemes within the firm. Whereas Raff emphasizes the importance of changing production techniques, Nelson argues that the coordination techniques employed by firms may be affected by broader intellectual movements and by the motives of the leading figures behind them. He links the rise and decline in the popularity of incentive pay schemes to the rise and decline of the industrial engineering movement. The article explains the spread of these schemes in terms of incentives for quick results built into the commercial relationships between industrial-engineering consultants and their client firms. The consultants advertised "a complete mental revolution," but they focused their efforts on changes that could be implemented promptly and would have observable consequences, a very different thing. Together, the Raff and Nelson papers encourage the reader to think about compensation systems as a part of a larger organizational design problem for the firm. They also raise the question of why radically new ideas and profound organizational innovations might, as they often do, actually diffuse quite slowly.

Nelson's article also raises the possibility that the conflicting ideas and interests of different managers within a firm might inhibit the adoption of innovative techniques. In the concluding essay of part I, Bernard Carlson uses the case of the Thomson-Houston Electric Company to argue that similar disagreements could prevent a firm's managerial hierarchy from functioning smoothly. Even when managers were all thoroughly committed to the success of the enterprise, their different perspectives within the firm gave rise to different visions of what policy should be—conflicts that had to be mediated for the firm to operate successfully. As Carlson shows, the history of a firm's institutions must be understood at least in part as the history of the comparative influence of these interests within the firm. The relative position of the contenders in one period affected the balance of power in the next. In other words, path dependency plays an inevitable and in fact highly salient role in such a history.

Part II extends the book's focus to the institutions that define the boundaries of firms and so to the location and porosity of those boundaries. Michael Enright's chapter is a contribution to the literature on alternatives to the large integrated firm. It shows that the markets-versus-firms distinction is far too simple. Related industries are often clustered near each other in a highly stable fashion, creating the informational conditions that permit vertically disintegrated firms to develop a variety of heterodox coordination mechanisms. Enright discusses three case studies and identifies the benefits in flexibility that can derive from alternative methods of coordination. He also points out the potential costs of such arrangements if investment in local alliances results in conservatism about change.

David Mowery turns the reader's attention from the coordination of work and production to the coordination of technical change. He explains in information-theoretic terms why large firms developed their own research laboratories rather than buying research from independent providers. He also points out that these facilities did not completely internalize the R&D function. Rather, labs provided firms with the capability they needed to engage in the information-intensive business of assessing technical developments in the external environment. Mowery argues that after World War II large firms increasingly turned within themselves and relied more exclusively on innovations generated by their own research organizations. This change, he suggests, was a response to government regulation rather than to strictly economic factors and may have negatively affected the pace of technical change.

Tony Freyer continues Mowery's point that the regulatory environment can have an important effect on the boundaries of firms and the institutional mechanisms that firms choose to coordinate their activities. He argues that the different paths that antitrust law took in the United States and Britain encouraged the development of large firms in the former nation but not in the latter. Tolerance for cartels in Britain permitted small firms to survive and prosper. By contrast, the more vigorous anticartel policies pursued by the U.S. government forced firms that engaged in anticompetitive practices to merge with each other and bring within their bounds all the elements they needed to coordinate the industry. Ironically, then, antitrust policy in the United States operated to stimulate the very concentrations of capital it originally aimed to prevent.

Part III explores problems of coordination in the financial markets. Kenneth Snowden shows that imperfect information posed severe problems for firms that attempted to coordinate interregional lending in the mortgage market. Although some kinds of organizations functioned more effectively than others, private solutions to information problems inevitably had a destabilizing effect under certain unfortunately recurrent conditions. Only government intervention solved the underlying problems of asymmetric information.

The final article in the volume, by Charles Calomiris, compares the role that banks in the United States and Germany played in economic development. Because of regulatory restrictions, Calomiris argues, banks in the United States took a form that was much less capable of solving the information problems (referred to above) that firms face when they seek external finance. As a result, the cost of capital was significantly higher in the United States, and a more restricted group of firms had access to the equity markets.

Conclusion

The aim of this volume is to highlight some of the complexities that need to be addressed in the analysis of economic coordination under conditions of imperfect information. As the contributors show, methods of coordination vary with production technique. They can also be affected by intellectual movements and by the activities of those movements' entrepreneurs. Bigness itself is not a guarantee of superior coordination, for large multifunction firms have unique coordination problems that have to be worked out. In some situations large firms function better if boundaries are porous. Moreover, in some situations small, vertically disintegrated firms have advantages over managerial hierarchies.

The contributors have also shown that regulation can have important consequences for the way economic activities are coordinated. Implausible as it may seem to some, regulation can sometimes have a positive effect. The interregional mortgage market depends upon it, for example. The information-oriented perspective developed in this volume helps explain why, and it also helps us understand how regulation can under different circumstances force firms to choose less effective coordination mechanisms. The cases of commercial banking and technical change are good examples.

The study of economic coordination has important practical implications, but these can only be uncovered and effectively developed with appropriate conceptual tool kits. Economists have recently improved the helpfulness of the available tools, but the possibilities are far from exhausted. Here business historians have a great deal to offer. We hope that they will be stimulated by recent theoretical developments to ask more cogent questions of their evidence and that their work will in turn stimulate economic theorists to develop more useful models. Only through such dialogue will we gain greater understanding of the logic and real-life dynamics of the allocation of economic activity within and among firms.

References

Abernathy, W. J. 1978. *The Productivity Dilemma: Roadblock to Innovation in the Automobile Industry.* Baltimore: Johns Hopkins University Press.

Burroughs, B., and J. Helyar. 1990. *Barbarians at the Gate: The Fall of RJR–Nabisco.* New York: Harper and Row.

Calomiris, C. W., and R. G. Hubbard. 1993. Internal Finance and Investment: Evidence from the Undistributed Profits Tax of 1936–1937. NBER Working Paper no. 4288. Cambridge, MA: National Bureau of Economic Research.

Chandler, A. D., Jr. 1962. *Strategy and Structure: Chapters in the History of the American Industrial Enterprise.* Cambridge: MIT Press.

——. 1977. *The Visible Hand: The Managerial Revolution in American Business.* Cambridge: Harvard University Press.

——. 1990. *Scale and Scope: The Dynamics of Industrial Capitalism.* Cambridge: Harvard University Press.

Coase, R. 1937. The Nature of the Firm. *Economica,* n.s., 4:386–405.

Jensen, M. 1993. The Modern Industrial Revolution, Exit, and the Failure of Internal Control Systems. *Journal of Finance* 48:831–80.

Koopmans, T. C. 1957. *Three Essays on the State of Economic Science.* New York: McGraw-Hill.

Kreps, D. 1990. *A Course in Microeconomic Theory.* Princeton: Princeton University Press.

Lazonick, W. H. 1990. *Competitive Advantage on the Shop Floor.* Cambridge: Harvard University Press.

——. 1991. *Business Organization and the Myth of the Market Economy.* New York: Cambridge University Press.

Milgrom, P., and J. Roberts. 1992. *Economics, Organization, and Management.* Englewood Cliffs, NJ: Prentice-Hall.

Nelson, R. R., and S. G. Winter. 1982. *An Evolutionary Theory of Economic Change.* Cambridge: Harvard University Press.

Piore, M. J., and C. F. Sabel. 1984. *The Second Industrial Divide: Possibilities for Prosperity.* New York: Basic Books.

Schelling, T. C. 1960. *The Strategy of Conflict.* Cambridge: Harvard University Press.

Teece, D. J., G. P. Pisano, and A. Shuen. 1994. Dynamic Capabilities and Strategic Management. Manuscript.

Temin, P., ed. 1991. *Inside the Business Enterprise: Historical Perspectives on the Use of Information.* Chicago: University of Chicago Press.

Williamson, O. E. 1975. *Markets and Hierarchies: Analysis and Antitrust Implications.* New York: Free Press.

——. 1981. The Modern Corporation: Origins, Evolution, Attributes. *Journal of Economic Literature* 19:1537–68.

——. 1985. *The Economic Institutions of Capitalism: Firms, Markets, and Relational Contracting.* New York: Free Press.

I   Within the Firm

1 The Puzzling Profusion of Compensation Systems in the Interwar Automobile Industry

Daniel M. G. Raff

1.1 Introduction

The American automobile industry employed a fantastic diversity of compensation systems to pay its blue-collar employees during the interwar period. Some employees were paid according to a linear piece rate—that is, they received a fixed fee per unit of output. Others were paid according to more complex piecewise linear systems in which the piece rate was constant at a relatively low value over an initial range of output and then increased sharply for one or even several higher ranges of output. There were also systems in which the piece rate rose continuously with output. There were nonlinear piece-rate systems in which the piece rate increased continuously with output but at a decreasing rate. There were nonlinear systems that were concave upward rather than downward, that is, in which the payment per piece increased at an increasing rate as output grew.[1] There were even more varieties of group incentive schemes. These involved the same set of formal relations between output and compensation, but the output in question was that of a group of workers. The

Daniel M. G. Raff is associate professor of management at the Wharton School and a faculty research fellow of the National Bureau of Economic Research.

The author owes thanks for stimulating conversations or comments over the years to Chris Argyris, Michael Beer, Steven Berry, Alfred Chandler, Donald Critchlow, Russell Eisenstat, Avner Grief, Naomi Lamoreaux, Margaret Levenstein, James Mirrlees, Daniel Nelson, John Sutton, Peter Temin, and, most particularly, to David Landes. He also learned from discussants and audiences at the Econometric Society and Business History Conference annual meetings, the Columbia University, University of Michigan, and Washington Area Economic History workshops, and Bengt Holmstrom's brown-bag seminar at the Yale School of Organization and Management. Naomi Lamoreaux and Walter Licht made detailed and helpful comments on the penultimate manuscript. The author's research has been supported by the Division of Research of the Harvard Business School and the National Science Foundation. The usual disclaimer applies.

1. Emerson [n.d.] surveys the basic varieties of individual compensation systems in use at the time. Helpful diagrams accompany the text.

sizes of these groups varied widely. And there was more heterogeneity still. At Ford, employees were—and had been for years—paid by the hour.

The infancy of the American automobile industry may be said to have ended in the winter of 1913–14 when the idea of mass production and the implications of Ford's $5 day burst upon the public consciousness. At the time, many journalists noted, Ford was the only firm in the industry paying its employees exclusively by time rates. Individual piece rates were by far the commonest means of remuneration. About a decade later, a study conducted by the U.S. Department of Labor's Bureau of Labor Statistics (1926) reported on compensation practices in ninety-nine establishments (whose employment was said to represent about one-third of the industry as observed in the census of manufacturers conducted two years previously). It showed nearly 40 percent of the establishments with some sort of bonus scheme in place. In some of these establishments, the bonus was based on individual performance. In some, it was based on the performance of groups. Which type of scheme predominated is not clear, but there had definitely been some movement to the group basis. A 1934 article on compensation systems by the Detroit editor of *Automotive Industries* makes it clear that by the early thirties group schemes had become dominant and even ubiquitous. The point of the article is that the whole of the assembly industry seemed to be in the midst of a shift to time rates.[2] The diversity of the midtwenties is thus striking, but it also appears as one stage in a longer sequence. By the 1920s, payment systems had evolved from very individualistic schemes to ones oriented predominantly toward medium-sized groups. In the next decade, the focus would continue to evolve toward very large groups, even entire factories.

How are we to understand these patterns? It is widely believed that the industry switched briskly over to mass-production methods when the $5 day brought reporters and photographers into the Ford factories. I argue below that this is false. Ford's production techniques actually diffused quite slowly. In the mid- and even late twenties, production technology remained heterogeneous. This is the key to understanding the contemporary diversity of compensation systems.

Compensation schemes can function as important mechanisms of control in factories in which production is carried out by many independent decision makers (that is, workers). Compensation systems offer workers incentives that help shape their decisions about how hard to work and how to allocate their effort and attention. Which compensation system is best for a given factory depends on how the work tasks of these decision makers are related to product performance and to one another, which in turn depends on the nature of the production technology. With some technologies, these tasks might be

---

2. Denham 1934. The author remarks, in passing, that "group bonus methods of worker compensation have never been as general in parts plants as in car factories" (703). I will come back to this remark below.

relatively independent. With others, they might be coupled together extremely tightly.

This general perspective suggests that compensation systems ought to evolve with the production technology (or, more precisely, with the production system) deployed. Similarly, the diversity of such schemes ought to be a function of the diversity of production systems. The midtwenties' heterogeneity of compensation systems was driven by heterogeneity in the organization of production. The convergence of predominant types of compensation systems over time basically reflected a convergence of approaches to organizing production in the population of automobile plants. There was relatively great variety in the production systems in place in the midtwenties. Ford-style mass production did not triumph until later.

This paper begins with a sketch of the technological history of the automobile industry and an analysis of the implications of this history for workforce control and compensation. I then show that Ford's ideas really did diffuse at a slow pace and that there was considerable variety in the production systems employed by automobile firms in the 1920s. Finally, I use anecdotal evidence and some formal tests to explore the relationship between the production system and the method of compensation employed. The test results confirm the main hypothesis, but there is some unexplained variation as well. The paper closes with a discussion of the significance of such unexplained variance in the history of economic institutions.

1.2   Mass Production and Compensation

In the early years of the industry, all cars were assembled on sawhorses in the center of a low-ceilinged room. Workers fetched parts from bins around the edges of this area. They kept their tools on or near workbenches running around the perimeter. Most of the work involving tools took place on the workbenches. The parts themselves were often irregular, requiring careful filing and fitting. Most of this filing and fitting went on away from the sawhorses. Anyone who wanted to observe the fit, worker or manager, had to be physically very close to the piece to do so.

Lighting in these work spaces was often poor. Sightlines were frequently physically obscured. Because it was difficult to monitor the pace of work, material inputs spent a lot of time sitting around under this system; and labor certainly spent a lot of time walking around. The extent to which the latter was appropriate or simply a means of working less hard was quite difficult for managers to judge.

The best compensation system in such a setting is a piece rate. The early production process was a highly decoupled system. Roughly speaking, extremely small groups of people assembled each car from start to finish. For any particular assembler, then, there were very few other assemblers whose work pace could constrain his own. Put slightly differently, the outputs of most individuals were close substitutes for one another. From the perspective of the owners of the company, more output was therefore unambiguously better, whoever it came from. Furthermore, the owners did not have much money tied up in physical capital in these factories. Most of their machinery was relatively inexpensive and general-purpose. The artisans owned many of their tools. The owners' main stake in the pace of production came from their ownership of materials and work in progress.

Ford perfected two improvements to this way of proceeding. The first of these, progressive assembly, made managing the chaos of the early shop floor much easier. Under this system, the men stayed put, and the parts and work flowed wherever they were needed. Monitoring and logistical control became much easier, and productivity increases were quite substantial. The Studebaker Corporation reorganized the layout of its automobile production facilities in 1913 to install progressive assembly. We can derive from its experience a rough rule of thumb of what shop-floor reorganization without any major capital investment might yield a competitive firm circa 1913, holding constant the degree of design complexity.[3] In this, the one example that has been documented, man-hours per car fell by about 47 percent.

This innovation coupled the work of assemblers far more tightly together. More precisely, it coupled tightly the work of all assemblers whose stations were not separated by buffer stocks. Within these groups, coordination of pace became much more valuable. This in turn increased the value of incentive systems that encouraged the workers to coordinate with one another. All other things equal, the optimal size of the group whose output should be measured would have grown.

Note, however, that this innovation by itself simply changed the layout of work. Job content remained, at least in principle, untouched. Controlling the expense of materials stocks had been rendered easier. But control over the flow of work itself remained elusive because the jobs remained highly artisanal. What more did the managers know, after all—and what more could they then control—about the work remaining? In the absence of other changes, the tasks themselves remained suitable only for highly skilled machinists working with a great deal of autonomy and exercising very great control over their time.

Ford's second essential innovation, which at Ford (but not at Studebaker and other firms) was apparently more or less simultaneous with the first, changed all this as well. Ford brought American-system production of parts—that is, production of parts standardized to such high tolerances that they were for all practical purposes interchangeable—into automobile manufacturing, and he did this on a more or less comprehensive basis. Suppliers were reluctant to dedicate their own capital equipment to making parts for a single customer

---

3. I have argued at length in Raff 1992 that the company did not begin to deploy American-system parts production on any substantial scale until the war years at the earliest. The shift to progressive assembly is the only important change in the production process going on during the period in question.

(see Helper 1991). The risks of holdup were too great.[4] If Ford wanted the investment, he had to do the bulk of it himself. The resources thus required from Ford for physical and organization capital were huge. But a direct consequence of committing them was that assembly, and most production jobs as well, could be completely routinized. The main effect was to allow central coordination and control of the work pace: the need for judgment, and with it the artisan's discretion, was banished from his shop floor forever.[5]

The deployment of the American system put much more shareholders' capital into the factories. Progressive assembly made the production system much more highly interconnected. Together these two changes increased the importance—to the owners of the capital—of actually keeping the equipment fully utilized and the output flowing smoothly. Workers executing their tasks in an uncoordinated fashion became potentially quite expensive, raising questions of control and compensation in an extremely salient form (Raff 1988). Ford's procedure was to pay time rates. Why precisely was this strategy wise?

The discussions of compensation systems one finds in the economics literature are not particularly helpful in resolving this question. The analyses come in two basic varieties. The first focuses on risk sharing between the firm and its employee; the other is directed toward the problem of getting differentially productive employees to identify themselves. The models in both theories are set up to focus attention on problems in the labor market and on decentralized incentives—the price system—as a solution. Firms need to undo as best they can a fundamental informational imperfection so as to get each worker to work as hard as he or she efficiently can and to enroll the most productive group of workers in the enterprise to begin with. In both cases, the basic underlying assumption is that the firm desires as much output as it can get from each and every worker. Both models put essentially all their emphasis on labor supply. In the name of analytic tractability, they ignore the imperatives of the production technology itself. Yet anyone who can visualize Charlie Chaplin on the assembly line will recognize that models such as these cannot help us understand what was going on at Ford.

The point of this intuition is that the assembly line is a setting in which all inputs and activities need to be precisely coordinated. In mass production of the assembly-line variety, uncoordinated increases in output are generally simply wasteful: they do nothing but increase work-in-process inventories and so tie up working capital. If the rate of production is high, this can be very expensive.

Theory appropriate to this setting would instead be written in the spirit of Martin Weitzman's famous paper "Prices versus Quantities" (1974). Weitzman's article is about the choice between decentralized (price-guided) systems

---

4. Klein, Crawford, and Alchian 1978. For the testimony of one supplier, see Sloan 1941.
5. It was this routinization and central control that allowed the efficient use of the expensive capital stock, the large-scale economies, and so forth. See Raff 1995, chap. 3.

of national resource allocation and central planning. The "peripheral units" of his article are factories. In the present setting, they would be the suppliers of effort and, through that, intermediate inputs into the automobile production process. Weitzman's central concern is the balance of costs and benefits in the peripheral units induced by two alternative schemes of telling them how to decide what to do. The first is the decision rule "expand production until marginal cost rises to some specified price," where in our case marginal cost is the marginal disutility of effort to the worker. The specified price is the piece rate he receives. Under the second decision rule, managers simply tell the effort suppliers what to do, paying them compensation based on obedience rather than on output per se. If workers keep the centrally determined pace, they are paid for their time. If not, they are fired.

The objective in Weitzman's model is to maximize the total net benefit, that is, profits. Weitzman shows that which control mode is best depends crucially upon the degree to which costs and benefits shift when output is not at just the desired level. When the level of marginal benefit is less sensitive to changes in quantities than is the level of marginal cost, it pays to focus attention on getting the cost side exactly right. The price-guided system is best for that. When the level of marginal benefit is more sensitive to changes in quantities than is the level of marginal cost, it pays to focus on the benefit side. A quantity-guided system is better for that. How was automobile production changing? The two most obvious examples may suffice to make the point. As production runs grew longer and new setups became less frequent, costs grew less sensitive. As the production process grew more tightly coupled and more employees and work in process had to stand idle whenever particular parts were, however temporarily, unavailable, benefits become more sensitive. In the progressive introduction of mass-production methods to the various production and sub-assembly processes and ultimately to final assembly itself at Ford, costs were becoming less sensitive and benefits were becoming more sensitive. The system was shifting in a direction favoring quantity controls.[6]

1.3   The Diffusion of Mass Production

Neither of the two central principles of the organization of mass production were original or distinctive to Ford. Progressive assembly was tried relatively early on at Studebaker, and the earliest attempts at truly interchangeable parts production in the automobile industry came well before the Model T.[7] But Ford

6. I should note that Weitzman (1974) speculates about this sort of situation without modeling it formally. But that task has been carried out in an unpublished Ph.D. thesis by one of his students, Gary Yohe. Technically, the question is what happens to the "coefficient of advantage" of, say, the price-setting mode over the quantity-setting mode when there are multiple producers of complementary goods and the degree of complementarity is rising. The answer comes down to a shift toward quantity setting. Montias 1976, 226, summarizes the argument.

7. On progressive assembly at Studebaker, see Raff 1992. The best example of interchangeable parts manufacturing is Ransom Olds' Curved Dash Oldsmobile of 1904. Raff 1992 discusses this in detail.

did innovate. Ford combined the two principles and deployed them relentlessly throughout the production system. Moreover, he used them to control centrally the pace of work so as to keep all fixed and quasi-fixed assets working at capacity.

How swiftly did the Ford system diffuse? The economist's intuition—prompted by all the attention the Highland Park plant received and by the attention paid to Henry's millions too—is probably "quickly." But an examination of the equipment in place in automobile plants during this period shows this intuition to be false.[8]

The most familiar outward sign of the system was conveyors. Moving assembly lines certainly were in place in a number of other firms by mid-1916. Articles in the trade press suggest that these were responsible for Ford-style quantity production, but there is good reason to doubt these claims.[9] Conveyors indicated only that the firm was using progressive assembly techniques, and we have seen that these could be deployed (and yield substantial savings) in the absence of American-system production. But the essence of the American system was the intensive use of purpose-built machine tools or general-purpose machine tools dedicated through the use of devices known as jigs and fixtures. Ford implemented the system through large-scale investment in precisely these sorts of machines and tools. Records from the Studebaker company, one of the handful of firms at which one might expect to find Ford methods if one could find them anywhere, indicate that Studebaker was certainly not investing in single-purpose machine tools on any serious scale.[10] Surviving records listing all major machine-tool purchases during the period 1913–16 indicate that the company was buying general-purpose tools.[11] For Studebaker to engage in American-system production, it would have to dedicate these tools using jigs

8. Confirming any sort of answer statistically is a difficult sort of exercise. There are no census statistics that could serve as even relatively unequivocal proxies. Company balance sheets of the day, when issued at all, are occasionally helpful (see below), but much more often they offer no useful information whatsoever. A single line item for "real estate, plant, and equipment" sheds little light on the particular patterns of capital investment suggested by a changeover to American-system production. The investigator is driven to articles about new developments in the trade journals and to surviving company archives for photographs, records of purchases of physical capital, and traces of discussions among knowledgeable managers.

9. For an example of the claims with some photographs and shop-floor diagrams, see "Conveyor System Aids Big Production," *Automobile,* 20 July 1916, 100–104.

10. One might expect to find Ford methods there because the Studebaker automobile operation had been run for some years by Walter Flanders, the engineering manager who came to automobile manufacturing from the Connecticut Valley gun trade (the seedbed of the American system) and who had brought progressive assembly to Ford. See Raff 1991a.

11. There are, of course, some exceptions. Page 5 of the *Studebaker News* for January 1915 gives a splendid photograph of one of them. But the records of the Finance Committee (which considered all capital investment proposals, down to $200 common machine tools) suggest that the company was investing only reluctantly in machinery. The minutes of the meeting of 2 September 1915 record that "[m]uch delay in production has occurred from old machinery breaking down. . . . The Production Department feel the importance of purchasing additional machinery to take the place of that which is antiquated, and also of adding to the present machinery new equipment as much as will be necessary from time to time to equip some of the proposed new buildings." The attitude toward investment at Ford was very different.

and fixtures. The telltale sign would therefore be substantial investment in these kinds of devices. but there is no evidence of such purchases in the records. Moreover, balance sheets for both Ford and Studebaker covering the year 1915 are sufficiently detailed to enable us to calculate the unit output per dollar of investment in such tools. The more Americanized the production, the higher this ratio should be. Ford used these tools roughly two-and-a-half times as intensively as Studebaker.

This is not to suggest that Studebaker failed to devote a good deal of time and energy to efficiency-enhancing improvements. Board and committee minutes for 1914 and 1915 are replete with references to shop-floor reorganizations (implementing, for example, progressive assembly and otherwise minimizing the excuses employees had to wander around the plant), attempts to plan plant workloads farther in advance, and the introduction of conveyor belts. But the general tenor is well summarized by the discussion concerning conveyor belts. The Finance Committee considered and approved putting in a number of them, including one for chassis. The advantages cited included eliminating five hundred men from the payroll (this was about one-seventh of their average monthly workforce in the Detroit operation that year) and lowering works and inventory expense as well as certain vaguely stated gains in flexibility. One official remarked that "[t]his runway and these conveyors will more than pay for themselves in the first year's labor savings." [12] The gains were admittedly substantial, but the point to emphasize is that this was labor saving, not labor control. It was certainly not mass production à la Ford.

Two vignettes fill in this portrait of pre–American system operations. The first concerns the reaction of Studebaker's directors to the $5 day. Finance Committee minutes describe this in considerable detail. All the members of the committee were close to their enterprise. Yet they could not fathom what Ford was up to. Minutes of the meeting of 19 January 1914, for example, include both false scents—"Ford . . . undoubtedly will have the pick of men"— and nervous reassurance—"It is believed in the city that his plan contravenes all economic laws and must in the end fail because of competition." Committee members were sure that the new measures would bring financial disaster to Ford's company. It is plain they had no idea where any increased productivity that might pay for them—and more—could come from. [13]

Indeed, when they decided later that winter that a considerable short-term increase in their own productivity was called for, centralized control was the farthest thing from their minds. The means they seized upon to increase output was to change their workers' compensation scheme to an extremely individualized incentive scheme: "In order to counteract the possibility of [labor] trouble

---

12. See the finance committee minutes for 19 January 1914. For shop-floor reorganization, see the minutes for 2 September. For advance planning, see 23 March.
13. Raff 1995, chap. 6, reconstructs the calculations Ford management seems to have done for itself on this point.

in our factory, and at the same time increase the production of the intervening months so that we will be best prepared for trouble if it comes, [our managers] feel it would be desirable to change our wage method to a piece rate system so that our men can make more money and at the same time turn out more product."[14] The vice president in charge of construction and engineering reported to the board of directors the following August that the company had "always believed an incentive wage system to be a very important factor in promoting efficiency."[15] The context makes plain that he was using the phrase "promoting efficiency" here to mean maximizing each individual's output. He went on to say that, having received the approval of the Finance Committee, he and his colleagues had instituted a piecework system in the production departments earlier in the fiscal year. He then devoted most of a page to statistics demonstrating how helpful this has been: one department's output had grown 66 percent, another's 141, another's 223. "The resulting condition," he concluded, "is one highly satisfactory to both employer and employee." This was not a factory in which the central principle was coordination.

David Hounshell suggests that the first large-scale implementation of Ford-style mass production came in the Chevrolet Division of the General Motors Corporation circa 1923 (1984, chap. 7; on the economics of this, see Raff 1991a). With the end of the war and the postwar depression, business prospects again looked expansive. GM had hired away Ford's senior production manager, William Knudsen. His first post was on the corporate staff. As Alfred P. Sloan's overall competitive plans became clear, however, Knudsen was given command of Chevrolet and told to start competing seriously with Ford.

Until this point, to judge from the trade journals and the researches of Alfred D. Chandler, Jr., there had been only two attempts at standardization at GM. When the Du Pont interests came in, they had attempted to integrate the accounting and control systems (Chandler and Salsbury 1971, 17). There had also been a direct effort after the war to cut down on the variety of screws and nuts on order, an exercise primarily in inventory control.[16] Now, however, GM began to focus on assembly.

Writing retrospectively in 1927, Knudsen detailed his steps (65–68). The company purchased new machine tools. "Sequence lines" were established to pave the way for the conveyors that were to follow. Gauges and indicators (to measure tolerances) were devised for all operations of importance. A decision was made simply to abandon all scrap work rather than redo it. Only then could volumes seriously be increased.[17]

14. Finance committee meeting of 9 February 1914. The labor trouble they feared was a return of the Wobblies, whose agitation had shut down their plants the previous spring for a period.

15. "Report of the Vice-President in Charge of Construction and Engineering," Secretary of the Corporation files, Supporting Matter for Minutes, Directors Meeting of 4 August 1914.

16. Baird 1923, 334–37. The two efforts were not unrelated, of course.

17. Indeed, we know that the interdependence went even further than these actions suggest. Raff 1991a gives the details. GM introduced a new model called the Pontiac in 1926. It was for

GM led the charge, but the rest of the industry ultimately followed. Perusal of the pages of the *American Machinist* for the decade of the twenties leaves a much more vivid impression of diffusion than does the analogous exercise a decade earlier. The installation of major conveyor operations is still news. But it is now nested among news of extraordinarily dedicated machine tools and complaints from machine-tool builders that the balance of demand ought to swing back in the other direction.[18] Chrysler's new Plymouth model in 1929 was obviously aimed at the economies as well as the markets pioneered by Ford and by Knudsen's Chevrolet.[19] The manuscript returns to the 1929 manufacturing census show the growing strength of the mass producers: the Big Three firms made two-thirds of the vehicles (Bresnahan and Raff 1991). On the other hand, the returns show signs of considerable and persistent heterogeneity as well: the Big Three may have made most of the output, but they operated only 26 percent of the establishments. The model product in 1929 was manufactured by mass-production methods, but the model factory did not use them. It took the Depression to kill off the artisanal enterprises and to establish the hegemony of mass production (Bresnahan and Raff 1993).

What happened to skill, autonomy and judgment, and the general idiosyncrasy of work tasks in automobile production as mass-production methods diffused? The number of firms manufacturing à la Ford had grown. Jobs in them were overwhelmingly routinized.[20] So too were the products, superficial differences and distinctions notwithstanding. Yet other enterprises operated, even opened, and flourished; and those establishments seem to have sold products that were often genuinely differentiated and that seem to have had a much higher skill content. The production runs were all much, and sometimes very much, shorter. Many of these firms produced for a clientele that valued handwork.[21] The rest had a clientele with needs sufficiently special that they had no choice.[22] The artisanal producers thus had a market niche. Elasticities of

---

practical purposes some odds and ends of new body panels, an Oldsmobile engine, and otherwise entirely parts from the current Chevrolet. The basic purpose of this strategy was to sell Chevrolet parts to persons who would not buy Chevrolet cars and by so doing enlist even these reluctant soldiers in the campaign to drive down Chevy unit costs. This enabled all the main Chevrolet supply plants to support even more corporate revenue.

18. On this latter point, see especially Heidey 1925 (a paper presented to a production meeting of the Society of Automotive Engineers). On the (postwar) timing of the great burst of machine-tool investment, see Pletz 1926.

19. The Pontiac strategy was also on Chrysler's mind. The company had one central engineering and design staff, not one for each brand as at GM. The next attempt at large-scale entry, Studebaker's unsuccessful one, had a similar strategy of common use of resources across product lines.

20. Babson's study focuses on the beliefs, attitudes, and actions of the remnant in the toolrooms.

21. Some of this handwork was visible, as in the body and interior. Some was invisible but could be felt: careful balancing of rotating parts was taken to great extremes at Packard, for example, and even today old-car buffs say of Packard engines that nickels can be balanced on them.

22. Thus, if the mass-production firms employed most of the people, then the typical employee in the industry could have a highly routinized job without the typical factory's doing highly routinized work.

substitution were low. At the margin, Ford and Chevy were not going to drive them out of business.

But the business cycle could. The change the Great Depression wrought on this heterogeneous population of firms and product/production strategies was a striking one. The cycle winnowed out the relatively artisanal producers, leaving the mass-production firms and those tending in that direction intact (Bresnahan and Raff 1993). Economists might be tempted to speculate that the mass-production firms survived because they had the lowest long-run average costs. Competition would drive out the less "efficient" competitors. But Bresnahan and Raff (1993) demonstrate that this was not in fact the selection mechanism at work. Jobs were simple at mass-production plants; training costs per worker were low; and abrupt scaling back in the face of slack demand was relatively easy. The artisanally organized cohort, in contrast, had major sunk costs in the indentification of personnel and the organization of production that it could not lightly reincur. It seems to have hung on to its workforce like grim death, ever hoping demand was about to return, until closure was the only alternative. Average practice changed through change in the population of firms as well as through changes in the practice of representative agents.

1.4   Production Methods and the Puzzling Profusion

We can now return to the subject of compensation systems and hope to test this technological explanation of their incidence. There are two sets of facts that require explication. The first is the heterogeneity of compensation schemes employed by auto manufacturers during the midtwenties crosssection. The second is the stylized time series, that is, the trend over time away from individual piece rates to group incentives to time rates.

There is certainly suggestive anecdotal evidence in support of the theory. Speeches by factory managers and their technical support staff to the annual production meetings of the Society of Automotive Engineers show actual decision makers addressing their colleagues on the subject of compensation systems and articulating precisely the germ of the logic advanced here. In the 1923 meetings, for example, the supervisor of time study at the Chandler Motor Car Company of Cleveland said straight out that manufacturing conditions, as well as the manufacturing processes in the departments of a large plant, vary considerably and cause entirely different problems to arise (Bouton 1923, 380–81). A single wage-incentive plan that would fit all departments in an automobile plant satisfactorily had yet, he asserted, to be evolved. Chandler had adopted the group piecework plan for the major assembly units and machining departments and straight individual piecework for small parts that involved one, two, or at most three steps to complete.

The following year an industrial engineer from Maxwell discussed imposing a particular group bonus scheme across many departments (Perkins 1924). He analyzed in detail one brilliant success and indicated that there had been crashing failures as well. He attributed the difference to a series of factors, the first in the list of which was (in the language of this paper) the organization of the production processes and the interrelationships between the work tasks in question.

Are these merely isolated instances? The firms are, of course, unknown today. One would like to test statistically whether compensation schemes varied systematically across departments or at least across firms using broadly different production techniques. Unfortunately, the Bureau of Labor Statistics reports cited above cannot be used for this purpose: the reports' authors guarded the identities of the plants and firms they described extremely carefully. Without knowing which was which, there is no hope of associating compensation systems with production strategies. This defect is worse in the widely cited studies of the National Industrial Conference Board, which provide even less detail about firms and their industries.[23] There is in fact no really satisfactory broadly based source of data. But the trade journal literature is of some use here.

An article in *Automotive Industries* for 1925 gives a small cross-sectional sample of the sort required (Shidle 1925). Twenty-one firms were included—some relatively large, some small, some parts suppliers, some solely assembly firms, and only three withholding their names. The article details the wage system used most extensively by each firm and lists other systems in place where applicable. Matching firms with systems reveals that relatively unintegrated and relatively artisanally organized firms (i.e., those making specialist parts or entire cars substantially by hand) employed relatively individualized compensation schemes. Other firms used more group-oriented schemes. The relationship is not without exceptions and the sample is small, but the basic pattern does seem clear.[24] The contingency table analysis summarized in table 1.1 indicates, moreover, that the pattern is statistically significant.[25]

This impression is strengthened by two glimpses of compensation practices within GM in 1927. At that time, GM used a variety of production systems in its plants. The first glimpse emerges from a survey of methods of payments and wage-setting protocols conducted for the members of the Special Conference Committee by its secretary, E. S. Cowdrick.[26] Cowdrick reported that hourly

23. The best of these is National Industrial Conference Board 1930. For a typical citation, see Nelson 1991.

24. This thrust is clearer once one understands that Packard, one of the exceptions, made efforts to routinize at least part of its production processes beginning in 1922, its advertising notwithstanding. See Parker 1949.

25. This is, strictly speaking, a test of the joint proposition that the claim is true and that the categories are the appropriate ones. The categories seem appropriate to me. But the test statistic should be interpreted cautiously. (Even if the test statistic were decisive, there still would remain the question of why the table shows any off-diagonal elements at all. This question of why there might be noise in the pattern is important and is discussed in section 1.5.)

26. For more on this extraordinary but shadowy organization, see Gitelman 1990 and the sources cited therein. A copy of "Methods of Wage Payments" can be seen at the Hagley Museum. Page citations are not given below, since the eccentric organization of the manuscript deprives them of any real usefulness.

Table 1.1   **Cross-Section of Motor-Vehicle-Industry Plants, 1925**

	Individualized Compensation Systems	Group-Based Systems
Relatively unintegrated production process	1	2
Relatively integrated	4	11

Note: The test statistic for this distribution is 45.64 $>>$ 5% critical F.

rates, individual piece rates, group and pool piece rates, and group bonuses were all being deployed somewhere in the company. Those responsible for choosing the schemes were relatively low level but themselves received performance-related pay, thus providing an incentive favoring the adoption of the most efficient schemes. The trend, Cowdrick wrote, was toward group bonuses.[27]

The rationale for group schemes was clearly stated by one of the interviewees: they "lessen the need for supervision, since it is in the interest of every man in a group to have every other man working at his maximum efficiency" while enabling management to set the standards so that the well-managed factory with satisfactory employees "can reach an average efficiency of from 108–110 percent [of a technical standard]. The actual average efficiency of the General Motors Corporation is not far from this figure." So the corporation was able to plan production relatively precisely and get the employees to monitor straightforward shirking as an extra. This was clearly an advantageous outcome in situations in which coordination was valuable.

Only one fragment of data on particular GM plants and systems survives, and it is strongly consistent with the analysis of this paper. Again, individualized compensation systems are coupled with relatively unintegrated production processes, and group-based compensation systems are coupled with relatively integrated processes. Table 1.2 gives the numbers. The pattern is statistically significant well beyond conventional confidence intervals.

The time-series pattern then runs as follows. Production organization within surviving firms shows a progressive tendency toward integration. Compensation practices show a progressive tendency away from individualized compensation schemes. The movement to straight time rates is a lurch, and it comes under the shadow of the National Industrial Recovery Act and the New Deal labor legislation—a regime change as sure and deep as Ford's once new idea, and in its implications quite similar.[28] The legislation made it much easier to organize assembly and parts plants, thus giving small groups greater ability to

27. It would be particularly interesting to know the history of compensation systems at Chevrolet. Research has not turned up any time-series evidence concerning this during the period of transition in the Chevrolet production system.

28. See "Johnson Warns Industry of Impending Wave of Strikes," *Automotive Industries,* 10 March 1934, 321, and, for example, "Drive to Unionize All Automotive Workers Seen in New Council Setup," *Automotive Industries,* 30 June 1934, 790.

Table 1.2   Cross-Section of GM Plants, 1927

	Individualized Compensation Systems	Group-Based Systems
Relatively unintegrated production process	6	2
Relatively integrated	0	20

Note: The test statistic for this distribution is 1266.03 $>>$ 5% critical F.

shut down the whole and so increasing management's incentive to view the whole system in unitary terms. While all this was going on, the Depression was, roughly speaking, wiping out the plants with relatively less routinized production systems (Bresnahan and Raff 1993). For both reasons, the attractions of decentralized motivation systems were markedly on the wane.

1.5   Patterns in Organizations and the Meaning of Unexplained Variance

The main conclusions I draw from this story and evidence are as follows. First, there was a microeconomic logic to these historical decisions and events. As the opportunity costs of particular ways of organizing production grew, manufacturers adopted new techniques. Mass-production methods changed the opportunity costs of uncoordinated workforce activity. They changed the structure of measurement and supervision costs. It should not be surprising to discover that administration methods in general, and compensation systems in particular, evolved and adapted to fit the circumstances in roughly the ways these changes would favor.[29] The data available to test this hypothesis are far sparser than is usual in empirical microeconomics late in the twentieth century. But they do support the story.

Second, the tools required to do very microeconomic history such as this need not be confined to models of black-box firms, perfect competition, complete and symmetric information, and continuous equilibrium, blown up from the textbook's page to the scale of historic plants and firms. The sort of history this paper develops is not rooted in any mystical a priori belief in the pervasiveness of markets and competition. This microhistory is nothing but a study of the evolution of microlevel facts, seen in a particularly orderly way. Efficiency—in the usual sense of the survival of only facilities and methods that minimize long-run average costs—is certainly not the only tale being told here. Artisanal firms continued to fill an important market niche long after Ford introduced mass production. They disappeared during the Great Depression

29. For an interindustry cross-section of data in the mid-1920s covering more than 500,000 employees, in which the incidence of time and piece rates can be statistically explained in this spirit, see Malcolmson 1992 and Lytle 1942, 57. For a more recent econometric exercise in this general spirit (though with a quite different model), see Goldin 1986.

not because they were inefficient but because the costs associated with holding together their skilled labor forces were too great to withstand the downturn in demand. Thus bottom-up labor history and marketing history as well probably have as much of a role to play as bare-bones neoclassical microeconomics in explaining why industries and production methods evolve as they do.

My third conclusion concerns that which thus far has been passed over in silence: the unexplained variance in regressions or in regressionlike tests and stories. Cross-sectional tests never, as a practical matter, end up explaining everything. More concretely, the explanation I have sketched above leaves unexplained why innovations in methods and administration diffuse slowly.[30] Such a gap in the argument might undermine its appeal. So I should say something about this in closing.[31]

Economists have traditionally identified firms with production possibilities—that is, with possible outputs.[32] Economists take the market for granted. This would strike any businessman as bizarrely abstracted. Businessmen organize production. They take finding "markets" to be a big part of their job. So they identify their enterprises not with outputs but with needs and with the resources and capabilities to meet them distinctively well. Businessmen thus identify the firm not with what they could purchase, turnkey, in competitive factor markets, but rather with what is either unique or developed through (collective) experience within their firms.

The relationship between these capabilities and the institutions and routines of organizational life is a close one. Firms and their employees make huge investments in these. (Some are firmwide rules, some are individual- or job-specific. Generally speaking, they could not be replicated through a manual, since an important part of them concerns what individuals should do when the manual does not say or is not to be believed.) These investments are in effect sunk costs. Aside from situations of crisis or true watershed opportunity, it is often easiest for individuals to continue to operate in the way they are used to than to undergo the sunk costs of learning a new way. This induces conservatism even in the face of opportunities that might be quite attractive were there no other alternatives.

Where the traditional economist's vision of organizational life makes one wonder why the take-up of innovations is slow, this vision suggests, if anything, the opposite problem. It has economic rationality at its core, but the composition overall is well leavened with culture, meanings, and the heavy

---

30. This paper has even presented a clear example, namely the compensation systems at Studebaker discussed in section 1.3 above.

31. See Raff 1991b for a (somewhat) better-worked-out version of these ideas. Nelson and Winter 1982 is in a similar spirit.

32. In recent years, real progress has been made in developing a deeper analysis that might explain actual organizational institution within firms. The key development was the recognition of how commonly economic actors even within an enterprise will be less well informed than the traditional theory allowed. See Raff and Temin 1992 for a nontechnical introduction and Holmstrom and Tirole 1989 for a lucid guide to the technical literature.

hand of history. Firms are not the sort of entities brought turnkey in competitive markets. They are complex organizations that develop over time as people in them respond to perceived needs and opportunities. That process often gives firms distinctive capabilities that can be a source of sustained abnormal profits. It also has a darker side. It can create resistance to change and adaptation as the firm may come to be, to its employees, a commitment to certain ways of doing things.

This being so, it is entirely possible that the evolving incidence of within-the-firm institutions one observes owes less to radically innovative ("heroic") managers than to the relatively mundane optimizing of operations, given the slow evolution of firm-specific resource bases and competences and given the evolution of competitive conditions in product markets. Economics thus has a role in illuminating the history of business. History has an equally central role in useful economics.

References

Baird, D. G. 1923. Eliminating Needless Cost and Confusion. *Industrial Management* 65:334–37.

Bouton, D. C. 1923. Wage-Incentive Systems. *Journal of the Society of Automotive Engineers* 13:380–83.

Bresnahan, T. F., and D. M. G. Raff. 1991. Intra-Industry Heterogeneity and the Great Depression: The American Motor Vehicle Industry, 1929–1935. *Journal of Economic History* 51:317–31.

———. 1993. Technological Heterogeneity, Adjustment Costs, and the Dynamics of Firm Shut-down Behavior: The American Motor Vehicle Industry in the Time of the Great Depression. Working Paper no. FB-93-09. New York: Columbia University Graduate School of Business.

Chandler, A. D., Jr., and S. Salsbury. 1971. *Pierre S. Dupont and the Making of the Modern Corporation.* New York: Harper and Row.

Denham, A. F. 1934. Day Rates Supplant Group Bonus. *Automotive Industries* 71:702–3.

Emerson, H. N.d. *A Comparative Study of Wage and Bonus Systems.* New York: Emerson Company.

Gitelman, H. M. 1990. The Special Conference Committee: Reality and Illusion in the Industrial Relations of the 1920s. Manuscript.

Goldin, C. D. 1986. Monitoring Costs, and Occupational Segregation by Sex. *Journal of Labor Economics* 4:1–27.

Heidey, R. M. 1925. The Machine Tool Needs of the Automobile Industry. *American Machinist* 63:533–35.

Helper, S. 1991. Strategies and Irreversibility in Supplier Relations: The Case of the U.S. Automobile Industry. *Business History Review* 64(4):781–824.

Holmstrom, B., and J. Tirole. 1989. The Theory of the Firm. In *Handbook of Industrial Organization,* ed. R. Schmalansee and R. Willig, 61–133. Amsterdam: North-Holland.

Hounshell, D. A. 1984. *From the American System to Mass Production: The Development of Manufacturing Technology in the United States.* Baltimore: Johns Hopkins University Press.

Klein, B., R. A. Crawford, and A. A. Alchian. 1978. Vertical Integration, Appropriable Rents, and the Competitive Contracting Process. *Journal of Law and Economics* 21:297–326.

Knudsen, W. S. 1927. For Economical Transportation. *Industrial Management* 76:6–68.

Lytle, C. W. 1942. *Wage Incentive Methods.* New York: Ronald Press.

Malcolmson, J. M. 1992. Contract Inefficiency, Wages, and Employment: An Assessment. Manuscript.

Montias, J. M. 1976. *The Structure of Economic Systems.* New Haven: Yale University Press.

National Industrial Conference Board. 1930. *Systems of Wage Payment.* New York: National Industrial Conference Board.

Nelson, D. 1991. *Masters to Managers: Historical and Comparative Perspectives on American Employers,* ed. S. M. Jacoby. New York: Columbia University Press.

Nelson, R. R., and S. Winter. 1982. *An Evolutionary Theory of Economic Change.* Cambridge: Harvard University Press.

Parker, J. 1949. A History of the Packard Motor Car Company. M.A. thesis, Wayne State University.

Perkins, H. G. 1924. The Group Wage-Payment Plan. *Journal of the Society of Automotive Engineers* 15:464–66.

Pletz, A. C. 1926. The Effect of Mass Production on Machine Tool Design. *American Machinist* 64:854.

Raff, D. M. G. 1988. Wage Determination Theory and the Five-dollar Day at Ford. *Journal of Economic History* 48(2):387–99.

———. 1991a. Making Cars and Making Money in the Interwar Period: Economies of Scale, Economies of Scope, and the Manufacturing That Stood behind the Marketing. *Business History Review* 65:721–53.

———. 1991b. Sunk Costs inside the Black Box: Why Organization Change Takes So Long and Is So Hard. Manuscript.

———. 1992. Studebaker and the Idea of Mass Production: Close Encounters of the First Kind and Their Quantitative Contribution to Productivity Growth. Manuscript.

———. 1995. *Buying the Peace: Wage Determination Theory, Mass Production, and the Five-Dollar Day at Ford.* Princeton: Princeton University Press.

Raff, D. M. G., and P. Temin. 1992. Business History and Recent Economic Theory: Imperfect Information, Incentives, and the Internal Organization of Firms. In *Inside the Business Enterprise: Historical Perspectives on the Use of Information,* ed. P. Temin, 7–35. Chicago: University of Chicago Press.

Shidle, N. G. 1925. How Industry Is Approaching the Wage Payment Problem. *Automotive Industries* 53:495–502.

Sloan, Alfred P., with Boyden Sparks. 1941. *Adventures of a White-Collar Man.* New York: Doubleday Doran.

U.S. Department of Labor. Bureau of Labor Statistics. 1926. *Wages and Hours of Labor in the Motor Vehicle Industry, 1925.* Bureau of Labor Statistics Bulletin no. 438. Washington, DC: GPO.

Weitzman, M. L. 1974. Prices versus Quantities. *Review of Economic Studies* 41:477–91.

Comment   Walter Licht

Daniel Raff's paper appeals to my historian's instincts. There is a simple message here: life is complicated, appreciate the details; or, more specifically, business is complicated, appreciate the details. Raff shows that the introduction of mass-production techniques in the American automobile industry in the first decades of the twentieth century formed a slow and staggered process. The implementation of systems to assemble cars on moving conveyors with highly standardized components that were also fashioned on an assembly-line basis occurred only in fits and starts. Car factories into the late 1920s remained complex entities with a variety of manufacturing regimes, and as a result, a vast array of worker compensation schemes prevailed.

Raff's paper makes many contributions. First, his essay accords with and supplements an expanding economic history literature that places great emphasis on the unevenness of American industrial development. Fully integrated, bureaucratically managed firms represented but one path toward industrial growth. Small-to-medium-sized, family-owned and -operated custom producers persisted alongside the new behemoths and added greatly to employment and the prosperity of the nation. There was money to be made through specialization, as well as through the achieving of economies of scale (and scope).

Similarly, scholars recently have shown that the vaunted American system of manufacturing was more myth than reality. True standardization in parts production—and the elimination of skilled-work assembly—did not occur in gun manufacturing in the 1810s, in the sewing machine industry in the 1870s, or, as Raff argues, in automobiles in the 1910s. Some have suggested that the technological wherewithal for precision-parts making had not yet been achieved; others, that there was insufficient demand for standardized products in a still parochialized American marketplace and thus there existed little pressure for greater technical development. Whatever slowed history, Raff succeeds, I believe, in bringing this story into the 1920s.

He also succeeds in raising an issue that, as far as I can tell, has received practically no attention from scholars—and that is the bizarre mix of formulas that existed to calculate the earnings of workers in American manufactories. Scholars have too glibly taken published wage or income data and assumed that they are straightforward reflections of labor supply, demand, and marginal productivity. Forays into company archives and perusal of payroll accounts reveal complicated, shifting, confusing, and unfortunately, too often, non-annotated calculations at work. Raff has made a contribution in bringing this to our attention, and I hope that his research stimulates investigation into the subject for other trades and time periods.

Raff's paper does raise a number of questions. The first concerns the Ford Motor Company. Ford figures strongly in the opening pages of the paper and

Walter Licht is professor of history at the University of Pennsylvania.

then disappears from view, with attention turned toward Studebaker and General Motors. Ford appears as an odd case here (actually, for business and labor historians, Ford for a variety of reasons has always been somewhat exceptional). Early in the paper, Raff notes that in 1913 the firm was the only one in the automobile industry compensating its workers through time rates (piece rates represented the norm). Later, he provides a quote that indicates that fifteen years later the company still paid by the hour and eschewed piece-rate systems (of any kind). This raises some questions for me. Because Ford still had a complex production regime, why did it not use varied compensation programs? Why was it exceptional? Ford remained heavily reliant on outside contractors for parts; purchased components represented more than 80 percent of the value of materials in Ford cars built in 1913 (Lewchuk 1989, 27). Does this or anything else help to explain the firm's uniform system of compensation?

A second issue relates to the main subject of the paper, that is, accounting for the varied compensation programs that existed in the automobile industry at least into the late 1920s (Raff does not deal with the entire interwar years as implied in the title). Raff rejects a number of possible answers and opts for diversity in production, and here I find myself entirely in agreement but desirous of greater specification. First, though, some thoughts about rejected explanations.

Raff rejects the notion that different kinds of firm endowments could be responsible for variations in payment schemes; that makes sense to me because variations within firms are as important as variations between firms. Second, he rejects emulation. A small army of industrial consultants were peddling their ideas at the time; although there was a great deal of dialogue and experimentation with labor arrangements because of this salesmanship—and I would not totally deny an influence—too many studies have convinced me that Frederick Winslow Taylor, his loyal and lapsed disciples, and his competitors rarely succeeded in getting their schemes accepted on a comprehensive or sustained basis. Practice was fashioned on the shop floor with and without fashionable ideas.

Raff, too, rejects agency on the part of a highly politicized workforce, but I would leave that possibility open for further research. Studies of the Ford Motor Company in England, for example, have found that piece rates were instituted largely at the behest of organized and militant workers who hoped to gain a modicum of shop-floor autonomy (Lewchuk 1989, 28–29). (This and the above statements on Taylor do raise a question about the implementation of payment schemes. Who were the chief architects? Top, middle, or lower-level managers? And were there inputs from below?)

Finally, although not explicitly stated, Raff does reject the role of whim in the profusion of compensation arrangements. There is a rationale for him in the profusion. If the "imperatives of the production system" is the key, however, I believe greater details should have been provided. If this was a rational process, one might expect different compensation systems to have emerged from different sites in the overall production process. Were pattern makers, core makers, and molders in foundry areas, for example, paid by time because of the uncertainties in the casting process? Were drill-press and lathe operators, on the other hand, paid by the piece (with or without bonus incentives)? Were axle assemblers paid on a group piece rate and magneto assemblers on a group or individual-time basis? Were all final assemblers compensated by group piece or time rates? A host of examples can be rendered. If, in fact, diversity of unroutinized tasks led to diversity in compensation programs, then the actual links should be drawn (of course, if documentation permits).

Raff's paper raises for me another set of questions regarding events after the 1920s. Raff actually isolates two developments: the move toward group-based systems of compensation and the shift toward time-rate payments (although Ford remained consistent here).

On the emergence of group-based compensation, Raff argues that the true implementation of mass-production techniques allowed for this, that is, the institution of progressive assembly in all aspects of production (parts manufacture as well as sub- and final assembly) and the use of highly standardized components (made with single-purpose tools and machines). Greater routinization then leads away from individualized compensation schemes. I accept Raff's tables showing a relationship between integration and group-based compensation systems, but I am not convinced of the explanation. The new General Motors' plants of the late 1920s may have approached the ideal of mass production, for example, but they remained, and actually became more, complex entities. The diversified product lines pushed by Alfred Sloan led to frequent shifts in production, and as a result the firm moved away from single-purpose tools not quite to full all-purpose ones, but to what were termed "semispecial" (Meyer 1989, 75–76, 82–83). I do not necessarily see a more homogeneous situation appearing and would expect continued diversity of compensation schemes. Are there other developments at work here leading to unified group-based systems of compensation? What of the role ultimately of unionization?

As to the general move to time-rate methods of payment, the explanation rendered by Raff also seems cloudy. He mentions that New Deal legislation and regulations played a part. But how important a role? Greater elaboration was necessary here. This aspect of the story might force qualification of Raff's overall argument.

I would like to conclude with a few comments on thoughts expressed by Raff at the end of his paper on the tense relationship that exists between economists and historians. I am one of a small group of historians who have taken as their subject of inquiry the organization of work and labor markets in the past. We have tried to bridge gaps that prevail between labor, business, and economic historians, labor economists, and students of industrial relations.

To date there has been a mixed dialogue between those scholars who share a common interest in what can broadly be labeled the labor process. There has been no cross-fertilization between labor historians and business historians, for example; for reasons I do not quite understand, business historians have shown little interest in the so-called personnel function. Dialogue between labor historians and students of industrial relations has always existed—John Commons is a common discipline-founding father—and there has been some and remains great potential for exchange between labor historians and labor economists. Labor historians can use all the help they can get with theory and methods to aid in the interpretation of their findings. And I am struck by the number of economic historians and labor economists who have moved toward historical labor study (Claudia Goldin, Gavin Wright, Richard Sutch, and Michael Piore, to mention a few).

I believe, though, that if a wider exchange is to occur, tolerance will be in order, and here I can circle back to Raff's paper. He has focused on some messy details—the stuff of history—and specifically, the complex compensation systems that existed in the automobile industry. That complexity should give pause to easy theorizing about wages. Raff does theorize, though, about developments, but developments that are not readily translated into supply and demand models or regression equations (I will note here the simple contingency tables that he provides).

Good relations between scholars can occur if (labor) historians open themselves to unfamiliar language and ways of conceptualizing and economists leave themselves open to be excited by the particulars (or the "heavy hand of history" as Raff calls it). While I have criticized Raff here for not providing ample specifics, I will conclude by applauding his great respect and appreciation for the details.

References

Lewchuk, W. 1989. Fordism and the Moving Assembly Line: The British and American Experience, 1895–1930. In *On the Line: Essays in the History of Auto Work,* ed. N. Lichtenstein and S. Meyer. Urbana: University of Illinois Press.

Meyer, S. 1989. The Persistence of Fordism: Workers and Technology in the American Automobile Industry, 1900–1960. In *On the Line: Essays in the History of Auto Work,* ed. N. Lichtenstein and S. Meyer. Urbana: University of Illinois Press.

2 Industrial Engineering and the Industrial Enterprise, 1890–1940

Daniel Nelson

The growth of industry during the last quarter of the nineteenth century inspired one of the most influential efforts to promote the coordination of economic activity: the industrial engineering movement of the early twentieth century. Although railroads had devised elaborate methods of internal communications and record keeping by midcentury, the late-nineteenth-century factory remained a loosely organized cluster of operations. Coordination depended on the leadership of plant executives and personal relationships between supervisors. Indeed, the distinguishing feature of factory management was the conspicuous role of the first-line supervisor; foremen organized materials and labor, directed machine operations, recorded costs, hired and fired employees, and presided over a largely autonomous empire. In the 1870s and 1880s, however, critics began to attack the "chaotic" condition of contemporary industry and to propose a more systematic, centralized approach to production management. Their critique became the basis for the best-known effort to encourage coordination within the firm during the first half of the twentieth century. Under various labels—systematic management, scientific management, efficiency engineering, and, by the 1920s, industrial engineering—it fostered greater sensitivity to the manager's role in production and greater diversity in industrial practice, as managers selectively implemented ideas and techniques.

2.1 Systematic and Scientific Management

The attack on traditional management originated in two late-nineteenth-century developments (see Nelson 1992a, 6–9). The first was the maturation of the engineering profession, whose advocates sought an identity based on

Daniel Nelson is professor of history at the University of Akron.

formal education and mutually accepted standards of behavior and who rejected empiricism for scientific experimentation and analysis. The second development, closely related, was the rise of systematic management, an effort among engineers and sympathizers to substitute system for the informal methods that had evolved with the factory system. Systematic management was a rebellion against tradition, empiricism, and the assumption that common sense, personal relationships, and craft knowledge were sufficient to run a factory. The revisionists' answer was to replace traditional managers with engineers and to substitute managerial systems for guesswork and ad hoc evaluations.

By the late 1880s, cost accounting systems, methods for planning and scheduling production and organizing materials, and incentive wage plans were staples of a burgeoning literature of industrial management. Their objective was an unimpeded flow of materials and information. In human terms, systematic management sought to transfer power from the first-line supervisor to the plant manager and to force all employees to pay greater attention to the manager's goals. Most threatening to the status quo, it promoted decisions based on performance rather than on personal qualities and associations (see Yates 1989, 1991; Levenstein 1991).

In the 1890s, an ambitious young inventor, manager, and consultant, Frederick Winslow Taylor, became the most vigorous and successful proponent of systematic management. As a consultant, he introduced accounting systems that permitted managers to use operating records to guide their actions, production-control systems that allowed managers to know more precisely what was happening on the shop floor, piece-rate systems that encouraged workers to follow orders and instructions, and various related measures. In 1895, he employed a colleague, Sanford E. Thompson, to help him determine the optimum time to perform industrial tasks; their goal was to compute, by rigorous study of the worker's movements and the timing of those movements with stopwatches, standards for skilled occupations that could be published and sold to employers. Between 1898 and 1901, as a consultant to the Bethlehem Iron Company, Taylor introduced all of his systems and vigorously pursued his research on the operations of metal-cutting tools. This experience, punctuated by controversy and escalating conflict with the company's managers, was the capstone of his creative career. Two features of it were of special importance. Taylor's discovery of high-speed steel, which improved the performance of metal-cutting tools, assured his fame as an inventor. In the meantime, his effort to introduce systematic methods in many areas of the company's operations forced him to take an additional step: to develop an integrated view of managerial innovation and a broader conception of the manager's role. By 1901, Taylor had fashioned scientific management from systematic management (Copley 1923; Nelson 1980; Kakar 1970).

As the events of Taylor's career make clear, the two approaches were intimately related. Systematic and scientific management had common roots, attracted the same kinds of people, and had the same business objectives. Yet in retrospect the differences stand out. Systematic management was diffuse and utilitarian, a series of isolated measures that did not add up to a larger whole or have recognizable implications beyond day-to-day industrial operations. Scientific management added significant detail and a larger view. It was the first step toward the utopian vision of the 1910s. In 1901, when he left Bethlehem, Taylor resolved to devote his time and ample fortune to promoting his new conception of industrial management. His first report on his work, *Shop Management* (1903), portrayed an integrated complex of systematic management methods, supplemented by refinements and additions such as time study.

In the following years, as Taylor's reputation grew, he modified his presentation to make it more appealing. Two changes were notable. First, he began to rely more heavily on anecdotes from his career to emphasize the links between improved management, greater productivity, and social melioration to audiences that had little interest in technical detail. He liberally interpreted his records and recollections to make his point. His parable of "Schmidt," a laborer who supposedly prospered because of an incentive wage, was largely apocryphal, but it captured the imaginations of legions of readers (Wrege and Perroni 1974). Second, apart from the object lessons, Taylor spoke less about factory operations and more about the significance and general applicability of his ideas. Between 1907 and 1909, with the aid of a close associate, Morris L. Cooke, he wrote a sequel to *Shop Management* that became *The Principles of Scientific Management* (1911) (Wrege and Stotka 1978). Rather than discuss the specific methods he introduced in factories and shops, Taylor relied on colorful stories and language to illuminate "principles" of management. To suggest the integrated character and broad applicability of scientific management, he equated it to a "complete mental revolution."

Taylor's reformulation of scientific management was the single most important step in the popularization of industrial engineering. *The Principles* extended the potential of scientific management to nonbusiness endeavors and made Taylor a central figure in the "efficiency craze" of the 1910s (Haber 1964). To engineers and nonengineers alike, he created order from the diverse prescriptions of a generation of technical writers. By the mid-1910s, he had achieved wide recognition in American engineering circles and had attracted a devoted following in France, Germany, Russia, and Japan (Fridenson 1987; Moutet 1975; Homburg 1978; Beissinger 1988; Daito 1989; Gordon 1989). His growing body of admirers at universities such as Pennsylvania State College, which introduced the first industrial engineering major in 1907, was another measure of the potency of his message (Nelson 1992b).

Taylor also had a major influence on the diffusion of scientific management in industry. His insistence that the proper introduction of management methods required the services of an expert intermediary linked the progress of industrial engineering to the activities of independent consultants and accelerated the rise of a new profession.

2.2 The Role of the Consultant

Initially, the spread of systematic and scientific management occurred largely through the work of independent consultants, a few of whom, such as the accountant J. Newton Gunn, achieved prominence by the end of the nineteenth century. By 1900, Taylor overshadowed the others; by 1910, he had devised a promotional strategy that relied on a close-knit corps of consultants to install his techniques, train the client's employees, and instill a new outlook and spirit of cooperation. The expert was to ensure that the spirit and mechanism of scientific management went hand in hand. The formula did not always work smoothly, as many accounts have emphasized (Nelson 1980, 137–67; Aitken 1960; Nadworny 1955). Nevertheless, it produced a number of successful consulting firms and the largest single cluster of professional consultants devoted to industrial management.

Between 1901 and 1915, Taylor's immediate associates introduced scientific management in nearly two hundred American businesses, 80 percent of which were factories (Thompson 1917, 36–104). Some of the plants were large and modern, like the Pullman and Remington Typewriter works; others were small and technologically primitive. Approximately one-third of the total were large-volume producers for mass markets. A majority fell into one of two broad categories. First were those whose activities required the movement of large quantities of materials between numerous workstations (textile mills, railroad repair shops, automobile plants). Their managers sought to reduce delays and bottlenecks and increase throughput. On the other hand were innovative firms, mostly small, that were already committed to managerial reform. Their executives were attracted to Taylor's promise of social harmony and improved working conditions. A significant minority of the total fell in both categories. Many of the textile mills, for example, were leaders in welfare work (Nelson 1984, 56–57).

The records that have survived suggest that the consultants provided valuable services to many managers. They typically devoted most of their time to machine operations, tools and materials, production schedules, routing plans, and cost and other record systems. Apart from installing features of systematic management, their most notable activity was to introduce elaborate production-control mechanisms (bulletin boards and graphs, for example) that permitted managers to monitor operations. At the Franklin Automobile Company and a number of textile mills, the consultant's work consisted almost exclusively of improvements in scheduling and routing (Babcock 1917; Nelson 1980, 149–54). Critics complained of excessive detail and red tape, but most executives expressed satisfaction with the engineers' work.

The records do not support the contention, common to many later accounts, that the experts' central concern was the work of the individual employee. In one-third of the factories, the consultant's activities generated such controversy that time and motion studies were never undertaken. Many workers in other plants were unaffected. At least one-half of the employees of the industrial companies must have been essentially onlookers. They may have experienced fewer delays, used different tools, or found that their supervisor's authority had diminished, but their own activities were unchanged (Nelson 1992b, 11–12).

What about those who were directly affected? Judging from the available evidence, neither Taylor nor his critics provided an accurate guide to the experts' activities. Supervisors lost much of their discretionary authority as they became subject to centrally imposed policies and regulations. Machine operators worked more steadily and performed fewer peripheral tasks. They also earned higher wages, though there were enough exceptions to blur the effect. Some unskilled jobs disappeared as improved scheduling and routing reduced the need for gangs of laborers and encouraged the introduction of materials-handling machinery. But few firms embraced functional foremanship, which called for substituting specialists for the traditional supervisor, and even fewer tried to substitute management systems for the expertise of skilled operatives. While no systematic accounting is possible, improvements in production and costs resulted overwhelmingly from the elimination of delays and bottlenecks, improved communications, and the introduction or extension of wage incentives, not from new techniques of work or work organization.

Initially, at least, social harmony was more often a casualty than a consequence of scientific management. Supervisors opposed the erosion of their powers and autonomy, while production workers often resisted the introduction of time study. The proper use of time study became and remained a delicate issue. The consultants' promises of harmony and prosperity depended on the fair and "scientific" application of time study, but many workers suspected that it would be a pretext for rate cuts and lower wages. In many cases their fears were warranted. Labor disputes (and strikes at Watertown Arsenal, Joseph & Feiss, and American Locomotive) resulted from the inability of many managers to resist the temptation to use time study for short-term cost cutting. Such abuses led to vigorous union campaigns against time study and incentive plans in the mid-1910s.

The contrast between the theory and practice of industrial engineering reflected several factors. The most obvious was the tradition of decentralized production management and the established web of interests that resisted innovation. A second factor was closely related: in most settings prior investment in machinery and other equipment limited the engineer's ability to introduce changes, regardless of the liberality of his or her mandate. An ideal arrangement would have required a new plant as well as new attitudes and responsibilities. A third element, ironically, was the role of the consultant, which contributed to a short-term, cost-cutting perspective. By definition a consultant was a transient, short-term employee. Taylor had proclaimed that a thorough reorganization required three or four years, but few of his successors had the temerity or financial security to make similar demands on their clients. They promised results and concentrated on goals that would justify their employment. Taylor's reliance on the consultant had been a way to accelerate the diffusion of his ideas. In practice, however, it undermined the likelihood of a "complete mental revolution."

Between 1910 and 1920, industrial engineering spread rapidly. Although large firms introduced staff departments devoted to production planning, time study, and other industrial-engineering activities, the most notable development of those years was the proliferation of consulting firms. By 1915, the year of Taylor's death, he and his immediate followers no longer controlled the diffusion of his methods. Professional organizations, notably the Taylor Society (1910) and the Society of Industrial Engineers (1911), provided forums for the discussion of techniques and the development of personal contacts. But after brief and unsuccessful trials, they did not try to regulate entry to the profession or certify the competence of practitioners (Nelson 1980, 181–85; Haber 1964). Financial success and professional recognition increasingly depended on entrepreneurial and communications skills rather than technical expertise. Several of Taylor's closest associates, including Carl G. Barth and H. K. Hathaway, failed as consultants, while a new generation of practitioners, including many university professors who had had no direct contact with Taylor and whose credentials would have been viewed with suspicion a decade earlier, developed successful consulting practices.

Competition for clients and recognition—especially after the recession of 1920–21 made executives more cost-conscious—produced other changes. Some consultants began to seek clients outside manufacturing. Spurred by the growing corps of academicians who argued that the principles of factory management applied to all businesses, they reorganized offices, stores, banks, and other service organizations (Davies 1982, 97–108; Strom 1989, 64–69; Rotella 1981, 51–58; Yates 1989, 21–64). Others specialized. A Society of Industrial Engineers survey of leading consulting firms in 1925 reported that many confined their work to plant design, accounting systems, machinery, or marketing (Quigel 1992, 403). A third trend was an increasing preoccupation with labor issues and time study. This emphasis reflected several postwar developments, most notably and ominously the increasing popularity of consultants who devoted their attention to cost cutting through the aggressive use of time study.

By the early 1920s, industrial engineers who worked in industry had divided into two separate and increasingly antagonistic camps. On the one hand were the pioneers and their heirs who viewed scientific management as an interrelated group of techniques that included increasingly sophisticated policies for managing production workers. Taylor and his associates had devoted little attention to labor issues apart from wage incentives. The attacks of labor unions and their political allies exposed the limitations of this approach, and the World War I economic boom showed that other personnel activities such as recruitment and training programs, representation schemes, and employee benefit plans were as important to improved economic performance as time study and the incentive wage. In the postwar years, the most influential group of industrial engineers, centered in the Taylor Society, embraced personnel management and combined it with orthodox industrial engineering to form a revised and updated version of scientific management. A handful of Taylor Society activists, Richard Feiss of Joseph & Feiss, Henry S. Dennison of Dennison Manufacturing, Morris E. Leeds of Leeds & Northrup, and a few others, mostly owner-managers, implemented the new synthesis. They introduced personnel management and more controversial measures such as profit sharing, company unionism, and unemployment insurance that attacked customary distinctions between white- and blue-collar employees and enlisted the latter, however modestly, in the management of the firm (Goldberg 1992; Heath 1929; Berkowitz and McQuaid 1992; Nelson 1970).

A larger group emphasized the potential of incentive plans based on time and motion study and disregarded or deemphasized other features of orthodox scientific management. Their more limited approach reflected the competition for clients, the trend toward specialization, and the continuing attraction of rate cutting. Indicative of this tendency was the work of two of the most successful consultants of the post-1915 years, Harrington Emerson and Charles E. Bedaux. Emerson (1853–1931) was a restless, creative, and flamboyant personality. Attracted to Taylor at the turn of the century, he briefly worked as an orthodox practitioner and played an influential role in Taylor's promotional work. He soon became a respected accounting theorist and a successful reorganizer of railroad repair facilities. As his reputation grew, however, he broke with Taylor and set up a competing business with a large staff of engineers and consultants. Between 1907 and 1925, he had over two hundred clients (Nelson 1980, 127–30; Johnson and Kaplan 1987, 51; Quigel 1992, 279–325). He also published best-selling books and promoted a mail-order personal efficiency course. He was probably the best-known industrial engineer of the late 1910s and early 1920s.[1]

Emerson's entrepreneurial instincts defined his career. An able technician, he was capable of overseeing the changes associated with orthodox scientific management. He also recruited competent assistants, such as Frederick Parkhurst and C. E. Knoeppel, who later had distinguished consulting careers, and E. K. Wunnerlund, who became the head of industrial engineering at General Motors. But Emerson always viewed his work as a business and tailored his services to this customer's interests. In practice, this meant that his employees spent most of their time conducting time studies and installing incentive wage systems. By the mid-1920s, General Motors, Westinghouse, the Baltimore & Ohio Railroad, Aluminum Company of America, American Radiator, and many other large and medium-sized industrial firms had introduced the Emerson system and in many cases an industrial engineering department staffed by former Emerson employees.[2]

---

1. "Harrington Emerson, 1853–1931," Harrington Emerson Papers, box 9, Pennsylvania State University Library, University Park, Pennsylvania.
2. Emerson Papers, boxes 2–9.

Bedaux (1886–1944) was even more adaptable. A French immigrant who was a clerk at a St. Louis chemical company in 1910 when an expert arrived to conduct time studies, Bedaux quickly grasped the essentials of time study and replaced the outsider. During the "efficiency craze" that followed the publication of *The Principles,* he found other clients. The turning point in his career came in 1912, when he accompanied several Emerson engineers to France as an interpreter. In Paris he struck out on his own, reorganized several factories, and studied the writings of Taylor and Emerson. Returning to the United States during World War I, he launched the Bedaux Company and began to cultivate clients. Bedaux rejected the promotional strategy that Taylor, Emerson, and Frank and Lillian Gilbreth, other Taylor disciples, had perfected. He gave no speeches, wrote no books or articles, avoided professional meetings, and never discussed his methods in public. Instead he relied on personal contacts and a simple, compelling promise: he would save more money than he charged. Although Bedaux employed able engineers and usually made some effort to reorganize the plant, his specialty was the incentive wage. His men worked quickly, used time studies to identify bottlenecks and set production standards, installed a wage system similar to Emerson's, and explained their activities in incomprehensible jargon. Bedaux's clients included General Electric, B. F. Goodrich, Standard Oil of New Jersey, Dow Chemical, Eastman Kodak, and more than two hundred other American firms by the mid-1930s. His European offices were even more successful (Kreis 1992).

Bedaux's secretive approach makes it impossible to generalize about his services in the United States, but the records of his British subsidiary, recently opened, reveal a consistent effort to pressure workers for greater output. Whereas Taylor and his followers opposed wage cutting and "speed-up" efforts, Emerson was more flexible, and Bedaux made a career of forcing workers to do more for less. One notable result was a resurgence of strikes and union protests. By the 1930s, Bedaux had become infamous on both sides of the Atlantic. In response to his notoriety, he revised his incentive plan to increase the worker's share and dropped much of his colorful terminology, including the famous B unit. Bedaux's business survived, though neither he nor his firm regained the position they had enjoyed in the late 1920s and early 1930s (Kreis 1992).

Bedaux's unsavory reputation was a substantial burden for other industrial engineers. The growth of labor unrest in the 1930s and the frequent appearance of the "Be-do" plan on grievance lists revived the association of industrial engineering with labor turmoil. Regardless of their association with Bedaux and his tactics, industrial engineers became the targets of union leaders and their allies. In industries such as autos and tires, worker protests paralyzed the operations of industrial engineering departments and led to the curtailment or abandonment of many activities.

These problems were closely related to a longer-term threat to industrial engineering. The growth of labor unrest and government regulation of labor relations in the mid-1930s led many large industrial firms to create or strengthen personnel departments (Jacoby 1986). In theory, industrial engineers and personnel and industrial relations experts subscribed to the same values and objectives. In practice, however, they were often antagonists and competitors. Apart from influencing wage, salary, and employee-benefit policies, industrial-relations managers had a strong intellectual and professional interest in maintaining stability on the shop floor. They helped curb the work of Bedaux and others like him, but they also resisted other changes that might lead to unrest.[3] Managerial innovation became more difficult, and industrial engineers found themselves increasingly confined to activities that did not directly affect wages or working conditions (Kochan, Katz, and McKersie 1986).

2.3 The Impact of Industrial Engineering in the 1920s and 1930s

Although the archives of the major consulting firms and the publications of professional associations document the evolution of industrial engineering as an intellectual discipline and a professional specialty, they provide only the most general indications of the effects of this activity on the firm and its employees. The client lists that have survived generally do not explain what was done, who was affected, or, in most cases, how influential the work was on operations or the viewpoint of executives. The thrust of Bedaux's work and of the expansion of industrial-relations management is clear, but its practical effects are less obvious. What, if anything, can be concluded from the experiences of later years?

There are at least three partial measures of the diffusion of industrial engineering that help answer this question. First, the many references to cost accounting, centralized production planning and scheduling, systematic maintenance procedures, time study, and employment management in the trade press and in the records of industrial corporations indicate that these activities were no longer novel or unfamiliar to executives. The promotional work of the consultants, the "efficiency craze," and the growth of management education in universities had made the rudiments of industrial engineering widely available; only the oldest or most isolated executives were unaware of them. The critical issue was no longer the desirability of the new management; it was the particular combination of techniques suitable for a given firm or plant, the role of the outside consultant, if any, and the authority of the staff experts.

Second, the information on industrial wage systems that the National Industrial Conference Board assiduously collected in the 1920s and 1930s documents widespread acceptance of incentive wage plans, particularly among large corporations. In 1928, for example, 6 percent of the smallest companies (1–50 employees) had incentive wage plans, while 56 percent of the largest

---

3. Unions had a similar impact, although their influence was comparatively short-lived. See Harris 1982.

firms (more than 3,500 employees) had such plans. In earlier years, small firms devoted to industrial reform had been among the most vigorous proponents of industrial engineering. But their ranks did not grow, and they were soon overshadowed by large corporations, which found in industrial engineering an effective answer to the problems that often prevented large, expensive factories from achieving their potential (Nelson 1991, 79). Incentive wage plans were an indicator of this trend, but—Bedaux notwithstanding—they were also indicators of more extensive managerial initiatives.

The popularity of incentive plans did not mean, however, that industrial engineering had a more uniform or predictable effect on work organization and job content than in earlier years. Feiss, Dennison, and others hoped to transform the character of industrial work through the use of incentives and personnel programs; judging from the information that survives, big business managers had more modest goals. Their principal objective was to make the best use of existing technology and organization by enlisting the workers' interest in a higher wage. In the early 1930s, many managers were attracted to the "work simplification" movement that grew out of the Gilbreths' activities, but the effects were apparently negligible, at least until the World War II mobilization effort. To most manufacturers, industrial engineering provided useful answers to a range of shop-floor problems; it was a valuable resource but neither a stimulus to radical change nor a step toward a larger goal.

A third source, contemporary surveys of the industrial engineering work of large corporations, provides additional support for this conclusion. The most interesting of these surveys, by Stanley Mathewson in 1928, found no difference in attitude between workers at General Motors, Westinghouse, and other giants noted for their advanced managerial practices, and workers in smaller, less modern plants. Mathewson discovered widespread efforts to restrict production in order to protect wages or jobs (Mathewson 1931). Clearly, the mental revolution had not reached the shop floor at these plants. A 1928 survey by the Special Conference Committee, an elite group of large industrial firms, emphasized related problems.[4] It reported wide differences in the practice of time study, in the duties of time-study technicians, and in the degree of commitment to time study as an instrument for refining and improving the worker's activities. At Western Electric, which had one of the largest industrial engineering staffs, a manufacturing planning department was responsible for machinery and methods; the time-study expert was simply a rate setter. At Westinghouse, which also had a large industrial engineering department, time-study technicians were responsible for methods and rates. However, a report from the company's Mansfield, Ohio, plant indicated that the time-study engineer could propose changes in manufacturing methods "in cooperation with the foremen." Most companies had similar policies. The time-study expert

---

4. E. S. Cowdrick, "Methods of Wage Payment," Bethlehem Steel Company Papers, accession 1699, Hagley Library, Wilmington, Delaware.

was expected to suggest beneficial changes to his superiors, often after consulting the foreman, but had no independent authority to introduce them. Essentially, the "expert" was a rate setter. In most plants, industrial engineering focused on detail, seldom threatened the supervisors or workers, and even more rarely produced radical changes in methods. Except in the hands of a Bedaux, it was not a serious threat to the status quo.

A recent, detailed examination of industrial engineering at E. I. Du Pont de Nemours & Company, a Special Conference Committee member, suggests the range of possibilities that could exist in a single firm (Rumm 1992, 175–204). Du Pont executives created an Efficiency Division in 1911 after the company's general manager read *The Principles*. Rather than employ an outside consultant, they appointed two veteran managers to run the division. These men conducted time and motion studies, "determined standard times and methods for tasks, set standard speeds for machinery, and made suggestions for rearranging the flow of work, improving tools, and installing labor-saving equipment." Yet they encountered a variety of difficulties; their proposals were only advisory, they clashed with the new employment department when they proposed to study fatigue and the matching of workers and jobs, and they found that many executives were indifferent to their work. Worst of all, they could not show that their activities led to large savings. In 1914, after the introduction of functional supervision in the dynamite-mixing department apparently caused several serious accidents, the company disbanded the Efficiency Division (Stabile 1987).

Although some Du Pont plants introduced time-study departments in the following years, the company did nothing until 1928, when it created a small Industrial Engineering Division within the larger Engineering Department. The IED was to undertake a "continuous struggle to reduce operating costs." That battle was comparatively unimportant until the Depression underlined the importance of cost savings. In the 1930s, the IED grew rapidly, from twenty-eight engineers in 1930 to over two hundred in 1940. It examined "every aspect of production," conducted job analyses, and introduced incentive wage plans. Like Taylor's associates a quarter century before, IED engineers began with surveys of existing operations. They then "consolidated processes, rearranged the layout of work areas, installed materials-handling equipment, and trimmed work crews." To create "standard times" for particular jobs, they used conventional stopwatch time study as well as the elaborate photographic techniques the Gilbreths had developed. By 1938, they had introduced incentive wage plans in thirty plants; one-quarter of all Du Pont employees were affected (Rumm 1992, 181–87).

Du Pont introduced a variety of incentive plans. Three plants employed the Bedaux Company to install its incentive system. Other managers turned to less expensive consultants, and others, the majority, developed their own "in-house" versions of these plans. Some executives, and workers, became enthusiastic supporters of incentive wages; others were more critical. Despite the work of the aggressive and ever-expanding IED, many workers found ways to take advantage of the incentive plans to increase their wages beyond the anticipated ranges. Wage inflation ultimately led the company to curtail the incentive plans. Time and motion study, however, remained hallmarks of Du Pont industrial engineering (Rezler 1963).

The Du Pont experience illustrates several larger themes. The diversity of manufacturing operations in large corporations such as Du Pont militated against a "complete mental revolution" and a more aggressive approach to shop-floor problems than had been characteristic of the engineers' activities in earlier years. Like other novel proposals, industrial engineering at Du Pont had to compete for resources. The failure of the Efficiency Division to produce immediate benefits compromised its position and ultimately led to its downfall, despite its appealing message. Only the collapse of the economy, the rise of new cost pressures, and, concomitantly, the company's success in avoiding or deflecting labor unrest revived interest in industrial engineering and created the consensus that sustained the IED in the 1930s. By 1940, IED technicians approached the goals of the original scientific management movement. Still, Du Pont did not entirely escape the pattern of opportunistic cost cutting. The executives who employed Bedaux or who introduced Bedaux-like wage plans with minimal prior study and reorganization were examples of the other, more controversial side of industrial engineering.

The eventual success of the IED obscured a more central problem. By 1910, Du Pont was supposedly one of the best-managed American corporations. It had reorganized successfully and had absorbed much of the spirit of the scientific management movement. Yet Du Pont's top executives had little interest in extending managerial reform to the shop floor. During the depression of the 1930s, when they developed a new sensitivity to the value of industrial engineering, they defined it as a way to cut factory costs. They transcended the Bedaux approach but remained surprisingly parochial. One reason for this perspective was bureaucratic: Du Pont had developed an extensive personnel operation in the 1910s and 1920s, which had authority over employee training, welfare programs, and labor negotiations. Equally important was the apparent assumption that industrial engineering only pertained to the details of manufacturing activities, especially the work of machine operators. Despite mounting pressures to reduce costs, the company's offices, laboratories, and large white-collar labor force remained off-limits to the IED. Despite these handicaps, the IED had a significant impact because rapid technological change in the industry created numerous opportunities for organizational change and Du Pont avoided relations with powerful unions.

Apart from its timing, the Du Pont experience was consistent with the evidence noted above. Like most manufacturers, Du Pont executives were receptive to the "principles" of industrial engineering but focused on the particulars, which they assessed in terms of their potential for improving short-term economic performance. As a result there was little consistency in their activities until the 1940s; even then, industrial engineering was restricted to the company's manufacturing operations. This approach, fragmentary and idiosyncratic by the standards of Taylor or Dennison, was logical and appropriate to executives whose primary objective was to fine-tune a largely successful organization.

2.4 Conclusions

During the first third of the twentieth century, industrial engineers successfully argued that internal management was as important to the health of the enterprise as technology, marketing, and other traditional concerns. Their message had its greatest impact in the 1910s and 1920s, when their "principles" won wide acceptance and time study and other techniques became commonplace. Managers whose operations depended on carefully planned and coordinated activities and reformers attracted to the prospect of social harmony were particularly receptive. By the 1930s, the engineers' central premise, that internal coordination required self-conscious effort and formal managerial systems, had become the acknowledged basis of industrial management.

Although the popularity of industrial engineering was due in large measure to the writings of Taylor and other pioneers, few executives took those statements literally or introduced all or most of the changes that Taylor and other industrial engineers advocated. Their customary approach was pragmatic and selective. This selectivity was apparent in their relations with consultants and in the work of corporate industrial engineering departments. It was also evident in the treatment of factory employees, the feature of industrial engineering that received the greatest attention. Time-study techniques differed from firm to firm, with diverse effects, and incentive wage plans were equally varied in conception and application. In view of these tendencies, it is hardly surprising that industrial engineering had no consistent or predictable effect on the character of industrial work.

Industrial engineering thus contributed to the growing diversity of industrial management in the early twentieth century. Using techniques developed by proponents of systematic management, by Taylor and his followers, and by their successors of the 1920s and 1930s, industrialists were able to adjust their organizations to market pressures, technological innovations, and their conceptions of how a factory or business ought to perform. If they were unsure how to proceed, armies of eager consultants, of varying degrees of fidelity to the tenets of orthodox scientific management, were available to assist them. In the nineteenth century, few industrialists had recognized the potential of this form of internal coordination. By the 1930s, they took it for granted. Although the expansion of industrial relations activities in the late 1930s threatened to reverse this pattern and impose a new uniformity, it affected only a small percentage of plants and industrial workers before World War II.

The variability in the practice of industrial engineering, evident from Taylor's day to the 1940s, greatly complicates any effort to assess its economic impact. In a minority of cases, it led to the realization of Taylor's original objectives and long periods of growth and prosperity. In other instances, it precipitated unrest, disruption, and organizational turmoil. In the majority of cases, however, it contributed in numerous ways, large and small, to improvements in manufacturing operations and firm performance. This mixed legacy, apparent by the eve of World War II, became the foundation for a second, more complex, and even more controversial chapter in the history of industrial engineering that extends to the present.

References

Aitken, Hugh G. J. 1960. *Taylorism at Watertown Arsenal.* Cambridge: Harvard University Press.

Babcock, George D. 1917. *The Taylor System in Franklin Management.* New York: Engineering Magazine Company.

Beissinger, Mark R. 1988. *Scientific Management, Socialist Discipline, and Soviet Power.* Cambridge: Harvard University Press.

Berkowitz, Edward D., and Kim McQuaid. 1992. *Creating the Welfare State: The Political Economy of Twentieth-Century Reform.* Rev. ed. Lawrence: University of Kansas Press.

Copley, Frank Barkley. 1923. *Frederick W. Taylor: Father of Scientific Management.* 2 vols. New York: Harper and Brothers.

Daito, Eisuke. 1989. Railways and Scientific Management in Japan, 1907–1930. *Business History* 31:1–28.

Davies, Margery W. 1982. *Woman's Place Is at the Typewriter: Office Work and Office Workers, 1870–1930.* Philadelphia: Temple University Press.

Fridenson, Patrick. 1987. Un Tournant taylorien de la société française, 1904–1918. *Annales: Economies, Sociétés, Civilisations* 42:1032–42.

Goldberg, David J. 1992. Richard A. Feiss, Mary Barnett Gilson, and Scientific Management at Joseph and Feiss, 1909–1925. In *A Mental Revolution: Scientific Management since Taylor,* ed. Daniel Nelson, 40–57. Columbus: Ohio State University Press.

Gordon, A. 1989. Araki Toichiro and the Shaping of Labor Management. In *Japanese Management in Historical Perspective,* ed. Tsunehiko Yui and Keiichiro Nakagawa, 173–91. Tokyo: Tokyo University Press.

Haber, Samuel. 1964. *Efficiency and Uplift: Scientific Management in the Progressive Era.* Chicago: University of Chicago Press.

Harris, Howell John. 1982. *The Right to Manage: Industrial Relations Policies of American Business in the 1940s.* Madison: University of Wisconsin Press.

Heath, Charlotte. 1929. History of the Dennison Manufacturing Company: Part 2. *Journal of Economic and Business History* 2:163–202.

Homburg, Heidrun. 1978. Anfange des Taylorsystems in Deutschland vor dem Ersten Weltkrieg. *Geschichte und Gesellschaft* 4:170–94.

Jacoby, Sanford M. 1986. *Employing Bureaucracy: Managers, Unions, and the Transformation of Work in American Industry, 1900–1945.* New York: Columbia University Press.

Johnson, H. Thomas, and Robert S. Kaplan. 1987. *Relevance Lost: The Rise and Fall of Management Accounting.* Boston: Harvard Business School Press.

Kakar, Sudhir. 1970. *Frederick Taylor: A Study in Personality and Innovation.* Cambridge: MIT Press.

Kochan, Thomas A., Harry C. Katz, and Robert B. McKersie. 1986. *The Transformation of American Industrial Relations.* New York: Basic Books.

Kreis, Steven. 1992. The Diffusion of Scientific Management: The Bedaux Company in America and Britain, 1926–1945. In *A Mental Revolution: Scientific Management since Taylor,* ed. Daniel Nelson, 156–74. Columbus: Ohio State University Press.

Levenstein, Margaret. 1991. The Use of Cost Measures: The Dow Chemical Company, 1890–1914. In *Inside the Business Enterprise: Historical Perspectives on the Use of Information,* ed. Peter Temin, 71–116. Chicago: University of Chicago Press.

Mathewson, Stanley B. 1931. *Restriction of Output among Unorganized Workers.* New York: Viking Press.

Moutet, Aimée. 1975. Les Origins du système de Taylor en France: Le point de vue patronal, 1909–1914. *Le Mouvement Social* 93:17–21.

Nadworny, Milton. 1955. *Scientific Management and the Unions, 1900–1932.* Cambridge: Harvard University Press.

Nelson, Daniel. 1970. "A Newly Appreciated Art": The Development of Personnel Work at Leeds and Northrup. *Business History Review* 44:520–35.

———. 1980. *Frederick W. Taylor and the Rise of Scientific Management.* Madison: University of Wisconsin Press.

———. 1984. Le Taylorisme dans l'industrie américaine, 1900–1930. In *Le Taylorisme,* ed. Maurice de Montmollin and Olivier Pastre, 51–66. Paris: Éditions La Découverte.

———. 1991. Scientific Management and the Workplace, 1920–1935. In *Masters to Managers: Historical and Comparative Perspectives on American Employers,* ed. Sanford M. Jacoby, 74–89. New York: Columbia University Press.

———. 1992a. Scientific Management in Retrospect. In *A Mental Revolution: Scientific Management since Taylor,* ed. Daniel Nelson, 5–39. Columbus: Ohio State University Press.

———. 1992b. Scientific Management and the Transformation of University Business Education. In *A Mental Revolution: Scientific Management since Taylor,* ed. Daniel Nelson, 77–101. Columbus: Ohio State University Press.

Quigel, James P., Jr. 1992. The Business of Selling Efficiency: Harrington Emerson and the Emerson Engineers, 1900–1931. Ph.D. diss., Pennsylvania State University.

Rezler, Julius. 1963. Labor Organization at DuPont: A Study in Independent Local Unionism. *Labor History* 4:178–95.

Rotella, Elyce J. 1981. The Transformation of the American Office: Changes in Employment and Technology. *Journal of Economic History* 41:51–58.

Rumm, John C. 1992. Scientific Management and Industrial Engineering at DuPont. In *A Mental Revolution: Scientific Management since Taylor,* ed. Daniel Nelson, 175–204. Columbus: Ohio State University Press.

Stabile, Donald R. 1987. The DuPont Experiments in Scientific Management: Efficiency and Safety, 1911–1919. *Business History Review* 61:365–86.

Strom, Sharon Hartman. 1989. Light Manufacturing: The Feminization of American Office Work, 1900–1930. *Industrial and Labor Relations Review* 43:53–71.

Taylor, Frederick W. 1903. Shop Management. *Transactions of the American Society of Mechanical Engineers* 24:1337–1456.

———. 1911. *The Principles of Scientific Management.* New York: Harper.

Thompson, C. Bertrand. 1917. *The Theory and Practice of Scientific Management.* Boston: Houghton Mifflin.

Wrege, Charles D., and Amedeo G. Perroni. 1974. Taylor's Pig-Tale: A Historical Analysis of Frederick W. Taylor's Pig Iron Experiments. *Academy of Management Journal* 17:6–27.

Wrege, Charles D., and Anne Marie Stotka. 1978. Cooke Creates a Classic: The Story behind F. W. Taylor's *Principles of Scientific Management. Academy of Management Journal* 3:736–49.

Yates, JoAnne. 1989. *Control through Communication: The Rise of System in American Management.* Baltimore: Johns Hopkins University Press.

———. 1991. Investing in Information: Supply and Demand Forces in the Use of Information in American Firms, 1850–1920. In *Inside the Business Enterprise: Historical Perspectives on the Use of Information,* ed. Peter Temin, 117–60. Chicago: University of Chicago Press.

Comment   Michael J. Piore

Daniel Nelson's paper reviews the impact of Frederick Taylor, scientific management, and industrial engineering upon American manufacturing in the early part of the twentieth century. It is difficult not to read it in the context of the current debate about the competitiveness of the U.S. economy. Many analysts (including myself) have attributed the problems of U.S. manufacturing in the 1970s and 1980s to the persistence of a set of managerial principles and practices developed earlier in the century and built into standard operating procedures of most large American corporations. As a result, it is argued, American manufacturing lacks the flexibility required to adjust to the rapidly changing business environment. Its practices and procedures are also too rigid to use new information and communication technologies effectively. This view has spawned a number of institutional reforms designed to make American business more supple.

On the shop floor, these reforms include pay for knowledge, as opposed to payment linked to output or to particular job assignments; the broadening, even the wholesale elimination, of job categories; the elimination of in-process inventories which isolate individual production operations from one another; increased use of production teams in place of individual work assignments. Reform is not of course limited to shop-floor practice. Indeed, the changes elsewhere in the organization are, if anything, more revolutionary: efforts to reduce hierarchy and eliminate intermediate management positions, matrix management which blurs the clear lines of authority of the traditional organizational charts, efforts to draw suppliers and customers into the design process, parallel engineering through cross-functional teams. We do not have a single name for all of the practices under attack taken as a group. Many organizational structures that are now being eliminated are those whose origin and development were heralded by Alfred Chandler in his monumental work *The*

Michael J. Piore is the David W. Skinner Professor of Economics and Management at the Massachusetts Institute of Technology.

Visible Hand; the reform movement might be called anti-Chandlerian were it not somewhat anachronistic to use his name to describe a set of practices that are on the verge of elimination even as he arrived to celebrate them. But the shop-floor practices are generally linked to Frederick Taylor and the industrial engineering profession, and are often referred to as Taylorism.

Read in this context, the paper constitutes an attack on the use of this term. Its central argument is that industrial engineering, as it was incorporated into American managerial practice in the 1920s, was little more than the view that good management involved "self-conscious effort and formal managerial systems"; it was a "systematic, centralized approach to production management," an attack on "the 'chaotic' condition of contemporary industry," on "guess-work and ad hoc calculations."

The practitioners of industrial engineering (Taylor, his disciples, and other management consultants who delivered similar messages but with whom Taylor generally competed) championed a variety of specific techniques, including job evaluation and time study, but, Nelson insists, U.S. managers were "pragmatic and selective" in the way they absorbed these lessons. "Techniques differed from firm to firm. . . . industrial engineering had no consistent or predictable effect on the character of industrial work." If there was uniformity in the patterns that replaced the "chaotic" conditions that prevailed in the 1880s and 1890s, it affected only a small percentage of plants and industrial workers prior to World War II. There is a strong suggestion at the end of the paper that the uniformity implied by the term "Taylorism" emerged later, in the 1940s. We will have to wait for Nelson's subsequent work to find out how this happened. One imagines that it was imposed by government regulators and industrial unions.

A good deal of what we know about industrial engineering comes from Nelson's own work, and one would be hard-pressed to dispute his scholarship. At one level, I am sure that he is correct: there was much more diversity among industrial engineers and the particular managerial practices that were instituted at their behest than most recent accounts of the development of modern management admit and more diversity still in the way in which the industrial engineering movement was felt in individual firms. In this sense, we have probably been rather sloppy in the way in which we have used the term. But "industrial engineering" and "Taylorism" may nonetheless be an appropriate shorthand for the old managerial approaches in contrast to the new.

The evolution of recent managerial practice suggests that what the industrial engineers viewed as "objective" and "scientific" was in fact a particular way of looking at production operations. The contrast between the older views and the current prescriptions for managerial practice is suggested by two recent titles promoting what their authors clearly conceive of as a revolution: *Thriving on Chaos* and *When Giants Learn to Dance.* Space does not permit a detailed examination of the differences between the new practices and the old. Indeed, we may be too close to the revolution to fully assess its character. Some part of what is going on may be a fashion that will not survive the moment. But the underlying principle seems to be related to the distinction between two fundamental dimensions of organization form, specialization and integration. Taylor, and the industrial engineering profession more broadly, emphasized the dimension of specialization, the division of the production process into neat and well-defined pieces with clearly new tasks that could be unambiguously assigned to particular workers or work groups. In this, they applied on the shop floor principles that analysts such as Weber, and later Schumpeter, thought of as modern and bureaucratic, and Chandler views as the hallmark of the organizational revolution heralded by the advent of the modern cooperation. The newer managerial practices, inspired by Japan, stress the integration of the different elements of the production process with each other. Matrix management, for example, and cross-functional teams break down and blur the lines of authority around which Chandler's exemplary corporate organization was built. The parallel reforms on the shop floor are typified by the effort to eliminate in-process inventories. Production is then brought to a halt by the failure of any single operation, and each operator is thereby forced to pay attention not only to his or her own immediate tasks but to all related tasks as well. This reform requires changes in accounting procedures that were once thought of as modern, since these typically focus on individual components rather than the process as a whole; more important in the present context, it is incompatible with the payment systems pioneered by industrial engineering, which for all their diversity nonetheless shared a predisposition to reward workers for the performance of individual tasks in ways that failed to take account of the system as a whole.

It turns out, then, that what practitioners of industrial engineering viewed as "systematic" and "scientific" is in fact a way of looking at the world that emphasizes specialization at the expense of integration. Alternative practices that emphasize integration appear in this perspective to be, as the titles of the texts that promote them suggest, "chaotic." One is thus led to ask whether the "chaos" of the perspective that Taylorism began to replace at the end of the last century was not actually different, but an equally coherent way of looking at the world, whether Nelson's perspective is not as limited by this way of looking at the world as that of the American managerial community.

This does not completely vitiate Nelson's conclusions about the limited impact of industrial engineering before the war. It does suggest that his view of what industrial engineering was all about is both too broad and too limited. It is too limited because it reduces industrial engineering to the specific shop-floor practices that its practitioners recommended; on these specific practices, the industrial engineers differed among themselves and with the managers whom they advised and who were evidently quite selective in what they actually introduced. But it is too broad in the sense that it accepts the engineers' claim that their role was to impose an objective systemization and order upon a set of practices that, before them, was objectively chaotic. Industrial engineering was much more than a set of specific practices: it was a general way of viewing the productive process. But it was also a limited perspective, one that spread at the expense of alternatives that were, in other times and places, at least valid.

Nelson is probably right in his assertion that the specific practices that we associate with industrial engineering gained dominance in the 1940s. But it may be that the critical moment for the ascendancy of the perspective out of which these practices emerged was the two decades before that. Indeed, reading Nelson against the background of Chandler and the new managerial literature, one might well argue that the relatively late arrival of Taylorism on the shop floor simply reflected the fact that the broader perspective upon management that it embodied rose to dominance in the shop last, only after other, higher-priority managerial practices had been changed to reflect it. Given the central place that industrial engineering gave to shop-floor practice, this would also be consistent with Nelson's argument in the narrow sense; but again it is not consistent with the broader thrust of the paper.

3 The Coordination of Business Organization and Technological Innovation within the Firm: A Case Study of the Thomson-Houston Electric Company in the 1880s

W. Bernard Carlson

3.1 Introduction

Most Americans assume that new technological innovations will revolutionize both the economy and society; they fervently believe that new products and processes will automatically enhance jobs, increase productivity, and make American corporations more competitive in global markets. Yet in order for a new technology to have revolutionary impact, it has to be linked with existing business practices. Managers and engineers often struggle to develop an appropriate business organization for manufacturing and marketing a new technology. Significantly, without an effective business organization, a new technology may not be used and may instead lie dormant for years.

Despite the importance of linking technology with business organizations, we know surprisingly little about how businessmen build business organizations. Few economists or historians have investigated how businessmen convert firms from the entrepreneurial startup characterized by one or two charismatic individuals to a more formal or elaborate organization where managers coordinate key activities.[1] During this crucial transition, the first generation of

W. Bernard Carlson is associate professor of technology, culture, and communication in the School of Engineering and Applied Science and associate professor of history at the University of Virginia.

This paper was prepared with the support of a grant from the Bankard Fund of the University of Virginia. The author thanks the conference organizers (Peter Temin, Naomi Lamoreaux, and Daniel Raff) and the conference participants for their comments and suggestions. He also thanks Jack Brown, Regina Carlson, Stephan Fuchs, and Bryan Pfaffenberger for their advice.

1. In historiographic terms, the unexplored territory lies between the entrepreneurial firm of Joseph Schumpeter (1934) and the managerial firm of Alfred D. Chandler, Jr. (1977). However, one should note that not all firms shift from the entrepreneurial to the managerial hierarchy emphasized by Chandler. Other firms acquire more formal structures without hierarchy or managers; for instance, as John K. Brown (1992) has shown in the case of the Baldwin Locomotive Works, many of the functions we associate with managers were handled by a group of partners who owned the Baldwin Works.

managers define the boundaries of the firm, selecting which activities the firm will undertake and which will be performed outside by suppliers, customers, or other intermediaries. Within the firm, the pioneering managers have to determine who will perform the key tasks and who will make decisions about different areas such as marketing, production, or research. Equally important, it is during the shift from the entrepreneurial to managerial stage that the firm defines its corporate culture, modes of internal communications, and ways of resolving differences between groups or departments. And finally, for the history of a particular technology, this transitional period is significant because it is then that inventors and their business associates often make a series of interrelated decisions about manufacturing and marketing an invention; because production and selling require substantial investments of capital, personnel, and resources, it is in this transition that the character of a technology and its impact on society are defined (David 1985).[2]

To understand how firms move from the entrepreneurial to the managerial stage, this paper investigates the rise of the Thomson-Houston Electric Company in the 1880s. Created by Charles A. Coffin and Elihu Thomson, this firm evolved an internal organization that allowed it to exploit successfully the new technology of electric lighting. Combining Coffin's vision of selling equipment to newly forming central-station utilities with Thomson's creation of new systems for generating and distributing electric light and power, Thomson-Houston played a major role in defining the electrical technology used in the United States during the past century. Thomson-Houston quickly came to dominate the electrical manufacturing industry, and in 1892, it absorbed the rival Edison General Electric Company to become the General Electric Company.[3]

In studying Thomson-Houston and GE, I have found that the intellectual challenge has been not so much understanding the technology as developing ways of thinking about the evolution of the business organization. The central question is to understand how Thomson, Coffin, and other members of this firm coordinated the key activities of marketing, manufacturing, and product innovation. To a certain extent, one can analyze their organization-building efforts in terms of rational actors who used economic or functionalist criteria to guide their choices. One can use Alfred D. Chandler, Jr.'s (1962, 1977) notions of strategy and structure to describe the evolution of Thomson-Houston, but I have been troubled that these concepts do not explain the dynamics of individuals and groups within the organization. In particular, the Chandlerian paradigm does not help explain why Thomson-Houston struggled to create an effective organizational arrangement for product innovation. In order to fill this

2. Frequently, historians of technology have treated this transition by focusing on what they call the development phase of technological change, a phase that they see as coming between invention or conceptualization and innovation or designing for manufacture and marketing. See Hughes 1976 and Staudenmaier 1985.

3. For a complete history of the Thomson-Houston Electric Company and how it became General Electric, see Carlson 1991.

gap between theory and data, I will introduce in this paper a model of the business firm as a coalition of interest groups and use this model not only to describe Thomson-Houston but to narrate the development of a specific product, an alternating-current system for incandescent lighting in the 1880s.

With these goals in mind, this paper begins with a section that briefly outlines the rational-actor approach and my model of the firm. Section 3.3 introduces the Thomson-Houston Electric Company and describes the interest groups within that organization. Section 3.4 narrates how the company developed its AC lighting system and reveals the problems that the managers and inventors encountered as they tried to coordinate business organization with technological innovation. In the conclusion, I discuss how the model allows us to sort out this complex historical case and enhances our understanding of the coordination of functions within the business firm. Thus, this paper should help link economic and historical studies of American business enterprise.

3.2 The Business Firm: Economically Rational Actors or Politically Motivated Interest Groups?

Over the past fifty years, economists have frequently considered business firms to be "atoms," or irreducible units of analysis. In taking this approach, they have created powerful and insightful models of how markets and industries behave, and they have been able to frame macroeconomic policy for American society (Temin 1991, 1–2).

Nevertheless, the view that individual firms are indivisible atoms works best when one is studying an industry or market in which numerous small firms are competing. It is an entirely different matter when one considers the more typical situation in American business history, an oligopolistic industry dominated by several large firms possessing complex internal structures (Galambos 1991). Made up of numerous groups and individuals, large business enterprises do not necessarily make decisions simply using the economics of supply and demand, but often make choices in response to a variety of internal and external pressures (Cyert and March 1963). Moreover, even a cursory comparison of American and Japanese firms reveals that businessmen using the same technology may organize their firms in substantially different ways, and this suggests that we need to know much more about how and why companies acquire their internal organization (McCraw 1986). Consequently, if economists and policymakers are going to develop more sophisticated models of markets and industries, then the next step is to move away from treating the firm as a black box and to look more closely at how firms evolve and acquire their internal structures.

To look inside the firm, one can turn to two extensive bodies of literature.[4]

---

4. The discussion in the next few paragraphs has been shaped by a reading of major treatises in economic and organizational theory and critical overviews of these two fields. As a historian look-

One can follow the lead of economists and business historians who often view the firm in terms of rational actors using economic or functional criteria to make choices. Alternatively, one can use the ideas of organizational theorists to interpret the inner workings of the firm in terms of political give-and-take among groups. Because these perspectives will be compared and contrasted in this paper, let me discuss what each contributes to investigating how firms select and coordinate functions in the transition from the entrepreneurial to the managerial stage.

The rational-actor approach begins with the assumptions that managers attempt to make reasonable decisions on the basis of the knowledge they have at hand and that they make decisions to direct their organizations toward specific goals. As Alfred D. Chandler, Jr. (1962, 1977, 1990) has argued, managers often articulate goals in form of a strategy that they then use to shape the structure of the organization. In the late nineteenth and early twentieth centuries, as managers took up new high-speed, energy-intensive industrial processes and pursued national and then international markets, the linking of strategy and structure required them to select carefully which activities or functions should be brought inside the firm. In coordinating a select group of activities, managers reduced uncertainty and improved efficiency and profitability. To select which functions to integrate and coordinate, managers presumably used some economic criteria such as transaction costs. As shown by Ronald H. Coase (1937) and Oliver Williamson (1985), a transaction-cost analysis consists of determining what it would cost the firm to contract with an outside agent to perform a task and then comparing that with what it would cost to perform the same activity internally. As Chandler (1990) has demonstrated, managers frequently lowered internal costs by exploiting the economies of scale and scope available through new production technologies, improvements in organization, and the opening of new markets. Acting in a rational manner, managers presumably brought into the firm those tasks that could be performed more cheaply and efficiently inside the organization.

Although I agree with Chandler's maxim that structure follows strategy, this maxim does not tell us much about the processes by which historical actors created and linked strategic goals with an effective organizational structure. How did the pioneering businessmen in a particular industry identify and develop an effective strategy? How did they choose which functions to emphasize and which to subordinate in their organizations? How did the first generation of managers draw on existing social structures to fashion new corporate hierarchies? And how effective were these new hierarchies? From their inception, did these organizations allocate resources and coordinate tasks effi-

---

ing into these two literatures, I recommend to other outsiders that they begin with the overviews provided by the following works: Davidson and Lytle 1982, 320–55; Allison 1971; and Pfeffer 1981, 18–33, especially table 1 on page 31.

ciently? Or in some cases, did early managers make mistakes in trying to link strategy and structure (Galambos 1979)? I would suggest that, while structure does follow strategy, the processes by which these were joined are not automatic but rather complex and contingent. Indeed, what is needed is a historically based model of how actors create and link business strategy and structure.

As a first step toward such a model, I find it is useful to think of the firm as a collection of interest groups, each with its own mind-set. Within a firm there are different aggregates of individuals promoting their own interests and, at times, seeking to control the organization. Each of these aggregates may be called an interest group, and they may be differentiated by their leaders, functions, or, most important, business-technological mind-sets. Each group may articulate ideas about how new technology should be used to capture particular markets or perform certain production steps and hence ensure the growth and prosperity of the firm. The central point here is that groups within the firm may possess very different ideas about how the firm should operate. For the firm to make a decision about technological innovation, marketing programs, or anything else, several of the interest groups must negotiate and compromise portions of their mind-sets and then direct other groups to implement the plan on which they agree. When the resources and rewards available to different intrafirm groups are ample, they often find it easy to negotiate and implement decisions. Similarly, groups work well together when they feel that their positions within the firm are respected by the other groups. Conversely, should a group perceive that its position in the organization is being challenged or that it may lose access to resources and rewards, then cooperation may give way to conflict and disorder.

This model of the firm is drawn from several sources. First, it is based on the social construction of technology approach of Trevor Pinch and Wiebe Bijker (1987).[5] These two sociologists have suggested that technological artifacts are defined and shaped through the interaction of social groups. Although I am impressed with Bijker and Pinch's model, I am troubled that it fails to locate social groups in a larger framework of relationships. Without understanding the positions of the groups relative to each other, it is difficult to comprehend how they will use and shape technology.

To offset this problem, one can turn to organizational theory. Within this intellectual tradition, scholars concentrate less on individual leaders and rational decision making and more on groups within the organization. The choices and activities of the organization are the result of the behavior of different internal groups. Within this field, there has been much debate on how groups interact. Some investigators have argued for a garbage-can model in which the interaction of groups is anarchical, and that choices made within an organization are based on the random confluence of needs and resources (March and

---

5. In analyzing how groups shape technology, sociologists of technology have also created a network approach. For example, see Law and Callon 1992.

Olsen 1976). Other theorists have posited a bureaucratic model in which each group within an organization has a task or mission to perform, and each group does whatever is related to or justified by its mission (Allison 1971). And still other scholars have proposed political or power models that reveal how groups may engage in political give-and-take wherein they compete for resources, bargain with each other, and create coalitions. Within power and political models, the choices of the organization are the result of intraorganization groups coming to agree or disagree with one another (Pfeffer 1981, 1992).

For the purposes of understanding the evolution of business firms, the political model of Samuel B. Bacharach and Edward J. Lawler (1980) seems especially appropriate. They emphasize that interest groups and coalitions are the basic units of analysis. Organizations make choices as a result of different internal groups bargaining with each other and creating alliances or coalitions. Once coalitions are created, the allied groups then select tactics to achieve their shared objectives. For instance, in his study of the founding of the General Electric Research Laboratory, George Wise (1980) demonstrated that the laboratory flourished because its first directors succeeded in integrating the professional aspirations of research scientists with the commercial needs of the company. Like Wise, I shall suggest that progress occurs in the firm when the leaders of groups strive for cooperation rather than overtly challenge each other.

Whereas Bacharach and Lawler's model implies that each group has a particular viewpoint, Bacharach and Lawler say little about how and why each group chooses to articulate different goals, needs, and perceptions. Consequently, a third idea informing this model of the firm is Reese V. Jenkins's (1975) concept of the business-technological mind-set. In his study of the photographic industry, Jenkins observed that major changes took place in the industry when entrepreneurs succeeded in matching new technology with new marketing techniques, thus creating what he called a business-technological mind-set. For Jenkins, a mind-set was a set of ideas and perceptions businessmen had of the market and of the potential of different technological options. Guided by their mind-sets, various entrepreneurs were able to create effective organizations and dominate the industry at different times.

One should note that while Jenkins attributed different mind-sets to individual firms within the photographic industry, in this paper I shall be arguing that different groups within the firm may possess different business-technological mind-sets. Several historians have investigated how different leaders and groups within a firm may articulate and act on different visions of what the company should do to grow and be profitable (Leslie 1979; Carlson 1992).

The business-technology mind-set is an important ingredient in the model proposed here, providing an element of purposeful behavior in an otherwise deterministic model. Without developing a way of talking about the values and goals of individuals within the firm, one is left with a model in which individuals are simply the pawns of larger political or economic forces that they cannot change. As I will show below, individuals within Thomson-Houston developed their own distinctive mind-sets about their work, their roles in the company, and the strategy of the company. In turn, individuals used their mind-sets to build groups, perform their key tasks, and move the firm in the direction of their mind-set. In this sense, I am trying to make room for individual choice in the face of economic and organizational theories that previously have been uncertain about how to include the individual.

3.3   The Strategy and Structure of Thomson-Houston

The interest-group model is useful because it permits us to trace how entrepreneurs and inventors in the Thomson-Houston Electric Company struggled to link business organization and technological innovation. This company was created in 1882 by a group of shoe manufacturers in Lynn, Massachusetts, to exploit the inventions of Elihu Thomson and Edwin J. Houston. Beginning in 1878, these two men developed an arc-lighting system. Unlike the Edison incandescent lighting system which powered hundreds of small, sixteen-candlepower incandescent lights, the Thomson-Houston system featured fifty to sixty large (2,500 candlepower) lights. Because of these technical characteristics, the Thomson-Houston system was used for lighting factories, department stores, and streets (Carlson 1991, 193–200).

Along with other early electrical manufacturers in the early 1880s, the Thomson-Houston Electric Company quickly realized that the challenge in electric lighting was to improve the technology while devising new marketing techniques. Initially, electrical manufacturers tried to sell lighting systems outright to customers, but there was a limited market for free-standing, isolated stations. There were few industrial or large retail concerns that had both the need for artificial illumination and the capital required to purchase a steam engine, dynamo, and lights. (Even the first lighting systems with four to six arc lights cost between $3,000 and $5,000.) Instead, it soon became clear that electric-lighting equipment required a new marketing arrangement. What was needed was a strategy that reduced the cost of lighting to each consumer by spreading the capital costs of the steam engine, generator, and distribution network across a large customer base. The marketing arrangement that answered these requirements was the central-station utility. Although pioneered by local businessmen in San Francisco in 1879, this strategy was promoted by Thomas Edison, who built a central station for incandescent lighting at Pearl Street in New York in 1882 (Carlson 1991, 173–75).

Although Edison is remembered in the history books for his Pearl Street station, the individual responsible for the perfection of the central-station strategy was the vice president of Thomson-Houston, Charles A. Coffin. A shoe manufacturer, Coffin built a successful firm in Lynn in the 1870s by taking advantage of new shoemaking machinery and by aggressively developing his marketing organization.[6] In 1882, he helped organize the Thomson-Houston Electric Company and focused his efforts on the problems of marketing the new technology of electric lighting. Rather than sell equipment for isolated plants, Coffin had Thomson-Houston concentrate on promoting central stations. Coffin perceived that the central-station strategy would permit the development of a substantial market for electric lighting. By offering an extensive product line of different-sized dynamos, the firm could provide the equipment needed to supply electric lighting to nearly every town and city. Furthermore, by selling both arc and incandescent lighting systems, it was possible to encourage utilities to add machines to expand their business to include lighting for streets, shops, and homes. From the standpoint of the manufacturer of electrical equipment, central stations were ideal customers in that they provided a ready demand for the product that was free of the risky business of convincing consumers to install lights in their businesses and homes. In that sense, the central-station strategy was similar to the manner in which Henry Ford externalized the risk of marketing his Model T by developing a network of franchised dealers who were required to purchase a certain quota of cars (Chandler 1977, 359, 457).

In order to implement the central-station marketing strategy, Coffin and his associates organized Thomson-Houston along functional lines (fig. 3.1). Just as American railroad companies in the 1850s had organized departments to carry out the tasks of operating trains, repairing rolling stock, and maintaining the roadbed, Thomson-Houston had groups that handled the key jobs of designing, manufacturing, marketing, and financing electrical equipment (Chandler 1977, 81–121). Significantly, the firm organized these activities because they were the functions that had to be performed in order to sell electrical equipment for use in central stations. Had Coffin, Thomson, and other managers conceptualized either their marketing strategy or their technology in other ways—for instance, had they chosen to build and sell isolated systems—then they would have created a different business organization.

At Thomson-Houston, three interest groups appeared in response to the central-station strategy. Each performed a key function, and each was headed by a strong individual who ensured that the function was performed properly. While Coffin handled marketing and finance at the Boston headquarters, Edwin Wilbur Rice, Jr., supervised manufacturing and engineering at the Lynn plant, and Thomson concentrated on invention and design in his Model Room. As each of these men pursued his function, each developed a mind-set that reflected his role in the firm and how he thought the firm should operate. Because the interaction of those mind-sets influenced how Thomson-Houston pursued product innovation, let us examine each group and its mind-set.

6. For biographical details on Charles A. Coffin, see his obituary in *Lynn Historical Society Register* 26, pt. 1: 32–33 (1934); and Wilson 1946.

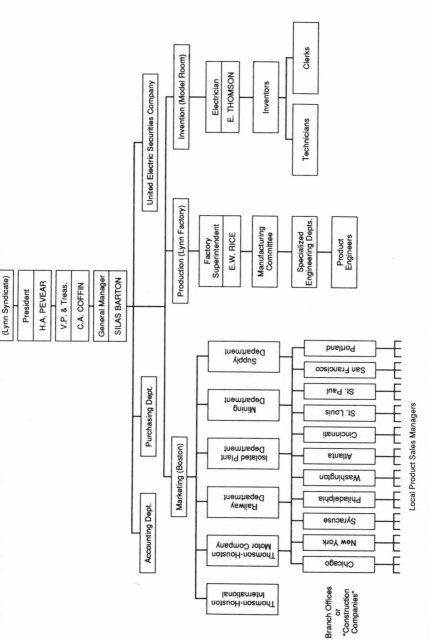

Fig. 3.1 Organization of Thomson-Houston Electric Company, 1883–92
Sources: Annual reports of Thomson-Houston Electric Company, 1888–91; various documents in Hammond File, General Electric Company, Schenectady, New York.

3.3.1 Selling Dynamics: Coffin and the Marketing Group

The central-station strategy led Coffin to establish a distinctive group around the functions of marketing and finance. This group was centered in the company's Boston office and thus physically and intellectually separate from the groups located at the Lynn factory. Coffin himself worked in this office, aided by four or five sales managers. Each manager was assigned to a product area, such as arc lighting, incandescent lighting, or street railways, and each manager worked with the Lynn factory to coordinate production with sales. Given that the company sold each product as a separate system, it made sense to have a manager for each; notably, this was quite different from the Edison organization, which at that time had seven sales managers at its headquarters, each of whom was assigned a selling territory in the United States. To assist Coffin and the sales managers, the Boston office also had a staff of bookkeepers and clerks who handled the details of advertising, sales transactions, and bond and stock issues.[7]

Beyond the Boston headquarters, Coffin established district sales offices in major cities. Each district office promoted Thomson-Houston products in the city and the surrounding region and handled the local details of each sale and installation. Because the district offices permitted the company to reach into new territory, Coffin carefully selected his district managers; for example, Coffin had Silas Barton move from being general manager to being the manager of the first district office in Chicago in 1885.[8]

Finally, below the managers in the Boston headquarters and the district offices were the salesmen, or "drummers." Traveling to towns and cities, they were the men who sold electric-lighting equipment to the organizers and operators of the new utility companies. In addition to selling equipment, salesmen were trained to help secure local capital, obtain the necessary franchise from the municipal government, and organize the operating company. Following the salesmen, an "expert," or construction engineer, was sent from the Lynn factory to install the electrical machinery. With this sales staff in place, the number of central stations using Thomson-Houston arc lights grew rapidly; whereas there were 31 companies using their equipment in July 1884, two years later there were 100 (table 3.1).[9]

7. "Methods of C. A. Coffin in Building a Commercial Organization: Story Told by J. R. McKee," 20 April 1927; "Recollections of C. B. Davis, J. P. Felton, and C. B. Burleigh, All of Boston Office," 29 May to 1 June 1925; both in John W. Hammond File, J757-8 and J194-8, General Electric Company, Schenectady, New York; Passer 1952, especially 382.

8. By 1890, Thomson-Houston had district offices in Chicago, New York, Atlanta, Washington, San Francisco, Kansas City, Saint Paul, Cincinnati, and Philadelphia; see "The Thomson-Houston Electric Company," [general catalog], 1 December 1890, Lynn Historical Society, Lynn, Massachusetts. See also A. L. Rohrer to J. A. McManus, 4 July 1945, Thomas Collection, General Electric Hall of History, Schenectady, New York (hereafter cited as Hall of History Collection); and "Further Recollection of T. A. McLoughlin . . . District Office Organization," 18 June 1925, Hammond File, L1028-9.

9. For information on how Coffin organized the sales staff, see "Further recollection of T. A. McLoughlin . . . District Office Organization," 18 June 1925, Hammond File, L1028-9. The num-

One of the most serious problems faced by many fledgling utility companies was raising sufficient capital to pay for equipment. According to one estimate, utilities in the 1880s had to invest between $4 and $8 in plant and equipment for each dollar of sales (Mitchell 1960, 45). Consequently, in building up his sales organization, Coffin was obliged to look for ways to help central stations finance their purchases. As one solution, Coffin had Thomson-Houston accept bonds as partial payment from utilities. Coffin then converted the local utility bonds into capital by organizing a series of trust funds that sold bonds representing local utility securities to Thomson-Houston stockholders. Using this financial innovation, Coffin prevented utility securities (some of which were of little value) from accumulating in the company's treasury, while at the same time generating $2.6 million in capital.[10]

Coffin used the income from the trust series and surplus profits to strengthen the firm. First, he plowed these funds back into the firm and enlarged the Lynn factory. As will be discussed later, the factory grew rapidly, with a new building added each year between 1884 and 1891. Second, Coffin used these funds to buy up smaller rival firms. Between 1888 and 1891, Thomson-Houston spent approximately $4 million to acquire eight electrical companies. Several of these companies, including Brush Electric, Fort Wayne, Schuyler, Excelsior, and Indianapolis Jenney, were competitors in arc lighting; others, such as Van Depoele Electric Manufacturing and Bentley-Knight Electric Railway, were purchased for their street-railway and motor patents. Several of the arc-lighting firms had encountered various problems in manufacturing and marketing their systems, but Coffin hastened their decline by having Thomson-Houston lawyers vigorously prosecute them for infringement of Thomson's patent for a dynamo regulator. It does not appear that Coffin undertook the merger campaign to acquire additional production capacity, because most of the purchased factories were closed. Instead, Coffin eliminated these rivals to increase Thomson-Houston's market share and secure control of key patents. Still another important benefit of the merger campaign was that it brought several inventors into the Thomson-Houston organization, and they were soon designing products and filing for patents for the company (Passer 1953, 52–56).

As Thomson-Houston was successful in selling arc lighting to central stations, Coffin had the company move into new product areas (table 3.1). With

---

ber of arc stations installed is from "Exhibit. The Following List of Thomson-Houston Plants . . . ," circa 1888, Notebooks, Elihu Thomson Papers, American Philosophical Society, Philadelphia (hereafter cited as TP). Hereafter, this pamphlet is cited as "List of T-H Plants."

10. Coffin appears to have structured each trust fund so as to include bonds from both high- and low-performing utilities. In this way, each trust fund probably paid a return to its investors, since the higher value of the bonds of the profitable utilities offset the unprofitable utilities. In this situation, the trust series served not so much to transfer risk from Thomson-Houston to the stockholder, as to function as another instrument for raising capital. See M. F. Westover, "History of the T-H Trusts, Series A, B, C and D," January 1916, Hammond File, J767; Passer, 1953, 29; Hughes 1983, 395.

Table 3.1   Spread of Thomson-Houston Lighting and Street Railway Systems, 1883–92

	Arc Lighting		DC Incandescent[a]		AC Incandescent[b]		Street Railways[c]		
Year	Number of Companies	Lamps	Number of Companies	Lamps	Number of Companies	Lamps	Number of Companies	Cars	Miles of Track
1883[d]	5	365							
1884	31	2,478							
1885	59	5,867							
1886	100	13,227							
1887	171	21,840	29	11,275					
1888	303	39,936	78	59,330	23	11,100			
1889	419	51,621	200[f]	120,380			30[f]	200[f]	
1890	587	68,203	400[f]	281,555			92	701	420
1891	755[e,f]	87,131		616,355			145	1,532	1,160
1892	873[e]	100,293		806,500			204	2,769	2,364

Sources: Annual Reports of the Thomson-Houston Electric Company, 1888–1891; "*Exhibit: The Following List of Thomson-Houston Plants*," 1888, Thomson Papers, American Philosophical Society, Philadelphia.

[a]First introduced in 1886.
[b]First introduced in 1887.
[c]First introduced in 1888.
[d]As of 1 January 1883.
[e]These totals include both arc and incandescent lighting stations. Approximately five hundred companies operated both arc and incandescent systems.
[f]There is a discrepancy in the sources as to how many companies were using Thomson-Houston equipment in 1891. Whereas the *annual report* gives 755, Thomson-Houston also published a list claiming 666 central stations; see table 3.2.

the business organization in place to market, finance, and install arc-lighting stations, it was easy to have the same salesmen and engineers sell and service other electrical products. As early as 1883, Coffin asked Thomson to develop an incandescent-lighting system, and the company began installing incandescent plants in 1885. Similarly, Coffin took an interest in selling DC motors that could be installed on arc-lighting circuits, in building AC stations, and in entering the field of electric street railways. Anxious to expand and diversify their customer loads, utilities readily purchased such new products. Hence, the manufacturer was taking advantage of economies of scope, and the utilities were capitalizing on economies of scale.

These actions reveal that Coffin favored product innovation. Just as he had been willing to use new machines in his shoe factory to produce more shoes to reach new markets, so Coffin supported the development of new electrical products. With new products such as motors and AC lighting, he believed that he could better serve existing markets as well as expand into new areas. As Thomson recalled, Coffin frequently visited the Lynn factory to see the latest inventions, and he invariably asked, "How soon can you have that done?" or "How long will it take to do that?"[11] As long as product innovations facilitated market development (which they generally did), Coffin was an ardent supporter of Thomson's efforts. Thus, along with the development of central stations, Coffin helped establish production innovation as a key component of Thomson-Houston's overall strategy.

In sum, Coffin and his group possessed a market-oriented mind-set: respond to the market quickly, give the people the products they want, and, if necessary, devise the means whereby customers can finance their purchases. In general, they favored product innovation, because it promised to help them increase market share.

3.3.2   Manufacturing Dynamos: Edwin Wilbur Rice, Jr., and the Engineering Group

In implementing the central-station strategy, the marketing and finance group contributed much to the rapid growth of the Thomson-Houston Electric Company. But marketing and finance are not the only functions that a machine-building firm must perform; to be successful, it must also address a host of manufacturing and engineering problems. Frequently it is not easy to transfer a new invention from the laboratory to the factory floor. Often the invention must be redesigned to simplify manufacture. Occasionally it may require new materials and production methods. At Thomson-Houston, for instance, Thomson and the other engineers were obliged to find better insulating materials as well as to devise faster ways to wind the coils used in dynamos, transformers, and arc lights. Once any invention goes into production, raw materials must be

11. Elihu Thomson (hereafter cited as ET), "He Invented Methods of Business," in "Charles A. Coffin Mourned by Industry," *Electrical World,* 24 July 1926, 189.

kept in stock, machine tools installed and maintained, and workers hired, trained, and paid. As the volume of production grows, the layout of the plant and the work flow must be carefully planned, and cost accounting is needed to prevent waste and confusion. Naturally, if new inventions are introduced or existing products modified, then the entire factory process may have to be revised and reestablished.

Because neither Coffin nor the Lynn syndicate was familiar with the intricacies of electrical manufacture, Coffin and the syndicate willingly delegated responsibility for the company's factory in Lynn to Edwin Wilbur Rice, Jr. Rice had served as Thomson's assistant, helping out with the drafting, building models, and winding armatures. Working with Thomson, Rice learned not only the craft of electrical invention but also how to convert Thomson's inventions from experimental models to manufactured products. On coming to Lynn, he was put in charge of assistants in the Model Room, or Experimental Department, but in February 1885, he was promoted to factory superintendent.[12]

As factory superintendent, Rice was responsible for all the work done at the Lynn works. Referred to by the workmen as the Lights, this plant was initially run like other New England factories. Various rooms or departments were equipped for machining dynamo parts, assembling lamp mechanisms, and testing dynamos. As long as the firm's product line consisted only of dynamos, arc lights, and regulators, Rice probably supervised operations by watching and participating in the work on the factory floor; there was no need for specialization or formal procedures. Wherever possible, Rice sought to improve production by rearranging the machine tools, introducing better assembly techniques, and designing special-purpose machinery. As a typical factory superintendent, Rice strove to lower manufacturing costs, thus permitting the firm to cut prices or expand its profit margin.[13]

Changing circumstances, however, soon forced Rice and the factory crew to modify their routine. As the company's salesmen sold more arc-lighting systems, production had to be expanded. By November 1886, for example, the company had so many orders that Thomson estimated that the factory had a backlog of two thousand lights. In response to the growing demand, Thomson-Houston constructed at least one new factory building every year from 1883 to 1892 (see figs. 3.2 and 3.3). Each new factory had to be planned and built in a short time. During these years, the workforce jumped from forty-five to thirty-

12. "Career of the New President," *Electrical World,* 21 June 1913, 1345–46; testimony of E. W. Rice, in "Testimony for Thomson in Rebuttal," Patent Interference no. 9,421, Thomson v. Joseph Olmsted (subject: cutout apparatus for electric lamps), Records of the Patent Office, RG-241, National Archives, Washington Records Center, Suitland, Maryland (hereafter cited as NARS), 16–17.

13. "The Thomson-Houston Factory, Lynn, Mass.," *Electrical World,* 29 August 1885, 83; "Testimony for Thomson," paper 48, Patent Interference no. 15,876, Thomson v. Dyer (subject: insulating materials), NARS, 28 (hereafter cited as "Testimony for Thomson," Intf. 15,876); "Misgivings as to Business . . . ," Lynn *Item,* 24 October 1933, Lynn Historical Society; "Electric Light machinery. Sept. 1883. Completion of the Factory at West Lynn . . . ," Hall of History Collection.

Fig. 3.2 Thomson-Houston factory in Lynn, Massachusetts, in 1884
Source: Scrapbook 1, Thomson Collection, Lynn Historical Society.

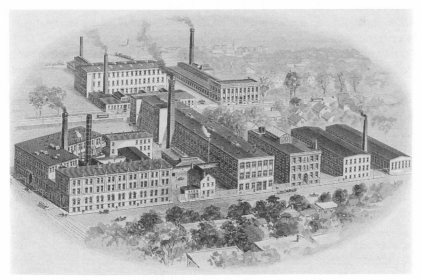

Fig. 3.3 Thomson-Houston factory in Lynn, Massachusetts, in 1891
Source: Scrapbook 1, Thomson Collection, Lynn Historical Society.

five hundred men. And just as demand was increasing, the company was also introducing new products; from 1885 to 1892, the Lynn factory turned out incandescent lamps, transformers, motors, meters, and trolley cars. To be competitive with Brush, Edison, and Westinghouse, Thomson-Houston offered those products in a variety of sizes and continually strove to improve them.[14]

To cope with the growing volume of production and the complexities of an expanding product line, Rice gradually created his own functional staff (fig. 3.4). To equip and maintain the factories, Rice selected Isaac F. Baker, an Englishman who had formerly installed incandescent stations for U.S. Electric, to serve as mechanical superintendent. Daniel M. Barton monitored the flow of work through the factory and ordered supplies. Making up the weekly payroll, which typically was over $40,000, was George E. Emmons.[15]

As the number of products manufactured in Lynn grew, Rice hired more engineers and assigned them to the major product areas. Again, that arrangement reflected the fact that the company sold different products for different applications. Walter H. Knight, a pioneer in electric traction, served as chief engineer. It appears that the product engineers were self-educated, but many of the engineers on the staff below them were college graduates. By 1887, Thomson-Houston was regularly hiring young men from MIT's Electrical Engineering Department and Cornell's Sibley College of Engineering. Some novice engineers also served as "experts," who were sent out to install electrical plants. Through his staff of engineers, Rice was able to monitor the work flow, improve manufacturing procedures, and design products.[16]

Whereas the engineering staff provided advice and information, a Factory Committee, organized by Rice in 1890, made decisions about operations. Consisting of Barton, Baker, and Emmons, the committee met at least once a week to handle employee problems, discuss new products, set production targets, and "exercise a general control over the foremen" (Shaw 1892, 657). Rice and the Factory Committee exerted final control over all aspects of the factory, and the managerial and engineering staff primarily played an advisory role in day-to-day operations.

In running the Lynn factory, Rice and his staff developed their own mindset. Deeply involved in the details of manufacturing, their basic premise was that they should help the firm earn money by reducing production costs. Wher-

14. ET to Edward F. Peck, 13 November 1886, TP, LB 9/86–3/87, 88–89; *Annual Statement of the Thomson-Houston Electric Company,* 2 February 1891 (hereafter cited as *T-H Annual Statement,* 1891), Historical File, General Electric Company, Schenectady, New York.

15. Shaw 1892, especially 655–56; memoir of Hermann Lemp, 2 July 1938, TP, Biographical Material; for information on Isaac F. Baker, see his testimony in "Testimony for Elihu Thomson," paper 129, Patent Interference no. 15,511, Pratt and Johns v. Thomson (subject: composition for insulating material), NARS (hereafter cited as "Testimony," Intf. 15,511); for biographical information on George E. Emmons, see his recollections, Hammond File, L13–19.

16. Shaw 1892, 658; ET to Theodore H. Seyfert, 23 September 1887, TP, LB 3/87–4/88, 489–90; E. E. Boyer, "Observations on Historical Notes . . . ," Hall of History Collection; C. B. Burleigh to J. W. Hammond, 20 June 1925, Hammond File; Wise 1979; Rosenberg 1984.

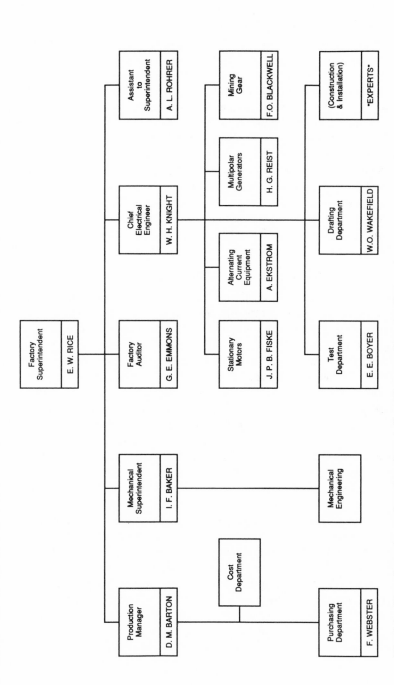

Fig. 3.4 Manufacturing and engineering staff at Thomson-Houston factory in Lynn, circa 1890
Sources: Shaw 1892; various documents in Hammond File, General Electric Company, Schenectady, New York.

ever possible, they strove to modify products so that they would be simpler to manufacture and install. The group also supported procedures that permitted greater control over the flow of work through the factory; Barton was quite proud of his system of wallboards, in which plugs were inserted to track the construction of large machines on the factory floor. Rice and the production managers also instituted a system of written work orders that allowed them to assign workers to specific projects and at the same time monitor costs.[17]

As to product innovation, however, Rice and the engineers were cautious. Although some innovations were necessary for the firm to remain competitive, Rice and his staff soon learned that other changes upset the factory routine.[18] Their tendency to approach product changes skeptically was exacerbated by the fact that the factory was continually expanding in order to meet demand. Consequently, even though Rice had worked closely with Thomson in developing new products, Rice's group was not always supportive of Thomson's efforts to improve his inventions. There was a limit to the confusion and change they could tolerate and still get the dynamos out the door.

3.3.3   Designing Dynamos: Thomson and the Model Room

Although Rice and the manufacturing group may have had mixed feelings about innovation, it was nonetheless essential to the well-being of the Thomson-Houston Electric Company. Throughout the 1880s, the firm generally supported product innovation. First, Coffin and the marketing group favored innovation because they saw it as a means to reach new customers and to acquire a larger share of the central-station market. Second, innovation was necessary for survival in a highly competitive industry. By the mid-1880s, there were nearly fifty arc-light manufacturers, all competing for a portion of the evolving market. Whereas creative financing arrangements and price cutting could be used to sell more equipment, customers also responded favorably to manufacturers with high-quality products. As Harold Passer (1953, 43–45) has observed, electric lighting was a capital good whose purchasers had to make complex calculations concerning both original investment and operating costs; consequently, they frequently chose equipment on the basis of its efficiency and reliability, rather than simply its price. In that situation, Thomson-Houston sought additional improvements and accessories that would accentuate those characteristics in their lighting systems. Third, but hardly the least important, the firm pursued innovation because of Thomson's presence. A key member of the firm, Thomson considered invention his personal domain, and he actively encouraged the company to make full use of his expertise.

Unlike Edison and Westinghouse, who took an active part in the manage-

---

17. Shaw 1892, 655–56; "Testimony," Intf. 15,511, 121–23; samples of the work orders can be found scattered throughout GE Transfiles, TP.
18. ET to F. P. Fish, 1 October 1889, TP, LB 4/89–1/90, 502–4.

ment of their companies, Thomson concentrated on invention and engineering. Having developed a distaste for business matters prior to coming to Lynn, he was content to leave the problems of raising capital and selling lights to Coffin and the Boston office. "I have as little as possible to do with the business of the Company," Thomson explained in 1888, "my work being in the line of development of apparatus and the production of new inventions."[19]

Instead of playing a prominent role in the day-to-day management of Thomson-Houston, Thomson created a niche for himself in the Model Room at the Lynn factory. Although his work area could have been called a laboratory, Thomson referred to it as his Model Room, because the primary work performed there was the construction of models for testing and patenting. The Model Room was equipped with machine tools, electrical instruments, and a special switchboard for supplying electricity at various current strengths and voltages. In addition, the Model Room had its own supply room, patent library, and offices for Thomson and his assistants. Although adjacent to the factory floor, the Model Room was "off-limits" to employees and visitors, in order to prevent industrial espionage.[20]

Assisting Thomson in the Model Room were skilled machinists and clerks (fig. 3.5). The machinists were responsible for constructing models of Thomson's inventions, and the clerks handled correspondence and the paperwork related to patents. Thomson's clerks followed with great interest the technical work in the Model Room and sometimes even made technical suggestions. For instance, J. W. Gibboney, Thomson's personal secretary, suggested using jeweled bearings in order to reduce friction and hence the current necessary to drive the earliest recording wattmeter. Supplementing the machinists and clerks were a draftsman and one or two office boys.

Although Thomson preferred to work with a small group of handpicked machinists, after 1888 he was joined in the Model Room by several inventors who came to Thomson-Houston as a result of Coffin's merger campaign. Whereas Charles Van Depoele appears to have worked independently on electric motors and streetcars, Merle J. Wightman and Hermann Lemp worked on projects under Thomson's direction. Unlike the machinists, Van Depoele, Wightman, and Lemp shared with Thomson the privilege of filing patent applications for their ideas.[21]

19. ET to H. B. Rand, 28 December 1888, TP, LB 4/88–4/89, 586.
20. Shaw 1892, 653, 656; "Testimony," Intf. 15,511, 53; "Recollections of A. L. Rohrer," Hammond File, J217–23, especially J221; ET to Charles A. Coffin (hereafter CAC), 12 April 1887, TP, LB 3/87–4/88, 37–38.
21. See the following letters in TP: ET to S. A. Barton, 19 February 1885, LB 5/85–8/85, 130; ET to H. C. Townsend, 6 September 1886, LB 3/86–9/86, 243–44; ET to James J. Wood, LB 4/88–4/89, 557–58; ET to CAC, 1 November 1888, LB 4/88–4/89, 431–33; ET to J. P. Caveling, 6 September 1890, LB 1/90–11/90, 841. See also "Recollections of L. T. Robinson," Hammond File, L1109–14; Lemp memoir; and "Testimony in Chief and Rebuttal on Behalf of Thomson," paper 94, Patent Interference no. 13,332, Edison v. Thomson (subject: incandescent-lamp cutout), NARS, 19–29.

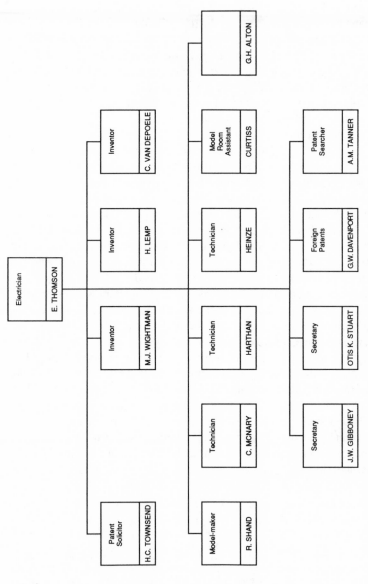

Fig. 3.5 Organization of invention and development at Thomson-Houston, circa 1888

Source: Various letters in the Elihu Thomson Papers, American Philosophical Society, Philadelphia.

Working with the Model Room staff, Thomson believed in building the best possible products. Thomson chose to design high-quality products because he found them personally and intellectually satisfying. Moreover, by being dedicated to regular improvement of the firm's products, Thomson ensured that he and the Model Room would have a continuing role to play in the company.

But beyond these reasons, Thomson was confident that the best product would, in the long run, capture the largest share of the market. Seeing that his arc-light system sold well because it was efficient and reliable, he strove to maximize similar characteristics in his other inventions. What is significant about Thomson's mind-set is that it was not shared by all groups within the firm. As has been suggested, the marketing and manufacturing groups had their own distinctive mind-sets about how the firm should operate and the role that product innovation should play in the firm's strategy. In sum, the management of Thomson-Houston was hardly monolithic, but rather made up of several groups, each with their own mind-set.

3.3.4   How Did Thomson-Houston Compare with Its Rivals?

Thomson-Houston became a leading firm in electrical manufacturing because it brought together marketing strategy, manufacturing capability, and product innovation. Led by the triumvirate of Coffin, Rice, and Thomson, the firm committed itself to selling electrical equipment to a customer it helped invent, the central-station utility. To help reach this new class of customers, the triumvirate organized Thomson-Houston along functional lines. Coffin personally supervised the marketing function and built a strong organization for sales and finance. At the same time, Rice built a large factory in Lynn for manufacturing dynamos and lights. Significantly, Coffin realized that to develop the central-station strategy fully it would be necessary for Thomson-Houston to offer a range of electrical products; in order to sell equipment to central stations in every town and city, the firm had to offer generators, lights, motors, and distribution networks suitable to a variety of needs. This realization led Coffin to encourage Thomson to invent new devices and systems.

Thomson-Houston's strength can be readily seen by comparing its performance with its competitors, both large and small. As table 3.2 reveals, Thomson-Houston surpassed all other firms in installing central stations. Not surprisingly, its substantial investment in a large sales force, factory, and product improvement allowed it to surpass and then absorb many of the smaller firms in the industry.

At the same time, Thomson-Houston performed better than its major competitors, Edison and Westinghouse, because neither of these firms was able to effectively integrate marketing, manufacture, and innovation. During the 1880s, Edison and his associates maintained a loose and poorly coordinated confederation of companies for manufacturing and distributing his incandescent system. Only in 1889 did Henry Villard succeed in welding these companies together as the Edison General Electric Company. Even then, however,

Table 3.2   Electric-Lighting Central Stations, 1891

Thomson-Houston	669[a]	Excelsior	25
Westinghouse	323	Sperry	24
Edison	202	National	16
Brush	199	Remington	4
Fort Wayne	144	Eickemeyer	2
American	67	Hawkeye	2
Western Electric	53	Standard	1
United States	51	Hochhausen	1
Schuyler	49	Beard	1
Heisler	49	Knowles	1
Waterhouse	41	Mayo	1
Ball	31	Keith	1
Van Depoele	31		

Source: "Electric Light and Electric Railway Statistics," Electrical World, 14 February 1891, 110.
[a]Presumably includes stations using arc, DC incandescent, and AC incandescent lights.

Edison General had difficulties with coordinating the key functions. Edison had opened a substantial laboratory at West Orange, New Jersey, which he assumed would be funded by Edison General but where he refused to work exclusively on the products needed by the company. Samuel Insull successfully created a national sales organization for Edison General, but he found it more difficult to improve manufacturing at the firm's Schenectady plant. Insull's efforts to enlarge the plant were limited by a scarcity of capital. Intent on gaining control of the utility industry through a holding company, the North American Company, Villard directed most of Edison General's assets in that direction, and left Insull in the difficult situation of paying for long-term factory improvements with short-term banknotes. Thus, while Edison General possessed a marketing organization, it was weak in terms of product innovation and production. Not surprisingly, Edison General was badly damaged when Villard's North American Company failed during the Baring financial crisis of 1890.

Like Edison General, the Westinghouse Company failed to integrate all three functions, but its problems stemmed more from finance and marketing. In shifting his attention from his railroad inventions (the air-brake and signaling systems) in the mid-1880s, George Westinghouse wisely hired a number of electrical inventors and engineers, including William Stanley and Nikola Tesla, and hence ensured that he had ready access to new technological developments. To manufacture the electrical systems developed by his inventors and engineers, Westinghouse built factories in Pittsburgh and Newark. However, his weakness was in marketing; Westinghouse depended on a small sales force working on commission out of offices in six or seven major cities, and he insisted on closing many of the major deals himself. Westinghouse also bankrolled the early development of his electrical company himself, which meant that he never developed the strong relationship with a banking house needed to float bond and stock issues or to help finance central stations purchasing his equipment. Consequently, again like the Edison organization, the financial crisis of 1890 found Westinghouse bankrupt, and he was only able to reorganize with the help of financiers August Belmont and Henry L. Higginson (Carlson 1991, 275–91).

Of the three major firms in the electrical industry, Thomson-Houston was thus the only firm that successfully coordinated all three functions. As a result, Thomson-Houston was able to take over Edison General in 1892 to form the General Electric Company. Moreover, throughout the 1890s and into the twentieth century, Coffin and GE were able to continually maneuver Westinghouse into a secondary position in the electrical industry.

The significant differences in structure and performance of Thomson-Houston, Edison General, and Westinghouse highlight the weakness of the rational-actor approach and the need for an organizational model. Following the rational-actor model, one would assume that the managers at each of these firms had access to approximately the same information about markets and technology and that the forces of competition would have led them to create similar organizations. Yet the historical record shows that the managers of these companies followed diverse paths, either because they perceived the markets and technology in different ways or because they were unable to build the necessary internal coalition of business and technical experts. Consequently, if we wish to understand how firms evolve their strategy and structure, we must look beyond a rational-actor model of the firm and supplant it with an organizational approach.

3.4   Taking an Organizational Approach: The Case of AC Lighting System

Although Coffin, Thomson, and Rice clearly made a series of sound decisions and brought the right functions inside Thomson-Houston, one should not assume that the decision-making process was smooth and orderly. Indeed, if we peek inside Thomson-Houston during the 1880s, we do not discover the logical world suggested by the organizational chart in figure 3.1, but rather one marked by the give-and-take of interest-group politics. To illustrate this, let us look at how the company developed an AC system for incandescent lighting. This system was vital to Thomson-Houston because it permitted the company to compete directly with Westinghouse and Edison for a new segment of the central-station market, namely, small cities and towns. In telling the story of this system, we shall see how the process of innovation at Thomson-Houston was strongly influenced by the interaction of the three groups within the firm.

3.4.1   Identifying AC Incandescent Lighting as a Product

Thomson had been fascinated by alternating current from the outset of his career as an inventor. In 1878, he and Houston had built a set of arc lights and a generator that employed alternating current and induction coils. The purpose of the induction coils was to render each lamp in a series circuit independent. In this way, Thomson and Houston solved the problem of subdividing the electric light. Previously, electrical inventors had been able to run only one large arc light from a single dynamo, but now they were able to use a dynamo to power several smaller lights. The two men drew up patent applications for their AC system, but they soon set them aside when two Philadelphia businessmen offered to fund a DC arc-lighting system (Carlson 1991, 96–105).

In 1885, after he had successfully introduced an arc-lighting system with Coffin's help, Thomson reviewed his earlier work with induction coils and began to sketch several new systems. Like other inventors, he sensed that it would be desirable to develop a distribution system whereby power could be transmitted to incandescent lights over distances greater than one or two miles, then the physical limit for existing DC systems. Because of this limitation, DC incandescent stations were erected only in towns and cities with sufficient population density to pay for the costs of installing large copper mains. To overcome these difficulties, in March 1885 Thomson sketched an AC system using induction coils with their primary windings in parallel, a system that would step the voltage down from 1,000 to 110 volts.

The advantage of using the higher voltage was that it permitted efficient transmission of power over long distances. Thomson also included several safety devices to minimize the danger of electrocution from the high voltage. On the primary or high-voltage side of the transformer, he inserted a fuse, and on the secondary or low-voltage side, he added a ground connection. In case of a short circuit between the primary and secondary coils, that ground connection would conduct the high-voltage current away from the electric lights. Inclusion of such safety devices was part of Thomson's business-technological mind-set: build a system that is both reliable and not harmful to the customer.[22]

In designing that system in early 1885, Thomson was not especially concerned with introducing it commercially; rather, he considered the invention as one of several projects he might pursue. Instead, it was Coffin who first realized the commercial potential of an AC lighting system. During a trip to Europe in 1885, Coffin saw a demonstration of an AC system developed by the Hungarian inventors Zipernowsky, Blathy, and Deri (ZBD). Although Coffin always claimed that he knew nothing of the intricacies of electrical technology, he quickly realized from the ZBD system that alternating current could be used to build central stations in smaller cities and towns. On his return, he urged

22. Foster 1920, especially 81; "System of Electrical Distribution by Means of Induction Coils, Mar 5. 85," Exhibit no. 12, "Testimony on Behalf of Elihu Thomson and Edwin J. Houston . . . ," Patent Interference no. 13,761 (subject: transformer distribution systems), Hall of History Collection, 307; ET, "Induction Apparatus Interf. with Gravier," July–August 1884, TP; ET to H. C. Townsend, 10 April 1885, TP, LB 5/83–8/85, 65–67, and 110–12; ET to J. A. Fleming, 12 October 1885, TP, LB 8/85–3/86, 82–83; ET to Townsend & MacArthur, 6 January 1887, TP, LB 9/86–3/87, 223.

Thomson to pursue his work with induction coils and to file additional patent applications for parallel circuits as soon as possible.[23] Through late 1885 and early 1886, Thomson tested an AC system.

Because safety was to be an important feature of his system, Thomson continued to improve the designs of the fuses and other safety devices. By June 1886, he had run an experimental AC power line between two buildings at the Lynn plant to deliver current to incandescent lamps. By the year's end, the company was advertising AC generators in its catalog, emphasizing that it could furnish power to incandescent lights over long distances using wires that were smaller than those used in DC systems. Although the catalog described four generator models, none had actually been sold or installed.[24] From an organizational perspective, work went forward on the AC system because two interest groups agreed that it was a worthwhile project: Thomson's group had already done preliminary work in the area, and Coffin's group had decided that an AC system would help them reach new customers.

In the meantime, however, George Westinghouse was making progress in developing his own AC system for incandescent lighting. First, with the help of Frank L. Pope, an independent consulting engineer, Westinghouse purchased the American rights to a transformer distribution system developed in England by Lucien Gaulard and John Gibbs. Second, Westinghouse supported William Stanley's research aimed at improving the transformer, which led to a successful demonstration of AC distribution in March 1886 in Great Barrington, Massachusetts. Westinghouse engineers followed up Stanley's success by redesigning the transformer during the summer of 1886. By intensively funding development in this way, Westinghouse was able to install its first AC system in Buffalo in November 1886.[25]

23. For a discussion of the work of Gibbs and Gaulard and Zipernowsky, Blathy, and Deri, see Hughes 1983, 86–98. For an early description of the ZBD system, see "Alternating Electric-Current Machines," *Electrical World,* 31 May 1884, 173–74. For Coffin's interest in European developments, see ET to G. Cutter, 7 October 1885, TP, LB 8/85–3/86, 76–80. and ET to H. C. Townsend, 23 October 1885, TP, LB 83–11/85, 249–50. On learning of the ZBD system, Thomson wrote to several people and claimed that the ZBD system was a duplicate of the one he had sketched in 1879; see ET to C. J. Wharton, 21 September 1885, TP, LB 8/85–3/86, 35–37; ET to Edwin J. Houston (hereafter EJH), [28 September–3 October 1885], TP, LB 8/85–3/86, 55–56; ET to Laing, Wharton & Down, 15 October 1885, TP, LB 8/85–3/86, 93–94; and ET to EJH, 17 October 1885, LB 8/85–3/86, 103.

24. ET, "Electric Induction Apparatus," 11 June 1886, TP, LB 3/86–2/89, 168–72; ET to CAC, 5 February 1887, TP, LB 9/86–3/87, 334–37; ET to Townsend & MacArthur, 6 January 1887, TP, LB 9/86–3/87, 223; ET to Townsend & MacArthur, 1 and 19 March 1888, TP, LB 3/87–4/88, 884, 921–22; "Extracts (or Summaries) of Testimony in Patent Infringement Suit of General Electric Co. vs. Butler Company," Hammond File, J457–59; "Catalogue of Parts of Apparatus Manufactured by the Thomson-Houston Electric Co . . . ," 1886, Thomson Collection, MIT Archives, Cambridge.

25. Frank L. Pope, in discussion of "The Distribution of Electricity by Secondary Generators," *Telegraphic Journal and Electrical Review,* 15 April 1887, 349–54, especially 349; Hughes 1983, 98–105; Rice 1929; Drew and Chapman 1985, especially 7–19; Wise 1988.

Westinghouse gained an important advantage over Thomson-Houston by securing a broad patent for an AC distribution system with transformers in parallel. In contrast, all of Thomson's patent applications for AC distribution were rejected in the fall of 1886. This put the Thomson-Houston Electric Company in the defensive position of having to contest or else bypass the Westinghouse patent.[26]

Thomson responded to the Westinghouse patent for AC distribution by filing additional applications based on his early work with induction coils and arc lamps. Thomson submitted these applications not only to claim what he thought he had previously invented but also to "render it inconvenient for rivals to get around them."[27] In addition, he continued to experiment in the Model Room with different circuit configurations, hoping to find a way to circumvent the Westinghouse patent

3.4.2   The Groups Bargain and Fight

Nonetheless, by early 1887 Coffin and the marketing group were beginning to wonder whether perhaps the Model Room was not working fast enough. Why was Westinghouse already installing AC equipment, and not Thomson-Houston? Had not Thomson been working on patent applications for several months before Westinghouse had even ordered a Gaulard-Gibbs transformer from Europe? In February 1887, Thomson admitted to Coffin that work on the AC system was proceeding slowly. First, Thomson explained that although they had been working as rapidly as possible, "the development of the system had outgrown the model room, which is only adapted to producing small models and nothing of very large size." Thomson would have drawn on the resources of the factory as a whole, but the production department was overwhelmed with filling back orders. In other words, manufacturing was too busy to help development. But rather than simply blame manufacturing, Thomson offered a second revealing reason: he was determined to introduce a complete AC system, with generators, regulators, lamps, transformers, and safety devices all matched to each other, and designing such a system would take time. He believed that an AC system designed as a single entity would be the most reliable; to quote him again, "when we enter this field we wish to . . . be sure of success from the start with a complete and economical system, and the pre-

26. L. Gaulard and J. D. Gibbs, "System of Electrical Distribution," U.S. Patent 351,589 (26 October 1886); Kennedy 1887; "Specification of Elihu Thomson, Lynn, Mass. Distribution of Electric Currents," 9 October 1886, TP, LB 3/86–2/89, 232–40; ET to T-H Elec. Co., 28 September 1886, TP, LB 9/86–3/87, 18–19; ET to Townsend & MacArthur, 19 November 1886, TP, LB 9/86–3/87, 95–96; ET to H. N. Batchelder, 8 December 1886, TP, LB 9/86–3/87, 133–34; ET to Townsend & MacArthur, 10 December 1886, LB 9/86–3/87, 141.

27. ET to CAC, 5 February 1887, TP, LB 9/86–3/87, 334–37. See also ET to H. C. Townsend, 9 November 1886, TP, LB 3/86–2/89, 241–43; ET to Townsend & MacArthur, 23 November 1886, TP, LB 9/86–3/87, 103; ET to Townsend & MacArthur, 21 January 1887, TP, LB 9/86–3/87, 279–81; and ET to EJH, 18 February 1887, LB 9/86–3/87, 376–77.

paratory work that we have done will, we think, tell in the end."[28] Here is a clear statement of Thomson's belief that the best-designed product will in the long run be the most profitable.

In terms of group dynamics, the situation had progressed to the point that marketing was mistrustful of development, and the development group responded with a statement of its goals. The situation might have deteriorated further, but Thomson improved matters by adjusting his technology to the marketing strategy. Rather than insist that innovation could proceed only toward his technically perfect system, Thomson redirected his efforts so as to improve the company's short-term marketing position. To reduce the threat of patent litigation, Thomson helped the company arrange a patent-sharing agreement with Westinghouse. During a meeting of the American Institute of Electrical Engineers in March 1887, Thomson met with Pope and discussed the desirability of cooperating rather than competing in the AC field. After several meetings, officials from Thomson-Houston and Westinghouse reached an agreement in August 1887. In return for a license to sell Thomson-Houston arc-lighting equipment, Westinghouse allowed Thomson-Houston to manufacture AC systems without fear of infringing the Westinghouse AC distribution patent. Although this agreement was terminated within two years because the Westinghouse patent was ruled invalid in court, it did give Thomson-Houston time in 1887 and 1888 to improve its AC equipment.[29]

Knowing that a patent-sharing agreement could be only a temporary expedient, Thomson next initiated a new strategy to bypass the Westinghouse patent. Because Westinghouse controlled the right to the broad principle of using transformers for distribution, Thomson filed patents in 1888 on the designs of the most efficient transformers. Thus, the Westinghouse company would be unable to use its rights to apply the broad principle, because all of the best transformer designs would be owned by Thomson-Houston. In pursuing that strategy, Thomson filed patents for transformers with laminated cores of different shapes, and he began using an oil insulation bath.[30]

Still another way in which Thomson directed invention toward short-term marketing needs was through the exploitation of what he called "the principle of induction-repulsion." In 1886 Thomson discovered how a magnetic field created by an alternating current passing through an electromagnet could be used to create rotary motion. Excited by this discovery, Thomson used it to develop an AC motor and improved measuring instruments. In staking out his

28. ET to CAC, 5 February 1887, TP, LB 9/86–3/87, 334–37; ET to E. F. Peck, 22 March 1887, LB 9/86–3/87, 470–71.

29. Frank L. Pope to ET, 23 March 1887, Collected Letters; ET to CAC, 24 March 1887, TP, LB 3/87–4/88, 1; Passer 1953, 145–47.

30. ET to Townsend & MacArthur, 18 January 1887, TP, LB 9/86–3/87, 265–66; ET to CAC, 20 November 1889, TP, LB 4/89–1/90, 729–30; Walter S. Moody to J. W. Hammond, 15 April 1927, Hammond File, L2598–99.

claims for these inventions, Thomson emphasized that he had discovered a principle, in the belief that it could provide the company with general control over the applications derived from it. Over the next two years, Thomson perfected these inventions, giving Thomson-Houston new AC products that helped it gain a share of the market.[31]

Thomson began to redirect his development work toward short-term marketing needs in early 1887 and pursued that approach into 1889. Early on, Thomson's efforts began to pay off. In May 1887, the firm shipped its first AC machine to the Lynn Electric Lighting Company, and by the year's end it had installed twenty-two more systems. The first Thomson-Houston AC systems were installed in smaller cities, such as New Rochelle, New York; Kansas City, Missouri; Putnam, Connecticut; and Syracuse, New York, where the population density was too low to offset the initial cost of a DC incandescent system. Anxious to show his confidence in the new system and to have a full-scale circuit on which to test new devices, Thomson installed one of the new transformers and incandescent lamps in his home in Lynn. Because of his concern with safety, he employed in his home all of the safety devices he had created— the grounded secondary, fuses, and lightning arresters. He offered to promote the completed AC lighting system by writing an article for *Electrical World,* but he did so asking "whether my time would be more valuable to the Company employed on new work and in new fields rather than in describing apparatus and arrangements that are comparatively old with us."[32]

As Thomson directed the work of the Model Room to suit the needs and expectations of the marketing team, he proposed that marketing help implement some of his ideals. In particular, Thomson was anxious to see that his notions about the safe use of alternating current be implemented. Maintaining that the best system was a safe system, Thomson remarked that "I am a believer in the establishment of all safeguards which conduce to the good working of a system, especially when they do not add greatly to the cost of making the installation." More than just fulfilling his technological idealism, Thomson was confident that his safety inventions should be part of the marketing strategy used to fight Westinghouse. Once Westinghouse's broad patent for transformer distribution had been ruled invalid, Thomson suggested that all central stations

31. [ET], "Specification—Alternating Current Motor Device," 22 December 1886, TP, LB 3/86–2/89, 265–76; ET to G. Cutter, 17 December 1886, TP, LB 9/96–3/87, 163–67; ET to CAC, 5 February 1887, TP, LB 9/96–3/87, 334–37; Thomson 1887a; H. G. Hamann and F. G. Vaughen, "Developmental Work by Prof. Thomson on Electric Meters," TP, Biographical Materials; [ET], "Specification [for liquid electric meter]," 14 October 1887, TP, LB 3/86–2/89, 19–36; ET to CAC, 12 March 1888, TP, LB 3/87–4/88, 913; J. W. Gibboney to S. C. Peck, 26 October 1889, TP, LB 4/89–1/90, 611–12.

32. ET to Thomson-Houston Elec. Co., 13 June 1887, TP, LB 3/87–4/88, 163–64. The first Thomson-Houston AC incandescent plants are from "List of T-H Plants." Descriptions of AC lighting used in Thomson's home can be found in ET to Chas. C. Fry, 7 October 1887, TP, LB 3/87–4/88, 522–23; and ET to Prof. S. W. Holman, 21 October 1887, TP, LB 3/87–4/88, 572–75; ET to Lynn Elec. Lighting Co., 8 May 1888, TP, LB 4/88–4/89, 13–14; J. A. McManus, memorandum, 6 March 1936, Hall of History Collection; and Thomson 1887b.

using Thomson-Houston AC equipment be fitted with the latest safety devices. The company should then emphasize in its advertisements how safe its installations were in comparison with the Westinghouse plants. As a result of adverse publicity, Westinghouse would then be forced to install safety equipment as well. Because Thomson-Houston controlled the patents for the best safety features, Thomson believed that such a strategy would block Westinghouse from acquiring a larger share of the market for alternating current.[33]

As Thomson soon learned, the difficulty with his plan was that it presumed that Thomson-Houston would encourage its customers to install safety devices. Unfortunately, that was hardly the case in 1889. Instead, it appears that Thomson-Houston customers frequently ignored safety equipment and careful installation procedures in the rush to get "on line." Pushed by investors to begin selling electricity as soon as possible in order to make a return on the capital invested, utility operators were forced to keep their construction and installation costs to a minimum. Utilities did not always purchase all the necessary safety accessories; they used poorly insulated wire, and their linemen often were careless and indifferent to the special requirements of alternating current. Although Thomson realized that such poor practices were influenced by the competitiveness of the electric-lighting field, they nonetheless offended his mind-set. "I do not believe in this kind of economy," he warned Coffin. "Rather it would be better not to have the business than incur the risks which are thus involved."[34] As an inventor, Thomson would have liked to have had control of his creations from the initial conception to the final installation, but he soon realized that the marketing group was unwilling or unable to help him accomplish this. In this situation, although Thomson and the development group had adjusted their efforts to suit marketing's short-term interests, marketing had failed to reciprocate by promoting development's ideas about safety.

In failing to endorse Thomson's ideas about safety, the marketing group soon discovered that it had lost a key ally needed for fighting in the AC-DC controversy. Lasting from 1886 to 1895, that controversy involved whether AC systems should supplant DC systems, and it was a debate that soon included not simply technical matters but political and emotional issues as well. The controversy became particularly heated in 1888 as it became clear that AC systems could be used to supply incandescent lighting to small cities and towns lacking the population density needed to support a low-voltage DC system. Unable to compete with Westinghouse and Thomson-Houston for that market, the Edison organization decided to challenge the AC system by questioning its safety.

33. ET to T. F. Gaynor, 7 March 1888, TP, LB 3/87–4/88, 900–901. See also ET to CAC, 11 December 1888, TP, LB 4/88–4/89, 547–50.

34. ET to CAC, 13 February 1889, TP, LB 4/88–4/89, 761–66. See also ET to CAC, 16 February 1889, TP, LB 4/88–4/89, 780–82; ET to John J. Moore, 19 October 1889, TP LB 4/98–1/90, 594–96; ET to Narragansett Elec. Light Co., 22 April 1890, TP, LB 1/90–11/90, 443–44; Thomson 1888.

The higher voltages required for efficient transmission by alternating current, argued the Edison group, were more likely to cause injury and death.[35]

By the summer of 1889 Coffin and the marketing group were anxious to participate in the AC-DC debate. In all likelihood, they saw it as an opportunity to surpass their two rivals, Edison and Westinghouse. Defensively, they also may have been concerned that the publicity about "deadly" alternating current might harm sales, and they wanted to reassure customers that it was safe to buy Thomson-Houston equipment. Because the company was already manufacturing safety equipment, all that was necessary for a strong position in the debate was to have a leading authority promote the general use of alternating current. Given his established interest in electrical safety, Thomson was the obvious choice for this public-relations effort.

In October 1889, Coffin asked Thomson to write an article titled "How to Make Electricity Safe." Along with addressing the general issue of the safety of alternating current, Coffin wanted Thomson to provide a defense for AC power in the wake of an accident that had recently occurred at a utility in New York City. The utility had been using a Thomson-Houston AC system, and it was short-circuited when a telephone wire fell across the 1,000-volt power lines. Much to Coffin's dismay, Thomson turned down the assignment. The utility had done a poor job of installing its AC equipment, and Thomson felt that he could not personally defend such work. Unsafe installation was unacceptable to Thomson, and what was more, Thomson-Houston would not have been in that unfortunate defensive position had they listened to Thomson several months earlier.[36]

At first, Thomson simply suggested that he should remain quiet rather than be "a stumbling block in the way of the Company's business transactions." However, when Coffin pressed for a general endorsement of alternating current, Thomson exploded. In anger, he informed Coffin that he felt like quitting, because "my position with the Company has no attractions for me if my ideas of what is needed to constitute good substantial work are not followed but personally neglected." In a letter written on Christmas Eve 1889, he advised Coffin that the firm would have to recognize that he was primarily an inventor and would not be distracted by writing articles for publicity purposes. With respect to the safety of alternating current, he refused to give a blanket endorsement. "I have no method" he wrote, "I have no panacea—for all the ills which may follow the use of high potential currents under conditions usually found in large cities. I can no more say how to make electricity safe in such cases than I can say how to make railroad travel safe, or how to make steamship travel safe, or how to make the use of illuminating gas safe, nor the use of

35. Hughes 1983, 106–9; Passer 1953, 164–75; [Harold P. Brown] to Spencer Aldrich, 6 February 1889, TP, LB 4/88–4/89, 771–74; ET to CAC, 16 May 1889, TP, Collected Letters.
36. [A. C. Bernheim] to CAC, 16 October 1889, TP, LB 4/89–1/90, 589; ET to CAC, 6 November 1889, TP, LB 4/89–1/90, 658–61.

steam boilers safe. No improvement of our modern civilization has ever been introduced but that involved considerable risk."[37] Because he had designed the AC system, Thomson knew well the risks involved in using it. He lived by the principle that the best system was a safe system. But when he found that the marketing group was interested only in promoting safety as a short-term, defensive measure, he refused to cooperate. They had not been willing to adapt marketing policy to his technological goals, and so he was unwilling to compromise his principles about safety. As a result, the Thomson-Houston Electric Company took no public position in the AC-DC controversy, leaving the debate to be settled by Edison and Westinghouse.[38]

Viewed in terms of the clashing of group interests, it is easy to see why Thomson and the development group came to refuse to cooperate. First, Thomson was finding it difficult to work with the manufacturing group. Previously, although they had been unable to help him with the development work in early 1887, they had, for the most part, been willing to manufacture AC equipment according to Thomson's designs. By 1889, however, the firm's business was rapidly growing and expanding into the new field of electric trolleys; as a result, the factory mushroomed in size, and the tasks of coordinating production became immense. These changes made the production engineers quite cautious about modifying and improving other products, because this would mean more confusion in the factory. Modifications might well mean that manufacturing costs would go up and reduce profits. Production's conservative outlook soon became apparent to Thomson, as when he tried to introduce an improved transformer design in mid-1889. Manufacturing turned it down on the grounds that the new form would cost more to make than the old version, an argument with which Thomson had to agree. Nonetheless, he was disturbed by the event because it signaled that it was becoming more difficult to introduce the minor improvements that would ensure that the company was manufacturing the best possible system.[39]

A second issue that concerned Thomson was that patent litigation was distracting him from working on new inventions. By 1889, Thomson had filed 375 patent applications, which had unfortunately led to a sizable amount of litigation. By the end of that year, he had been named in over sixty interference cases, many of which required extensive testimony. In addition, Thomson-

37. ET to CAC, 19 October 1889, TP, LB 4/89–1/90, 579–83; ET to CAC, 20 December 1889, TP, LB 4/89–1/90, 867–78; ET to CAC, 24 December 1889; TP, LB 4/89–1/90, 903–8.

38. Thomson-Houston's nonparticipation in the AC-DC controversy is sometimes credited to Coffin, who chose not to enter the public debate and instead concentrated on selling systems. See, for example, Woodbury 1944, 173–74.

39. Thomson summed up his difficulties in introducing new inventions as follows: "The more our facilities grow the harder it seems to be to get through any special work of a new character, simply because we have no department that is absolutely set aside for this kind of work outside of the model department." From ET to S. C. Peck, 30 August 1889, TP, LB 4/89–1/90, 422. See also ET to J. S. Bell, 21 January 1888, TP, LB 3/87–4/88, 791–92; ET to T. C. Martin, 16 August 1889, TP, LB 4/89–1/90, 363–65; ET to F. P. Fish, 1 October 1889, TP, LB 4/89–1/90, 502–4; and "Recollections of L. G. Banker," Hammond File, J677–83.

Houston was actively suing firms that had infringed Thomson's patent for an automatic dynamo regulator. Accustomed to having Thomson assist them with the infringement litigation, the Thomson-Houston lawyers soon began using him as an expert witness in other cases. Although Thomson understood the importance of defending his patents, he came to question his participation in litigation, as it took him away from invention. Eventually he informed Coffin that he would no longer testify. "If I am to act as *inventor* for the Company," he wrote, "I shall not hold myself in readiness to be called upon as patent expert and handy man . . . for the more I invent, the more will my inventions . . . embarrass me in the future. . . . [It] is simply wasting my time to have to do . . . patent expert work."[40]

More than his difficulties with manufacturing or the troublesome patent litigation, Thomson was troubled by a third issue in 1889: his role within the company. As the preceding quotation indicates, Thomson saw himself as the firm's chief inventor. Many of Thomson-Houston's products were his handiwork, and his creative efforts had yielded handsome profits for the firm. Yet there were signs that Thomson might be losing his position as chief innovator. Beginning in 1888, Thomson was joined in the Model Room by other inventors who came to Lynn as their companies were bought out by Thomson-Houston. Although Thomson was nominally in charge of their work, he may have been worried that his own inventions would no longer be highly valued by management.[41]

In addition to the output of these new inventors, Coffin and the marketing group began to purchase more outside patents in 1888. Thomson intensely opposed this policy, and in 1888 and 1889 he approved the purchase of only a few patents. His opposition appears to have been based on fear that such a policy would jeopardize his control over innovations within the firm. Not only might the company no longer need him, but the policy of purchasing outside patents diluted the firm's product line with worthless items. One questionable patent purchased by the company in 1889 was for "electric water." When he learned that the company planned to test this substance, Thomson was enraged. He wrote the Boston office: "If our Company should go seriously to work to expand any money in making tests . . . I should feel like resigning on the spot. I have plenty of material which I do not have the opportunity to work up."[42] The purchase of outside patents and the arrival of other inventors must have

40. Quotations are from ET to CAC, 24 December 1889, TP, LB 4/89–1/90, 903–8. See also ET to Capt. E. Griffin, 9 October 1888, TP, LB 4/88–4/89, 374; ET to Ernst Thurnauer, 26 October 1889, TP, LB 4/89–1/90, 613; and ET to T-H International Electric Co., 4 January 1890, TP, LB 4/89–1/90, 945.

41. Along with Thomson, Rice, A. L. Rohrer, Wightman, Lemp, Van Depoele, and Priest filed patents in 1889; see J. W. Gibboney to Bentley & Knight, 6 June 1890, TP, LB 1/90–11/90, 597.

42. ET to Robert C. Clapp, 23 October 1889, TP, LB 4/98–1/90, 602–3. See also ET to Fish, 1 October 1889, TP, LB 1/90–11/90, 502–4; and ET to Capt. E. Griffin, 21 February 1890, TP, LB 1/90–11/90, 185–87.

suggested to Thomson that other members of the firm were implicitly challenging his control over innovation.

Thomson's decision not to accommodate Coffin may also have been informed by his contractual arrangements with the company. When the Thomson-Houston Electric Company was formed in 1882, Thomson agreed to serve as the firm's electrician in return for an annual salary of $5,000 and 15 percent of any new stock issued by the company. (Both the president of Thomson-Houston, Henry A. Pevear, and Coffin received stock when the company was formed, but the size of their holdings is unclear.) In 1887, Thomson signed a new agreement that extended his appointment to July 1890. In this agreement, Thomson gave up his share in any new stock issue in return for $8,000. Up to that time, the firm had not increased its capital stock, and Thomson may have concluded that he was better off taking the lump-sum payment. In May 1887, however, the company did increase its capital stock to $500,000. One source suggests that Coffin deliberately tricked Thomson into giving up his stock option, but I have not found any documents in which Thomson complained about losing his stock option. Nevertheless, by December 1889, Thomson may have decided that the early months of 1890 were the best time to put pressure on Coffin since it was then that they would have renegotiated his contract.[43]

Disappointed with the production group, tired of the patent litigation, and worried about this position as chief innovator, Thomson was in no mood to compromise his business-technological mind-set in the fall of 1889, especially as it related to the subject of safety. He had cooperated fully in the rapid introduction of the AC system and other products, only to find that other groups did not respect his efforts and authority. In fact, he even perceived them as undercutting his "power base" within the firm. And given that his contract was due to expire in July 1890, Thomson knew that it was time to force a change in his role with the company.

3.4.3   An Organizational Denouement

Even after his angry Christmas Eve letter, it took some time for Thomson-Houston managers to realize that Thomson expected to be treated differently. During the first months of 1890, he refused to evaluate any outside patents or to serve as an expert witness in court. Furthermore, Thomson expressed his anger by not corresponding with Coffin for nearly two months, even though previously they had exchanged letters and memos almost daily. Instead of coming in early and staying late at the Model Room, he spent more time at home and worked only half days. Using these tactics, Thomson communicated that he wanted his role within the firm to change.

---

43. [Agreement between ET and the T-H Electric Co.], 20 April 1887, TP, Collected Letters; *T-H Annual Report,* 1891; Pound and Moore 1931, 39.

Sensing Thomson's unwillingness to handle certain kinds of work, Coffin and Rice assigned routine product improvement to the engineering staff in the manufacturing group, and they established a legal department in 1891 to handle patent matters.[44] In the summer of 1890, Thomson replaced his contract with an informal agreement with Coffin by which he was permitted to work on projects of his own choosing, as well as those needed by marketing or production. Under this agreement, Thomson continued to develop new products, but he also looked for opportunities to direct his work toward scientific and professional goals. Although he filed for patents for improved transformers and electric welding equipment, Thomson also conducted research and published articles on high-frequency and high-voltage phenomena. Professionally, Thomson began to take a more active part in the affairs of the American Institute of Electrical Engineers, and he was elected president of that society in 1889 and 1890. To express his concerns about the safety of electric lighting systems, he served on the National Electric Light Association's subcommittee for overhead wiring, and he presented a paper, "Safety Devices in Electrical Installations," at their annual meeting in 1890.[45] In redefining his position, Thomson knew that he was relinquishing some of his power over product innovation within the firm; other inventors and engineers were becoming responsible for improving the company's products. However, he must have sensed that only by shifting his interests could he overcome the dissatisfaction he had felt so sharply in the fall of 1889.

Thomson's anger over the AC-DC controversy signaled to Coffin and others that the innovation function was neither fully understood nor properly located within the firm. Only after pushing Thomson to the brink did the firm realize that innovation involved a variety of tasks—inventing, patenting, giving expert testimony, and designing for manufacture—and that these activities needed to be institutionalized in separate departments. Furthermore, by buying outside patents and bringing in additional inventors, Coffin had wanted to expand the firm's sources of innovation, but he did so at the cost of upsetting the firm's original innovator. As a result of that experience, Coffin was much more circumspect about bringing in additional "star" inventors; for instance, Charles

44. See ET to Robert P. Clapp, 11 January 1890, TP, LB 4/89–1/90, 991–92; ET to Capt. E. Griffin, 3 March 1890, TP, LB 1/90–11/90, 220–22; and ET to Robert P. Clapp, 29 April 1890, TP, LB 1/90–11/90, 468. For the absence of letters from Thomson to CAC, see the first 175 pages of TP, LB 1/90–11/90. For the new patent department, see "Testimony," Intf. 15,511, 99.

45. For Thomson's informal agreement with Coffin, see J. A. McManus, confidential memorandum, 12 September 1935, Hall of History Collection. For his new research projects, see Thomson 1890a, 1891. Because of the demands placed on him by the company, Thomson was angry that he was not able to be more active as president of the American Institute of Electrical Engineers. As he complained to T. C. Martin, "this state of affairs is indeed very galling to me, and I hope to take steps to have the condition remedied sometime in the near future" (ET to T. C. Martin, 13 January 1890, TP, LB 1/90–11/90, 3–4). For Thomson's efforts to promote safety, see ET to Capt. Eugene Griffin, 27 December 1889, TP, LB 4/89–1/90, 902; ET to E. R. Weeks, 13 January 1890, TP, LB 1/90–11/90, 2; and Thomson 1890b.

Steinmetz came to the Lynn factory in 1892 only after he had been carefully interviewed by Thomson and Rice.[46]

These organizational changes meant neither a triumphant victory for Coffin and the marketing group nor a resounding defeat for Thomson and product innovation. Rather, as often happens in organizations, these two groups and their leaders made just enough adjustments to ease the immediate tension. Indeed, these changes marked the start of a decade of gradual reshuffling of various activities related to product development and engineering. During the 1890s, as Thomson-Houston became General Electric, Coffin and Rice continued to expand the engineering staffs at both the Lynn and Schenectady factories, assigning different engineering teams to improve existing products and production processes. Under the leadership of Albert G. Davis, the patent and legal office grew in size and importance. At the same time, the company continued to look to Thomson to develop new products. Because the depression of the mid-1890s curtailed the growth in the utility industry, GE asked Thomson to develop new products that used its existing manufacturing capabilities. Thomson designed an X-ray system that could be manufactured using the lamp production facilities in Harrison, New Jersey, and he experimented with automobiles, a product Coffin contemplated manufacturing at Lynn or Schenectady. However, in both cases, Thomson was frustrated that the equipment and manpower needed to build, test, and patent these new products was scattered across the company, making it very difficult to guide the development of these products. Consequently, in 1899, Thomson began calling for a central research and development facility in the company, and in 1900, GE responded by creating the industrial research laboratory at the Schenectady factory (Carlson 1991, 301–39). Although this laboratory brought together the resources and personnel needed for product innovation, its first leader, Willis R. Whitney, found himself in 1910s and 1920s bargaining and building coalitions for products much as Thomson did during the 1880s (Wise 1979, 1985).

3.5   Conclusion

Applying the interest-group model to the Thomson-Houston Electric Company reveals that it is possible to get inside the firm and trace how historical actors converted a small, entrepreneurial start-up to a large firm with a formal managerial structure. Significantly, this approach focuses our attention not only on how key activities were brought inside the firm but also on how these functions were coordinated by managers.

As the Thomson-Houston case reveals, the managers of this company responded to the challenges of electric lighting by taking up the tasks of organizing a national sales force, building a substantial factory, and undertaking con-

46. ET to CAC, 24 December 1889, TP, LB 4/89–1/90, 903–8.

tinual improvement and expansion of their product line. The triumvirate of Coffin, Thomson, and Rice perceived clearly the complexities of the market, organized these perceptions into an effective strategy and structure, and out-performed the rival Edison and Westinghouse companies.

Although the rational-actor approach suggests that a firm will acquire a particular structure to implement a particular strategy, form does not automatically follow function. Once functions are brought within the firm, there is no guarantee that the managers will know how to create a set of organizational arrangements that will permit employees to develop each function fully. Rather, managers such as Coffin had to make choices about which functions they could fully develop in the organization. Given finite resources and a rapidly growing market, Coffin chose to devote resources and personnel first to organizing marketing, not product innovation. Coffin understood marketing, and in a complex environment, businessmen tend to do what they know how to do best. Even though innovation was as important to the firm's well-being as marketing, neither Coffin nor Thomson fully understood all of the activities related to developing new products, and so they organized this function on a trial-and-error basis. Although the firm did establish the Model Room for Thomson, the company came to understand all of the tasks related to product innovation only after Thomson became overextended and angry in 1889. Thus, although it may be obvious to us with our functionalist hindsight that the marketing strategy of central stations called for having the firm perform the function of product innovation, the historical record reveals that members of the firm did not automatically or instinctively create the organizational structure needed to fully pursue innovation. Instead, based on a variety of factors—the personalities, skills, and perceptions of the actors—a firm may integrate different functions or activities at different times and different ways. Indeed, that the managers at Edison and Westinghouse presumably had access to the same information and opportunities but created very different organizations underlines the contingent nature of how managers chose to institutionalize the key functions associated with electric lighting.

To make sense of the contingency associated with how functions are coordinated within the firm, we need a organizational/political perspective. Using an interest-group model, we can see how the strong personalities in Thomson-Houston strove to create groups or departments to use their talents and implement their business-technological mind-sets. Choosing at times to bargain and cooperate with each other and at other times to disagree, these interest groups determined how the key functions of design, manufacture, and marketing were coordinated in the process of introducing a new product such as AC lighting. Clearly, the coordination of the functions within the firm did not follow automatically from any strict logic but rather was the result of the political give-and-take of interest groups.

It is important to note that while the give-and-take of groups within firms is highly contingent, the consequences of this interaction can be long-lasting and difficult to change. As entrepreneurs and inventors make the transition from start-up firm to formal managerial hierarchy, they create patterns of social interaction that can be difficult to alter. Once the members of the Thomson-Houston organization became accustomed to emphasizing marketing over product innovation, Thomson had to use rather dire tactics to alter his position in the company. Similarly, it took GE's brush with bankruptcy during the Panic of 1893 before Coffin and the other former Thomson-Houston managers were able to rethink their marketing strategy and move into new areas such as the electrification of factories (Carlson 1991, 304–11).

This observation of the conservative nature of organizational culture complements points made by Daniel Raff and Daniel Nelson in this volume. In his paper (chap. 1 in this volume), Raff suggests that the proliferation of compensation schemes in the U.S. auto industry in the 1920s must be explained in part by the tendency of firms to evolve their own internal practices in response to their own peculiar needs and customs. Likewise, Nelson (chap. 2 in this volume) reveals that while industrial engineering is a significant cultural and intellectual development in twentieth-century America, we should be cautious in assuming it significantly altered business practice. According to Nelson, managers tended to employ industrial engineering consultants to fix short-term problems and instead made decisions within the framework of existing corporate practice. Taken together, these three papers suggest that the need to pay attention to how the structure and culture of a firm influence its ability to change and take up new innovations (see also Mokyr 1992).

Using the interest-group model to study the development of the AC system also reminds us that there is no "one best way" to develop and use an innovation. Market forces may suggest some ways that a technology may develop, but only when groups within the firm perceive those market opportunities and link them to particular innovations. Moreover, within an organization, different groups will perceive markets and technologies differently, and a new product can only be brought to market when different groups negotiate and coordinate their efforts. As Langdon Winner (1986) has suggested, technological artifacts do have politics. Significantly, this political process—whereby a technological development is linked to interests of different groups—is not a "bad thing," in the sense that the technology is compromised. Indeed, if the story the Thomson-Houston AC system teaches us anything, it is that negotiation among groups is the only way that firms can ensure that a product will possess an effective set of attributes that will permit it to be manufactured and marketed. To some extent, this is a lesson that American engineers and manufacturers have relearned, given the recent interest in development teams and concurrent engineering (Wheelwright and Clark 1992).

In highlighting the importance of how individuals and groups negotiate within the firm, I am not denying the rational quality of the outcome. Thomson-Houston did perform better in the marketplace, beating out Edison General and Westinghouse, because its leaders created a winning combination of strategy and structure. Rather, in taking an organizational approach, I want to suggest that what is interesting is the *process* by which Coffin, Thomson, and Rice created and maintained the winning combination. To study this process, we need to integrate the analytical tools of the economist and the historian. From the economist, we need the perspective that presents the firm as a set of production possibilities and helps us to analyze how firms with various production possibilities interact in a market or industry. Within the firm, an economics perspective is also essential in making sense of mind-set of individuals and groups; how do groups organize their perceptions of markets and technology into a coherent set of practices? At the same time, we need the historian's perspective to identify the social dynamics of groups inside and outside the firm and to address the subtle and contingent roles that personality, values, and culture play in shaping business decisions. Thus, it is only by combining economics and history that we will be able to understand that central institution of capitalism, the business firm.

References

Allison, Graham T. 1971. *Essence of Decision: Explaining the Cuban Missile Crisis.* Boston: Little, Brown.

Bacharach, Samuel B., and Edward J. Lawler. 1980. *Power and Politics in Organizations: The Social Psychology of Conflict, Coalitions, and Bargaining.* San Francisco: Jossey-Bass.

Brown, John Kennedy. 1992. The Baldwin Locomotive Works, 1831–1915: A Case Study in the Capital Equipment Sector. Ph.D. diss., Department of History, University of Virginia.

Carlson, W. Bernard. 1991. *Innovation as a Social Process: Elihu Thomson and the Rise of General Electric, 1870–1900.* New York: Cambridge University Press.

———. 1992. Artifacts and Frames of Meaning: Thomas A. Edison, His Managers, and the Cultural Construction of Motion Pictures. In *Shaping Technology/Building Society: Studies in Sociotechnical Change,* ed. Wiebe E. Bijker and John Law, 175–98. Cambridge: MIT Press.

Chandler, Alfred D., Jr. 1962. *Strategy and Structure: Chapters in the History of the American Industrial Enterprise.* Cambridge: MIT Press.

———. 1977. *The Visible Hand: The Managerial Revolution in American Business.* Cambridge: Harvard University Press.

———. 1990. *Scale and Scope: The Dynamics of Industrial Capitalism.* Cambridge: Harvard University Press.

Coase, Ronald H. 1937. The Nature of the Firm. Reprinted in *The Firm, the Market, and the Law* 33–56 (Chicago: University of Chicago Press, 1988).

Cyert, Richard, and James G. March. 1963. *A Behavioral Model of the Firm.* Englewood Cliffs, N.J.: Prentice-Hall.

David, Paul A. 1985. Clio and the Economics of QWERTY. *American Economic Review* 75:332–37.

Davidson, James West, and Mark Hamilton Lytle. 1982. *After the Fact: The Art of Historical Detection.* New York: Knopf.

Drew, Bernard A., and Gerard Chapman. 1985. William Stanley Lighted a Town and Powered an Industry. *Berkshire History* 6 (fall): 1–36.

Foster, W. J. 1920. Early Days in Alternator Design. *GE Review* 23 (February): 80–90.

Galambos, Louis. 1979. The American Economy and the Reorganization of the Sources of Knowledge. In *The Organization of Knowledge in America,* ed. A. Oleson and J. Voss, 269–84. Baltimore: Johns Hopkins University Press.

———. 1991. The Triumph of Oligopoly. Unpublished paper.

Hughes, Thomas P. 1976. The Development Phase of Technological Change. *Technology and Culture* 17:423–31.

———. 1983. *Networks of Power: Electrification in Western Society, 1880–1930.* Baltimore: Johns Hopkins University Press.

Jenkins, Reese V. 1975. *Images and Enterprise: Technology and the American Photographic Industry, 1839 to 1925.* Baltimore: Johns Hopkins University Press.

Kennedy, Rankin. 1887. Electrical Distribution by Alternating Currents and Transformers. *Telegraphic Journal and Electrical Review,* 15 April, 346–47.

Law, John, and Michel Callon. 1992. The Life and Death of an Aircraft: A Network Analysis of Technical Change. In *Shaping Technology/Building Society: Studies in Sociotechnical Change,* ed. Wiebe E. Bijker and John Law, 21–52. Cambridge: MIT Press.

Leslie, Stuart W. 1979. Charles F. Kettering and the Copper-Cooled Engine. *Technology and Culture* 20:752–76.

McCraw, Thomas K., ed. 1986. *America versus Japan.* Boston: Harvard Business School Press.

March, James G., and Johan P. Olsen. 1976. *Ambiguity and Choice in Organizations.* Bergen: Universitetsforlaget.

Mitchell, Sidney Alexander. 1960. *S. Z. Mitchell and the Electrical Industry.* New York: Farrar, Straus and Cudahy.

Mokyr, Joel. 1992. Technological Inertia in Economic History. *Journal of Economic History* 52 (June): 325–38.

Passer, Harold C. 1952. Development of Large-Scale Organization: Electrical Manufacturing around 1900. *Journal of Economic History* 12 (fall): 378–95.

———. 1953. *The Electrical Manufacturers, 1875–1900: A Study in Competition, Entrepreneurship, Technical Change, and Economic Growth.* Cambridge: Harvard University Press.

Pfeffer, Jeffrey. 1981. *Power in Organizations.* Cambridge: Ballinger.

———. 1992. Understanding Power in Organizations. *California Management Review* 34:29–50.

Pinch, Trevor J., and Wiebe E. Bijker. 1987. The Social Construction of Facts and Artifacts: Or How the Sociology of Science and the Sociology of Technology Might Benefit Each Other. In *The Social Construction of Technological Systems: New Directions in the Sociology and History of Technology,* ed. W. E. Bijker, T. P. Hughes, and T. J. Pinch, 17–50. Cambridge: MIT Press.

Pound, Arthur, and Samuel Taylor Moore, eds. 1931. *More They Told Barron: Conversations and Revelations of an American Pepys in Wall Street.* New York: Harper and Brothers.

Rice, E. W. 1929. Missionaries of Science. *GE Review* 32 (July): 355–61.

Rosenberg, Robert. 1984. Test Men, Experts, Brother Engineers, and Members of the Fraternity: Whence the Early Electrical Work Force? *IEEE Transactions on Education* E27 (November): 203–10.

Schumpeter, Joseph. 1934. *Theory of Economic Development.* Cambridge: Harvard Economic Studies.

Shaw, A. C. 1892. "Thomson-Houston": Or Among the Dynamo Builders of Lynn. *Electrical Engineer,* 29 June, 647–61.

Staudenmaier, John M. 1985. *Technology's Storytellers: Reweaving the Human Fabric.* Cambridge: MIT Press.

Temin, Peter, ed. 1991. *Inside the Business Enterprise: Historical Perspectives on the Use of Information.* Chicago: University of Chicago Press.

Thomson, Elihu. 1887a. Novel Phenomena of Alternating Currents. *Electrical Engineer* 6 (June): 211–15.

———. 1887b. Systems of Electric Distribution. *Scientific American Supplement,* 23 July, 9632–34.

———. 1888. Insulation and Installation of Wires and Construction of Plant. *Electrical Engineer* 7 (March): 90–91.

———. 1890a. Phenomena of Alternating Current Induction. *Electrical Engineer,* 9 April, 212–14.

———. 1890b. Safety and Safety Devices in Electrical Installations. *Electrical World,* 22 February, 145–46.

———. 1891. Notes on Alternating Currents at Very High Frequency. *Electrical Engineer,* 11 March, 300.

Wheelwright, Steven C., and Kim B. Clark. 1992. *Revolutionizing Product Development: Quantum Leaps in Speed, Efficiency, and Quality.* New York: Free Press.

Williamson, Oliver E. 1985. *The Economic Institutions of Capitalism: Firms, Markets, and Relational Contracting.* New York: Free Press.

Wilson, Charles E. 1946. *Charles A. Coffin, 1844–1926: Pioneer Genius of General Electric Company.* New York: Newcomen Society.

Winner, Langdon. 1986. Do Artifacts Have Politics? In *The Whale and the Reactor: A Search for Limits in an Age of High Technology,* ed. L. Winner, 19–39. Chicago: University of Chicago.

Wise, George. 1979. "On Test": Post-Graduate Training of Engineers at General Electric, 1892–1961. *IEEE Transactions on Education* E22 (November): 171–77.

———. 1980. A New Role for Professional Scientists in Industry: Industrial Research at General Electric, 1900–1916. *Technology and Culture* 21:408–29.

———. 1985. *Willis R. Whitney, General Electric, and the Origins of U.S. Industrial Research.* New York: Columbia University Press.

———. 1988. William Stanley's Search for Immortality. *American Heritage of Invention and Technology* 4 (spring–summer): 42–49.

Woodbury, David O. 1944. *Beloved Scientist: Elihu Thomson, a Guiding Spirit of the Electrical Age.* New York: Whittlesey House. Reprinted Cambridge: Harvard University Press, 1960.

Comment   John Sutton

In an excellent recent book on Elihu Thomson and General Electric, W. Bernard Carlson developed a fresh and valuable perspective on a series of issues that have been much studied since the publication in 1953 of Harold Passer's *Electrical Manufacturers, 1875–1900.* In this admirable paper, he uses the history of the Thomson-Houston company to develop a new theme, which relates to the way in which early entrepreneurial firms grow into elaborate managerial

John Sutton is professor of economics at the London School of Economics, where he directs the Economics of Industry Group (STICERD).

organizations. Central to this theme is the notion that we must move away from the idea of the firm as a single maximizing agent, toward the more complex representation of the firm as a set of separate interest groups, with differing aims. These differing aims, the argument goes, may sometimes conflict, and may sometimes be reconciled. Only through an understanding of these processes can we hope to arrive at a satisfactory explanation of the firm's actions.

In Carlson's version of this approach, two ideas are emphasized: (i) progress occurs in the firm when the leaders of groups strive for cooperation rather than overtly challenge each other; (ii) the reason groups differ in their aims is that they differ in their "set of ideas and perceptions . . . of the market and of the potential of different technological options." Now as a description of how things are, this seems unobjectionable. What matters is whether our understanding of why things happened as they did is advanced by reference to this more complex model of the firm. Carlson argues that it is, and he does so by means of an appeal to two episodes in the firm's history.

The first episode relates to the success of Thomson-Houston in competing with Westinghouse and the Edison organization in installing central stations during the late 1880s. Carlson attributes Thomson-Houston's leading position to the fact that it successfully integrated its marketing, manufacturing, and innovation functions. That it succeeded in bringing these three groups into step is well established here, and I quite accept that this success was an important contributory factor in Thomson-Houston's rise. On the other hand, I am not convinced that this is the whole story.

The origins of Thomson-Houston's strength in this period can be traced to the arc-lighting era of the early 1880s, when it competed successfully against the two firms then dominant, Brush and Weston. Of the 6,000 arc lights in use at the beginning of 1881, 5,000 were made by Brush and the remainder by Weston (Passer 1953, 56). By 1890, Thomson-Houston, and the companies it owned or controlled, accounted for two-thirds of the 235,000 arc lights in service.

Thomson-Houston's success in this period can be attributed to several factors (Passer 1953, 57); it is arguable that two of these were crucial. The first lay in Thomson-Houston's strong focus on building up its position in the profitable "central-station" business; it was as a result of this that Thomson-Houston entered the next phase of competition—where its main rivals were to be the Edison organization and Westinghouse—with a head start. It had a strong position in supplying central stations, and usually placed clauses in its contract with the licensee company, requiring it to continue purchasing supplies from Thomson-Houston. The second factor distinguished Thomson-Houston from its less successful rivals: "After developing a workable system, Brush turned to other fields of interest and took out no arc-lighting patents after 1880. The Brush system of 1890 was essentially the one he had designed ten years before. Weston also turned to other matters and did almost nothing in arc lighting after 1880. But Elihu Thomson continued to improve and perfect his system all through the 1880s and the 1890s. He thus helped his company to secure and maintain its dominant position in arc-lighting equipment" (Passer 1953, 57).

Other factors also played a part; Thomson-Houston enjoyed the financial backing of a group of businessmen who were prepared to take the long view and to underwrite Thomson-Houston's policy of acquisitions, which played an important role in the company's growth. But whatever the view one takes of the relative importance of the several factors underlying Thomson-Houston's early growth, it is clear that the company was well established as a strong incumbent prior to the crucial period in the late 1880s when it had to face new competition from Edison and Westinghouse.

The interpretation of the events that followed, as developed in the present paper, goes like this: Thomson-Houston succeeded in fusing the aims of three crucial groups within the company, which dealt with marketing, manufacturing, and innovation. The Edison organization, by contrast, was a loose and poorly coordinated set of companies; it developed a sales organization but suffered from weaknesses in product innovation and production. Westinghouse, in spite of its strength in innovation, was weak both in marketing and in finance, where its lack of strong links to banks proved crucial in the crisis of 1890.

By the end of the decade, price competition intensified, while the pace of innovation demanded substantial investment. Increasing financial pressures, as Carlson has argued elsewhere (1991, 292–94), led to two initiatives by outside financiers to consolidate the industry. They first attempted to arrange that Thomson-Houston should take over the ailing Westinghouse. The failure of this initiative led them to encourage Coffin at Thomson-Houston, and Villard at Edison, to investigate a merger of their two companies.

So what, then, are we to conclude from this first example? We can certainly agree that it is important and arguably even crucial to long-term success that an integration of aims between functions should be achieved. But Carlson argues for more than this; his concern is to convince us that a proper understanding of how the industry evolves demands that we come to grips with his "intrafirm groups" model, rather than treat each firm as a "single agent." Relative to this argument, his first example is suggestive rather than convincing; much depends on how much importance we attach to the factors that he emphasizes in drawing up the strengths and weaknesses of the three main players on the eve of the financial reorganization of 1892, in which the future General Electric was born of a fusion between Thomson-Houston and the Edison organization.

The second episode that Carlson chooses to advance his thesis is more convincing; it relates to the approach taken by Thomson-Houston to the emergence of alternating current, where Westinghouse led the field. The issue is, why did Thomson-Houston take so long to make a serious commitment to this field? On Passer's interpretation, which fits nicely into a "single agent" framework, Thomson-Houston played a cautious, sensible, and successful low-risk strategy by being a "fast follower"; when, and only when, a first mover had shown that a new system could be established profitably in the market would Thomson-Houston then follow. Given the company's strength in the market, it could afford to wait, knowing that it could in due course establish itself in the new regime.

Carlson will have none of this: for him, the slowness of Thomson-Houston's entry into the field did not reflect the rational calculation of a single agent. Rather, it was born of an impasse within the company between people whose vision of the technology and the marketplace were in sharp conflict. Carlson's account of the differing priorities, preconceptions, and goals of Thomson and Coffin is telling. His interpretation of slow advance as the outcome of this stalemate is persuasive.

But, like Oliver, I would like to ask for more. Will this kind of example persuade economists to open up the black box that is their "firm," and delve into its internal organization, the better to understand the evolution of market structure? Perhaps. But I have some niggling doubts. Not only do we have to rule out Passer's "single agent" interpretation, but we are told by Carlson that the eventual outcome was, in some sense, a "good" one for Thomson-Houston. If I wanted to convince someone to adopt this more complex model of the firm, I would feel best armed if I had some examples in which the outcome was both difficult to reconcile with any reasonable "single agent" interpretation and was highly unsatisfactory to the firm in question.

The kind of example I would appeal to is well illustrated by Foster's discussion of DuPont's actions in the U.S. tire market in the late 1960s, when the dominant nylon-based tire was about to be overtaken by the technically superior polyester tire (1986, 123ff.).

DuPont was the market leader in nylon-based tires; it was also the leading producer of tire cord. It seemed ideally positioned to take over leadership in the new polyester-tire business. But it did not. Instead, the Celanese company, which had no interests in nylon, took a 75 percent share of the market with its polyester-based tires.

The reason for DuPont's failure lay in its internal organization. Foster gives a fascinating account of the internal maneuverings of the nylon department, which had a big investment in the "old" technology, versus the innovators in the polyester department, who wished to champion the new. All companies find it hard to accept that sunk costs are sunk, and the advent of a new technology means that we may have to write off investments whose true economic value has suddenly collapsed. These difficulties can be reconciled if there is a strong center, or if—in Carlson's framework—all groups are cooperating. In practice, there may be some game playing of the kind Foster describes at DuPont: First, the polyester champions develop a new product. The performance of the prototype is just below that of nylon, but is improving fast. This is met by a delaying tactic; the nylon department regards the case as unproven, and in the interval that intervenes before polyester really proves itself, a major new nylon tire plant is built. Now it becomes even harder to argue that sunk costs are sunk—and by the time DuPont moves, Celanese has taken the lead.

Before I close, I would like to turn to Carlson's final remarks, in which he takes up a question that is central to the present volume: Why should economists and historians talk to each other? Here I take a stronger line than Carlson. What is involved is not the usual sort of argument that we hear whenever "multidisciplinary studies" are mentioned: the point, for once, is sharp, specific, and should—for the economists at least—be compelling, for it derives directly from the central core of economic theory itself.

A decade of work on game-theoretic models in industrial organization has made it plain that, in representing any market of interest, there will usually be many a priori reasonable models, whose design differs in respect of features that we cannot observe, identify, or proxy empirically. As a result, many outcomes are "consistent with theory." Now if *all* outcomes are possible, we are in the historian's realm of accident and personality; and the business historian need pay little heed to what the economist has to say. But this is not, in fact, the case. Many outcomes are possible, but by no means all. It turns out that there are certain competitive mechanisms whose operation across *all* reasonable candidate models constrains the set of possible outcomes. These "robust" mechanisms include, notably, the process of price competition and the process of competitive escalation of innovative efforts—whose operation serves to delimit the set of outcomes that can emerge (Sutton 1991).

Carlson's first example, which he elaborated more fully in Carlson 1991, shows these two mechanisms leading to just the kind of breakdown of market structure that economic theory predicts (compare the story of Carlson 1991, 293ff. with that of Sutton 1991, chaps. 6 and 8, for example). What the economist has to offer the historian here is the statement that *some* shift of structure involving exit, merger, or consolidation was probably inevitable by 1890–92. This observation suggests that we should not try to explain too much by claiming that this firm was strong, or that one weak. Something had to give.

But many outcomes were possible: economic theory places only weak constraints on the data. And it is for this reason that the economist cannot do without the historian. Only by delving into the details can we hope to understand why one configuration emerged rather than another. Coffin's angry retort that he'd prefer to see Westinghouse go bankrupt rather than merge with him is hardly the kind of mechanism on which we can build models—yet it probably had as much to do with the emergence of the General Electric–Westinghouse duopoly, as opposed to a THW–Edison duopoly, as did anything else in this fascinating story.

References

Carlson, W. B. 1991. *Innovation as a Social Process: Elihu Thomson and the Rise of General Electric, 1870–1900.* New York: Cambridge University Press.

Foster, R. 1986. *Innovation: The Attacker's Advantage.* New York: Simon and Schuster.
Passer, H. 1953. *The Electrical Manufacturers, 1875–1900: A Study in Competition, Entrepreneurship, Technical Change, and Economic Growth.* Cambridge: Harvard University Press.
Sutton, J. 1991. *Sunk Costs and Market Structure.* Cambridge: MIT Press.

II At the Boundaries

4 Organization and Coordination in Geographically Concentrated Industries

Michael J. Enright

Economic activity requires the coordination of a variety of functions within and between firms. The organization of economic activity and the mechanisms used to coordinate such activity have become increasingly central issues for industrial economists and business strategists. While economists explore the advantages of markets versus hierarchies, business strategists are turning their attention to the notion of the boundaryless firm, and historians are studying the evolution of coordination mechanisms in particular companies and industries (see Williamson 1985; Hirshhorn and Gilmore 1992; papers in this volume). In this regard, geographically concentrated industries, industries in which many or most of the competitors are located in close proximity, provide unique opportunities to examine the organization of economic activity and the nature of coordination both within and among firms. The main reason is that geographic concentration increases the effectiveness of the external coordination mechanisms available to firms, and therefore allows for a wider variety of organizational forms and coordination mechanisms than might otherwise be observed. The boundaries between firms in such industries are sometimes blurred and often fluid, tending to respond to changes in product, technology, markets, competition, and government policy.

The first section of this paper introduces the phenomenon of geographic concentration, or localization, in industry. Particular attention is paid to the industrial organization of localized industries and the influence of localization on firm structures and incentives. Section 4.2 discusses the evolution of organizational forms and coordination mechanisms in three localized industries: the Hollywood motion picture industry, the Prato-area textile industry, and the Swiss watch industry. Though each example discusses the historical develop-

Michael J. Enright is professor of business administration at the Harvard Business School.

ment of organization and coordination in the localized industry, the focus is on the transformations that have taken place in the twentieth century. Section 4.3 explores some of the implications of the present work for students of economic and business organizations.

4.1 Geographically Concentrated Industries

Firms in a given industry are often located in close proximity to each other.[1] Geographic concentration within industries is pervasive, spanning large portions of the economies of most nations. In the United States, Detroit, Hollywood, Wall Street, Madison Avenue, Silicon Valley, and Route 128 are associated with particular industries. The world's two leading motorcycle companies and two leading musical instrument producers grew up in the Japanese city of Hamamatsu. Three of Japan's forty-seven prefectures produce the vast majority of the nation's silk and woven synthetic fabrics, whereas nearby companies account for the bulk of Japanese textile machinery, synthetic fiber, and carbon-fiber production. All of Germany's leading cutlery firms are located in Solingen, whereas the pen and pencil industries are centered in Nuremberg, optical equipment in Oberkochen and Wetzlar, tooling in Remscheid, and jewelry in Pforzheim. In Switzerland, Geneva and the Jura area are the centers of the watch industry; Basel is the home of the Swiss dye, pharmaceutical, and freight-forwarding industries; and Zurich is the center for banking, trading, and other financial services. Some of the most striking examples of localized industries are found in Italy. Sassuolo, a small town near Bologna, produces roughly 35 percent of the world's ceramic tiles. Montebelluna, in the Dolomites, supplies approximately 50 percent of the world's ski boots. Carrara is by far the world's leading center for stonecutting. Two areas, Arezzo and Valenza Po, account for more than $2 billion in precious-metal jewelry exports each year. Bologna is the home of nearly two hundred packaging machinery firms. Prato and Biella account for approximately 80 percent of Italy's wool textile output.

Despite the importance of geographically concentrated industries in most economies, such industries have only recently begun to capture the imagination of economists and business strategists.[2] Efforts to explain the development and dynamism of areas such as northern Italy and to explore what might be termed non-Chandlerian business development, or development through clusters of small firms rather than large managerial firms (see Chandler 1990), have inevitably focused on geographically concentrated industries. The present work seeks to add to the growing literature on this important topic.

1. For a more complete description of the industrial organization of geographically concentrated industries, see Enright 1990.
2. Porter (1990) emphasizes the role of localization in the development of internationally successful industries. Krugman (1991) terms localization the most striking feature of the geography of economic activity.

There are two types of localized industries. The first is characterized by increasing returns that are internal to the firm, while the second is characterized by increasing returns that are external to any single firm. Some industries are dominated by a small number of firms with production concentrated at one or a few facilities. One would expect such industries to be geographically concentrated. In the extreme case of ever-increasing returns at the plant level, one would expect to see an industry with a single-facility monopolist exhibiting maximum geographic concentration. The large commercial airframe and large jet engine industries in the United States have structures that approach this extreme.

The second, and in many ways more interesting, phenomenon is that of geographic clusters of firms in an industry. In such industries, the structure of firms influences, and is influenced by, the localization of industry. Localization leads to the development of external economies in terms of information flow, knowledge spillovers, and contacts with suppliers and buyers. Localization is often associated with low levels of vertical integration and diversification. In localized industries, geographic concentration may serve to limit the disadvantages that small firms face with respect to larger, vertically integrated firms. Localization can also facilitate the negotiation and monitoring of collusive arrangements among firms.

4.1.1 Clusters of Firms and External Economies

Firms within a geographic cluster are often able to draw advantage from their local environment. Marshall (1920, 1923) pointed out the importance of external economies that can arise from the concentration of many similar firms in the same location in the development of firms, especially in industries that require specific skills. Marshall's description of localized industries remains perhaps the most insightful in the literature.

> When an industry had chosen a locality for itself, it is likely to stay there long: so great are the advantages which people following the same skilled trade get from their neighborhood to one another. The mysteries of the trade become no mysteries; but are as it were in the air, and children learn many of them unconsciously. Good work is rightly appreciated, inventions and improvements in machinery, in processes and the general organization of the business have their merits promptly discussed: if one man starts a new idea, it is taken up by others and combined with suggestions of their own; and thus becomes the source of further new ideas. And presently subsidiary trades grow up in the neighborhood, supplying it with implements and materials, organizing its traffic, and in many ways conducing to the economy of its material. (1920, 225)

External economies encourage the localization of production in industries characterized by limited economies of scale. Although one might expect such industries to spread over space to serve geographically dispersed customers, significant requirements for industry-specific expertise or specialized inputs can cause clusters of firms to develop around sources of the necessary expertise and inputs. The Sassuolo-area ceramic-tile industry provides a good example. Demand for ceramic tiles is widespread, both in Italy and the rest of the world. Many other building-materials industries are geographically dispersed rather than concentrated. The efficient scale for ceramic-tile production is the single production line, which represents a small fraction (well under 1 percent) of the total market. Economies of scale in ceramic tile production are limited, but access to knowledge of the complex material transformation process and specialized suppliers (several of which operate in industries with significantly larger economies of scale than tile production) helps keep the industry localized in Sassuolo.

The evolution of clusters of suppliers, customers, and competitors is extremely important to the development of localized industries.[3] The external economies that such clusters create in terms of information flow and the spread of knowledge appear to give localized firms advantages in a wide range of industries. In many cases, suppliers and equipment manufacturers work closely with their local customers to develop new and improved products. Ongoing contact between buyer and supplier promotes rapid information flow and joint efforts to solve pressing problems. Local firms often serve as test sites for new ideas, or for the optimization of inputs and equipment. In return, they tend to receive exclusive use of the ideas, inputs, and equipment, at least for a short period of time. Outsiders must often be content with older inputs and equipment. The Sassuolo ceramic-tile industry, in which many technical advances were developed through the efforts of tile firms and equipment manufacturers, provides a good example of joint problem solving. One such advance, the single-firing process, reduced the cycle time for a batch of ceramic tiles from forty-eight hours to fifty minutes (Enright and Tenti 1990). Although the new technology caught on rapidly in and around Sassuolo, it was several years before equipment embodying the new technology was sold outside the area.

4.1.2 Firm Structures in Localized Industries

Firms within a geographic cluster often exhibit lower levels of vertical integration than their dispersed counterparts. Bologna-area packaging-machinery firms, for example, subcontract out a far higher proportion of their production than their competitors both inside and outside Italy. The same is true of Sassuolo ceramic-tile manufacturers. In Prato, there is no such thing as a vertically integrated textile firm. Each company concentrates on a single stage, such as spinning, in the production process. A single wool textile can go through five or six firms before it is finished. The synthetic fabric industry in Fukui, Ishikawa, and Toyama exhibits a similar level of disintegration. There are hundreds of small firms in Solingen that perform a single step in the cutlery production

3. See, for example, Hoover and Vernon 1959; Brusco 1982; Oakey 1985; Becattini 1987, 1989; and Scott 1987, 1988a, 1988b.

process. A single product will normally pass through many craft shops before it is finished. The Piacenza-area manufacturers of factory automation equipment are among the least vertically integrated in the world. Several companies actually do no metal bending, preferring to subcontract for all component production and to concentrate on assembly and software development.

Localization can influence the vertical structure of industries in two ways. The first is through the impact of the extent of the local market on the vertical structure of firms. Stigler (1951) points out that, as an industry increases in size, firms may start to specialize in certain activities, particularly those subject to increasing returns to scale over some range of output. He concludes that localization increases the effective economic size of an industry, allows for gains from specialization, and results in lower levels of vertical integration than are seen among geographically dispersed firms. Evans (1972) predicts that functions with an optimal scale larger than that required by a single firm will tend to be performed by separate firms. Co-location of firms in a given industry allows each activity to achieve its optimal scale. Though such activities could be undertaken by one of the firms in the original industry, Evans concludes that firms will generally not wish to buy from a competitor. Thus localization results in the emergence of supplier firms and lower levels of vertical integration than would otherwise occur.

Localization can also influence the vertical structure of firms through its impact on the costs of transactions, including the costs of negotiating and monitoring contracts and the costs associated with the potential for opportunistic behavior. When suppliers and buyers are physically close together, negotiations and monitoring become less costly. This will be true if information is transmitted through personal contact, communication costs increase with distance, or if there is a degradation in communication with increased distance. In addition, some localized industries develop standardized transactions and a common language that lower the cost of negotiation. In the Prato wool textile industry and the Japanese synthetic weave industry, standard contracts have developed that reduce the time and cost of negotiation. The Hollywood motion picture industry routinized the casting of extras through Central Casting in the 1920s. More recently, area-specific guild and union contracts have standardized many of the industry's transactions.[4] The repeated close-quarter transactions and cultural similarities often allow localized industries to develop such mechanisms even when dispersed firms do not.

Localization can also improve the effectiveness of market transactions by reducing the chances that a firm might engage in opportunistic behavior. A firm is unlikely to make an investment if its buyers or suppliers can renege on agreements after the investment is made. The more specific the investment

---

4. An interesting aside on the geographic concentration of the motion picture industry is that the three national officers of the Screen Actors Guild, the president, treasurer, and secretary, must reside in the Los Angeles area for the duration of their terms.

(the fewer alternative uses it has), the greater is the danger of such behavior.[5] Geographic concentration can reduce the specificity of investments (or assets), since the presence of several local firms in an industry provides alternative transaction partners should one firm renege on its agreements. Reduction of asset specificity greatly reduces the frequency of the potential holdup problems that might force firms to integrate vertically. Geographic concentration also allows news of opportunistic behavior to spread rapidly through the industry, making it more difficult for the offending party to make further contracts, thereby increasing the costs of engaging in opportunistic behavior. Finally, localized industries often develop additional governance structures, including social as well as economic strictures, that lower the risk of opportunistic behavior and therefore the costs associated with market transactions.[6]

The net result is that geographic concentration allows for the development of vertically disintegrated structures by allowing each activity to be performed at its optimal scale, reducing the transaction costs involved in market transactions, and by supplying additional mechanisms that foster firm interdependence.

4.1.3   Incentive Structures in Localized Industries

Markets and hierarchies each have advantages and disadvantages as mechanisms to coordinate transactions. The principal advantage of markets lies in the clear incentives that they provide firms, whereas the principal disadvantage of markets lies in their inability to coordinate certain complex or difficult transactions. The principal advantage of hierarchies lies in their ability to coordinate complex or difficult transactions, whereas the principal disadvantages of hierarchies are problems of incentives and bureaucracy, such as principal-agent problems (the incentives of the principal and the agent might differ), needless intrusion by upper management, a tendency to forgive deficiencies within hierarchies (failure to hold individuals or groups responsible for outcomes reduces their incentive to give an optimal effort), and the politicization of investment and operating decisions (decisions are based on politics rather than economics) (Williamson 1985). The disintegrated structures common in many localized industries allow market, or "high-powered," incentives to permeate the system. Firms operating in each stage of the production process face local markets that force them to be efficient and to improve their skills and capabilities continually. The structures can also increase overall industry efficiency by eliminating the incentive and bureaucratic features that limit the efficiency of hierarchical arrangements. In many instances, localized clusters of firms are able to obtain the benefits of organization through markets, though they can do so only if

5. Klein, Crawford, and Alchian (1978) link opportunism with specific assets. Williamson (1985) provides a complete treatment of the effect of specific assets on transactions.
6. dei Ottati (1987), for example, concludes that the sense of community present in Italy's industrial districts helps govern transactions within the districts. Piore and Sabel (1984) identify "social cohesion" as a factor that limits the range of behavior in industrial districts.

they develop coordination mechanisms that limit the disadvantages of the absence of hierarchy.

Other incentives also come into play in localized industries. In such industries, interpersonal and interfirm rivalry can be particularly fierce. In an environment in which industry participants know each other and the local press continually compares firms, the desire to be number one in the local industry becomes particularly acute. When Yamaha announced its intention to become the world leader in motorcycles, Honda moved quickly and decisively to meet the challenge from its local rival (both firms were from Hamamatsu).[7] The Sassuolo-area tile companies are owned by the leading citizens of the same town. Their place in the local pecking order is determined by the position and prestige attained by their firms. The same is true in the Hollywood motion picture industry, where a quick glance at the seating arrangements at leading restaurants shows the relative positions of industry participants.[8]

The economic literature on rank order tournaments indicates that this type of behavior may have adaptive value for localized industries. Rivalry for ordinal position (rivalry to outperform other participants rather than to achieve a particular level of performance), or "playing to win," can result in greater efficiency than other forms of behavior when it is costly to monitor effort and common shocks (environmental factors that affect all participants and are beyond their control) are relatively large. The basic argument is that when common shocks are large, absolute performance levels depend more on the shock than the efforts or capabilities of the participants. In these circumstances, rewards based on absolute performance outcomes do not induce optimal levels of effort. Instead, rewards based on ordinal position can induce superior levels of effort on the part of participants. In localized industries, where common shocks are large and monitoring, by those outside the firm, is costly, "playing to win" through investment in firm capabilities can increase the efficiency of the entire cluster of firms.[9] Thus the constant comparison among firms and the interpersonal and interfirm rivalry found in localized industries can contribute to the efficiency and competitiveness of the local industry.

Conversely, geographic concentration can also increase the level of cooperation among firms. Some forms of cooperation, such as bulk purchasing, joint

7. The president of Yamaha was forced to publicly apologize for attempting to take over the number one spot.

8. Several authors note that the interaction of economy and society within localized industries can lead to greater cooperation than would be observed among dispersed firms. The rationale is that economic activity is embedded in a larger set of social relationships that foster trust and cooperation. Less attention has been paid to the idea that social interaction can be competitive as well as cooperative and that the competitive aspects may spill over into economic behavior.

9. See Lazear and Rosen 1981; Green and Stokey 1983; and Nalebuff and Stiglitz 1983. In these papers, compensation schemes that depend on ordinal positions rather than absolute levels of output are shown to be superior (more efficient) when monitoring is costly and common shocks are large. As the number of participants increases, competition through investment in individual capabilities becomes more intense. Rewards based on ordinal positions provide the proper incentives for participants to expend effort and invest in their capabilities.

training programs, and industry-specific infrastructure investments, are often not possible when firms are dispersed. Localization can increase the political power of an industry, increasing the ability of its firms to lobby local authorities and giving it a greater voice in local affairs. Finally, the ease of communication within a geographically concentrated industry makes it easier to negotiate and monitor collusive agreements. If coordination is allowed to insulate firms from competitive pressures, however, incentives can become skewed, and the localized industry can lose its vitality. Coordination through collusion, by reducing competitive pressures, can actually reduce the pressure to coordinate productive activities effectively. Again we see that geographic concentration does not determine industry behavior, but allows for a greater range of behavior than might otherwise be observed.

4.2   Coordination of Productive Activities in Localized Industries

In general, there are a number of mechanisms that can be employed to co-ordinate activity within an industry, including spot markets, short-term coalitions, long-term relationships, and hierarchical organizations. The coordinating mechanisms used in a given industry will depend on production technologies, the nature of demand, the competitive environment, firm strategies, and government regulation. They will often change over time. Each coordinating mechanism employs its own set of coordinating tools and coordinating agents (see fig. 4.1). Prices and specifications are the tools used to coordinate the activities of spot markets. Spot markets require marketmakers to match supply with demand, or to take the place of the auctioneer of the neoclassical economist. Specific contracts of limited duration typically bind the members of short-term coalitions. These coalitions usually require an organizer or promoter to act as the coordinating agent. Economic or social interdependence, which is often formalized in general long-term contracts, serves to bind the members of long-term relationships. Usually, the members of such relationships are themselves the main coordinating agents. Finally, hierarchical organizations (firms) use compensation schemes to coordinate the activities of employees. The firms' managers are typically the main coordinating agents. (All the papers in this volume address one or more of these aspects of coordination.)

Simply listing the various organizational forms and coordinating mechanisms, however, does not tell us why a particular form or mechanism is used in a particular industry or situation. Only historical analysis of individual industries and firms can provide such an understanding. The following examples describe the evolution of coordination between firms in some well-known localized industries, each of which has seen dramatic change in organization and coordination in the twentieth century. Hollywood has been synonymous with the motion picture industry since the 1920s. Prato is perhaps the prototypical Italian industrial district. The watch industry has been one of Switzerland's

Coordination Mechanism	Coordinating Agents	Coordinating Tools
Spot Markets	Marketmakers	Prices, Specifications
Short-term Coalitions	Organizers	Short-term Contracts
Long-term Relationships	Partners	Interdependence
Hierarchy	Managers	Compensation

Fig. 4.1   Types of coordination

major success stories for centuries. The examples are not meant to provide a detailed explanation of why these industries are localized; I have done so elsewhere (Enright 1990). Instead, the examples take localization as a given and attempt to show the range of coordination mechanisms employed in localized industries and how these mechanisms have evolved in response to changes in products, technology, markets, competition, and government policies.

4.2.1   Coordination through Short-Term Coalitions: The Hollywood Motion Picture Industry

Hollywood, or more properly the Los Angeles area, has dominated the U.S. motion picture industry since the 1920s. In 1939, for example, Hollywood produced 90 percent of the feature-length motion pictures made in the United States and 65 percent of those produced in the world (Rosten 1970, 4). According to the Department of Commerce's census of service industries, in 1987 California accounted for 75 percent of U.S. motion picture production and 70 percent of U.S. television show production. The Los Angeles–Long Beach Primary Metropolitan Statistical Area (PMSA) accounted for 96 percent of California's motion picture and 85 percent of its television show production in that year. This translated into 71 percent of the nation's motion picture and 60 percent of the nation's television show production.

Industry History

Hollywood's rise to prominence began shortly after the turn of the century. In 1909, William Selig, a Chicago moviemaker frustrated by Chicago's weather (all movies were shot outdoors at the time) and running battles with the New York–based Motion Picture Patents Company (MPPC),[10] moved his

---

10. The MPPC was created in 1908 to pool and control the various patents that had been awarded on motion pictures and motion picture equipment. The trust sought to enforce its monopoly on motion picture production through the courts and through strong-arm tactics. The U.S. Justice Department eventually sued the MPPC for antitrust violations. The MPPC was dissolved by the courts in 1918.

business to Los Angeles. Another company, the Nestor Film Corporation, set up the first studio in Hollywood in 1910. Within three months, there were fifteen companies shooting films in Hollywood, which was soon transformed from a sleepy residential community into the motion picture capital of the world. The movie companies were initially attracted to Hollywood by the weather, the proximity of Los Angeles (which provided infrastructure and workers), location near other film companies (which stimulated the development of specialized services and suppliers for the industry), and low land prices. Another attraction was distance from New York (and the MPPC's strong-arm tactics) and proximity to Mexico (which permitted escape beyond the jurisdiction of U.S. marshals). The physical geography of the Los Angeles area allowed film companies to find a wide range of locations, including mountains, deserts, rivers, and ocean, within a day's journey. According to Schatz (1983, 35), the forces that were to become the major Hollywood studios were in place by 1914. By 1915, the local film industry payroll was already estimated at $15 million (Palmer 1938, 191, 198).

During the "studio era" (mid-1920s to 1949), the U.S. motion picture industry was controlled by eight corporations. The five so-called majors, Paramount, Loew's, Twentieth Century–Fox, Warner Brothers, and Radio-Keith-Orpheum (RKO), were fully integrated into production, distribution, and exhibition. Of the "little three," Universal and Columbia produced and distributed films but owned no theaters, whereas United Artists distributed films for independent producers but did no production and owned no theaters. The majors developed strategies based on creating stars, controlling distribution, and dominating exhibition through ownership of a small number of first-run theaters. This strategy allowed the majors to receive roughly 75 percent of the motion picture rental fees during the studio era. The "little three" received around 20 percent of the film rentals in the studio era; all other companies combined received around 5 percent.[11]

Coordination of the industry's activities was carried out within the vertically integrated firms. The majors' overall production and release schedules were set by corporate management in New York. The Hollywood studio chief and a small number of producers then organized the writing, pre-production work, filming, editing, and post-production work using actors, staff writers, directors, and crews, as well as pre- and post-production workers who were under long-term contracts (the so-called contract system). The studios attempted to utilize fully their fixed production assets to supply their other, larger fixed assets in exhibition and distribution.[12] Specialized skills and rigid union work rules (by the mid- to late 1930s) meant that a large number of individuals performed

11. Although the majors dominated motion picture production during the studio era, some independent producers, such as Samuel Goldwyn and David O. Selznick, producer of *Gone with the Wind*, were able to make their way during the period.

12. According to Gomery 1986, 8, production accounted for only 5 percent of the major studios' assets in the 1940s. Distribution accounted for 1 percent and exhibition (theaters) 94 percent.

sharply defined specialized tasks for a given film (Gomery 1986, 15). Hollywood and New York negotiated over budgets, schedules, wages, and investments. Final decisions usually rested with the CEO in New York, not the studio boss in Hollywood. The physical separation of management allowed the production chief to be part of the Hollywood creative milieu while corporate remained part of the New York financial and distribution community. The separation also allowed the studio chief a certain autonomy, providing some insulation from the very different tasks of distribution and exhibition.

Under the studio system, motion picture production in Hollywood became a standardized process tightly controlled and coordinated by the studio boss. Many believe the mass production of motion pictures reached its zenith (or nadir) at MGM, under Louis B. Mayer, and Warner Brothers, under Jack Warner, in the 1930s and 1940s. Mayer, MGM studio boss from 1924 to 1947, was reportedly the highest-paid executive in the United States in the 1930s. At MGM, producers could only sign stars and initiate projects with Mayer's express approval. Warner Brothers was particularly known for its assembly-line methods of moviemaking. Jack Warner and his assistants made all the important movie production decisions, generally trying to produce large volumes of films on small budgets, reusing stories, and operating with an overworked and underpaid studio staff (Gomery 1986, 68–69, 112–15).

An antitrust suit initiated by the Justice Department against the eight largest motion picture companies in 1938 had a dramatic impact on the movie industry. In 1948, the U.S. Supreme Court found that the companies had illegally monopolized the distribution and exhibition of motion pictures.[13] In what became known as the "Paramount Decision," the Court ordered the firms to divest their theaters and outlawed block booking, the practice of forcing exhibitors to take blocks of films, sight unseen, in order to obtain any films at all. The decision influenced organization and coordination in the motion picture industry in two ways. The direct effect was the separation of exhibition from distribution. The indirect effect was the separation of distribution and production. The divestiture of the theaters and the end of block booking meant that each film had to be marketed individually. A studio could no longer guarantee the run of its motion pictures, or whether they would actually be run at all. Faced with greatly increased uncertainty, the Paramount defendants curtailed production (even though the Paramount decision did not force them to do so), further decreasing their level of vertical integration, and ended the contract system. Directors, writers, producers, and performers began to freelance on a picture-by-picture basis, while the "studios" focused on distribution rather than production.[14]

Another result was a dramatic increase in the importance of independent

---

13. Charges of monopolization of production were dismissed.
14. I will continue to use the term "studio" (following industry practice) to refer to the production/distribution companies.

production. In 1949, independently produced films accounted for only 20 percent of the films released by the eight Paramount defendants. United Artists, which did not produce at all, accounted for half of that 20 percent. In 1957, independent production accounted for 58 percent of the large distributors' releases, with United Artists releasing less than one-third of that 58 percent (Conant 1978, 117–18). The separation of production from distribution had unanticipated benefits. The major studios found that independent producers were able to provide films that were more creative and lower cost than in-house production, with its large overhead expenses and risk-averse formula-film tradition, indicating that there had been significant inefficiencies in the vertically integrated structure. The studios actually accelerated the process of vertical disintegration by renting studio space, distributing independent films, and investing in independent production. Warner Brothers, for example, advanced $1.6 million to independent producers in 1946. Ten years later the figure was $25.1 million.[15]

Actually, the motion picture industry had begun to change even before the Paramount decision. During the boom years of the Second World War, leading stars, directors, and producers set up production companies to take advantage of favorable corporate and capital gains tax rates.[16] By the 1950s, most important stars had formed their own production companies (Gomery 1986, 9–10). Bitter but successful unionization drives in the 1930s and 1940s left Hollywood a fully unionized shop by the time of the Paramount decision. Extremely detailed work rules limited the flexibility of the studios, while wage agreements increased the integrated studios' labor expenses. Even before the decision, studios had begun efforts to reduce their fixed costs and payrolls. Paradoxically, industry-wide union contracts, which gave workers protection without the need to negotiate a detailed agreement for each film, and the roster system, in which the craft unions acted as hiring halls to allocate temporary jobs, allowed independent filmmakers to find qualified personnel without incurring search and negotiation costs. After the Paramount decision, more and more filmmakers found they could increase flexibility and decrease expenses by hiring independent contractors rather than permanent employees. The result was a further "casualization" (use of temporary workers and contractors) of motion picture employment.[17]

The structure of the motion picture industry was also influenced by changes in demand due to demographic changes and increased competition from television. As population shifted from city to suburb, it became more difficult to attract crowds to the large inner-city theaters that had provided the bulk of

---

15. Warner Brothers Annual Reports, quoted in Conant 1978, 117.

16. Some artists were able to reduce their effective tax rates from 81 percent to 60 percent by incorporating. Others were able to sell interests in motion pictures as assets and therefore qualify for the 25 percent capital gains rate in effect at the time.

17. This process has continued to the present. See Christopherson and Storper 1989; and Storper and Christopherson 1987.

movie revenues in the 1930s and 1940s. A more important phenomenon was the advent of television. In 1949, there were 1 million sets in use in the United States; by 1969, there were 84 million. The penetration of television went from 2.3 percent of American households to 95 percent of households over the period. By 1960, the average American was watching twenty-five hours of television a week (Schatz 1983, 18). U.S. motion picture admissions peaked in 1946 and fell dramatically until levelling off in the mid-1960s at less than one-third of the peak. Competition from television forced motion picture producers to find ways to differentiate their films. One result was an increased focus on large-budget, star-studded blockbuster (and would-be blockbuster) films. The focus on blockbusters was reflected in the growth in average movie production, or negative, costs. During the studio period, production costs averaged $500,000 per movie. By 1952, the figure was $1 million. By 1970, it was $1.5 million. Costs rose dramatically in the 1970s and 1980s. The average production cost was $9.4 million in 1980, and by 1992, it cost between $40 million and $50 million to make, distribute, and advertise a major motion picture.[18] The rise of the blockbuster resulted in increased volatility in the industry. The success of a studio could now depend on the results of a single motion picture.[19]

Increased volatility led to the evolution of a variety of organizational forms that developed to manage or share the risks involved in motion picture production. The three principal organizational forms used for motion picture production in the early 1990s reflected this evolution. Nine major studios[20] still engaged in in-house production (vertical integration of production and distribution), where the studio financed the movie internally; hired producers, directors, and actors (usually to a one-picture contract); and then distributed the film through its distribution arm.[21] A second organizational form was the fully independent production company in which an independent producer (there were literally hundreds in the industry) financed and made the picture and then attempted to sell the film to a major studio that would distribute it, in what was known as a "negative pickup deal" (an arm's-length transaction on what was essentially a spot market).[22] A third form was independent production with a studio guarantee, in which the independent producer put together a script,

---

18. See *The Motion Picture Almanac,* several years. Much of the increase was attributable to a dramatic increase in fees commanded by Hollywood's leading stars. The wages of the director, writer, producer, and stars accounted for roughly 10 percent of the typical film's budget in 1982, but 50 percent in 1992 (Stein 1992).

19. *Cleopatra* (1963), which lost some $18 million, nearly drove Fox into bankruptcy. Two years later *The Sound of Music,* which grossed more than $75 million, became the most successful motion picture ever released to that point. *E.T.* (1982) cost $12 million to make and grossed more than $228 million in revenues. *Ishtar* (1987), on the other hand, cost $45 million to make and grossed only $7.5 million.

20. Buena Vista (owned by Disney), Columbia (owned by Sony), MGM/UA (owned by Credit Lyonnais), Orion, Paramount, TriStar, Twentieth Century–Fox (owned by Rupert Murdoch's News Corporation), Universal (owned by Matsushita), and Warner Brothers (owned by Time-Warner).

21. Paramount presently makes most of its pictures in this way.

22. Producer Saul Zantz financed *Amadeus,* which he then sold to the highest bidder.

actors, director, and crew and then sold the idea to a major studio, which guaranteed that it would buy the film as long as it met certain requirements (an intermediate form of coordination). The producer then took this guarantee to a bank that extended a loan to cover production costs.[23] Variations on these organizational forms included coproduction, in which two or more studios shared production responsibilities,[24] and cofinancing, where studios took on outside financial partners (often foreign distributors) for films they produced in-house. Another variation was affiliated production, which involved cooperation between a studio and a large entertainment/production company to produce a feature film.[25]

Negative pickup deals increased in importance in the late 1980s. In 1987 and 1988, the major distributors picked up more than half of the films they distributed (see table 4.1). This trend was somewhat reversed in the 1990s, as many independents faced financial difficulties or bankruptcy.[26] The late 1980s and early 1990s also saw an increase in multipicture deals, in which the Hollywood studios signed exclusive contracts with leading stars and filmmakers for a fixed number of films. Multipicture deals provided filmmakers and stars with financial security, while giving the studios the chance to lock up proven moneymakers for several pictures in medium-term relationships. Multipicture deals tended to be risky for the studio, since they gambled on the continued popularity and creativity of the artists.[27] Some of the more noteworthy multipicture deals involved Paramount and Eddie Murphy, Orion and Woody Allen, and Twentieth Century–Fox and writer-director James Cameron (of *Terminator 2* fame).[28] Industry sources estimated this last deal, reached in April 1992 and covering up to twelve pictures, could be worth $500 million (Eller and Fleming 1992). Multipicture deals linked individual artists with the studio. A new short-term coalition still had to be put together for each individual film.

Coordination within the Hollywood Motion Picture Industry

Coordination mechanisms in the Hollywood motion picture industry have evolved to meet changes in the regulatory and economic environment. In the

23. Spike Lee has made all his films in this way.

24. The latter is rare, but does occur. Warner Brothers and Universal coproduced *Gorillas in the Mist*, a film for which both owned production rights.

25. There were several large entertainment/production companies, including Amblin Entertainment (owned by Stephen Spielberg) and Mal Passo (owned by Clint Eastwood). Such companies often worked with different studios on different films.

26. Independent production has been a difficult business. Roughly 40 to 50 percent of the independent productions produced in the early 1980s in the United States never received U.S. theatrical distribution. See Cohn 1991.

27. Most multipicture deals involved either cofinancing (the producer's own company agreed to raise part of the cost of making the movie, the studio agreed to pick up the rest) or equity participation (in which the artist would be paid a percentage of the gross or a portion of the profits of the films) to make sure that the interests of the studios and the artists coincided.

28. Murphy's 1991 agreement guaranteed him $12 million a film for four films. See Wechsler 1990; Landro 1991; and Weinraub 1991b. Allen made nine pictures for Orion between 1982 and 1991 and was committed for three more until Orion's financial difficulties left them unable to finance Allen's projects. See Weinraub 1991a.

Table 4.1   **In-House Production versus Acquisitions for the Major Film Distributors**

Year[a]	In-House Productions	Acquired Productions	Percentage In-House
1982	52	75	41
1983	76	76	50
1984	81	75	52
1985	70	53	57
1986	67	61	52
1987	72	85	46
1988	73	82	47
1989	78	67	54
1990	90	66	58
1991	86	63	58
1992[b]	44	31	59

Source: Variety, 27 April 1992.

Notes: English-language films distributed by the major distributors in the United States. Companies covered are Buena Vista, Columbia, MGM/UA, Orion, Paramount, TriStar, Twentieth Century–Fox, Universal, Warner Brothers, Triumph, and Sony Pictures Classics.

[a]Year of commencement of production.

[b]First half of year.

studio era, the studio bosses and their assistants coordinated the actual making of motion pictures in extremely hierarchical structures. The large motion picture companies used personal negotiations between a studio chief based in California with corporate management in New York to coordinate production with distribution and exhibition. Individual films were placed under the control of a producer, generally a studio employee who organized film production at the behest of the studio boss. The Paramount case had a dramatic influence on the industry structure and coordination mechanisms within the industry. The separation of production and distribution from exhibition made the integration of production and distribution far less attractive than it had been. Changes in industry economics associated with competition from television, unionization, changing demographics, and changes in the bargaining power of the various parties also contributed to the disintegration of the industry. In fact, it is highly unlikely that the vertically integrated studio system would have survived these developments even in the absence of the Paramount decision.

In the modern industry, studio projects, studio-backed independent projects, and negative pickup deals provide coordination through hierarchy, quasi markets, and spot markets respectively. Although the precise organization may differ, in each case an individual film is created through the efforts of a short-term coalition. The minimum efficient scale for movie production is the single production unit or single project. Project-based coalitions of directors, actors, crew, contractors, and subcontractors are assembled for each major motion picture (see fig. 4.2). Virtually every credit for a major motion picture represents an independent entity contracted to work on the film. Large numbers of

Story Rights Acquisition	Concepts Books Screenplays	
Pre-Production	Script Development Set Design Casting Crew Selection Costume Design Location Scouting Budget	
Principal Photography	Above the Line: Actors Directors Producers Writers	Below the Line: Soundstage Wardrobe Set Construction Labor
Post-Production	Film Editing Scoring Titles and Credits Dubbing Special Effects Sound Track	

Fig. 4.2   Production cost components for motion pictures
Source: Vogel 1990, 72.

contracts must be written for each motion picture. Even the studios' in-house production involves the hiring of many individuals and subcontractors on a one-film basis. The costs of casting, negotiations, agents' and lawyers' fees, and monitoring can account for a substantial portion of the costs of a film.[29]

The many agreements and contracts necessary to produce a motion picture involve a huge amount of communication and an array of coordinating agents. Localization is vital for an industry whose participants are in constant communication. One industry executive estimated that he spent fifty hours a week on the phone, with roughly 80 percent of the time spent on local phone calls. Another executive stated, "In this business, it's all based on who you know— and you have to network—the agents are here and so are the writers. Everyone knows everyone. These people live, eat, and breathe the entertainment industry." In order to participate in the industry, one has to be part of the local sub-

29. Agents typically receive 10 percent of the fees paid to actors and directors; lawyers typically receive another 5 percent. Completion guarantee insurance once cost on the order of 5 percent of a movie's budget, but by 1992 cost around 1.5 percent of the production budget (Scholl 1992). The costs associated with negotiating the contracts and monitoring the production were at least 10 percent of the production budget for a typical movie in 1992. This was in addition to the search costs involved in casting and selecting a crew.

culture. Formal and informal networks have developed among the studios, directors, and local firms in the area. The motion picture community is relatively small; there are only a few dozen key decision makers. Since information flows so quickly and completely through the industry, a reputation for fair dealing is essential, and opportunistic behavior is often swiftly punished.

A bewildering number of intermediaries have emerged as coordinating agents within the industry. Producers, executive producers, talent agents, entertainment lawyers, and business affairs executives negotiate the multitude of deals that must be made for each motion picture, effectively matching supply and demand and setting prices for the services of film artists. The producer is usually the one who puts, and keeps, together the coalition required for the project. Today, a producer might be an independent filmmaker, a studio executive, a talent agent, a friend of a major star, or anyone who has access to a good story, a top director, a major studio, or a popular artist. The larger talent agencies have used their control over access to many top-name clients to become major forces in the industry.[30] The agencies keep constant track of ongoing and prospective deals and movies and are generally well informed about similar deals made in the recent past. Business affairs executives deal with artists, negotiate for distribution rights for finished films, and negotiate studio participation in the development and financing of in-house and independent productions on behalf of the studios. Business affairs executives frequently share information with their counterparts at other studios on a confidential basis (Brouwer and Wright 1990, 57). Information sharing on both sides has created a remarkably efficient market for motion picture talent in Hollywood.

Interfirm and interpersonal competition is a driving force in the industry. The studios compete fiercely with one another to attract talented individuals and promising projects, and to place their films at the most desirable theaters. Rivalry in the motion picture industry is highly personal. According to Rosten (1970), under the old studio system, battles between studio bosses often got in the way of potentially lucrative deals. Today, interpersonal rivalry is still intense, especially since each individual is constantly trying to find his or her next job and since each individual is considered only as good as the last film he or she was involved in. The local trade press heightens the rivalry by constantly comparing the performance of the movie companies, as well as individual actors, directors, and producers. The movie hierarchy is apparent for all in the industry to see. As was noted earlier, the seating arrangements at Spago's and other local restaurants reflect the fortunes of industry participants on an almost daily basis.

The disintegration of the studio system, which increased the number of face-to-face negotiations required to make a picture, actually resulted in an increase of geographic concentration in the industry. Christopherson and Storper (1986)

---

30. Michael Ovitz of Creative Artists Agency (CAA) is generally regarded as the most powerful individual in Hollywood.

measured a substantial increase in the number of firms in filmmaking services in the Los Angeles area. Given the stability of output of films during the period (1966–82), they conclude there was a substantial increase in vertical disintegration in the industry. Industry sources indicated that the trend was reversing only slightly in the 1990s as the complexity of some pre- and post-production activities (including some technically sophisticated special effects) caused the studios to bring them in-house. Even so, the number of specialized firms that serve the motion picture industry has grown dramatically in the Los Angeles area. Hollywood remains unparalleled in the availability of services (including casting and monitoring to ensure productions come in on time and on budget), contractors, subcontractors, state-of-the-art facilities, talent, and skilled craft workers for the motion picture industry. One can easily contract for services that a production company operating elsewhere would have to perform for itself. Formal and informal networks have developed among the studios, directors, and local firms in the area. These networks, combined with the contacts and reputations of individuals and the use of facilitators such as agents and lawyers, allow coordination within the motion picture industry through short-term coalitions.

4.2.2   Coordination by Entrepreneurs and Markets: The Prato Wool Textile Industry

Italy is by far the world's leading exporter of wool textiles. In 1989, for example, Italy accounted for 39 percent of world exports of wool fabrics and 46 percent of world exports of fine wool (United Nations 1991). The Italian industry is centered in three areas; the Prato area in Tuscany, the Piedmont town of Biella, and the Veneto region. Today, Prato, which is just outside of Florence, accounts for roughly 50 percent of Italian wool textile production, Biella 30 percent, and the Veneto region around 15 percent to 20 percent (Italian Wool Industry Association, private communication). The industry is even more localized than these figures suggest. Biella firms specialize in top-quality fabrics for men's clothing, whereas Prato firms generally supply medium-quality fabrics for women's wear. Prato firms account for roughly three-quarters of the medium-quality wool fabric produced in Italy.

Industry History

The Prato wool textile industry dates back at least to the early twelfth century. Local records document the operation of a fulling mill in Prato as early as 1108. Later in the twelfth century, the Bisenzio River was channeled through the city to serve local fulling mills and dyeing establishments. Prato authorities encouraged development of the textile industry by exempting from local taxes wool workers and dyers who had relocated from Verona and Lombardy. Although the different stages of textile production[31] in Prato had once been char-

---

31. The principal stages in wool fabric production were and are raw material preparation, spinning, weaving, dyeing, and finishing.

acterized by independent craftsmen selling on open markets, by the fourteenth century, capitalist wool merchants (*lanaiuolo*) controlled the industry. The Prato merchants imported raw materials from Spain, Africa, and, for the finest fabrics, England, subcontracted production, and then sold the finished fabric in local and foreign markets (Origo 1986, 46–47). Individual firms that supplied the merchants were organized and coordinated under the umbrella of the local cloth guild (Arte della Lana), which dominated the various stages of textile production and sales (Origo 1986, 36). Four consuls named by the city council settled quarrels between guild members and enforced guild regulations. Cloth sales were strictly controlled by guild statutes, which governed even the selection of a supplier for a given customer (Origo 1986, 45). Although the guild system eventually dissolved, the industry retained a structure in which merchants coordinated activities within the industry, subcontracting production to homeworkers and independent craftsmen, for more than four centuries.

A modern, mechanized textile industry began to develop in Prato in the mid–nineteenth century. Shortly after the industrial revolution began in the United Kingdom, textile technology and machinery began to find their way to Prato. Giovanni Mazzoni, a graduate of the University of Pisa, combined his theoretical knowledge with the practical experience he gained in French cotton mills to open his own cotton-spinning facility in Prato in 1819. Mazzoni, who switched over to wool production in 1823–24, is credited with bringing the latest textile developments of the time to Prato (Lugonelli 1988, 8). Pratesi soon left farming in large numbers to enter the textile industry. The local sharecropping system, which operated through a series of subcontracting relationships, had helped generate a population of independent, self-reliant artisans who readily took up the textile trades. By 1846, the textile industry accounted for more than 90 percent of industrial employment in the area (Tenti 1987).

By 1862, there were twenty-seven factories in the Prato textile industry. In 1878, after a difficult period for the industry, there were twenty-eight wool textile firms with more than ten employees in the area. Prato had become a leader in recycled wool (wool made from rags and scraps) and was the leading center for the collection, sorting, and distribution of rags in Europe. Protectionist tariffs instituted in 1887 had a profound effect on the Prato industry, increasing demand for Prato's fabrics and fostering the development of new factories. The most important of the new facilities was the Kossler-Mayer factory, founded in 1888. This factory, which was owned by Austrians and employed Germans and Czechs in technical positions, was huge by Prato standards, employing 900 workers and 640 mechanical looms (Lugonelli 1988, 33). Over the next several years, this and other factories grew up alongside more traditional handicraft production.

Mechanization was accompanied by the rise of vertically integrated textile mills, mills that performed all or nearly all textile production steps internally. By the end of the 1920s, approximately 80 percent of the Prato area's twenty thousand textile workers were employed by vertically integrated mills (Trigilia

1989). The industry further consolidated in the 1930s and 1940s due to large military orders[32] and a focus on long production runs of standard fabrics, which were exported to less developed countries, particularly India and South Africa. At the time, the industry's requirements for coordination with the outside world were limited. Raw materials were imported from Australia through British traders. Because their fabrics were not differentiated, the Prato firms did not need to develop sophisticated marketing capabilities. Instead, British intermediaries organized the important trade of commodity fabrics to British colonies (including India and South Africa). Coordination of productive activities within the Prato industry was carried out by owners and managers within the relatively large, vertically integrated firms that continued to dominate the local industry until after the Second World War. Throughout this period, the Prato-area textile industry remained much smaller than that of Biella, which concentrated on higher-quality wool fabrics.

A boom in the Prato industry created by United Nations relief operations and the rebuilding of Europe in the immediate post–World War II period proved to be short-lived (dei Ottati 1991b). In the early 1950s, competition from low-cost producers in Third World nations, reduced military demand, the recession of the early 1950s, and increased protection in India and South Africa (which instituted import substitution programs shortly after obtaining their independence) resulted in a crisis for the Prato textile industry. Collapsing wool prices (which fell by 65 percent between March and September 1951 [dei Ottati 1991b]) put further pressure on the textile firms, which saw the value of their stocks drop precipitously. In response to the crisis, the vertically integrated Prato firms closed their factories, dismissed their workers, and sold their machinery to former employees who went into business for themselves. The result was the disintegration of the industry and the founding of a large number of small specialized firms out of the remnants of the vertically integrated mills. Subcontracting of individual steps in the production process became the principal means of regulating relations among an increasing number of ever-smaller firms (Lorenzoni 1985). This division of labor was possible because the stages of wool textile production are separable and the technology relatively well known and mature. The number of Prato-area textile firms increased from 780 in 1951 to 14,500 in 1981 and to 15,000 in 1990. The average firm size decreased from twenty-eight employees to less than four employees over the same period (Balestri 1990; industry sources).

The vertical disintegration of the Prato-area textile industry was accompanied, and in part caused, by changes in product mix. In the pre–World War II era, Prato firms tended to supply long runs of standard fabrics. After the war, the Prato industry shifted to more differentiated production, both in the fabrics themselves and the timing of the production cycle. Prato's skilled workers became masters at the flexible, rapid-turnaround, short production runs needed

32. The Italian government preferred to deal with a few firms for large military orders.

for fashion apparel and prototypes of mass market apparel. Modern technology and machinery (mostly supplied by local machinery firms) and the short production runs required for fashion apparel allowed for efficient operation at small scale. Fragmentation led to an increase in variety, which, along with the geographic concentration of the industry, reduced shopping costs for customers and attracted buyers from around the world. According to Lorenzoni (1985), potential clients knew that in Prato they could find firms willing and able to produce virtually any fabric design. Design capabilities became key to the Prato industry. By the late 1980s, Prato firms introduced some 25,000 new designs and 60,000 new patterns every six months, as older patterns were copied and produced more cheaply elsewhere. The development of new patterns and the actual production of swatches of new designs were among the most important and costly activities of the Prato firms, many of which spent an amount equal to approximately 10 percent of sales on their pattern books.

The disintegration of the textile industry was further encouraged by attitudes toward entrepreneurship that developed within the Prato area. Owning a firm and being one's own boss became a nearly universal goal, fueled in part by the example of successful entrepreneurs. Workers, technicians, and managers acted on the widespread desire for independence found in the area (Mazzonis 1985, 7). Disintegration was also encouraged, unwittingly, by government policies. Italy's artisan industry laws provided support for the purchase of new equipment by small firms, while labor legislation passed in the 1970s contributed to the fragmentation of the industry by making it difficult to operate larger firms. Restrictions on hiring and firing, indexed wages, and tight work rules hit the cyclical textile industry particularly hard. Small firms, which were exempt from some of the more onerous provisions of the labor laws, proved to be more flexible.[33] ENEA, Italy's agency for atomic and alternative energy sources, concluded that Italian labor legislation that limits the freedom to hire and fire workers in firms with fifteen or more employees discouraged the growth and limited the vertical integration of Prato textile firms. This, in turn, contributed to the flexibility and adaptability of the system as a whole (ENEA 1985, 1).

By 1990, the Prato-area wool textile industry consisted of nearly 15,000 firms employing 57,000 people.[34] The latter figure represented more than 50 percent of the area's employment and over one-sixth of its population. Small firms, with fewer than ten employees, accounted for 40 percent of industry employment. Firms with fewer than fifty employees accounted for some 80 percent industry employment (see table 4.2). One out of every twenty local residents owned a textile firm (Unione Industriele Pratese 1991). Most Prato firms specialized in a single stage of production. A single batch of raw material often passed through five, six, or more Prato firms on its path from raw material

33. There was a reduction in the average firm size across the Italian manufacturing sector in the 1970s and into the 1980s.

34. The second-largest employer in the area was the textile machinery industry, which employed approximately ten thousand people.

Table 4.2   Employment in the Prato Textile Industry, by Firm Size, 1990

Number of Employees	Total Industry Employment (%)
1–9	41.6
10–49	38.0
50–99	7.4
Over 100	3.3
Did not report	9.7[a]

Source: Calculated from information provided by the Unione Industriele Pratese.
[a]Estimated.

to finished textile. There were no firms that engaged in all production stages. Nonetheless, the Prato textile industry, and the Italian wool textile industry as a whole, has dramatically outperformed the industries in the rest of Europe, which were not as localized or fragmented.

Coordination within the Prato Textile Industry

Coordination within the Prato textile industry has been influenced by the requirements of the product and its production process. In textile production, the same material is processed through several consecutive and separable stages. Coordination of production involves arranging and guiding the flow of material through and between these stages.

The mechanisms used to coordinate activities within the Prato-area textile industry have evolved in response to changes in the competitive environment, technology, and product market strategies. In the Middle Ages, the industry was coordinated by guild statutes that regulated almost every aspect of the relationships within the industry and between the industry and the outside world. The wool merchants coordinated the import of raw materials, organized production, and had the exclusive right to market finished product to local and foreign customers. Though the guilds eventually dissolved, merchants continued to coordinate the production of numerous craftsmen for centuries. In the nineteenth and early twentieth centuries, industrial entrepreneurs and factory owners coordinated the bulk of Prato's productive activities, while British merchants coordinated sales to some of Prato's major markets.

The fragmented industry structure that developed in the post–World War II period required different skills, such as marketing, creativity in design, and capacity to serve new markets. The relatively high quality and rapid turnaround that became the norm in the Prato textile industry involved a substantial amount of coordination and communication to mesh productive stages. The localization of the industry facilitated the organization of a complex system where each stage of production delivered just-in-time to each subsequent stage. The disintegrated structure and the size of the local industry also led (as Stigler [1951] and Evans [1972] might suggest) to the development of a large number of firms who provided services to the textile industry, a fact that further increased the importance of efficient flow of financial, organizational, commercial, and technical information within the district (Mazzonis 1985, 4). Brabant (1985) estimated that communication costs (including the value of the time used in communicating) in the Prato textile district was approximately 2.9 percent of total sales, or on the order of $70 million to $80 million each year. In comparison, sample production, one of the most important activities in the industry, often represented 10 percent of a company's sales. Of all textile-related communication originating in Prato, 54 percent was directed to others in the area, 34 percent was directed to the rest of Italy, and 12 percent was directed abroad. The vast majority of the communication within Prato took place over the telephone or in face-to-face meetings.

Information flows within the Prato industry have benefited from its localization. Virtually everyone in the Prato area is involved in the textile industry in some capacity. The industry is literally "in the air." Everyone speaks the same language, literally and figuratively. Social contacts and interpersonal networks help spread information about the industry and its firms. Standardized contracts, which reduce the information requirements for any particular transaction, have emerged. Recognizing the importance of information flow within the district, local and national authorities have cooperated in a program to develop advanced information systems and computerized ordering. Many in Prato, however, believe that information flows so freely through the area that local governmental efforts to install advanced information systems have been superfluous, and the efforts have been ignored by many Prato firms.

Today, most transactions in the Prato industry take place on spot markets. Coordination is achieved through contractual relationships and market parameters such as price, quality, timing, and reliability, rather than hierarchical authority (Lorenzoni 1985, 12). *Impannatori* have become the central coordinating agents of the Prato industry. Impannatori have occupied a unique position in the industry, supervising fabric design, finding clients, purchasing material, subcontracting production, coordinating logistics, and making final sales, often without directly controlling any production capacity.[35] Though impannatori existed in the pre–World War II industry, their importance grew dramatically in the postwar era with the need to coordinate the production of the new, fragmented firms. After receiving orders, impannatori subcontract productive activities on a spot basis. They tend to use many subcontractors, and each subcontractor tends to serve many customers, with the local market providing the principal coordination mechanism for firm activities. Most impannatori rotate their subcontractors periodically. Those that do not still use the presence of numerous local competitors and common knowledge of local quality and price standards to set contract parameters. This results in essentially market-mediated outcomes, even for what appear to be long-term relationships. As long as a subcontractor does not deviate from local standards of quality, or try

35. The only physical assets employed by many impannatori are their telephones.

to charge above the going price for a service, there is no reason to change subcontractors.

By 1990, there were approximately six hundred impannatori active in the Prato area. The impannatori have become the marketmakers of the Prato system, matching supply within the Prato area with demand, from Italy and from abroad. According to Becattini (1990, 42–43), the impannatori are "pure entrepreneurs" whose major function is to translate the capabilities of the district into products that can be sold on world markets. The impannatori coordinate activities within the district. They also coordinate the activities of the district with the outside world, obtaining information on improved machinery, new processes, and markets wherever it is available. As a result, the Prato system has been able to keep abreast of the most modern technology as it competes on the basis of quality, design, reliability, continuity of supplies, and punctual delivery (Mazzonis 1985, 5).

Despite their efficiency, Prato's spot markets cannot deal effectively with all contingencies, especially when capacity is constrained. Large rush orders sometimes strain the system. In such cases, firms may simply pay their subcontractors more to expedite their orders. In other instances, interpersonal and family ties provide a "market override" mechanism that allows the orders to be filled, while other, less important orders are slightly delayed. Implicit is the understanding that the debt will eventually be repaid, either in future business or in special contract terms.[36] Some of the larger Prato firms have invested in weaving and finishing firms in order to ensure rapid turnaround on special orders for large customers. These relationships augment rather than replace the spot market in the Prato system. Although most transactions take place on what may be described as a spot market, increases in equity cross-holdings show that the spot market is not adequate for all the district's transactions.

The organization of the Prato textile industry has evolved in response to changes in technology, market demands, government regulations, and competition from outside the district. Vertical disintegration created substantial needs for coordination among specialist firms. Mechanisms that have arisen to coordinate activities within the Prato district have allowed the district to gain the benefits of a vertically disintegrated structure, while mitigating its disadvantages. Geographic concentration offers reduced transaction costs through lower communication and transportation costs. Standardized contracts reduce

---

36. Lorenzoni (1985) states that understanding and trust in the capabilities of others in the district and the recognition of the need for mutual adjustment is characteristic of the Prato industry. dei Ottati (1987) emphasizes that cooperation between the district's buyers and suppliers aids in the coordination within the Prato industry. Trust has its limits in the Prato system, however. Prato firms frequently spread disinformation in an attempt to gain advantage. Prato weavers, for example, often make inflated demand projections to induce spinners to increase capacity, thus improving the weavers' bargaining position. A recent agreement among Prato spinners to hold the line on prices fell apart almost instantly as firms began to undercut each other. Jockeying for position through the selective use of disinformation is an acknowledged practice in the Prato industry.

negotiating costs. Social relationships recognize the interdependence of firms and promote cooperation between vertical stages of production, while fierce competition within each stage wrings inefficiency out of the system and forces firms to upgrade their expertise and equipment. The presence of hundreds of firms at each stage in the production process ensures essentially perfect competition at each stage of the process. According to ENEA (1985, 2), "The essence of the Prato system is competitive development." The types of imitation and innovation described by Marshall flourish. Interfirm and interpersonal rivalry within the district heightens the level of competition.[37] Even with such tough competition, the repeated nature of firm interactions, the importance of reputation in obtaining orders, and rapid information flow among industry participants preclude overtly opportunistic behavior.

Overall, the results have been impressive. The Prato system has proven better able to change from the production of commodities to the production of differentiated products than the textile industries in other European nations, which are not as localized or fragmented. The specifics of wool textile production, particularly the separability of productive stages, and the segments served by the Prato industry, particularly fashion-related segments, have been amenable to the fragmented structure of the Prato industry.[38] Prato firms remain unmatched in their ability to turn out short production runs of a wide variety of fabrics on short notice, making them ideal for the fashion-related segments of the garment industry, with their short seasons and production runs. In the process, the Prato area has become one of the most prosperous areas in Italy and indeed in Western Europe.

4.2.3 Coordination through Cartels and Consolidation: The Swiss Watch Industry

In 1991, Switzerland accounted for 15 percent of worldwide production of watches by unit volume, but 52.8 percent of the value (7.4 billion francs out of 14.0 billion) of world production. Japan, in contrast accounted for 46.6 percent of unit production and 25.6 percent of production by value. Hong Kong was the third leading producer, with a 20.5 percent unit production share and an 8.6 percent value share. Switzerland accounted for 55.3 percent of world exports (by value) of watches (Fédération de l'industrie horlogère suisse FH, private communication). The watch industry was concentrated in seven of Switzerland's twenty-six cantons and half cantons. These seven cantons accounted for 89.8 percent of the total employment in the Swiss watch industry in 1991 (see table 4.3). The low- and medium-priced watch firms were located throughout the Jura mountains in western Switzerland from Geneva to Schaff-

---

37. Prato's entrepreneurs compete for business and also for position in the local society. The leading entrepreneurs are also the town's leading citizens. One Prato industrialist recently commissioned a poll to determine his standing in local public opinion.

38. It is interesting to note that Italy has been internationally successful (with fragmented structures) in other industries with similar attributes, such as footwear, apparel, leather goods, and even some machinery industries.

Table 4.3   Employment in the Swiss Watch Industry, by Canton, 1991

Canton	Watch Industry Employment	Percentage of Swiss Watch Employment
Neuchâtel	9,080	27.5
Bern	6,158	18.7
Geneva	5,024	15.2
Solothurn	3,593	10.9
Jura	2,928	8.9
Vaud	1,880	5.7
Basel-Land	960	2.8
Seven-canton total	29,623	89.8

Source: Revue FH, 27 August 1992, 1.

hausen, whereas the luxury-watch producers were mostly located in Geneva, La Vallée de Joux, and Schaffhausen.

Industry History

The Swiss watch industry began in Geneva, whose jewelry makers and goldsmiths were known for their artistic flair and knowledge of metallurgy throughout the Middle Ages. The local gold and jewelry industries, however, declined sharply in 1541 when John Calvin issued his famous edicts against luxury, pleasure, elegant clothing, and "useless" jewelry. Calvin's edicts and a more detailed set of city regulations enacted twenty-five years later nearly put an end to the jewelry and goldsmithing industries in Geneva. At roughly the same time, Huguenots fleeing religious persecution in France, Italy, and Flanders arrived in the Swiss cantons. Among the refugees were a number of people who had been important watchmakers in their home countries. The smiths and jewelers of Geneva began to make watches and clocks under the tutelage of the refugees in order to escape the ban on "useless" jewelry. The world's first watchmaking guild was founded in Geneva in 1601, and by 1700 there were already some five hundred watchmakers in the city. Genevan craftsmen elevated watchmaking to an art form, with watches that were soon known throughout the world.

The Geneva industry developed a fragmented production process and extreme division of labor in what became known as the *établissage* system. Cardinal (1989) identifies approximately thirty specialized trades involved in the production of watches and clocks in Geneva at the end of the eighteenth century. Each trade supplied a particular component (such as watch springs, chains, and dials) or performed a particular operation (such as movement assembly, engraving, and watchcase gilding). Production within each trade took place in small workshops in which a few workers were directed by a master craftsman. *Établisseurs* coordinated production through a putting-out system and took charge of distribution and sales. This system encouraged the development of specialized skills critical to the production of precision components and watches. Cardinal concludes that this division of labor and coordination by the établisseurs "ensured the success of Genevan watchmakers" (1989, 57).

Watch production spread from Geneva to the Jura area in the latter portion of the seventeenth century. Daniel-Jean Richard and his family were said to have introduced the établissage system to the Jura, where watchmaking provided much needed employment in an area with long winters and limited agricultural potential. By Richard's death in 1741, hundreds, and later thousands, of artisans made individual watch components, which were assembled in workshops located in nearby towns, such as Neuchâtel, Bienne, and Solothurn. Entrepreneurs from these towns organized production and marketed the watches throughout Europe. The local industry grew dramatically; watch industry employment in Neuchâtel grew from 464 in 1752 to more than 2,000 in 1778 (Schweizer 1986 and sources within). Individual towns or valleys came to specialize in particular components or even in watches for specific end markets. An 1818 essay claimed that the advantage of the Jura region in watchmaking came from the "orderly coordination of the various work processes" (quoted in Landes 1983, 263). Cardinal agreed, concluding that the rise of the Jura watch industry depended on extreme division of labor and coordination by the établisseurs (1989, 60). The Swiss watchmaking towns had also begun to invest in education and training, setting up associations to promote the development of new designs and technology, while annual accuracy trials and invention contests spurred innovation in the industry (Schweizer 1986; Landes 1983).

By 1790, annual production of watches in the Jura reached approximately fifty thousand units. By 1817, the figure had doubled. The center of gravity of the Swiss watch industry had moved from Geneva to the Jura (which included the cantons of Neuchâtel, Solothurn, Vaud, and Jura as well as part of Bern). In 1790, six of Switzerland's cantons accounted for 92.1 percent of the industry's employment of 39,336 watchworkers. By 1820, employment in the watch industry had grown to 62,844. The leading cantons in terms of employment in 1790 were Neuchâtel with 34.8 percent of the nation's watchworkers, Bern with 37.4 percent, Vaud with 9.2 percent, and Geneva with 8.2 percent. By 1820, the six cantons accounted for 94.9 percent of Swiss watch industry employment, with Bern (41.5 percent), Neuchâtel (30.2 percent), Solothurn (10.1 percent), Geneva (5.4 percent), and Vaud (5.3 percent) as the leaders.[39]

Production methods for watches began to change in the nineteenth century. In the 1830s, machinery to make gears was introduced to the Swiss watch industry. Soon the Swiss developed machine tools to make parts precise enough to be used interchangeably. At first, these tools were used by homeworkers to improve precision and productivity. Eventually, the watchmakers began to group machine tools and workers together in a search for further efficiency gains. Between 1870 and 1910, the organization of the Swiss watch industry shifted as factory production began to replace homework. By 1905,

39. Calculated from Landes 1983, 380 and sources cited within.

there were thirty-eight thousand factory workers and twelve thousand home-workers in the Swiss industry. For the first time, substantial investments in fixed assets (watchmaking equipment and machinery) were required to compete. Even though component production became mechanized, watch assembly in the Jura continued to be dominated by small firms (Knickerbocker 1972). In contrast, several leading luxury-watch manufacturers founded in or around Geneva in the eighteenth and nineteenth centuries were more integrated than their Jura counterparts, producing intricate hand-made movements for their watches.[40] These firms vertically integrated in order to achieve total control in the production of complicated watches and movements that could sometimes take years to complete.

In the 1920s, in response to falling sales and rising unemployment during the post–World War I recession, Swiss watch companies organized themselves into several associations. Watch assemblers and vertically integrated watch-makers, the companies that sold completed watches to end markets, founded the Fédération suisse des associations de fabricants d'horlogerie FH in 1924. Seventeen *ébauche* (unfinished watch movement) makers were organized into a trust, Ébauches SA, in 1926. Component suppliers grouped together to form the Union des branches annexes de l'horlogerie (UBAH), an association with eighteen separate subgroups for producers of different types of components, in 1926. In 1928, the associations reached a series of cartel agreements that controlled manufacturing, pricing, and exporting within the Swiss watch industry (Knickerbocker 1972, 7).

The depression of the 1930s and deteriorating conditions in the industry created an unemployment problem in the watchmaking regions that prompted intervention by the Swiss federal government. In 1931, the government invested in a holding company, the Société générale de l'horlogerie suisse SA (commonly known as ASUAG, the acronym of the German form of its name, Allgemeine schweizerische Uhrenindustrie), which in turn acquired the majority of the shares of Ébauches SA and several leading component and watch manufacturers. In 1934, a federal statute ratified the industry's private controls and imposed new ones. FH members were allowed to make and sell finished watches. Ébauches SA was granted a monopoly on ébauche production, except for vertically integrated firms, which were allowed to manufacture ébauches for internal use, but was forbidden to make or sell finished watches. FH members could buy components only from Ébauches SA or from UBAH (both of which could only supply FH members) unless parts of comparable quality were available from foreign sources at prices 20 percent less than Swiss prices. UBAH and Ébauches SA sold components at specified prices that could be changed only through interassociation negotiations. FH members were forbid-

40. Leading firms founded in the period included Blancpain and Vacheron Constantin (founded in the eighteenth century), Jaeger–Le Coultre (1833), Patek Phillippe (1839), Audemars Piguet (1875), and Rolex (1878).

den to price watches below a floor price determined by adding component costs, a standard manufacturing cost, and a 23 percent margin. FH firms also agreed to reduce nonprice competition by limiting guarantees to one year on finished watches (Brengel and Rugo 1961).

The Swiss government enforced industry price agreements and attempted to protect watchmaking skills and secrets. Government permits were required to manufacture and export finished watches, movements, and components. All mergers, acquisitions, and new plant construction required government approval, as did exports of watchmaking machinery, tools, and designs for watchmaking, a move that effectively froze the structure of the industry (Knickerbocker 1972, 8). The 1934 law gave the associations, with government backing, control over the industry. Several new associations eventually formed. The Chambre suisse de l'horlogerie (Swiss watch chamber) represented the entire industry in international trade matters and in the administration of federal legislation. In addition to the Chambre suisse de l'horlogerie, FH, UBAH, and Ébauches SA, were the Association d'industries suisses de la montre Roskopf, a group of manufacturers of inexpensive pin-lever watches; the Délégations réunies (DR), which exercised general control over the industry's collective agreements; and the Convention patronale, the employers' organization that negotiated and administered agreements governing wages and working conditions with employees.

At first, the cartel proved successful. The industry prospered as demand rose in the 1930s and 1940s,[41] and in the immediate postwar period, Swiss firms held an estimated 80 percent share of the world watch market. In the 1950s, however, the system started to break down. The fragmented structure hindered the adoption of the newest production techniques. Jura firms found it difficult to standardize parts or make the investments required to automate production. Some FH members began to complain that the arrangements protected marginal assemblers, fostered inefficiency among the component producers, and resulted in a deterioration of the Swiss quality image. In 1957, the resignation of seventy-two watch assemblers from the FH prompted the appointment of a government-sponsored commission to investigate their complaints. In 1959, after several months of intensive discussions, a number of changes were made in the rules governing the watch industry. FH firms were allowed to use their own production costs rather than a standard cost in determining prices, but still had to add a 23 percent margin. Ébauches SA prices could be appealed to a joint FH–Ébauches SA commission, while UBAH prices were now negotiated individually. FH members were given the right to purchase foreign parts of "acceptable quality" if (after tariff) they were 13 percent, rather than 20 percent, cheaper than Swiss parts. Integrated manufacturers were allowed to sell ébauches to each other, provided that they did not sell more than 60 percent of their output or purchase more than 60 percent of their total needs from other

---

41. Swiss firms were able to supply both sides during the Second World War.

integrated producers. This change allowed integrated manufacturers to achieve some economies of scale in ébauche production (Brengel and Rugo 1961).

In 1961, the cartel law was repealed altogether. As of 1 January 1966, Swiss firms were free to expand, contract, merge, sell out to foreigners, or buy foreign companies. A watch standards committee was set up to ensure quality and maintain the reputation of the Swiss industry. The fixed-price system was abolished in 1966, and export permit requirements were phased out in 1971. The repeal of the cartel law changed the face of the Swiss watch industry. In the early 1960s, there were approximately 650 watch assemblers in Switzerland, 17 manufacturers of ébauches (all members of Ébauches SA), 650 manufacturers of special parts, and 500 other firms performing miscellaneous functions. Three groups, Fabriques d'assortiments réunies SA (escapement mechanisms), Fabriques de balanciers SA (balance wheels), and Groupements des fabricants suisses de spiraux (hairsprings), along with Ébauches SA supplied roughly three-quarters of the Swiss industry's requirements for ébauches and separate parts. By 1971, after a series of mergers, eight watchmaking firms accounted for almost three-quarters of all Swiss watch exports. In the same year, ASUAG, the trust that controlled a majority interest in Ébauches SA and the three largest component companies, combined seven watch brands into a single firm. The result was a direct link between companies that assembled and marketed watches with each other and with the component manufacturing sector (Knickerbocker 1972, 11–12).

The mergers, however, did not lead to changes in the underlying industry structure. Patterns that emerged in the cartel days, when the "Swiss made" trademark meant unrivalled precision, persisted. There was little coordination among the various entities that existed under ASUAG and the other major holding company, Société suisse pour l'industrie horlogère (SSIH).[42] Neither holding company had the power to enforce coordination among the different brands and suppliers. Limited production quantities resulted in inefficient production and limited planning.[43] Although quality remained high, coordination among firms was poor. There were no standard orders, parts often had to be redone, and orders were often late. The holding company structure had allowed for the injection of capital from the government (which was unwilling to deal with the individual companies directly) and the large Swiss banks, but had not resulted in professional managerial control.

Industry politics prevented the holding companies from acting against the old-line watch families, or "watch barons," who retained control but did not push for increased efficiency. Several of the families had acquired the "right" (tradition more than right) to have family members employed by the holding

---

42. The SSIH was founded in 1930. By 1980, SSIH included brands like Tissot and Omega.
43. The établisseurs tended to design watches that would require custom components. The result was lots that were often too small to justify the cost of tooling and dies. The specificity of tooling and dies often left assemblers at the mercy of individual suppliers.

company. The prerogatives of each entity were respected; no rationalization took place. There were still seventeen ébauche factories in the late 1970s, for example, with overlapping product ranges and strategies that remained for the most part uncoordinated (Wilhelm Hill and Urs Bumbacher, private communication). The mergers, in fact, represented an attempt to save the old structure, which had prevented market incentives from permeating the system of assemblers and suppliers. The result was that the industry had neither the efficiency of a vibrant disintegrated structure, nor the coordination advantages of hierarchy. Effective coordination at the level of production had largely ceased to exist. The fact that the system persisted as long as it did was a monument to the magnitude of the lead the Swiss industry had developed against outside competitors. Eventually, the rents that the system was devised to distribute, and that had allowed the system to persist, vanished.

The Swiss share of the world market decreased from 80 percent to around 40 percent by the end of the 1960s. Bulova, which became successful in the 1960s with the tuning-fork watch (developed by Swiss engineer Max Hertzel), and Timex, which sold more units than any other watch company in the world in 1970, had become important competitors. Despite losses in market share, growing demand kept capacity utilization and profits high in the Swiss industry. Prosperity disappeared, however, with the advent of the quartz watch in the mid-1970s. According to Bumbacher (1992), after reaching a new peak in sales of mechanical watches and movements in 1974, the Swiss watch industry virtually collapsed. Swiss firms rejected the quartz watch movement (which had actually been developed in Switzerland) because they felt it was unreliable, unsophisticated, and not consistent with Swiss standards. In addition, there was a fear that scale-intensive quartz technology would ruin the traditional fragmented industry structure and force many firms out of business. Vertically integrated foreign competitors had no such qualms. Seiko and Citizen (Japan) switched to quartz technology quickly and were soon followed by new competitors such as Casio (Japan) and Texas Instruments. Quartz technology underwent rapid improvement. Soon quartz watches exceeded the accuracy and reliability of mechanical movements by a wide margin. New entry, aggressive expansion, oversupply, and aggressive pricing caused industry prices and profits to plummet. Swiss watch output fell drastically (see table 4.4). By 1980, the Swiss had lost their position in low-priced and medium-priced watches, mostly to Seiko and Casio (Bumbacher 1992, 18). Total employment in the Swiss watch industry fell from 89,448 in 1970 to 46,998 in 1980, and would fall to 32,253 by 1990. The Jura area was faced with an economic crisis.

The need for a major restructuring of the Swiss watch industry became apparent. The restructuring was led by the large Swiss banks,[44] federal and local governments, and a management team recruited from outside the industry. The losses of the late 1970s and early 1980s meant that the banks and governments

---

44. The large Swiss banks wrote off hundreds of millions of francs during the reorganization.

Table 4.4   Growth Rates in Watch and Watch-Movement Production

Year	Switzerland (%)	Worldwide (%)
1970	2.8	
1971	−1.8	
1972	8.1	
1973	8.9	9.1
1974	4.3	6.8
1975	−20.2	−0.9
1976	−1.7	3.2
1977	1.7	14.2
1978	−3.5	4.3
1979	−12.4	3.0
1980	21.0	8.7
1981	−13.3	7.7
1982	−36.9	11.5
1983	−6.4	5.8

Source: Fédération de l'industrie horlogère suisse.

held control of the industry. The watch barons had seen their equity dissolve and were no longer a major factor. SSIH and ASUAG were joined to form the Société suisse de microélectronique et d'horlogerie SA (SMH) in 1983.[45] The formation of SMH involved substantial organizational and managerial changes. A controlling interest in SMH was sold to new CEO Nicholas Hayek and a friendly group of Swiss investors. By the end of 1985, the bulk of the share capital was held outside the banking industry. SMH management took active control, rationalizing and modernizing production, reorganizing the firm's activities, and breaking down the barriers that had existed between subsidiaries. Production schedules were streamlined and coordinated, as were design and marketing strategies. Finance, control, and production were managed centrally, while marketing for each SMH brand was managed separately but coordinated through an SMH management committee (SMH controlled the Swatch, Rado, Certina, Omega, Tissot, Longines, ETA, Hamilton, Blancpain, F. Piguet, Mido, and Flik Flak brands).

SMH was far more vertically integrated than either of its predecessors had been (and as or even more vertically integrated than its foreign competitors), controlling subsidiaries that supplied movements, electronic components, specialized integrated circuits, batteries, quartz oscillators, specialized materials, specialized machine tools, manufacturing systems, and distribution services. SMH's vertical integration ensured that it would not have to rely on its foreign competitors for key components. In 1983, for example, SMH founded EM Microélectronique Marin SA to reduce its dependence on Japanese suppliers of specialized integrated circuits. Vertical integration was accompanied by in-

45. The following paragraphs on SMH are based on interviews by the author.

creased differentiation of SMH's products as the company repositioned its lines to give them a clear identity. Tissot, for example, became identified with watches made from natural materials such as rock and wood as well as special designs such as the two-timer, while Rado became known for futuristic designs and space-age materials. The new hierarchical organization was able to coordinate marketing programs in a way the old holding company structure could not.

The new organization allowed SMH management to rethink the function and production of the watch, something that could not be done in the vertically disintegrated structure. The result was the Swatch, a revolutionary concept for the low- and medium-priced watch segment. The Swatch, with its distinctive designs produced in limited series with new models every six months, turned the low-priced watch into a fashion accessory. By 1991, more than 100 million Swatches had been sold. SMH had become the largest watch company in the world, accounting for approximately a third of the output (sales) of the Swiss watch industry, a quarter of its employment, and roughly three-quarters of its value added. SMH had come to dominate the low- and medium-priced segments of the Swiss watch industry and, with its Omega and Longines brands, had become the world's second leading supplier of luxury watches. Only Rolex had greater sales in this latter category.

Despite the great importance of SMH, there are several other firms in the Swiss watch industry representing different organizational forms. Switzerland's luxury-watch companies, which are mostly found in the Geneva area, have been virtually unchallenged by foreign competitors for more than two hundred years. In the early 1990s, Swiss firms accounted for approximately 85 percent of sales of luxury watches (Fédération de l'industrie horlogère suisse FH, private communication). Although several of the luxury-watch companies use quartz movements, others continue to produce handcrafted mechanical masterpieces. Some of these firms act as pure assemblers, relying on a large number of small shops for virtually all components. Rolex produces many of its own components in-house, but relies on a single supplier (which for the most part only supplies Rolex) for its watch movements. This supplier, in turn, purchases key components from SMH. Several other luxury-watch producers make their own movements. Jaeger–Le Coultre SA, probably the most vertically integrated Swiss firm other than SMH, produces its own movements and most of its own components, but relies on independent suppliers for certain specialized components such as hands, dials, and crystals.

The role of the main industry associations also underwent a dramatic change. In 1983, the Chambre suisse de l'horlogerie and the Fédération horlogère suisse FH merged to form the present Fédération de l'industrie horlogère suisse FH. The new association's primary tasks were to promote the Swiss watch industry, to ensure foreign markets remained open to Swiss watches, to obtain and disseminate information on the industry, to fight the counterfeiting of well-known Swiss brands, and to protect the "Swiss made" trademark. The association no longer played a role in fixing prices for watches and components. The association's foreign repair shops were turned over to the watch companies.

Coordination in the Swiss Watch Industry

As in the Prato textile industry, coordination requirements in the Swiss watch industry have depended on the nature of the product. Watches are complex products that contain between fifty and several hundred parts that must fit and work together with extreme precision. Coordination of production involves managing the design of the watch, the specification and fabrication of components, watch assembly, and scheduling each part of the process. This gives rise to a substantially more complex coordination task than that found in the textile industry.

In the early days of the Swiss watch industry, établisseurs organized production of components and assembly of watches, dealing with dozens of homeworkers and small shops to coordinate the activities of the industry. The établissage structure that developed first in Geneva and then in the Jura was closely linked to the geographic concentration of the watch industry within Switzerland. The structure, with its market-mediated price and quality standards, provided flexibility and variety in its early days, and was retained in the Jura area even as component production became mechanized. The early établissage system allowed the Swiss watch industry to take advantage of extreme division of labor by providing a means of coordinating the activities of hundreds and then thousands of craftsmen. This system allowed the Swiss watch industry to attain and maintain its position of world leadership for more than two centuries.

The importance of the watch industry to local economies, fear of outside competition, and the cooperation inherent in the system helped lead to the formation of a cartel. From the 1920s through the 1960s, the activities of the Swiss watch firms were coordinated by negotiations within and among associations of firms. The associations regulated competition, arbitrated differences among members, and spoke for the industry in its relations with government (Brengel and Rugo 1961, 12). The geographic concentration of the industry allowed the firms to negotiate and monitor tightly the collusive arrangements. Proximity and interdependence had drawn the watch firms together. Information about the industry, and in particular about attempts to deviate from industry norms, traveled quickly through the watchmaking portion of northwestern Switzerland, though little information was shared with those outside the area. Geographic concentration also prompted government intervention, as the Swiss government hoped its actions would improve employment prospects in an area that relied heavily on the watch industry. In freezing industry structure, the agreements ensured that watch production in the Jura area would remain fragmented.

Inefficient firms and organizations were protected by fixed-price arrangements. Changes in the Swiss industry had to be negotiated by the associations.

This combination of circumstances reduced incentives to innovate and reduced the chance that innovations would be adopted. The industry's responses to changes in markets and technology slowed. Over time, the Swiss industry lost much of its dynamism as coordination was carried out more through a local political process than through markets or hierarchies. The fundamental structure of watch production in much of the Swiss industry, batch assembly of mechanical components, became obsolete for low- and medium-priced watches. The Jura-area watch industry was especially affected. Its fragmented structure prevented the development of scale and unity of purpose required to rationalize production or make the large investments necessary to introduce plastics and quartz movements. In addition, the Swiss system limited the incentive to improve and innovate. Ironically, the very effectiveness of this form of coordination within the cartel prevented competitive forces from making the Swiss firms adjust to changes in the product, technology, demand, and competition until it was almost too late.

Only with the advent of SMH, a centralized, vertically integrated firm, did Switzerland regain a strong position in the low- and medium-priced watch segment. SMH's activities were coordinated through its hierarchical corporate structure; CEO and principal shareholder Nicholas Hayek remained involved in all major business decisions. The formation of SMH was the response of the system to changes that had been going on in the industry for decades. The geographic concentration of the industry again played a role. The watch industry was so important to the economy of northwestern Switzerland that abandoning the industry was unthinkable. Coordination through much of the Swiss watch industry had passed from markets, to cartels, to modern corporate management.

4.3   Conclusions

Geographic concentration, or localization, in industry is a widespread and complex phenomenon. There is a close relationship between localization and the structure of firms and industries. Geographic concentration within an industry may influence the boundaries between firms by increasing the efficiency and effectiveness of coordination across firms. It reduces the transaction costs associated with spot markets and the formation of short-term coalitions based on a nexus of contracts by reducing the costs of negotiations as well as reducing the likelihood of ex post opportunistic behavior. Finally, geographic concentration can also foster the formation of cartels by making the arrangements easier to monitor and enforce. Localized industries therefore provide a unique opportunity to examine coordination within and among firms.

The organizational forms and coordinating mechanisms employed by the industries profiled have shifted with changes in product, technology, markets, competition, and government actions. The interaction is complex; it is difficult to determine one-way causation. It appears that the competitive environment, technology, product market strategy, industry structure, and optimal coordination mechanisms are jointly determined. Each motion picture is a unique project that brings together a multitude of parties. Textiles are produced in a number of separable stages. Watches are complex products that contain many parts that must fit together with extreme precision. The nature of the product creates particular coordination requirements that influence coordination mechanisms. The greater complexity of coordination in the watch compared to the textile industry helps explain why the Swiss watch industry vertically integrated and the Prato textile industry disintegrated. The formation of cartels and associations that froze the structure of the Swiss watch industry, however, delayed this integration until the rents that propped up the system were no longer available. In Hollywood, the temporary nature of each project has fostered a certain amount of disintegration.

Changes in the external competitive environment provided a stimulus for changes in organization and coordination in the industries described. The loss of markets due to protection and greatly increased competition from the Far East reduced the viability of long production runs of low-quality wool fabrics in Prato. The Swiss watch industry was forced to restructure in the 1980s by competition from American and Asian competitors. Competition from television forced the Hollywood motion picture industry to try to differentiate motion pictures from television shows through the creation of the big-budget blockbuster film. Although each of the three industries has shown an ability to change from within, external competitive pressure figured prominently in the most dramatic of the changes in organization and coordination in each industry.

The evolution of firm strategy also influenced organization and coordination. Changes in the degree of vertical integration were associated with the development of greater levels of product differentiation in each of the three industries profiled. In Hollywood and Prato, increased differentiation was accompanied by a decrease in levels of vertical integration, whereas in the low-priced segment of the Swiss watch industry, increased differentiation was associated with an increase in vertical integration. In the first two cases, a disintegrated structure has proven better able to generate variety and flexibility. In the third, it took a vertically integrated firm to develop and carry out a strategy that brought fashion to low-priced watches. The main difference is that in textiles and motion pictures variety is linked to a production process with limited economies of scale, at least for the segments served by Prato and Hollywood, while the Swatch process is scale intensive, but permits flexibility in colors and styles around a limited number of base designs.

Government policies have influenced organization and coordination in the three industries. Antitrust enforcement unleashed a chain of events that dramatically influenced the structure of the Hollywood motion picture industry. The Swiss government codified and supported the Swiss watch cartel. Italy's artisan-firm laws favored the formation of small disintegrated firms. The industry examples also show that government action has had unforeseen consequences. The Paramount decision forced the studios to divest their theaters, but it was the uncertainty that this divestiture entailed, not the decision itself, that caused the studios to separate production and distribution. Italy's restrictive labor laws accelerated the process of disintegration in the Prato industry by making it difficult for large firms to operate in a cyclical industry. The Swiss government's efforts to support the watch cartel eventually contributed to the ossification of the industry.

The examples show that there is no single natural progression through which industries develop. While portions of the Swiss watch industry eventually consolidated into a vertically integrated managerial firm, the Prato textile industry and the Hollywood motion picture industry did just the opposite. The examples also show that geographic concentration does not in and of itself determine the boundaries of firms, but may allow for a range of productive organizations and a fluidity between organizational forms. Competing organizational forms and coordination mechanisms have coexisted in the three industries. In Prato, for example, fragmented production organized by impannatori existed even when the industry was dominated by vertically integrated firms. Today, however, there are no vertically integrated textile firms in the Prato wool textile industry. There were vertically integrated Swiss watch firms in the low- and medium-priced segments in the days when assemblers and fragmented production were dominant. Today, however, the importance of fragmented production processes in the Swiss watch industry has diminished. There were some important independent producers in Hollywood's studio era. Today, independent and studio production coexist. The persistence of competing organizational forms may be related to the selection environment faced within the industry. The textile and watch industries have provided particularly tough selection environments for alternative organizational forms, whereas the uncertainty inherent in the motion picture industry contributed to the persistence of alternative organizational forms.

Different organizational forms appear to have different abilities to foster or react to innovation. Fragmented structures appear to be quite flexible and adaptable to incremental innovation and change, such as changes in fashion, that do not require the rethinking of the entire product or production process. Fragmented structures on the other hand may not allow for the rethinking of an entire product and process. Small producers that focus on a single stage of production will not work on developments that eliminate their stage. Companies in other stages may not have the inclination or money to do so. The development of the decentralized structure of the Prato textile industry was accompanied by innovations and changes in marketing, but did not involve substantial changes in production processes. The Hollywood motion picture industry has seen technological and market changes, but has not had to rethink the entire production process. The advent of the quartz watch movement, on the other hand, required a dramatic reappraisal of the entire process of watch manufacture. The fragmented, collusive structure of the industry made it difficult to adapt to new circumstances. The Swiss watch firms proved too shortsighted to adopt the quartz movement until it was almost too late. Only a dramatic and painful restructuring, led by management from outside the industry, allowed the Swiss to regain a strong position in the low- and medium-priced segments of the watch industry. A group of localized firms may go into decline if the firms become ossified and too inwardly focused, and lose sight of their competitors and markets. This should serve as a warning to those that would view geographic clusters of small firms as a panacea for the problems of economic development.

References

Balestri, Andrea. 1990. *The Textile Industry: An Economic Profile.* Prato: Unione Industriele Pratese.

Becattini, Giacomo. 1990. The Marshallian Industrial District as a Socio-Economic Notion. In *Industrial Districts and Inter-Firm Co-operation in Italy,* ed. Frank Pyke, Giacomo Becattini, and Werner Sengenberger. Geneva: International Institute for Labour Studies.

———, ed. 1987. *Mercato e Forze Locali: Il Distretto Industriale.* Bologna: Il Mulino.

———. 1989. *Modelli Locali di Sviluppo.* Bologna: Il Mulino.

Brabant, François. 1985. Prato: Telematics Project. In Documentation on the Prato Case Study, by ENEA.

Brengel, Peter, and Marieve Rugo. 1961. Note on the World Watch Industry. In *Problems of General Management: Business Policy,* ed. Edmund Learned, C. Roland Christensen, and Kenneth Andrews. Homewood, Illinois: Irwin.

Brouwer, Alexandra, and Thomas Wright. 1990. *Working in Hollywood.* New York: Crown Publishers.

Brusco, Sebastiano. 1982. The Emilian Model: Productive Decentralization and Social Integration. *Cambridge Journal of Economics* 6:167–84.

Bumbacher, Urs. 1992. The Swiss Watch Industry. HBS Case N9-792-046. Boston: Harvard Business School.

Cardinal, Catherine. 1989. *The Watch: From Its Origins to the Nineteenth Century.* Translated by Jacques Pages. New York: Tabard Press.

Chandler, Alfred D., Jr. 1990. *Scale and Scope: The Dynamics of Industrial Capitalism.* Cambridge: Harvard University Press.

Christopherson, Susan, and Michael Storper. 1986. The city as Studio, the World as Back Lot: The Impact of Vertical Disintegration on the Location of the Motion Picture Industry. *Environment and Planning,* ser. D, 4:305–20.

———. 1989. The Effects of Flexible Specialization on Industrial Politics and the Labor Market: The Motion Picture Industry. *Industrial Labor Relations Review* 42:331–47.

Cohn, Lawrence. 1991. Greater Percentage of Films Now Reaching U.S. Screens. *Variety,* 15 April, 1991, 12.

Conant, Michael. 1978. *Antitrust in the Motion Picture Industry.* New York: Arno Press.

dei Ottati, Gabi. 1987. Il Mercato Communitario. In *Mercato e Forze Locali: Il Distretto Industriale,* ed. Giacomo Becattini. Bologna: Il Mulino.

———. 1991a. The Economic Bases of Diffuse Industrialization. *International Studies of Management and Organization* 21;53–74.

———. 1991b. *Prato, 1944–1963: Rinascita e Trasformazione di un Sistema Produttivo Locale.* Milan: Franco Angeli.

Eller, Claudia, and Charles Fleming. 1992. Cameron's Fat Fox Deal. *Variety,* 27 April, 1992, 8–9.

ENEA. 1985. Documentation on the Prato Case Study. Rome. Mimeo.

Enright, Michael. 1990. *Geographic Concentration and Industrial Organization.* Ann Arbor, MI: University Microfilms.

Enright, Michael, and Paolo Tenti. 1990. La Competitività Internazionale della Ceramica Italiana. *Harvard Espansione,* September, 28–41.

Evans, Alan. 1972. The Pure Theory of City Size in an Industrial Economy. *Urban Studies* 9:49–77.

Gomery, Douglas. 1986. *The Hollywood Studio System.* New York: St. Martin's Press.

Granovetter, Mark. 1985. Economic Action and Social Structure: The Problem of Embeddedness. *American Journal of Sociology* 91:481–510.

Green, Jerry, and Nancy Stokey. 1983. A Comparison of Tournaments and Contests. *Journal of Political Economy* 91:349–64.

Hirshhorn, Larry, and Thomas Gilmore. 1992. The New Boundaries of the "Boundaryless" Company. *Harvard Business Review* 70 (May–June): 104–15.

Hoover, Edgar, and Raymond Vernon. 1959. *Anatomy of a Metropolis.* Cambridge: Harvard University Press.

Klein, Benjamin, Robert Crawford, and Armen Alchian. 1978. Vertical Integration, Appropriable Rents, and the Competitive Contracting Process. *Journal of Law and Economics* 21:297–326.

Knickerbocker, Frederick. 1972. A Note on the Watch Industries in Switzerland, Japan, and the United States. HBS Case 9-373-090. Boston: Harvard Business School.

Krugman, Paul. 1991. *Geography and Trade.* Cambridge: MIT Press.

Landes, David. 1983. *Revolution in Time.* Cambridge: Harvard University Press.

Landro, Laura. 1991. Paramount Pictures and Eddie Murphy Sign Agreement to Make Four Movies. *Wall Street Journal,* 24 September, 1991, B6.

Lazear, Edward, and Sherwin Rosen. 1981. Rank Order Tournaments as Optimal Labor Contracts. *Journal of Political Economy* 89:841–64.

Lorenzoni, Gianni. 1985. A Strategy for Survival: The Example of Prato. In *Documentation on the Prato Case Study,* by ENEA.

Lugonelli, Michele. 1988. Dalla Manifattura alla Fabbrica: L'Avvio dello Sviluppo Industriale, 1815–1895. In *Prato Storia di una Città: 3 Il Tempo dell'Industria, 1815–1943,* ed. Giorgio Mori. Prato: Le Monnier.

Marshall, Alfred. 1920. *Principles of Economics.* 8th ed. London: Macmillan.

———. 1923. *Industry and Trade.* 3d ed. London: Macmillan.

Mazzonis, Danielle. 1985. A Project for Innovation in Prato. In *documentation on the Prato Case Study,* by ENEA.

Nalebuff, Barry, and Joseph Stiglitz. 1983. Prizes and Incentives: Toward a General Theory of Compensation and Competition. *Bell Journal of Economics* 14:21–43.

Oakey, Ray. 1985. High-Technology Industry and Agglomeration Economies. In *Silicon Landscapes,* ed. Peter Hall and Ann Markusen. Boston: Allen and Unwin.

Origo, Iris. 1986. *The Merchant of Prato.* Boston: Godine. Originally published 1957.

Palmer, Edwin. 1938. *History of Hollywood.* Garden City, New York: Doubleday.

Piore, Michael, and Charles Sabel. 1984. *The Second Industrial Divide.* New York: Basic Books.

Porter, Michael. 1990. *The Competitive Advantage of Nations.* New York: Free Press.

Rosten, Leo. 1970. *Hollywood: The Movie Colony, the Movie Makers.* New York: Arno Press. Originally published 1941.

Schatz, Thomas. 1983. *Old Hollywood/New Hollywood: Ritual, Art, and Industry.* Ann Arbor: University of Michigan Research Press.

Scholl, Jaye. 1992. Lights! Camera! Money! Hollywood's Bonding Companies Are Feeling the Pinch. *Barron's,* 8 June, 1992, 14.

Schweizer, Beat. 1986. The Swiss Watchmaking Industry. UBS Publication no. 100. Zurich.

Scott, Allen. 1987. Industrial Organization and Location: Division of Labor, the Firm, and Spatial Process. *Economic Geography* 63:214–31.

———. 1988a. *Metropolis.* Berkeley and Los Angeles: University of California Press.

———. 1988b. *New Industrial Spaces.* London: Pion.

Stein, Benjamin. 1992. Is Hollywood's Star Fading? *Across the Board,* May 1992, 50.

Stigler, George. 1951. The Division of Labor Is Limited by the Extent of the Market. *Journal of Political Economy* 59:185–93.

Storper, Michael, and Susan Christopherson. 1987. Flexible Specialization and Regional Agglomerations: The Case of the U.S. Motion Picture Industry. *Economic Geography* 61:260–82.

Tenti, Paolo. 1987. The Italian Wool Textile Industry. Manuscript.

Trigilia, Carlo. 1989. Il Distretto Industriale di Prato. In *Strategie di Riagiustamento Industriale,* ed. Marino Regini and Charles Sabel. Bologna: Il Mulino.

Unione Industriele Pratese. 1991. Il Sistema Economico Pratese alle Soglie degli Anni '90. *Sprint Notizie,* September–October, 1–4.

United Nations. 1991. *International Trade Statistics Yearbook.* New York: United Nations.

Vogel, Harold. 1990. *Entertainment Industry Economics.* Cambridge: Cambridge University Press.

Wechsler, Dana. 1990. Profits? What Profits? *Forbes,* 19 February 1990, 38–40.

Weinraub, Bernard. 1991a. Money Worries Force Orion to Shelve Several Films. *New York Times,* 23 October 1991, C17, C19.

———. 1991b. Paramount in Accord for 4 Films by Murphy. *New York Times,* 24 September 1991, C11, C12.

Williamson, Oliver. 1985. *The Economic Institutions of Capitalism.* New York: Free Press.

Comment   Kenneth L. Sokoloff

Over the past decade, there has been a welcome revival of interest in the integration of geographic variables into economic analysis. Several developments have contributed to this now unmistakable trend. Foremost among them is the apparent success of Japan and several other East Asian countries at cultivating world-class export-oriented industries behind trade barriers to foreign competition in their home markets. Both politicians and policy-oriented economists have suggested that this record reflects the existence of external economies operating at the industry level and within geographic units such as regions or nations. These gut reactions to real-world observations have been comple-

Kenneth L. Sokoloff is professor of economics at the University of California at Los Angeles and a research associate of the National Bureau of Economic Research.

mented nicely by advances on a different front—where abstract but well-meaning mathematical economists have been slogging around in the trenches. In their quest for a general theory of growth, they found that they could elegantly close their models with external economies of scale; moreover, they noted at least a superficial consistency of this sort of model with the cross-sectional evidence—high rates of economic growth among nations with high levels of per capita income and very low rates of growth among those with low incomes.

Of course, a major impetus to further study of the subject has also come from the observation that some of today's most dynamic industries in the United States, such as biotechnology and personal computers, are geographically concentrated in a few areas. Since these industries are intensive in human capital instead of a traditional immobile factor like iron ore or warm climate, there has been a tendency to attribute such spatial concentration to the operation of external economies. The magnitude and prevalence of such geographic externalities are not only relevant to issues of regional and national economic development, but also to questions concerning the boundaries, activities, and organizations of firms. If spatial clustering influences the costs of transacting or of coordinating the efforts of different agents or firms, many aspects of the behavior of these firms and agents could be affected, including how they organize their production, their locations, the characteristics of their products, their techniques of production, and the rates at which they invent or innovate.

As scholars have grown increasingly convinced of the significance of external economies operating at the local or regional level, they have had to confront our limited empirical knowledge of the subject. Virtually no systematic investigations have been conducted, so basic questions as to the source or specific content of externalities, the ease with which districts can realize them, their magnitude, the range of industries affected, and their durability over time remain unanswered. For this reason, Michael Enright's work is especially welcome. His paper is but one from a broad project on the localization of industries, and in it he recounts the evolution of the organization of three case industries that have long and fascinating histories of being geographically concentrated. In doing so, Enright discusses the relationships between an industry's degree of geographic clustering and the structure of its firms as well as the coordination mechanisms it employs. Although his treatment is not comprehensive, he also elucidates some of the competitive advantages that firms in certain types of industries enjoy when they are located in close proximity to one another. His principal hypothesis is that geographic proximity enhances the effectiveness of coordinating activities of agents through markets as opposed to relying on hierarchical structures within firms for coordination. Geographic proximity is of course only one of many factors that influence the degree of vertical integration, but Enright suggests that this effect is sufficient to account for a greater diversity in the organization of localized industries than one observes in nonlocalized industries. He notes how geographic clustering is advantageous for the operation of spot markets which facilitate the bringing together of teams of producers for short-term projects. The clear implication is that industries with short production runs will tend to be more geographically concentrated.

Enright's presentations of three case studies are elegant. But the paper highlights how economists' desire to establish simple lines of causation between geographic concentration and the organizational forms or coordinating mechanisms employed by industries may be frustrated by problems of simultaneity. While geographic localization may encourage more disintegrated industrial structures, part of the empirical association must be due to the tendency for workers in industries whose outputs are best produced (for either technological or demand-based reasons) in small batches or short bursts of time to locate near one another so as to facilitate contracting and fuller employment throughout the year. Similarly, although the extent of geographic concentration and the reliance on short-term coalitions for production will be influenced by the path of technical change, the character of the competition in both the factor and output markets, and government policy, the latter variables will in turn be partially determined in the long run by the historical structure of the industry. The simultaneity problem notwithstanding, Enright's emphasis on the line of causation from geographic concentration to the method of coordination is probably warranted in his examples of filmmaking in Hollywood and wool textiles in Italy—where the organizations of long-localized industries clearly became more disintegrated over time.

There is a powerful logic to Enright's argument. However, the familiar question of sample selection should be considered before drawing general inferences from this study. Although Enright identifies a number of features common to his three cases and outlines an appealing intuitive approach to understanding the linkages between organizational structure and localization, it is not at all clear that the Prato wool textile industry, the Swiss watch industry, and the Hollywood film industry are representative of geographically concentrated industries. Moreover, there is no systematic comparison with a control group of nonlocalized industries. If his goal is only to establish that diversity exists in the organizational structure of localized industries, then the lack of representativeness of his case studies and the lack of a control group do not matter and he succeeds admirably. If, however, he entertains the more ambitious agenda of establishing how firms in localized industries differ systematically from others in their form of organization, or demonstrating that any such difference is quantitatively or qualitatively important, then there may be a problem with his evidence.

For example, all three of his localized industries are characterized over the time period he focuses on by rather small scales and limited runs of production, as well as by labor forces with substantial individual investments in human capital. In such a technological context, one would indeed expect that there would be frequent expirations of old contracts and entrances into new ones—in order that all parties remain as fully employed as possible. Moreover, it is reasonable that industries in such technological circumstances would tend to be located in geographic clusters so as to reduce the transactions costs involved in recontracting—just as traders in a capital market tend to gather in the same locations to facilitate their trading.

My unease arises from the many cases of localized industries that do not resemble those treated by Enright: Los Angeles and aeronautical engineering for the military; New York and investment houses; Warsaw, Indiana, and artificial limbs and joints; Detroit and automobiles; Pittsburgh and steel; Silicon Valley and computer hardware; Hamamatsu, Japan, and motorcycles; and many other pairs. Admittedly none of these industries is perfectly vertically integrated, but they are nevertheless far from being characterized by fluid firm boundaries, small scale, fragmented production processes, or many of the other features that are associated with Enright's case studies. Instead, they reflect technological contexts other than those considered by Enright that would also serve to encourage the localization of industries. Examples of such other contexts include situations where a locality has a relative abundance of some relatively fixed factor of production for which there is no good substitute, or where technical change is rapid and the firms cluster geographically to keep abreast of the frontiers of knowledge and technology by means of informal channels through which information diffuses spatially.

The existence of nonlocalized industries characterized by extensive subcontracting also presents problems for Enright's analysis. The practice of obtaining parts from remote, independent, and diverse sources to assemble in yet another location is now widespread in many manufacturing industries, and analogous arrangements are also evident in the service sector. The increasing prevalence of this sourcing pattern raises the possibility that immediate geographic proximity may not actually have a large effect on the relative costs of alternative methods of coordinating factors of production. It also reinforces the view that a more systematic empirical investigation is necessary in order to establish Enright's hypothesis about the association between geographic concentration and the organization of the industry.

Concern about problems of sample selection is further heightened by Enright's suggestion that a review of his case studies supports the conclusion that small, disintegrated firms respond more quickly to incremental changes in technology or fashion, while larger, integrated enterprises have the advantage in adapting to revolutionary changes. As one who has been following the fortunes of mammoth firms like General Motors, IBM, and Sears and Roebuck, I find the proposition odd. The case of IBM appears especially telling, because this company appears to have been overwhelmed by the revolutionary changes in the power and design of computers, while the smaller gadflies in the industry thrived and multiplied.

Despite these caveats, I commend Enright for his pioneering efforts to study systematically the phenomenon of localized industries and its association with the ways in which firms are organized and in which technology evolves and is diffused. These are extremely important, if complex, subjects, and his work will advance our understanding of them.

5 The Boundaries of the U.S. Firm in R&D

David C. Mowery

5.1 Introduction

An important part of the restructuring of U.S. manufacturing firms during the late nineteenth and early twentieth centuries was the development of corporate research laboratories within the firm. The in-house industrial research laboratory first appeared in the German chemicals industry during the 1870s (Beer 1958), and a number of U.S. firms in the chemicals and electrical equipment industries had established similar facilities by the turn of the century. The growth of industrial R&D in both the United States and Germany was influenced by the dramatic advances in physics and chemistry during the last third of the nineteenth century, which created considerable potential for the profitable application of scientific and technical knowledge. Indeed, many of the earliest corporate investors in industrial R&D, such as General Electric and Alcoa, were founded on product or process innovations that drew on advances in physics and chemistry.

But change in the scientific and technological knowledge base does not suffice to explain the growth of industrial R&D within the U.S. corporation. Although changing technical opportunities influenced the decision to invest in industrial R&D, they do not account for the growing share of R&D activity within the boundaries of the firm. A substantial network of independent R&D laboratories provided research services on a contractual basis throughout

David C. Mowery is a professor in the Walter A. Haas School of Business at the University of California at Berkeley.

Preparation of this paper was aided by support from the Alfred P. Sloan Foundation. The paper benefited from the comments of Naomi Lamoreaux, Daniel Raff, Peter Temin, and other participants in an earlier meeting of contributors to this project.

the formative years of industrial R&D in the United States. These contract research organizations' share of total R&D employment, however, declined during the first half of the century, and their R&D services often complemented client firms' in-house R&D activities.

The expansion in the boundaries of the U.S. firm is central to any explanation of the growth of U.S. industrial R&D. The corporate R&D laboratory brought more of the process of developing and improving industrial technology into the boundaries of U.S. manufacturing firms, reducing the importance of the independent inventor as a source of patents (Schmookler 1957). But during much of the period before 1940, the in-house research facilities of large U.S. firms were not concerned exclusively with the creation of new technology. They also monitored technological developments outside of the firm and advised corporate managers on the acquisition of externally developed technologies.

Although their corporate laboratories were important devices for the acquisition of technologies from external sources before 1940, many large firms shifted to greater reliance on in-house sources of technology during the postwar era. In other words, the porousness of their boundaries in industrial research declined. This shift in the uses of intrafirm research was one response to the more stringent antitrust environment of the postwar U.S. economy. The relationship between the in-house R&D activities of large firms and innovative activities elsewhere in the economy also was affected by postwar expansion in defense-related federal R&D funding and procurement. These developments contributed to the creation of a postwar U.S. national innovation system that differed in important respects from the prewar system, and contrasted as well with the innovation systems of other postwar industrial economies.[1]

This paper surveys the historical development of U.S. industrial research. I discuss the reasons for the location of industrial R&D within the firm, and consider the historical and organizational implications of the changing boundaries of the firm in industrial R&D. The growth of U.S. industrial research was heavily influenced by R&D in other institutions, such as universities and government laboratories, and I briefly discuss the changing structure of these components of the U.S. national innovation system. Because federal R&D and antitrust policies of the postwar era significantly changed the industrial R&D strategies of U.S. firms in industrial research, I examine this period in some detail.

---

1. A "national innovation system" is the network of private- and public-sector institutions that exert the primary influence on the creation and adoption of new technologies. Like the Holy Roman Empire, national innovation systems may be in the process of becoming "none of the above," increasingly international in scope and boundaries; concerned with the adoption, as much as with the creation, of new technologies; and (especially in the United States) exhibiting few if any of the hallmarks of planning that one associates with the term "system." Nelson 1993 contains a set of studies of the national systems of a number of industrial and industrializing economies.

During the past decade, many U.S. firms have experimented with new organizational structures for their R&D operations, seeking ways to strengthen linkages to external sources of scientific and engineering knowledge such as universities, foreign and other domestic firms, and publicly financed national laboratories. Some of these experiments are genuinely novel, but others are simply a renewal of linkages that were weakened during and after World War II. I return briefly to this point in the conclusion.

5.2   Why Is Industrial R&D Located within the Firm?

In contrast to the predictions of George Stigler,[2] U.S. industrial research during this century has been located mainly within the firm, rather than being dominated by independent firms selling R&D via contract. Nevertheless, independent R&D contractors have played an important role in U.S. industrial research throughout the twentieth century, and were cited by early proponents as an important source of R&D services for small firms.[3] In addition, in-house R&D organizations were not wholly insulated from the market, but actively sought to purchase patents and technologies from external sources. In this section, I discuss the basis for the coexistence of markets and hierarchies in industrial R&D.

Two factors explain the failure of market-based forms of organization to dominate the organization of industrial R&D. First, the sources and characteristics of knowledge employed in the industrial innovation process tend to favor vertical integration among manufacturing, marketing, and R&D activities. Second, transaction-cost considerations make contractual R&D transactions feasible for only a narrow class of R&D activities.

The advantages of placing R&D within the firm reflect the fact that the sources of many commercially valuable innovations do not lie in scientific laboratory research. Instead, much of the knowledge employed in industrial innovation flows from the firm's production and marketing activities. The technical

---

2. "[W]ith the growth of research, new firms will emerge to provide specialized facilities for small firms. It is only to be expected that, when a new kind of research develops, at first it will be conducted chiefly as an ancillary activity by existing firms. . . . We may expect the rapid expansion of the specialized research laboratory, selling its services generally. The specialized laboratories need not be in the least inferior to 'captive' laboratories" (Stigler 1956, 281).

3. John J. Carty, director of Bell Telephone Laboratories, argued in 1916 that "[c]onditions today are such that without cooperation among themselves the small concerns cannot have the full benefits of industrial research, for no one among them is sufficiently strong to maintain the necessary staff and laboratories. Once the vital importance of this subject is appreciated by the small manufacturers many solutions of the problem will promptly appear. One of these is for the manufacturer to take his problem to one of the industrial research laboratories already established for the purpose of serving those who cannot afford a laboratory of their own. Other manufacturers doing the same, the financial encouragement received would enable the laboratories to extend and improve their facilities so that each of the small manufacturers who patronized them would in the course of time have the benefit of an institution similar to those maintained by our largest concerns" (512).

knowledge that is produced by the interaction of R&D and other functions within a given firm often is highly specific to that enterprise. Moreover, this information is difficult to transfer within an organization, let alone across organizational boundaries. Its transfer within or between organizations requires considerable shared expertise and knowledge, as well as sufficient expertise to absorb and apply the knowledge within the recipient division or firm.[4]

Because interaction among the different functions within the firm contributes to a stock of firm-specific knowledge that is not easily transferred across organizational boundaries, organizations that do not conduct "downstream" activities such as manufacturing or marketing may be unable to develop specific bodies of know-how. A free-standing contract research organization, for example, is not likely to produce the technological knowledge that results from the intraorganizational interaction of engineering, production, marketing, and research.

Contracting problems also limit a firm's reliance on market-based forms of organization in R&D, especially for specialized projects that involve fundamental research. These types of projects are likely to involve investments in specialized physical or human capital, they will typically involve small numbers of buyers and sellers, and their outcomes will be uncertain. Transaction-specific investments in an R&D project that cannot be easily redeployed to other uses or sold make it easier for one party to a contract to "hold up" the other, threatening to break the contract and negate the value of the other party's investment. The thin market, that is, the small number of buyers and sellers, for specialized research services makes opportunistic behavior more likely and discourages reliance on contracts for these forms of R&D (see Teece 1988 for a more detailed discussion of contracting problems).

When the knowledge or equipment needed for the research is less highly specialized or firm-specific, competition among research institutions is more likely, making it more difficult for a contractor to exploit its client. High uncertainty about outcomes means that contracts for such R&D services will be incomplete, incapable of specifying all contingencies, and therefore of limited use.

---

4. Arrow's "Classificatory Notes on the Production and Transmission of Technical Knowledge" pointed out that "[w]hen the British in World War II supplied us with the plans for the jet engine, it took ten months to redraw them to conform to American usage" (1969, 174). Concerning Japanese technology imports from the industrialized West, Caves and Uekusa (1976, 126) stated: "The level and pattern of research and development within Japan are closely related to the import of technology from abroad. Firms must maintain some research capacity in order to know what technology is available for purchase or copy and they must generally modify and adopt foreign technology in putting it to use. A 1963 survey of Japanese manufacturers showed that on average one-third of the respondents' expenditures on R&D went for this purpose. The moderate level, wide diffusion, and applied character of Japan's research effort are consistent with a facility for securing new knowledge from abroad." See also Evenson and Kislev 1975; Cohen and Levinthal 1989; and Mowery 1983a.

An additional limitation on firms' use of independent R&D contractors as a substitute for in-house R&D is the client firm's need for considerable internal expertise. A client firm needs an ability to select and evaluate an R&D contractor, to assess contractor performance, and even to pose a feasible project to a contractor. All of these requirements create a need for considerable project-specific and general knowledge within the client firm. In addition, the transfer and internal application of the results of the R&D rely on the in-house expertise of the client firm. Contract R&D services thus will complement, rather than substitute for, in-house R&D in many firms.

These arguments are consistent with two findings concerning the role of independent R&D firms during the formative years of U.S. industrial research: (1) they specialized in the provision of relatively simple R&D services, such as materials analyses, and tended to avoid open-ended, highly uncertain undertakings in advanced research; and (2) a large and growing share of their client population during the pre-1940 era consisted of firms with in-house R&D operations. For three major independent research laboratories (the Battelle Institute, the Mellon Institute, and Arthur D. Little, Inc.), for example, the share of client firms with in-house R&D laboratories during 1930–40 was 43.6, 51.8, and 22.8 percent, respectively, significantly higher than the share of firms with in-house R&D laboratories in the larger population (Mowery 1983c). The share of clients with in-house research facilities was higher still for the small number of more complex research projects undertaken by the Battelle Institute and Arthur D. Little during this period (these shares respectively were 47 and 69.6 percent).

R&D contractors thus provided a limited array of services, and for many of their clients, contractually governed R&D complemented in-house R&D. Firms lacking in-house R&D facilities were less likely to have access to a full range of R&D services, and were handicapped in obtaining even the limited services available via contract (Mowery 1983c). Reflecting these realities, the importance of independent contract research laboratories within the U.S. private industrial research system declined during the 1921–46 period. Although employment in contract and independent research organizations grew during this period, their share of overall industrial research employment in U.S. manufacturing shrank.[5]

In-house industrial R&D nonetheless was not completely divorced from markets for intellectual property and new technologies. The very uncertainties that discouraged firms from contracting for some R&D services also prevented them from relying exclusively on in-house R&D for new technologies; no firm could ensure that all technological threats and opportunities would be pursued

5. The employment of scientific professionals in independent research organizations, expressed as a fraction of employment of scientific professionals in all in-house and independent research laboratories, was 15.2 percent in 1921, 12.9 in 1927, 10.9 in 1933, 8.7 in 1940, and 6.9 in 1946 (Mowery 1981, chap. 2).

successfully in-house.[6] Precisely because the outcomes of many research projects cannot be known ex ante, the portfolio of in-house projects may not adequately explore all technological alternatives, and important technological developments are likely to emerge from sources other than intrafirm R&D. Many firms therefore used their in-house R&D for two "outward-oriented" activities: monitoring their technological environment, often through research links with universities, and acquiring innovations from external sources. Contractual governance was infeasible for the provision of some classes of R&D services, but market mechanisms could be and were used, with the aid of internal R&D, to acquire the products of independent inventors and other manufacturing firms. Internal R&D facilities also served to monitor and interpret the progress of research in other laboratories.

Firms generally purchased an innovation in the early stages of its development, rather than contracting for R&D services, with the attendant uncertainties relating to contractor performance, opportunism, and outcomes. Nevertheless, the considerable risks and uncertainty associated with the acquisition of a patent or an unproven technology meant that in-house expertise was essential to these technology acquisitions. In effect, the purchaser firm exploited its capabilities in development, manufacturing, distribution, and marketing to complement the inventive capabilities of another firm or individual. The in-house R&D facilities of the purchasing firm monitored opportunities for technology acquisitions, managed the transfer and absorption of the innovation, and undertook its further development and commercialization.

This "outward-looking" use of in-house R&D served as a hedge against one class of competitive risks. An exclusive reliance on intrafirm sources of new technologies, especially in an environment of rapidly expanding technical opportunities and intensified competition from other firms, could narrow the area of search and lead a firm to overlook technological developments or threats from other sources. But the ability to recognize and exploit these external opportunities, like the purchase of contract R&D services, required an effective in-house R&D organization.

5.3   The Growth of U.S. Industrial Research, 1921–45

Although recent historiography on U.S. industrial research has focused primarily on the electrical industry (an exception is Hounshell and Smith 1989), the data on the growth of U.S. industrial research during the early twentieth century suggest that chemicals and related industries were the leading sector. The chemicals, glass, rubber, and petroleum industries accounted for nearly 40 percent of the laboratories founded during 1899–1946. The chemicals sector also dominated research employment during 1921–46.

---

6. Swann (1988, 55) emphasizes this consideration in explaining U.S. pharmaceutical firms' use of university research during the 1930s and 1940s.

Chandler (1977, 1990) and Landau and Rosenberg (1992) have noted that the growth of research employment within the chemicals and chemicals-related industries was associated with the exploitation of high-pressure, continuous-flow production processes. The adoption of these process technologies by other industries, including petroleum, foodstuffs, and paper, increased their reliance on industrial research (Mowery 1983b). The dominance of research employment by chemicals-related industries was supplemented during 1921–46 by industries whose product and process technologies drew heavily on physics. Electrical machinery and instruments accounted for less than 10 percent of total research employment in 1921. By 1946, however, these two industries employed more than 20 percent of all industrial research scientists and engineers in U.S. manufacturing, and the chemicals-based industries had increased their share to slightly more than 43 percent of total research employment.

Table 5.1 contains data on research laboratory employment for 1921, 1927, 1933, 1940, and 1946 in nineteen two-digit manufacturing industries. Employment of scientists and engineers in industrial research within manufacturing grew from roughly three thousand in 1921 to nearly forty-six thousand by 1946.[7] As note 5 indicates, the growth of industrial research employment during this period was dominated by in-house research. By 1946, there were slightly more than twenty-three hundred industrial research laboratories within U.S. manufacturing firms, a dramatic increase from the number (slightly more than one hundred)[8] that appear to have been active in 1900 (Mowery and Rosenberg 1989, table 4.1).

The ordering of industries by research intensity in table 5.1 is quite stable—chemicals, rubber, petroleum, and electrical machinery are among the most research-intensive industries, accounting for 48–58 percent of all scientists and engineers employed in industrial research within manufacturing, throughout this period.[9] The geographic concentration of industrial research employment

7. The data in table 5.1 were drawn originally from the National Research Council surveys of industrial research employment, as tabulated in Mowery 1981. My discussion of these data draws on Mowery 1981, 1992 and Mowery and Rosenberg 1989.

8. As Hounshell (1993) has pointed out, the estimate of the number of industrial research laboratories in Mowery and Rosenberg 1989 may be high; he argues that the number of in-house research laboratories that did more than simple materials testing or quality control was in fact far smaller. The estimate in Mowery and Rosenberg is based on the reported foundation dates of laboratories listed in the 1940 edition of the National Research Council survey (1940), and therefore is subject to the vagaries of corporate memory, as well as differences among firms over the definition of an industrial research laboratory. The employment data reported in table 5.1 are less likely to suffer from this flaw, since they are gathered from contemporaneous surveys published by the National Research Council.

9. An exception to the pattern of stability in research intensity is transportation equipment, which increased in research intensity throughout the period, and by 1946 was among the five most research-intensive manufacturing industries. The upward movement in the relative research intensity of this industry (which includes aircraft) is attributable to federal support of research and federal procurement during 1940–46, and to the rapid growth of the automobile industry throughout 1921–46. Federal government funding of wartime research in industry also contributed to research employment within electrical machinery and instruments after 1940.

Table 5.1 **Employment of Scientists and Engineers in Industrial Research Laboratories in U.S. Manufacturing Firms, 1921–46**

	1921	1927	1933	1940	1946
Food/beverages	116	354	651	1,712	2,510
	(0.19)	(0.53)	(0.973)	(2.13)	(2.26)
Tobacco	—	4	17	54	67
		(0.031)	(0.19)	(0.61)	(0.65)
Textiles	15	79	149	254	434
	(0.015)	(0.07)	(0.15)	(0.23)	(0.38)
Apparel	—	—	—	4	25
				(0.005)	(0.03)
Lumber products	30	50	65	128	187
	(0.043)	(0.16)	(0.22)	(0.30)	(0.31)
Furniture	—	—	5	19	19
			(0.041)	(0.10)	(0.07)
Paper	89	189	302	752	770
	(0.49)	(0.87)	(1.54)	(2.79)	(1.96)
Publishing	—	—	4	9	28
			(0.015)	(0.03)	(0.06)
Chemicals	1,102	1,812	3,255	7,675	14,066
	(5.2)	(6.52)	(12.81)	(27.81)	(30.31)
Petroleum	159	465	994	2,849	4,750
	(1.83)	(4.65)	(11.04)	(26.38)	(28.79)
Rubber products	207	361	564	1,000	1,069
	(2.04)	(2.56)	(5.65)	(8.35)	(5.2)
Leather	25	35	67	68	86
	(0.09)	(0.11)	(0.24)	(0.21)	(0.25)
Stone/clay/glass	96	410	569	1,334	1,508
	(0.38)	(1.18)	(3.25)	(5.0)	(3.72)
Primary metals	297	538	850	2,113	2,460
	(0.78)	(0.93)	(2.0)	(3.13)	(2.39)
Fabricated metal products	103	334	500	1,332	1,489
	(0.27)	(0.63)	(1.53)	(2.95)	(1.81)
Nonelectrical machinery	127	421	629	2,122	2,743
	(0.25)	(0.65)	(1.68)	(3.96)	(2.2)
Electrical machinery	199	732	1,322	3,269	6,993
	(1.11)	(2.86)	(8.06)	(13.18)	(11.01)
Transportation equipment	83	256	394	1,765	4,491
	(0.204)	(0.52)	(1.28)	(3.24)	(4.58)
Instruments	127	234	581	1,318	2,246
	(0.396)	(0.63)	(2.69)	(4.04)	(3.81)
Total	2,775	6,320	10,927	27,777	45,941

Source: Mowery 1981.

Note: Figures in parentheses represent research intensity, defined as employment of scientists and engineers per one thousand production workers.

during this period exhibits similar stability. Five states (New York, New Jersey, Pennsylvania, Ohio, and Illinois) contained more than 70 percent of the professionals employed in industrial research in 1921 and 1927; their share declined modestly, to slightly more than 60 percent, by 1940 and 1946. The major prewar research employers remained among the most research-intensive industries well into the postwar period, despite the growth in federal funding for R&D in industry. Chemicals, rubber, petroleum, and electrical machinery accounted for more than 53 percent of industrial research employment in 1940 and represented 40.3 percent of research employment in industry in 1984 (National Science Foundation 1987).

The stable rank ordering of industries by research intensity may be attributable to enduring differences among industries in "technological opportunity," higher levels of which are associated with greater R&D investment (Scherer 1965; Levin, Cohen, and Mowery 1985). An additional factor contributing to such intertemporal stability is that the development of firm-specific innovative capabilities through R&D investment requires considerable time. The resulting high levels of serial correlation in longitudinal firm-level R&D investment data may influence these industry-level data.

Stability in the geographic concentration of R&D employment over long time periods suggests that the regional concentration of high-technology firms and R&D activities within the United States is not an exclusively postwar phenomenon. This intertemporal stability in the geographic distribution of industrial R&D activity is also consistent with Patel and Pavitt's observation (1991) that the widely remarked postwar globalization of manufacturing activity has not been accompanied by a similar international spread in the location of R&D activity, insofar as patent data are reliable indicators of such activity. In domestic as well as international markets and operations, proximity to a network of other firms, universities, and support services remains critical to innovation. The development or decay of such a regional or national infrastructure takes considerable time. The in-house R&D facilities of firms benefit from the regional agglomeration effects pointed out by Marshall (1910, chap. 10). These effects derive in part from the ability of labor and ideas to move among research facilities, reflecting the porousness of firms' boundaries in R&D.

5.3.1   U.S. Antitrust Policy and the Origins of Industrial Research

The development of U.S. industrial research was closely linked with the emergence of large-scale corporations during the late nineteenth and early twentieth centuries (Chandler 1977, 1990). Technically trained managers, a central office staff that focused on strategic rather than operating decisions, and the integration within the firm of functions such as marketing were necessary conditions for the development of in-house R&D. This relationship between the internal organization of the firm and in-house industrial research meant that the mergers and corporate reorganizations of the late nineteenth and early twentieth centuries hastened the growth of industrial research.

The structural change in many large U.S. manufacturing firms that underpinned investment in industrial research was influenced by U.S. antitrust policy. By the late nineteenth century, judicial interpretations of the Sherman Antitrust Act had made agreements among firms for the control of prices and output targets of civil prosecution. The 1895–1904 merger wave, particularly the surge in mergers after 1898, was in part a response to this new legal environment. Finding that the legality of informal and formal price-fixing and market-sharing agreements was under attack, firms resorted to horizontal mergers to control prices and markets.[10]

The incentives created by the Sherman Act for horizontal mergers were reduced by the Supreme Court's 1904 *Northern Securities* decision. But the influence of antitrust policy on the growth of industrial research extended beyond its effects on corporate mergers and remained important long after 1904. Justice Department opposition to horizontal mergers caused large U.S. firms to seek alternative means for corporate growth. For some firms, the threat of antitrust action created by their dominance of a single industry led to efforts to diversify into other areas. The commercialization of new technologies, developed internally or purchased from external sources, supported corporate diversification and growth. Threatened with antitrust suits from state as well as federal agencies, George Eastman saw industrial research as a means of supporting the diversification and growth of Eastman Kodak (Sturchio 1985, 8). Facing a similarly hostile political environment during the first decade of this century, the Du Pont Company used industrial research to diversify out of the black and smokeless powder businesses even before the 1913 antitrust decision that forced the divestiture of a portion of the firm's black powder and dynamite businesses (Hounshell and Smith 1989, 57).

Although it discouraged horizontal mergers among large firms, U.S. antitrust policy through much of the pre-1940 period did not discourage efforts by these firms' research laboratories to acquire new technologies from external sources. Du Pont obtained many of its major product and process innovations during this period, for example, from outside sources and proceeded to further develop and commercialize them within the U.S. market (Mueller 1962; Hounshell and Smith 1989). The research facilities of AT&T were instrumental in the procurement of the "triode" from independent inventor Lee De Forest, and also were involved in the corporation's decision to obtain loading-coil technology from Pupin (Reich 1985). General Electric's research operations inten-

10. See Stigler 1968. The Supreme Court ruled in the *Trans Missouri Association* case in 1898 and the *Addyston Pipe* case in 1899 that the Sherman Act outlawed all agreements among firms on prices or market sharing. Data in Thorelli 1954 and Lamoreaux 1985 indicate an increase in merger activity between the 1895–98 and 1899–1902 periods. Lamoreaux (1985) argues that other factors, including the increasing capital intensity of production technologies and the resulting rise in fixed costs, were more important influences on the U.S. merger wave, but her account (109) also acknowledges the importance of the Sherman Act in the peak of the merger wave. Lamoreaux also emphasizes the incentives created by tighter Sherman Act enforcement after 1904 for firms to pursue alternatives to merger or cartelization as strategies for attaining or preserving market power.

sively monitored foreign technological advances in lamp filaments and the inventive activities of outside firms and individuals, and aggressively pursued patent rights to innovations developed all over the world (Reich 1985, 61). The Standard Oil Company of New Jersey established its Development Department precisely to carry out development of technologies obtained from other sources, rather than for original research (Gibb and Knowlton 1956, 525). Alcoa's R&D operations also closely monitored and frequently purchased process innovations from external sources (Graham and Pruitt 1990, 145–47). To the extent that federal antitrust policy motivated industrial research investment by large U.S. firms before and during the interwar period, the policy paradoxically may have aided the survival of these firms and the growth of a relatively stable, oligopolistic market structure in some U.S. manufacturing industries.[11]

Historians are virtually unanimous in concluding that the stringency of U.S. antitrust policy was unique among the industrial economies during this period.[12] This antitrust climate contrasted with that of Great Britain, the only foreign industrial economy for which comparable R&D employment data are available for even a part of the 1900–1950 period. In Great Britain, weak antitrust policies allowed the establishment of informal cartels and market-sharing agreements that reduced firms' incentives to merge and prevented the rationalization of the internal structure of the firms created by these mergers (Hannah 1979). British antitrust policy was associated with levels of industrial R&D intensity that were lower than those of U.S. firms during much of the 1900–1950 period (Mowery 1984; Chandler 1990).[13] Even in large British firms that did invest significantly in R&D, such as Imperial Chemical Industries, historians have suggested that the weakness of the firm's central management structure reduced the returns to this investment (Reader 1975).

Since a weak antitrust climate in Germany was associated with what are widely believed to have been high levels of industrial research (no direct measures of German industrial R&D investment are available for the pre-1940 period), one cannot assert a simple cause-and-effect relationship between tough antitrust policy and high levels of intrafirm R&D. Although it was an important element of U.S.-U.K. contrast, antitrust policy was only one of several factors

---

11. During 1921–46, the growth of intrafirm industrial research was associated with a decline in turnover among the largest U.S. manufacturing firms (Mowery 1983b; Edwards 1975; Kaplan 1964; Collins and Preston 1961). Interestingly, and in contrast to the usual formulation of one of the Schumpeterian "hypotheses," these results suggest that firm conduct (R&D employment) was an important influence on market structure (turnover). They are also broadly consistent with the results of studies of more recent data on the market structure-R&D investment relationship that suggest that structure and R&D investment are jointly determined (Levin, Cohen, and Mowery 1985).

12. The argument is elaborated in Keller 1990, 23; Freyer, chap. 6 in this volume; McCraw 1981; Fligstein 1990; and Chandler 1977, 1990.

13. Cantwell's analysis of U.S. patenting during the interwar period by European firms (1991) also concludes that corporate R&D in Great Britain and France lagged behind the level of corporate R&D observed in the United States and Germany during this period.

affecting the unique path of development of U.S. corporate structure and industrial research. Nevertheless, the pre-1940 antitrust environment created strong incentives for U.S. firms to establish in-house research facilities and to use their internal R&D operations to exploit external sources of technology.

5.3.2   The Role of Patents in the Origins of U.S. Industrial Research

The effects of U.S. antitrust policy on the growth of industrial research were reinforced by other judicial and legislative actions in the late nineteenth and early twentieth centuries that strengthened intellectual property rights. The congressional revision of patent laws that took effect in 1898 extended the duration of protection provided by U.S. patents covering inventions patented in other countries (Bright 1949, 91). The Supreme Court's 1908 decision (*Continental Paper Bag Company v. Eastern Paper Bag Company*) that patents covering goods not in production were valid (Neal and Goyder 1980, 324) expanded the utility of large patent portfolios for defensive purposes. Other congressional actions in the first two decades of this century increased the number of Patent Office examiners, streamlined internal review procedures, and transferred the office from the Interior to the Commerce Department (Noble 1977, 107–8). These changes in Patent Office procedures and organization were undertaken in part to improve the speed and consistency of procedures through which intellectual property rights were established, while shifting the office to an agency charged with representing the interests of U.S. business.

Stronger intellectual property protection expanded the appropriability of the returns from innovation, increasing incentives for the establishment of industrial laboratories. In addition, stronger and clearer intellectual property rights facilitated the development of a market for the acquisition and sale of industrial technologies. Judicial tolerance for restrictive patent licensing policies (see below) further increased the value of patents in corporate research strategies.

Although the search for new patents provided one incentive to pursue industrial research, their imminent demise formed another important impetus for the establishment of industrial research laboratories. The impending expiration of patents protecting core technologies, as well as the growth of competing technologies, led to the establishment or expansion of in-house research laboratories. Both AT&T and General Electric, for example, established or expanded their in-house laboratories in response to the intensified competitive pressure that resulted from the expiration of key patents (Reich 1985; Millard 1990, 156). In both of these firms, intensive efforts to improve and protect corporate technological assets were combined with increased acquisition of patents in related technologies from other firms and independent inventors.

Patents also provided a mechanism for some firms to retain market power without running afoul of antitrust law. The 1911 consent decree settling the federal government's antitrust suit against General Electric left GE's patent licensing scheme largely untouched, allowing the firm considerable latitude in setting the terms and conditions of sales of lamps produced by its licensees, maintaining an effective cartel within the U.S. electric-lamp market (Bright 1949, 158). Patent licensing provided a legal basis for the participation by GE and Du Pont in the international cartels of the interwar chemical and electrical equipment industries. U.S. participants in these international market-sharing agreements took pains to arrange their international agreements as patent licensing schemes, arguing that exclusive license arrangements and restrictions on the commercial exploitation of patents would not run afoul of U.S. antitrust enforcement (Taylor and Sudnik 1984, 126).

Change in the structure of the U.S. intellectual property system in the early twentieth century, as well as the treatment of intellectual property by the judiciary, thus enhanced firms' incentives to internalize industrial research and to invest in the acquisition of technologies from external sources. Against the backdrop of tougher federal enforcement of antitrust statutes, judicial decisions affirming the use of patents to create or maintain positions of market power also created additional incentives to pursue in-house R&D. Stronger, more consistent intellectual property rights also improved the operation of a market for intellectual property, making it easier for firms to use their in-house research facilities to acquire technology and contributing to the porousness of their boundaries in R&D.

5.3.3 U.S. Universities and Industrial Research before 1940

University-based research and education also influenced the growth of U.S. industrial research. The reliance of many U.S. universities on state government funding, the modest scope of this funding, and the rapid expansion of their training activities all supported the growth of formal and informal linkages between industry and university research. U.S. universities formed a formal point for the external monitoring activities of many U.S. industrial research laboratories before 1940. In some cases, these university linkages involved industrial development and commercialization of new technologies or products. But most of these relationships appear to have supported industrial firms' observation of emerging developments in scientific and technological research.

Linkages between academic and industrial research were powerfully influenced by the decentralized structure and funding of U.S. higher education, especially the public institutions within the system. Public funding created a U.S. higher education system that was substantially larger than those of European nations such as Great Britain.[14] The source of this public funding, however, was equally important. The prominent role of state governments in fi-

---

14. In the early 1920s, roughly 42,000 students were enrolled in British universities; the figure rose to 50,000–60,000 by the late 1930s. By contrast, American institutions of higher learning awarded over 48,000 *degrees* in 1913 and more than 216,000 in 1940. With a total population 35 percent that of the United States, Britain had only about 6 percent as many students in higher education in the late 1930s. See Briggs 1982; U.S. Bureau of the Census 1975.

nancing the prewar U.S. higher education system led public universities to seek to provide economic benefits to their regions through formal and informal links to industry (Rosenberg and Nelson 1992).

Both the curriculum and research within U.S. higher education were more closely geared to commercial opportunities than was true in many European systems of higher education. Swann (1988) describes the extensive relationships between academic researchers, in both public and private educational institutions, and U.S. ethical drug firms that developed after World War I.[15] Hounshell and Smith (1989, 290–92), document a similar trend for the Du Pont Company, which funded graduate fellowships at twenty-five universities during the 1920s and expanded its program during the 1930s to include support for postdoctoral researchers. During the 1920s, colleges and universities to which the firm provided funds for graduate research fellowships also asked Du Pont for suggestions for research, and in 1938 a leading Du Pont researcher left the firm to head the chemical engineering department at the University of Delaware (Hounshell and Smith 1989, 295).

Many state university systems introduced new programs in engineering, mining, and metallurgy in response to the requirements of local industry. Although they never received federal financial support, the first engineering experiment stations were established early in the twentieth century, and by 1938 there were thirty-eight. These installations focused mainly on applied, rather than basic, research.[16] The University of Minnesota's Mines Experiment Station, equipped with a blast furnace and foundry, conducted research that led to techniques for the commercial exploitation of the state's vast taconite deposits (Mowery and Rosenberg 1989, 95). Purdue University maintained a testing facility for locomotive engines. Levine (1986, 52) notes that, during the 1920s, the University of Illinois offered degrees in disciplines ranging from architectural engineering to railway civil engineering and railway electrical engineering, and stated that virtually every Illinois industry or government agency was served by a department at the university.

Still another example of strong ties with local and national government is provided by the Massachusetts Institute of Technology, founded by Massachusetts in 1861 with Morrill Act funds.[17] In 1906, according to Wildes and Lind-

15. According to Swann (1988, 50), Squibb's support of university research fellowships expanded (in current dollars) from $18,400 in 1925 to more than $48,000 in 1930, and accounted for one-seventh of the firm's total R&D budget for the period. By 1943, according to Swann, university research fellowships amounting to more than $87,000 accounted for 11 percent of Eli Lilly and Company's R&D budget. Swann cites similarly ambitious university research programs sponsored by Merck and Upjohn.

16. The contribution of universities to U.S. technological performance is particularly interesting in view of the fact that for much of the pre-1940 period, there were few areas of scientific research in which U.S. universities or scholars could be described as substantially stronger than their European counterparts. This portion of the historical record suggests that the linkage between excellence in scientific research and growth in U.S. national income or productivity is tenuous, a point consistent with postwar evidence and with the conclusions of Nelson (1990) and Wright (1990).

17. The MIT example also illustrates the effects of reductions in state funding on universities' eagerness to seek out industrial research sponsors. Wildes and Lindgren (1985, 63) note that the

gren (1985, 42–43), MIT's electrical engineering department established an advisory committee that consisted of Elihu Thomson of General Electric, Charles Edgar of the Edison Electric Illuminating Company of Boston, Hammond V. Hayes of AT&T, Louis Ferguson of the Chicago Edison Company, and Charles Scott of Westinghouse. The department's Division of Electrical Engineering Research, established in 1913, received regular contributions from General Electric, AT&T, and Stone and Webster, among other firms.

Another important linkage between higher education and industrial research operated through the training by public universities of scientists and engineers for employment in industrial research. The Ph.D.'s trained in public universities were important participants in the expansion of industrial research employment during this period (Thackray 1982, 211).[18] The sheer scale of the U.S. higher educational system meant that it served as a device for the diffusion and utilization of advanced scientific and engineering knowledge by established firms. The foundation of entirely new firms by university-based researchers does not appear to have been prominent in the prewar period, in part because of the forbidding economic climate of the 1930s and in part because federal government programs and policies were so much less supportive of new, R&D-intensive firms than was true of the post-1945 era (see below).

5.3.4 Summary

Industrial research laboratories were a key part of a prewar U.S. R&D system in which federal funds played a modest role (accounting, according to one estimate, for 12–20 percent of total national R&D expenditures during the 1930s). Moreover, 39 percent of the federal R&D budget in 1940 was devoted to the Department of Agriculture. Industry, on the other hand, accounted for roughly two-thirds of total national expenditures on R&D (see Mowery and Rosenberg 1989, 93, and National Resources Planning Board 1942, 178). The remainder of national R&D spending was drawn from state, university, and private philanthropic sources.

The industrially funded R&D that loomed so large in the prewar period's R&D spending was conducted mainly within the boundaries of U.S. firms. Although located within the firm, these novel entities also looked outside the

---

1919 withdrawal by the Massachusetts state legislature of financial support for MIT, along with the termination of the institute's agreement with Harvard University to teach Harvard engineering courses, led MIT president Richard C. Mclaurin to establish the Division of Industrial Cooperation and Research. This organization was financed by industrial firms that gained access to MIT libraries, laboratories, and staff for consultation on industrial problems. Still another institutional link between MIT and a research-intensive U.S. industry, the institute's School of Chemical Engineering Practice, was established in 1916 (Mattill 1992).

18. Hounshell and Smith (1989, 298) report that 46 of the 176 Ph.D.'s overseen by Carl Marvel, longtime professor in the University of Illinois chemistry department, went to work for one firm, Du Pont. According to Thackray (1982, 221), 65 percent of the 184 Ph.D.'s overseen by Professor Roger Adams of the University of Illinois during 1918–58 went directly into industrial employment. In 1940, 30 of the 46 Ph.D.'s produced by the University of Illinois chemistry department were first employed in industry.

firm, monitoring the external environment of research in universities and industry, and supporting the technology acquisition strategies that played an important part in the development of large U.S. manufacturing firms during this period. By 1940, all of the components of this research system were about to undergo a dramatic transformation that would in less than a decade produce a very different national R&D system.

5.4   The Postwar Transformation

World War II and the cold peace that followed changed the roles of the three institutional pillars of the pre-1940 U.S. R&D system—universities, government, and industry. All of the influences that molded the pre-1940 industrial research laboratory, including antitrust policy, university research, and (to a lesser extent) intellectual property rights were affected by the postwar transformation. World War II propelled the federal government into a central role as research funder within both academia and industry.[19] The dramatic increase in federal defense-related spending on R&D and weapons procurement, which had no pre-1940 analogue, also exerted a strong influence on the development of industrial R&D.

U.S. antitrust policy continued to influence U.S. industrial research and innovation during the postwar period, but both the policy and the nature of its influence changed. The appointment of Thurman Arnold in 1938 to head the Antitrust Division of the Justice Department, combined with growing criticism of large firms and economic concentration (e.g., the investigations of the federal Temporary National Economic Committee), produced a much tougher antitrust policy that extended well into the 1970s. The cases filed by Arnold and his successors, many of which were decided or resolved through consent decrees in the 1940s and early 1950s, changed the postwar industrial research strategies of many large U.S. firms.

This revised antitrust policy made it more difficult for large U.S. firms to acquire firms in "related' technologies or industries,[20] and led them to rely more heavily on intrafirm sources for new technologies. In the case of Du Pont, the use of the central laboratory and Development Department to seek technologies or firms for acquisition was ruled out by senior management as a result of the perceived antitrust restrictions on acquisitions in related industries. As

19. According to Hounshell and Smith (1989, 331–32), the expanded wartime role of federal funding, the operation by competitor firms of large-scale chemical plants, and the sale of government-financed production plants after the war weakened the dominant technological position of Du Pont within the chemicals industry. Graham and Pruitt (1990, 239–42 and chap. 6) note that World War II had a similar effect on Alcoa's technological and economic dominance of the U.S. aluminum industry.

20. Hawley (1966) analyzes the shifting antitrust policies of the New Deal. Arnold took office in 1938, and during 1938–42 filed 312 antitrust cases, considerably more than the 46 filed during 1932–37 or the 70 filed during 1926–31 (Fligstein 1990, 168).

a result, internal discovery (rather than development) of new products became paramount (Hounshell and Smith [1989] emphasize the firm's postwar expansion in R&D and its search for "new nylons"),[21] in contrast to the firm's R&D strategy before World War II.

This shift in Du Pont's R&D strategy weakened the links between the growing central corporate research facilities, which increasingly concentrated their efforts on basic research, and the operating divisions of the firm. The R&D efforts of the established business units focused on increasingly costly improvements in existing processes and products, and the overall productivity of Du Pont R&D suffered (Hounshell and Smith 1989, 598). The inward focus of Du Pont research appears to have impaired the firm's postwar innovative performance, even as its central corporate research laboratory gained a sterling reputation within the scientific community.

A similar inward orientation developed within the R&D operations of Alcoa, according to Graham and Pruitt (1990, chap. 7), as a result of the federal antitrust suit against the firm and the creation of competitors through the sale of government-owned wartime production plants.[22] For Alcoa, however, the effects of this inward orientation were rather different than for Du Pont. The links between Alcoa researchers and external research institutions weakened to such an extent that both the scientific and technological contributions of the firm's laboratory declined.

Where large firms made acquisitions, they frequently did so in unrelated lines of business, creating conglomerate firms with few if any technological links among products or processes. In a number of instances, this extensive diversification led to a decline in the innovative performance of firms that prior to World War II had been leaders in R&D and innovation (see Chandler 1990; Ravenscraft and Scherer 1987; Fligstein 1990). RCA, for example, pursued a conglomerate diversification strategy while maintaining its large fundamental research "campus" near Princeton, New Jersey, which made important research contributions to military and consumer electronics technologies. But RCA found it difficult to reap the commercial returns to its research capabilities, pursuing the hugely expensive and unsuccessful videodisc project (Graham

---

21. Hounshell and Smith (1989) and Mueller (1962) argue that discovery and development of nylon, one of Du Pont's most commercially successful innovations, was in fact atypical of the firm's pre-1940 R&D strategy. Rather than being developed to the point of commercialization following its acquisition by Du Pont, nylon was based on the basic research of Carothers within Du Pont's central corporate research facilities. The successful development of nylon from basic research through to commercialization nevertheless exerted a strong influence on Du Pont's postwar R&D strategy, not least because many senior Du Pont executives had direct experience with the nylon project. Hounshell (1993) argues that Du Pont had far less success in employing the "lessons of nylon" to manage such costly postwar synthetic fiber innovations as Delrin.

22. Graham and Pruitt (1990, 270–71) also argue that patents played a much less prominent role in Alcoa's postwar R&D strategy, because of corporate concerns over the disclosure of technical information to competitors. Instead, process-related know-how, not subject to disclosure through patent applications, became central to the firm's R&D efforts.

1986), while failing to maintain its dominant position in color television receivers.

At the same time that established firms were shifting the R&D strategies that many had employed since the early twentieth century, new firms began to play an important role in the development of the technologies spawned by the postwar U.S. R&D system. The prominence of small firms in commercializing new electronics technologies in the postwar United States, for example, contrasts with their more modest role in this industry in the interwar period. In industries that effectively did not exist before 1940, such as computers and biotechnology, major innovations were commercialized largely through the efforts of new firms.[23] The postwar U.S. differs in this respect from both Japan and most western European economies, where established firms in electronics and pharmaceuticals dominated the commercialization of these technologies.

In semiconductors, the activities of new firms in the commercialization of new technologies often built on the R&D investments and patents of larger firms (Tilton 1971, 69). In a near-reversal of the prewar situation, the R&D facilities of large firms provided the basic technological advances that were commercialized by new firms. Small-firm entrants' contribution to semiconductor-industry patents grew steadily during 1952–68, but their most significant role was in introducing new products, reflected in their often-dominant share of markets in new semiconductor devices.[24] In mainframe computers, established firms, such as IBM, Burroughs, and NCR, retained important roles. In other emerging segments, however, such as minicomputers and supercomputers, new firms, including CDC, DEC, Data General, and Cray, achieved dominant positions, a point overlooked in Chandler's analysis (1990). Microcomputers also saw an influx of new firms, such as Compaq and Apple, along with established enterprises such as IBM. In the U.S. biotechnology industry, new firms have played an even more important role in developing and patenting new techniques and products than was true of semiconductors (Pisano, Shan, and Teece 1988, 189).

The arguments made by Chandler (1990) and Pavitt (1990) about large

---

23. This is not to deny the major role played by large firms such as IBM in computers and AT&T in microelectronics. In other instances, large firms have acquired smaller enterprises and applied their production or marketing expertise to expand markets for a new product technology. Nonetheless, it seems apparent that start-up firms have been far more active in commercializing new technologies in the United States than in other industrial economies. Malerba (1985) and Tilton (1971) stress the importance of new, small firms in the U.S. semiconductor industry; Flamm (1988) describes their significant role in computer technology; and Orsenigo (1989) and Pisano, Shan, and Teece (1988) discuss the importance of these firms in the U.S. biotechnology industry. Bollinger, Hope, and Utterback (1983) survey some of the literature on the "new technology-based firm."

24. The contribution of new firms to major innovations increased substantially after 1960, the era of integrated circuits that combined in a single chip the functions formerly performed by discrete semiconductor components. Levin (1982, 55) noted that only one of the firms (Motorola) identified as having produced major innovations or new product families during 1960–77 had been active in the electronics industry before the invention of the transistor.

firms' dominance of new technologies thus require some qualification when applied to these high-technology industries in the postwar United States. The significant technological contributions made by large firms in semiconductors, for example, have not been matched by their role in commercializing these technologies. In biotechnology, small firms have played a more important role in expanding the technology pool and in commercializing its contents. Moreover, in both semiconductors and computers, new small firms grew rapidly to positions of considerable size and market share.

Several factors have contributed to the prominent role of new, small firms in the postwar U.S. innovation system. The basic research establishments of universities, government, and large corporations served as important sources of scientific and technological knowledge that "walked out the door" with individuals who established firms to commercialize the innovations based on this knowledge. High levels of labor mobility and a supportive legal climate in intellectual property and antitrust policy facilitated the incubator role of universities and large firms.

The foundation and survival of vigorous new firms also depended on a sophisticated private financial system to support these firms during their infancy. The U.S. venture capital market played an important role in the establishment of new firms in microelectronics, computers, and biotechnology. According to the Office of Technology Assessment (1984, 274), the annual flow of venture capital into industrial investments ranged between $2.5 and $3 billion during 1969–77. Roughly $500 million in venture capital funds annually flowed into new firms during the 1980s (Florida and Smith 1993). Western European economies have yet to spawn similarly abundant sources of risk capital for new enterprises in high-technology industries (Sharp 1989, 9–10). Okimoto (1986, 562) estimated that Japanese venture capital firms provided no more than $100 million in financing in 1986.
firms provided no more than $100 million in financing in 1986.

U.S. antitrust policy also contributed to the importance of start-up firms in postwar high-technology industries, reducing patent-based entry barriers. The 1956 settlement of the AT&T case significantly improved the environment for start-up firms in microelectronics, because of the liberal patent licensing terms of the consent decree and because of AT&T's decision following the decree to avoid commercial activities outside of telecommunications. As a result, the firm with the greatest technological capabilities in microelectronics chose not to enter the commercial production of microelectronic components, enhancing the opportunities for entry by start-up firms. The 1956 consent decree that settled a federal antitrust suit against IBM also mandated liberal licensing by this pioneer computer firm of its punch-card and computer patents at reasonable rates (Flamm 1988, 223).

These antitrust consent decrees contributed to the development of an unrestrictive intellectual property regime in both semiconductors and computers, in which patent licensing at low royalty rates was common and patent enforce-

Table 5.2 **Sources of Funds for Research and Development, by Sector, 1953–91 (millions of 1982 dollars)**

	Total	Federal Government	Industry	Universities and Colleges	Other Nonprofit
1953	19,744	10,590	8,671	276	208
1954	21,445	11,895	9,023	303	224
1955	22,760	12,923	9,282	326	229
1956	29,822	17,311	11,910	344	257
1957	33,641	21,035	11,923	376	307
1958	36,076	22,826	12,494	406	350
1959	40,598	26,432	13,351	440	375
1960	43,648	28,191	14,591	479	387
1961	45,764	29,553	15,226	525	460
1962	48,176	31,011	16,039	578	548
1963	52,585	34,519	16,839	635	591
1964	57,202	38,023	17,877	711	591
1965	59,351	38,532	19,384	791	643
1966	62,589	40,047	20,962	875	706
1967	64,406	40,057	22,654	960	735
1968	65,458	39,788	23,869	1,049	752
1969	64,672	37,660	25,166	1,071	775
1970	62,405	35,636	24,851	1,111	807
1971	60,385	33,966	24,387	1,212	820
1972	61,414	34,146	25,190	1,246	832
1973	62,427	33,478	26,837	1,268	844
1974	61,467	31,726	27,578	1,298	865
1975	59,883	30,986	26,679	1,302	916
1976	62,134	31,813	28,058	1,305	959
1977	63,653	32,152	29,176	1,325	1,001
1978	66,769	33,172	31,087	1,446	1,064
1979	70,077	34,271	33,198	1,538	1,071
1980	73,255	34,557	36,065	1,574	1,059
1981	76,641	35,690	38,257	1,667	1,027
1982	80,018	36,578	40,692	1,731	1,017
1983	85,753	39,251	43,568	1,851	1,083
1984	93,790	42,286	48,456	1,945	1,102
1985	102,462	46,870	52,252	2,130	1,209
1986	104,866	47,555	53,639	2,436	1,235
1987	106,616	49,201	53,341	2,711	1,364
1988	110,166	50,635	55,181	2,856	1,495
1989	111,129	49,553	56,815	3,115	1,646
1990[a]	110,470	48,591	56,757	3,376	1,746
1991[b]	110,277	47,991	56,799	3,596	1,890

Source: National Science Foundation 1991.

[a]Preliminary.

[b]Estimated.

Table 5.3   **Defense R&D as a Share of Federal R&D Spending, 1960–92**

Year	%	Year	%	Year	%
1960	80	1971	52	1982	61
1961	77	1972	54	1983	64
1962	70	1973	54	1984	66
1963	62	1974	52	1985	67
1964	55	1975	51	1986	69
1965	50	1976	50	1987	69
1966	49	1977	51	1988	68
1967	52	1978	49	1989	65
1968	52	1979	48	1990	63
1969	54	1980	51	1991[a]	59
1970	52	1981	54	1992[a]	60

Source: National Science Board 1991.
[a]Estimated.

ment was relatively lax.[25] The postwar intellectual property rights environment in these industries that resulted from federal antitrust policy contrasts sharply with that of the early decades of industrial research, when large firms used patenting to maintain positions of market power that would not attract antitrust prosecution.

Defense spending on R&D and procurement, another element of the postwar U.S. R&D system that greatly increased in importance from pre-1940 levels, also benefited new firms in some industries. The share of national R&D spending accounted for by federal funds expanded to 40–50 percent of national R&D expenditures during the postwar period (table 5.2), although in contrast to other industrial economies, a large fraction of federally financed research was performed in nongovernment research laboratories. The military services have dominated this large federal R&D budget since the early 1950s, falling below 50 percent of federal R&D obligations in only three years during 1960–92 (table 5.3). But many of the most significant effects of postwar defense spending resulted from Department of Defense procurement, rather than R&D.[26] The U.S. military market in the 1950s and 1960s provided an important springboard for start-up firms in microelectronics and computers, who faced relatively low marketing and distribution barriers to entry into this market (Tilton 1971, 91; Flamm 1988, 78–79). The willingness of U.S. military

25. In biotechnology, according to Pisano, Shan, and Teece (1988), aggressive enforcement of patents has been discouraged somewhat by uncertainty over the breadth and strength of intellectual property protection.

26. The interaction of defense procurement spending and R&D investment is in fact more complex than this statement suggests; Lichtenberg's empirical estimates (1988) on the effects of federal defense procurement during 1979–84 indicate that federal procurement competitions induce increases in private R&D spending. Lichtenberg concluded that more than one-half of the increase in private R&D spending during 1979–84 could be attributed to the effects of increased defense spending.

policymakers to channel procurement contracts to relatively new firms contrasts with the military procurement policies of European governments, which tended to favor established firms (Flamm 1988, 134). The benefits of the military market were enhanced further by the substantial possibilities for technological spillovers from military to civilian applications in a broad array of high-technology industries.

The role of universities within the U.S. research system, including the interaction between U.S. industry and academic research, also was transformed by World War II. The wartime Office of Scientific Research and Development (OSRD) relied heavily on universities as research performers. The largest single recipient of OSRD grants and contracts during wartime (and the inventor of institutional overhead charges) was MIT, with seventy-five research contracts that amounted to more than $116 million. The largest corporate recipient of OSRD funds, Western Electric, accounted for only $17 million (Pursell 1977, 364).

Federal financial support for U.S. university research continued to grow during the postwar period, as Department of Defense support for university research was supplemented by funds from such agencies as the Atomic Energy Commission, the National Institutes of Health, and, more modestly, the National Science Foundation. Combined with increased reliance by large U.S. industrial firms on their internal R&D laboratories for new technologies, the upsurge in federal funding of university research appears to have weakened some of the prewar links between corporate and university research (Leslie [1993] presents a similar view of the effects of defense-related research funding on the postwar research activities of MIT and Stanford University). Universities no longer sought industrial research sponsors as aggressively as they had before 1940, since abundant research funding was available from federal sources. Du Pont's research director argued in 1945 that the firm no longer could rely as heavily on university research as it had before World War II (Hounshell and Smith 1989, 355), in part because the firm's competitors, strengthened by World War II, were equally capable of exploiting such research. No longer able to use its superior ability to commercialize the results of basic research performed outside the firm, Du Pont found another reason to rely more heavily on internal sources of new scientific and technical knowledge. Swann (1988, 170–71) also argues that research links between U.S. universities and the pharmaceuticals industry weakened significantly in the immediate aftermath of World War II by increased federal research funding for academic research in the health sciences.

The structure of the U.S. national innovation system, of which industrial R&D was a central component, underwent dramatic change during the 1940s, largely as a result of World War II and its aftermath. The huge expansion in the federal government's role as research funder and as a purchaser of the products of research-intensive industries changed the relationship between U.S. corporate research laboratories and universities, and created new markets with relatively low entry barriers for producers of innovative electronic components and systems. The antitrust policy of the late 1930s, which came to fruition in the 1940s, also led large U.S. corporations to reduce their use of in-house R&D facilities to seek out and acquire technologies from outside the firm, and aided the entry and growth of start-up firms. The overall effect of these changes was to reduce the relative importance of large U.S. firms as sources of R&D funding by comparison with their pre-1940 position. Large firms attempted to rely more heavily on their in-house R&D facilities as the exclusive source of new technologies. The boundaries of these firms in R&D effectively became less porous.

Two elements of the postwar transformation are noteworthy. First, the large federal role in R&D funding, the tough antitrust policies that accompanied it, and the importance of new firms in technology commercialization all were characteristics of the postwar U.S. that had no counterpart in the R&D systems of other industrial economies. In Japan and Germany, for example, public and defense-related R&D accounted for a much smaller share of national R&D investments, and established firms dominated the commercialization of new technologies in electronics and biotechnology. Second, this discussion suggests that much if not most of the postwar shift in the role of corporate R&D reflected change in the public policy environment within which U.S. firms operated, rather than originating either from technological factors or intrafirm developments.

5.5   Conclusion

U.S. firms were among the earliest investors in industrial research within the firm, as part of the late-nineteenth-century processes of corporate restructuring that extended the boundaries and range of products manufactured by industrial firms. Although intrafirm R&D substantially outstripped the importance of independent contract services, the two forms of R&D organization complemented one another. Before 1940, the in-house R&D facilities of major corporations monitored the external technological environment and guided the acquisition of new technologies from outside sources, which were then developed to the point of commercialization by the acquiring firm.

After 1945, changes in government policy transformed the role of R&D within many large firms. Rather than using it as a source of in-house innovations and a "listening post" for external technological opportunities, U.S. firms came to rely on intrafirm R&D to create new technologies for the firm. This shift toward an "inward orientation" in R&D strategy contributed to the important role of new firms as agents of technology commercialization in the postwar United States.

These observations on the changing role of corporate R&D need much more research, especially on the history of individual corporations and their R&D facilities, to be corroborated. Nevertheless, the evidence suggests that the emphasis in Chandler's comparative analysis (1990) on the continuity of the pre- and post-World War II corporate U.S. economy may be overstated. The consequences for corporate or national economic performance of these changes in the role of U.S. industrial research also require additional research. These effects are confounded with those of many other variables, and their identification is further hampered by the lack of reliable models linking innovative performance to internal corporate structure. Nevertheless, some evidence suggests that the changes discussed in this paper impaired the innovative performance of at least some large U.S. firms that had pioneered in industrial research.

Hounshell and Smith's historical account of Du Pont's R&D program (1989) concluded that the firm's postwar search for "new nylons" impaired its innovative and competitive performance. As was noted earlier, other scholars have argued that many of the conglomerate mergers and acquisitions of the 1960s and 1970s produced disappointing economic results. Recent empirical evidence suggests that the competitive strength of at least some Japanese manufacturing firms is associated with their ability to rapidly commercialize technologies based on external sources of knowledge (see Mansfield 1988). To the extent that large U.S. firms' shift to internal sources for innovations weakened their ability to exploit external sources of industrial technology, it may have weakened their ability to deal with new competitors that were especially adept at exploiting these sources.

Considerable uncertainty also remains about the consequences for national competitive performance of the large role played by new, small firms in postwar U.S. high-technology industries. Long hailed as a dynamic source of new technologies, entrepreneurial verve, and employment opportunities, the startup firm has more recently been criticized for being unable to move from the creation and commercialization of a new product to the sustained competitive improvement of a portfolio of products and processes (see, e.g., Florida and Kenney 1990; Gomory 1992).

Comparative studies of the U.S. and Japanese semiconductor industries, for example, have argued that the greater size and higher level of vertical integration in many Japanese electronics firms have strengthened their ability to compete against a U.S. industry populated largely by smaller firms (the descendants of start-ups) with much lower levels of vertical integration (Steinmueller 1988; Borrus 1988). But this debate has not reached a satisfactory conclusion. As of early 1993, at least, the putative advantages of large size and vertical integration have not prevented erosion in the profits and market share of these large Japanese firms, nor have they prevented a significant downturn in the performance of the largest, most highly vertically integrated U.S. producer of semiconductors, IBM.

Nelson (1988, 325) has referred to the industrial research laboratory as the "heart of the [innovation] system" in the United States. Even this pillar of the U.S. system, however, is undergoing change. Faced with escalating costs and intensified competitive pressures, many U.S. firms are exploring alternatives to exclusive reliance on intrafirm sources of innovation; their search is being supported by new state and federal government policies.[27] Alternatives include university-industry research partnerships, alliances with other domestic and foreign firms, and publicly sponsored cooperative research programs. These and other changes in the structure of the U.S. innovation system may revive several of the characteristic elements of the pre-1940 period, including state government funding of applied research and collaborative research relationships between universities and industry. These initiatives represent a partial revival of earlier relationships that were sundered by the dramatic changes in the structure of the U.S. national research system during and after World War II.

Since these changes also will affect several features of the postwar U.S. national innovation system that have distinguished it from those of other industrial economies, they may also reduce the structural differences between the U.S. and other national innovation systems.[28] As U.S. defense spending declines, the federal government's share of national R&D spending is likely to shrink to levels that more closely resemble those of other industrial economies. Some evidence also suggests that the civilian technological spillovers historically associated with postwar defense spending have shrunk (Rosenberg 1987; Mowery and Rosenberg 1989; Chinworth and Mowery forthcoming). The declining role and weaker civilian spillovers of defense procurement spending, along with tougher domestic protection of intellectual property rights, may raise the entry barriers faced by new firms in many R&D-intensive industries, reducing the important role of start-up firms in technology commercialization that has been unique to the postwar United States among the major industrial economies.

The seminal work of Chandler (1977, 1990) on the development of the modern corporation has drawn on and influenced the work of Williamson (1975, 1985) on market-based and intrafirm approaches to the organization of economic activity. This discussion of the development of industrial research, however, suggests that the distinction between "markets" and "hierarchies" should not be overstated. Market-based and intrafirm forms of governance of the industrial innovation process have coexisted throughout this century. Although the historical transformation in the boundaries of the firm is an important

---

27. Examples of such supportive public policies include changes in antitrust policy, public funding for industry-university research linkages, and state government support of industrial technology development.

28. Even as some historically unique characteristics of the U.S. national innovation system may be declining in importance, debate has intensified in other industrial economies (e.g., Japan) about the wisdom of developing R&D organizations and institutions that in some respects resemble those that were long important in the United States. Thus, Japanese policymakers and managers are considering policies to strengthen university research, industry-financed basic research, and military-financed research in ways that may reduce the salience of some of the unique structural characteristics of the Japanese innovation system (see Mowery and Rosenberg 1989, chap. 8, for further discussion).

development in modern economic history, the fact remains that, at least within corporate R&D, these boundaries have been porous to varying degrees during the development of U.S. industrial research. Moreover, changes in the porousness of U.S. firms' boundaries in R&D during the past seventy-five years probably have been more heavily affected by public policy than any other single factor. In R&D, no less than in other areas, many of the key influences on the evolution of the boundaries of the U.S. firm lie outside the corporation.

References

Arrow, K. J. 1969. Classificatory Notes on the Production and Transmission of Technical Knowledge. *American Economic Review Papers and Proceedings* 59:29–35.

Beer, J. J. 1958. Coal Tar Dye Manufacture and the Origins of the Modern Industrial Research Laboratory. *Isis* 49:122–31.

Bollinger, L., K. Hope, and J. M. Utterback. 1983. A Review of Literature and Hypotheses on New Technology-Based Firms. *Research Policy* 12:1–14.

Borrus, M. A. 1988. *Competing for Control: America's Stake in Microelectronics.* Cambridge, MA: Ballinger.

Briggs, A. 1982. Social History, 1900–1945. In *The Economic History of Britain since 1700,* vol. 2, ed. R. Floud and D. W. McCloskey. Cambridge: Cambridge University Press.

Bright, A. A. 1949. *The Electric-Lamp Industry.* New York: Macmillan.

Cantwell, J. 1991. The Evolution of European Industrial Technology in the Interwar Period. Economics Department Discussion Paper in Industrial Economics, ser. E, vol. 4, no. 33, University of Reading.

Carty, J. J. 1916. The Relation of Pure Science to Industrial Research. *Science* 44:511–18.

Caves, R. E., and M. Uekusa. 1976. Industrial Organization. In *Asia's New Giant,* ed. H. Patrick and H. Rosovsky. Washington, DC: Brookings Institution.

Chandler, A. D., Jr. 1977. *The Visible Hand: The Managerial Revolution in American Business.* Cambridge: Harvard University Press.

———. 1990. *Scale and Scope: The Dynamics of Industrial Capitalism.* Cambridge: Harvard University Press.

Chinworth, M. W., and D. C. Mowery. Forthcoming. Cross-Border Linkages and the U.S. Defense Industry: Outlook and Policy Challenges. Technovation.

Cohen, W. M., and D. Levinthal. 1989. Innovation and Learning: The Two Faces of R&D. *Economic Journal* 99:569–96.

Collins, N. R., and L. E. Preston. 1961. The Size Structure of the Largest Industrial Firms. *American Economic Review* 51:986–1011.

Edwards, R. C. 1975. Stages in Corporate Stability and Risks of Corporate Failure. *Journal of Economic History* 35:428–57.

Evenson, R. E., and Y. Kislev. 1975. *Agricultural Research and Productivity.* New Haven: Yale University Press.

Flamm, K. 1988. *Creating the Computer.* Washington, DC: Brookings Institution.

Fligstein, N. 1990. *The Transformation of Corporate Control.* Cambridge: Harvard University Press.

Florida, R., and M. Kenney. 1990. *The Breakthrough Illusion.* New York: Basic Books.

Florida, R., and D. Smith. 1993. Keep the Government Out of Venture Capital. *Issues in Science and Technology* (summer): 61–68.

Gibb, G. S., and E. H. Knowlton. 1956. *The Resurgent Years: History of Standard Oil Company (New Jersey), 1911–1927.* New York: Harper.

Gomory, R. G. 1992. The Technology-Product Relationship: Early and Late Stages. In *Technology and the Wealth of Nations,* ed. N. Rosenberg, R. Landau, and D. C. Mowery (Stanford, CA: Stanford University Press).

Graham, M. B. W. 1986. *RCA and the VideoDisc: The Business of Research.* New York: Cambridge University Press.

Graham, M. B. W., and B. H. Pruitt. 1990. *R&D for Industry: A Century of Technical Innovation at Alcoa.* New York: Cambridge University Press.

Hannah, L. 1974. Mergers in British Manufacturing Industry, 1880–1919. *Oxford Economic Papers,* n.s., 26 (March): 1–20.

———. 1979. Mergers, Cartels, and Concentration: Legal Factors in the U.S. and European Experience. In *Law and the Formation of the Big Enterprises in the Nineteenth and Early Twentieth Century,* ed. N. Horn and J. Kocka. Göttingen: Vandenhoeck and Ruprecht.

Hawley, E. 1966. *The New Deal and the Problem of Monopoly.* Princeton: Princeton University Press.

Hounshell, D. A. 1993. Industrial R&D in the United States: An Exploratory History. Paper presented at the conference "The Future of Industrial Research," Harvard Business School, 10–12 February.

Hounshell, D. A., and J. K. Smith. 1989. *Science and Corporate Strategy.* New York: Cambridge University Press.

Kaplan, A. D. H. 1964. *Big Business in a Competitive System.* Washington, DC: Brookings Institution.

Keller, M. 1990. *Regulating a New Economy: Public Policy and Economic Change in America, 1900–1933.* Cambridge: Harvard University Press.

Lamoreaux, N. 1985. *The Great Merger Wave in American Business, 1895–1904.* New York: Cambridge University Press.

Landau, R., and N. Rosenberg. 1992. Successful Commercialization in the Chemical Process Industry. In *Technology and the Wealth of Nations,* ed. N. Rosenberg, R. Landau, and D. C. Mowery. Stanford, CA: Stanford University Press.

Leslie, S. W. 1993. *The Cold War and American Science: The Military-Industrial-Academic Complex at MIT and Stanford.* New York: Columbia University Press.

Levin, R. C. 1982. The Semiconductor Industry. In *Government and Technical Progress: A Cross-Industry Comparison,* ed. R. R. Nelson. New York: Pergamon.

Levin, R. C., W. M. Cohen, and D. C. Mowery. 1985. R&D, Appropriability, Opportunity, and Market Structure: New Evidence on Some Schumpeterian Hypotheses. *American Economic Review Papers and Proceedings* 75:20–24.

Levine, D. O. 1986. *The American College and the Culture of Aspiration.* Ithaca, NY: Cornell University Press.

Lichtenberg, F. R. 1988. The Private R&D Investment Response to Federal Design and Technical Competitions. *American Economic Review* 78:550–59.

McCraw, T. K. 1981. Rethinking the Trust Question. In *Regulation in Perspective.* Cambridge: Harvard University Press.

Malerba, F. 1985. *The Semiconductor Business.* Madison: University of Wisconsin Press.

Mansfield, E. 1988. Industrial Innovation in Japan and the United States. *Science* 241 (30 September): 1769–74.

Marshall, A. 1910. *Principles of Economics.* London: Macmillan.

Mattill, J. 1992. *The Flagship: The MIT School of Chemical Engineering Practice, 1916–1991.* Cambridge: Koch School of Chemical Engineering Practice, MIT.

Millard, A. 1990. *Edison and the Business of Innovation.* Baltimore: Johns Hopkins University Press.

Mowery, D. C. 1981. The Emergence and Growth of Industrial Research in American Manufacturing, 1899–1945. Ph.D. diss., Stanford University.

———. 1983a. Economic Theory and Government Technology Policy. *Policy Sciences* 16:27–43.

———. 1983b. Industrial Research and Firm Size, Survival, and Growth in American Manufacturing, 1921–1946: An Assessment. *Journal of Economic History* 43:953–80.

———. 1983c. The Relationship between Contractual and Intrafirm Forms of Industrial Research in American Manufacturing, 1900–1940. *Explorations in Economic History* 20:351–74.

———. 1984. Firm Structure, Government Policy, and the Organization of Industrial Research: Great Britain and the United States, 1900–1950. *Business History Review* 58:504–31.

———. 1992. The U.S. National Innovation System: Origins and Prospects for Change. *Research Policy* 21:125–44.

Mowery, D. C., and N. Rosenberg. 1989. *Technology and the Pursuit of Economic Growth.* New York: Cambridge University Press.

Mueller, W. F. 1962. The Origins of the Basic Inventions Underlying Du Pont's Major Product and Process Innovations, 1920 to 1950. In *The Rate and Direction of Inventive Activity,* ed. R. R. Nelson. Princeton: Princeton University Press.

National Research Council. 1940. Industrial Research Laboratories of the United States. Bulletin 104. Washington, DC: National Research Council.

National Resources Planning Board. 1942. *Research: A National Resource.* Vol. 1. Washington, DC: GPO.

National Science Board. 1991. *Science and Engineering Indicators, 1991.* Washington, DC: GPO.

National Science Foundation. 1987. *Research and Development in Industry, 1986.* Washington, DC: National Science Foundation.

———. 1991. *International Science and Technology Data Update, 1991.* Washington, DC: National Science Foundation.

Neal, A. D., and D. G. Goyder. 1980. *The Antitrust Laws of the U.S.A.* 3d ed. Cambridge: Cambridge University Press.

Nelson, R. R. 1988. Institutions Supporting Technical Change in the United States. In *Technical Change and Economic Theory,* ed. G. Dosi, C. Freeman, R. Nelson, G. Silverberg, and L. Soete. London: Pinter.

———. 1990. U.S. Industrial Competitiveness: Where Did It Come From and Where Did It Go? *Research Policy* 19:117–32.

———. ed. 1993. *National Innovation Systems: A Comparative Study.* New York: Oxford University Press.

Noble, D. 1977. *America by Design.* New York: Knopf.

Office of Technology Assessment. U.S. Congress. 1984. *Commercial Biotechnology: An International Analysis.* Washington, DC: GPO.

Okimoto, D. J. 1986. Regime Characteristics of Japanese Industrial Policy. In *Japan's High Technology Industries: Lessons and Limitations of Industrial Policy,* ed. H. Patrick and K. Yamamura. Seattle: University of Washington Press.

Orsenigo, L. 1989. *The Emergence of Biotechnology.* London: Pinter.

Patel, P., and K. L. R. Pavitt. 1991. Large Firms in the Production of the World's Technology: An Important Case of Non-globalisation. *Journal of International Business Studies* 22:1–21.

Pavitt, K. L. R. 1990. What We Know about the Strategic Management of Technology. *California Management Review* 32:17–26.

Pisano, G., W. Shan, and D. J. Teece. 1988. Joint Ventures and Collaboration in the Biotechnology Industry. In *International Collaborative Ventures in U.S. Manufacturing,* ed. D. C. Mowery. Washington, DC: American Enterprise Institute.

Pursell, C. 1977. Science Agencies in World War II: The OSRD and Its Challengers. In *The Sciences in the American Context,* ed. N. Reingold. Washington, DC: Smithsonian Institution.

Ravenscraft, D. J., and F. M. Scherer. 1987. *Mergers, Sell-Offs, and Economic Efficiency.* Washington, DC: Brookings Institution.

Reader, W. J. 1975. *Imperial Chemical Industries: A History.* Vol. 2. Oxford: Oxford University Press.

Reich: L. S. 1985. *The Making of American Industrial Research.* New York: Cambridge University Press.

Rosenberg, N. 1987. Civilian "Spillovers" from Military R&D Spending: The U.S. Experience since World War II. In *Strategic Defense and the Western Alliance,* ed. S. Lakoff and R. Wiloughby. Lexington, MA: D. C. Heath.

Rosenberg, N., and R. R. Nelson. 1992. American Universities and Technical Advance in Industry. Manuscript.

Scherer, F. M. 1965. Firm Size, Market Structure, Opportunity, and the Output of Patented Inventions. *American Economic Review* 55:1097–1123.

Schmookler, J. 1957. Inventors Past and Present. *Review of Economics and Statistics* 39:321–33.

Sharp, M. 1989. European Countries in Science-Based Competition: The Case of Biotechnology. Designated Research Center Discussion Paper no. 72, Science Policy Research Unit, University of Sussex.

Steinmueller, W. E. 1988. Industry Structure and Government Policies in the U.S. and Japanese Integrated Circuit Industries. In *Government Policies toward Industry in the U.S. and Japan,* ed. J. B. Shoven. New York: Cambridge University Press.

Stigler, G. 1956. Industrial Organization and Economic Progress. In *The State of the Social Sciences,* ed. L. D. White. Chicago: University of Chicago Press.

———. 1968. Monopoly and Oligopoly by Merger. In *The Organization of Industry* (Homewood, IL: Irwin).

Sturchio, J. L. 1985. Experimenting with Research: Kenneth Mees, Eastman Kodak, and the Challenges of Diversification. Paper presented at the R&D Pioneers Conference, Hagley Museum and Library, Wilmington, DE, 7 October 1985.

Swann, J. P. 1988. *Academic Scientists and the Pharmaceutical Industry.* Baltimore: Johns Hopkins University Press.

Taylor, G. D., and P. E. Sudnik. 1984. *Du Pont and the International Chemical Industry.* Boston: Twayne.

Teece, D. J. 1988. Technical Change and the Nature of the Firm. In *Technical Change and Economic Theory,* ed. G. Dosi, C. Freeman, R. Nelson, G. Silverberg, and L. Soete. London: Pinter.

Thackray, A. 1982. University-Industry Connections and Research: An Historical Perspective. In *University-Industry Research Relationships: Selected Studies,* by National Science Board. Washington, DC: National Science Foundation.

Thorelli, H. B. 1954. *Federal Antitrust Policy.* Baltimore: Johns Hopkins University Press.

Tilton, J. L. 1971. *International Diffusion of Technology: The Case of Semiconductors.* Washington, DC: Brookings Institution.

U.S. Bureau of the Census. 1975. *Historical Statistics of the United States: Colonial Times to 1970.* 2 vols. Washington, DC: GPO.

Wildes, K. L., and N. A. Lindgren 1985. *A Century of Electrical Engineering and Computer Science at MIT, 1882–1982.* Cambridge: MIT Press.

Williamson, O. E. 1975. *Markets and Hierarchies.* New York: Free Press.
————. 1985. *The Economic Institutions of Capitalism.* New York: Free Press.
Wright, G. 1990. The Origins of American Industrial Success, 1879–1940. *American Economic Review* 80:651–68.

Comment   Joel Mokyr

Mowery's paper deals with the location of the source of technological progress. Specifically, it asks whether that location is within the boundaries of the firm that ends up using it, or whether it is purchased from other firms, either R&D labs or possibly competitors. Mowery provides a useful historical survey of the location of R&D, that is, whether most of it will be carried out in-house or purchased from other firms, and surveys the changes in its location as a result of government policy and other environmental factors. His paper, however, does not connect this question to some deeper and highly relevant issues in the theory of the firm and the theory of technological change and thus falls short of an altogether persuasive account of the issue.

The question of what economic activity will take the place *within* the firm as opposed to transacted *among* firms is not new, of course, and was first posed in its starkest form by Ronald Coase in his celebrated 1937 paper on the nature of the firm. Mowery's paper basically constitutes an extension of Coase's question to the realm of R&D (oddly without direct reference to Coase), clearly an important and timely issue.

Coase asked when activities will occur within the firm as opposed to when they will occur through the market by means of an explicit transaction. The answer is now quite obvious and well understood: firms will integrate and produce things for themselves in-house rather than buy them in the market when the costs of transaction between firms are higher than the gains from specialization that necessitate this transaction. The in-house production of inputs thus substitutes for the market, and internal decision rules are substituted for obeying price signals. The coexistence of conscious in-house decision making and spontaneous, decentralized market allocations was described by D. H. Robertson in an appetizing if mixed metaphor, cited with approval by Coase as follows: "we find islands of conscious power in this ocean of unconscious co-operation like lumps of butter coagulating in a pail of buttermilk."

Coase was thinking of intermediate products and inputs, not that elusive thing called new technological knowledge. As Mowery stresses, R&D is in many ways different from other inputs. There are obvious and well-understood contracting difficulties that come up in the market for technology (Teece

Joel Mokyr is the Robert H. Strotz Professor of Arts and Sciences and professor of economics and history at Northwestern University.

1988). Thinness of markets, the specificity of technical knowledge, the uncertainty involved in generating it, asymmetric information, the moral hazards of cost-plus contracts, and above all the pitfalls of intellectual property rights and public-good properties of technology—all are good reasons why obvious and well-undersood contracting difficulties come up in these markets. Opportunistic behavior is likely to be rampant, and markets of technical knowledge are often said to be deficient and incomplete. Yet they do exist, and licensing agreements, consultant firms, interfirm technological consortia, and other forms of contracting for technologies exist. After all, as Coase said, the firm is a "supersession of the price mechanism." When the price mechanism becomes expensive to use, vertical integration and in-house R&D are more likely to occur. The more tacit and firm-specific the knowledge, the more likely firms are to develop their technologies in-house. Yet there are clearly enormous advantages in specialization and interfirm trade in new technological ideas.

The basic microeconomic rule that governs the in-house versus outside purchase in technological progress is this: industrial R&D will be purchased from the outside the higher the gains to specialization and the lower the market transactions cost. In technological change, transactions costs may have been very high, but so were the gains from specialization. Comparative advantage is never more pronounced and powerful than when it comes to development and engineering of new products and processes, because that is where inspiration and expertise, intuition and experience come together as nowhere else. The lack of discipline and freedom in search for new ideas have always made universities and pure research-oriented think tanks more effective at developing new departures, and firms have traditionally recognized that. "Universities are much better at the basic sciences and discovery than we are," argues Joseph Patterson of Hoechst Celanese, after awarding $1 million each to three research schools (*Wall Street Journal* 22 October 1992). Comparative advantage patterns thus differ, and there are gains from a division of labor in R&D.

Theory, therefore, predicts a less than perfect specialization pattern. R&D will involve some modicum of cooperation and transaction between firms that will eventually use the technology and those that research the first stages of it, as well as a fair amount of in-house work. That still leaves a lot of slippage in the middle, and clearly the history of R&D in the United States indicates changing weights between in-house research and market transactions in new technology. The boundaries of the firm will be quite porous to relatively radical new technologies, where they will continue to rely on outsiders. If this relation gets very cozy, the firms might change from a market to a nonmarket relationship and merge or perhaps hire the consultant firm on a permanent retainer. Some of these mergers, like the GM-EDS fusion, were intended from the outset to revolutionize production methods in the firm. The fact that this happens proves there are transactions costs in using the market. The fact that it does not happen *invariably* proves that there are offsetting advantages to specialization and market transactions.

Unfortunately, explaining this process over time is difficult. Transactions costs are not measurable with any degree of accuracy, and so there is no way of knowing whether the growing dependence on in-house research after 1945 was the result of increasing difficulties in buying and selling components of an ever more complex technology or declining gains from interfirm trade in technology. Moreover, it is not clear whether the ratio of transactions costs to gains from specialization changed in one direction or another in the period under discussion. In the absence of any direct clues, the search for an explanation must remain tentative. Furthermore, unrecognized by the simple Coasian framework, there are transactions costs of doing business *within the firm* as well. In large corporate bureaucracies, information is generated in large quantities in part because there are economies of scale in information. All the same, the fact that it exists *somewhere* within a firm does not mean that it automatically flows from one branch of the bureaucracy to another and that it is accessible by those who need it. To judge from what Ross Perot had to say about GM, clearly intrafirm information is not all it is cracked up to be and does not flow necessarily better than interfirm. Indeed, it is often said of large firms that "the left hand does not know what the other left hand is doing." The incentive structure to *share* and *dispense* knowledge within the firm is not always as strong as it is in a market environment where the quid pro quo is more immediate. Much depends on the quality of top management. In the long haul, the obvious problems of appropriability, intellectual property rights, and opportunistic behavior notwithstanding, the competitive forces that lead to the sharing of information between firms may be more reliable.

One way of making some progress is to look not at the inputs of the innovation process (that is, R&D budgets or the number of employees in the research sector) but at the nature of the product that is generated. Teece and others do not distinguish sufficiently between R&D (essentially an input) and new technological knowledge, whether it qualifies as "inventions" or whether it is more in the nature of "product development," which is an output of inventive activity. Mowery treats technology more or less as an undifferentiated outcome of R&D input. Yet to answer his question about the locus of technological change, the *nature* of the technology generated may be quite crucial. Ever since Usher, we have understood that major breakthroughs create a new technique or a new industry, and constitute a shift *of* the marginal product curve of R&D rather than a shift *along* it. Following such a macroinvention, we observe a wave of smaller inventions (microinventions) that refine, debug, and perfect the new technique and make it workable. Many of those microinventions are part of experience and learning by doing or learning by using and often are so tacit and specific that they cannot be marketed. Others may be sold or licensed to other firms. Things are quite different with respect to major breakthroughs. On the whole, macroinventions are rarely made in-house, that is, by a firm that could use them best. The classic account of Jewkes, Sawers, and Stillerman (1969) provides a long list of examples and much of the rationale for this phenomenon: truly radical inventions require an uncommitted and unconventional mind, which is rarely welcome in the corporate world of conformist team-players. When they emerge, they are either licensed out, the inventing firm itself is acquired by the user, or it adapts its structure to accommodate the new technology. At times, what seems an ex ante invention ready to be licensed and traded becomes an ex post in-house invention as the inventing firm decides to go into the business itself. Aspartame was invented by G. D. Searle, which had no way of using it under its existing structure, not by Coca Cola, which did. To pick another example, when an in-house R&D lab at a German dye-making concern, Bayer's, stumbled upon the most successful analgesic in history, the firm diversified into pharmaceutics. Leo Godowski and Leopold Mannes, the two musicians who invented Kodachrome, received both financial support and necessary assistance from Eastman Kodak but did not work for it. Downstream inventions, determined by users and customers, may well be of critical importance in the overall picture, but few macroinventions were generated that way. In an age of technological consolidation rather than radical new departures, then, we would expect in-house R&D to become more important. In an age of fundamental innovations, such as the 1980s, interfirm trade in new knowledge seems more likely.

One testable hypothesis, then, that derives directly from this analysis is that in-house R&D will be more successful in older industries in which there have been few major breakthroughs, and that interfirm transactions in technology are more common in industries in which recent technological breakthroughs have occurred. Although this picture is confused by the fact that firms buy up other firms, the evidence presented in Mowery's paper bears it out. A single heroic inventor in the Jewkes, Sawers, and Stillerman tradition might be counted ex post as doing his work "in-house" when a large corporation acquires him, his lab, and his ideas in a package deal. All the same, really big and successful technological ideas are sufficiently rare that if a firm comes up with one, either through luck or through hard work, it is more likely to license or sell it, and thus it will enter the market rather than be counted as a purely in-house type of invention. As an invention becomes "smaller" this likelihood declines, other things equal.

A separate issue is whether existing and old firms are more suitable at innovating and carrying out industrial R&D or whether new firms entering are essential for continuous industrial progress. Mowery rightly takes issue with Chandler's exaggerated beliefs in the flexibility of big corporations, and points to "new firms" as indispensable loci where much of the R&D takes place. Yet at the same time some old corporations were able to rejuvenate themselves, with IBM, NCR, Motorola, Ford, and Du Pont the classic examples. Perhaps, then, firm "age" is not the only important variable in determining whether a firm will be innovative and engage heavily in industrial R&D, and whether it will get its new technology by doing its own research or buy the ideas from others. Instead we should look at the technology at stake itself: How novel is it? What is the appropriability of further advances? How firm-specific are microinventions that make it advance? Is the nature of the innovations highly patentable and licensable? Does it involve processes than can be kept secret and thus best developed and kept in-house?

A further issue is the quality of management and its openness to new ideas. On the whole, it seems to me that all we know about the long-term dynamics of bureaucracies suggests that within the same firm R&D departments tend to go stale unless they are subject to radical overhauls from time to time. Perhaps the strongest argument against in-house research then is that big corporations, like all bureaucracies, tend to become ossified and conservative, and so their managements may become hostile to innovations that make waves and threaten the stability of the status quo (Kuran 1988). Such sclerotic firms may not be able to generate much innovation themselves, but when faced with tighter conditions in the marketplace, the new technology is presented to them by their competitors rather than by their employees, and so their options are limited. Their large R&D departments then become scouting agencies, searching for new inventions on the markets that threaten the firm. Once identified, however, it is still an open question whether management will buy into the new technology. Mowery implicitly assumes that firms that cannot generate new technology will buy it from others if available. But management may not welcome new ideas at all. To be sure, competitive markets tend to deal summarily with firms that suffer from the "not-invented-here" syndrome and its more malignant relative "if it were possible we would have done it long ago." Yet in practice firms make these mistakes all the time. It is easier to dismiss a new idea when it comes from your own employee. When Henry Ford III was faced with radial tires, he contemptuously dismissed them. He then reluctantly had to purchase them from Michelin despite his distaste for "frog tires" (Frey 1991). Serious pockets of resistance in other parts of the corporation may block the introduction of new techniques, as the example provided by John Sutton regarding the introduction of polyester-based tires at Du Pont amply demonstrates. Firms that resist innovation might be clay-footed bureaucratic giants, or one-man empires in which a brilliant but erratic entrepreneur makes the decisions himself. Either way, they have three options: generate the new technology themselves, buy it from others, or languish and (perhaps) perish.

The recent work by Daniel Shiman (1992) on technological progress in Victorian Britain has found that a key variable in technological progress is the ability of the firm to delegate authority within its own hierarchy to the people in charge of R&D. British family firms, run by, through, and for old-boy networks, trusted few underlings, and management rarely lent the R&D departments, insofar that these existed at all, a free hand. Effective in-house research requires that management leave technical issues to its in-house specialists. In practice, this rarely happens, and the same scientist will produce very different results depending on whether he is working for a large firm that plans to use his invention or a smaller one (including himself) that will sell it. Yet continuous pressure on such labs to produce profitable results quickly mean that in-house and specialist research labs do not produce the same kinds of new knowledge. Only if the firm's management is fully committed to let its research lab do what it wants will they produce similar results.

An important element, allegedly, in the interpretation of the development of the U.S. R&D industry is the existence of antitrust laws. Antitrust policies, on balance, are said to have enchanced in-house research. A simple test of this proposition is to look at imperial Germany, where it flunks quite spectacularly. The hypothesis also implies that when antitrust legislation was loosely enforced, firms should have switched from in-house R&D to market-supplied new technologies. Yet one could argue that the reverse is equally plausible: firms that do a lot of in-house research might fear that their competitive advantage would become so overwhelming that the antitrust enforcers would attribute it to price-fixing rather than to technological superiority. If they are worried about intervention of this kind, they do not *have* to merge with the firms that generated the new technologies, and could license or rent it in some form. The market provides enough flexibility to overcome such fears. Moreover, in the vast bulk of technological mergers in which a large user company bought out a small but innovative supplier, the difference in size between the two companies was such that it can hardly have mattered to the authorities. In any event, if the antitrust policies had this effect, the outcome may have been the reverse of the intended one if intrafirm research tended to weaken competition as successful firms acquired technological niches in the products they developed and thus fostered a stable oligopolistic market. This hypothesis is never put to an exact test, and we have another tantalizing suggestion that makes sense, but is not directly confronted with the evidence. It is, of course hard to prove anything when the main variable to be explained (the proportion of new technology produced by in-house industrial research labs) is neither quantifiable nor directly observable.

Neoclassical economic theory is quite good in pointing out its own failures and carefully delineating when markets fail, and it is standard fare in any course in the economics of technological change to point out why markets involving technology are incomplete and unreliable. When they are, they can be superseded by mechanisms internal to the firm. But where do these internal procedures come from, what constraints are they subject to, and can they adapt over time to a changing environment? And, above all, are they capable of generating that flow of innovations that is necessary for a dynamic capitalist system to sustain itself? Many of the papers in this volume are making an effort to provide alternatives. An analysis in terms of the *nature* of the hierarchies involved and their tendency toward conservatism seems to me necessary to complement the emphasis on external environment, especially government policies. What happens when management is faced with a radical novel approach from its own R&D department? Will the firm willingly accept innovations that will make much of its physical and human capital obsolete? Does the R&D department anticipate management's response? To what extent does the R&D lab itself become a bureaucracy with entrenched vested interests?

On these issues we look in vain to standard theory for answers. To bend a hackneyed aphorism about the drunk looking for his keys a bit more: we have searched under the streetlight, and the keys we are looking for are not there. We can either go home without our keys, or try to get another source of light. In the new institutional economics, with its emphasis on transactions costs, its capability to characterize conventions and customs as Nash equilibria in bargaining models and coordination games, and its analysis of the internal dynamics of power structures and hierarchies, we may be in the process of erecting a new streetlight. I am not sure whether our keys are there either, but it is worth a look.

References

Coase, Ronald. 1937. The Nature of the Firm. *Economica,* n.s., 4:386–405.
Frey, Donald. 1991. Learning the Ropes: My Life as a Product Champion. *Harvard Business Review,* September–October. Reprint no. 91504.
Jewkes, John, David Sawers, and Richard Stillerman. 1969. *The Sources of Invention.* 2d ed. New York: Norton.
Kuran, Timur. 1988. The Tenacious Past: Theories of Personal and Collective Conservatism. *Journal of Economic Behavior and Organization* 10:143–71.
Shiman, Daniel. 1992. The Decline of the British Economy in the Late Nineteenth and Early Twentieth Centuries: Organizational Structure and Technological Performance. Ph.D. diss., Department of Economics, Northwestern University.
Teece, David. 1988. Technological Change and the Nature of the Firm. In *Technical Change and Economic Theory,* ed. G. Dosi et al., 256–81. London: Pinter.

6 Legal Restraints on Economic Coordination: Antitrust in Great Britain and America, 1880–1920

Tony Freyer

During the formative era of managerial capitalism, changes in legal rules had important consequences for the evolution of business forms. Alfred D. Chandler, Jr., and Leslie Hannah have argued that varying policies toward cartels in Britain and the United States help explain the different scale of the turn-of-the-century merger wave in the two nations. They also argued that diverging legal rules help explain why managerial capitalism and large-scale corporations became the norm in America, whereas family capitalism continued to characterize the British business order. Neither Chandler nor Hannah based this argument on a close consideration of the legal record, however.[1] This paper aims to provide a legal foundation for their thesis by surveying the development of antitrust policy in the two nations over the period 1880 to 1920.[2]

First, I give an overview of the legal rules governing cartel practices during the formative period and then, in sections 6.2 and 6.3, I examine more closely the evolution of court decisions in Britain and the United States. It is noteworthy that in Britain nearly all the cases were private suits involving the cartel practices of family firms or individually owned organizations. In the United States, however, there was a mix of cases. Many were private suits challenging cartels, but the most important cases involved state or federal prosecution of

Tony Freyer is University Research Professor of History and Law at the University of Alabama at Tuscaloosa.

1. Chandler 1977, 1990; Hannah 1980, 1981, 1983. Hannah (1979) does consider the relation between merger and cartel policy, but he acknowledges that the treatment was not exhaustive.

2. Freyer 1992 attempts to enlarge upon and provide a broad empirical basis for the Chandler and Hannah insights. A multilevel study encompassing political, social, and economic theory variables, as well as legal ones, the book strives to attain a holistic analysis. For the purposes of this conference, the present paper focuses primarily upon legalistic factors, leaving out the wider context with which they interacted. Although the isolation of legalistic variables is undoubtedly useful, such an approach is nonetheless, both empirically and interpretatively, incomplete.

large corporate consolidations. In section 6.4 I suggest more directly how changing legal rules influenced the economic behavior of managerially centralized corporations, particularly holding companies.[3]

6.1 Legal Rules Governing Cartels

In discussing legal policies toward formal cartels and other cartellike restraints of trade, it is useful to distinguish between unenforceability and criminal liability. In Britain the gradual evolution of legal rules led the courts generally to reject any form of criminal liability in cases involving restrictive trade practices and restraints. By the middle of the nineteenth century Parliament had repealed statutes that made it an indictable offense to try to secure control of commodities en route to market in order to raise prices. Within a short time British courts had similarly modified the common law. By the 1890s, as we shall see, British judges fashioned a formal principle of nonintervention in the *Mogul* case and a rule of reason in the *Nordenfelt* decision. In the United States, however, change proceeded largely in a contrary direction. By the 1880s and 1890s the number of trade restraints subject to criminal indictment had actually *increased,* facilitating the development of per se rules against such restraints. During the same period, moreover, an American rule of reason emerged that further enlarged the ground for raising legal challenges to monopolistic practices (Freyer 1992, esp. 121–58).

In both Britain and America by the mid–nineteenth century the enforceability of a contract in restraint of trade cases depended on whether the restraint was "partial" or "total." An agreement whereby a producer might sell to another the right to make something in a local community was a "partial" restraint which under certain circumstances was enforceable even though a monopoly might result. A similar restrictive agreement, however, applying to all procedures was a total restraint and hence not enforceable. Courts applied the same principles to various price-fixing agreements (including resale price maintenance), refusal-to-deal cases, and boycotts. A related principle applicable to this test involved the idea of "public policy." The courts would not enforce contracts found to be contrary to "public policy," but that did not mean the contracts were criminal. Instead, unenforceability meant that the courts treated such contracts "as if they had not been made at all," even though the "parties have agreed" (Freyer 1992, 126).

By the end of the nineteenth century, however, the decisions of American and British courts increasingly diverged. Take the case of horizontal restrictive agreements, whereby one party agreed to sell out to another and establish a monopoly. In Britain not only did such agreements remain free of criminal

3. Chandler 1977, 375; 1990, 398; Hannah 1979; McCraw 1984, 67, suggest the importance of "enforceability" in understanding the cartel/merger issues, but again, the treatment is not exhaustive. See also Cornish 1979 and Dennison 1980.

liability, but by the 1890s British judges began to employ a reasonableness standard that allowed certain of these agreements to be enforced, regardless of whether they were partial or total. At this time, British courts permitted, but still did not enforce, horizontal price-fixing agreements among potential competitors. After 1900, however, even these restraints increasingly became enforceable where British judges found them to be reasonable. By contrast, in America, horizontal restraints were generally unenforceable even under a reasonableness standard. More important, such agreements increasingly were found to be per se criminally illegal (Freyer 1992, esp. 76–140).

Vertical price-fixing agreements further suggest the contrast. Throughout the nineteenth century in both nations it was common for producers to impose upon retailers contractual restraints that governed the selling price. In both nations these were generally accepted but not enforced by the courts. After the turn of the century, however, legal rules in the two nations again diverged. In Britain vertical price restraints increasingly were enforceable under the standard of reasonableness. In the United States, however, such agreements were rarely if ever enforceable. Moreover, in the *Dr. Miles* decision of 1911, the U.S. Supreme Court held that vertical restraints were per se illegal. Although in later years the Court upheld a few exceptions, the per se policy remained dominant (Freyer 1992, 20–35, 153, 157, 191–94).

At issue in all of these cases were two fundamental forms of economic liberty: freedom of trade versus freedom of contract. Freedom of trade meant that individuals and firms should be free to enter into transactions without interference from the restrictive practices of others. Freedom of contract meant that the law should force parties to adhere to contractual obligations. By the turn of the century, British and American courts had come to balance these two freedoms in very different ways. Although the British courts had initially embraced a noninterventionist policy, favoring competition and refusing to enforce restraints that impeded it, over time they moved to enforce contracts that met their reasonableness tests. In the United States, the courts moved in precisely the opposite direction, not only refusing to enforce restrictive contracts but increasingly finding them actionable as violations of criminal law.

6.2 Evolution of British Laws

The 1890s were a turning point in British law because it was then that the courts decided the new controlling precedents. A key decision was *Mogul Steamship Co. v. McGregor Co.* The case arose in 1888 between a conference of steamship companies engaged in the lucrative China tea trade and the Mogul Company, which sought to enter the same market. The shipping conference was an effectively organized cartel system of private governance, permitting its members to allocate markets, regulate prices, control entry, and enforce agreements through persuasion or, if necessary, intimidation. Briefly, the conference permitted Mogul a piece of the business. When the outsider demanded that it become a cartel member as well, the conference balked, whereupon Mogul threatened to cut its rates low enough to "smash" its opponent. The conference responded by reducing rates to such a level that Mogul could not survive. It was a straightforward case of using predatory pricing to destroy a competitor. The steamship company sued, arguing that the conference had conspired to prevent it from competing "fairly," violating common-law rules forbidding conspiracies to enter into restrictive commercial contracts. In several lower and appellate rulings between 1888 and 1892, British courts, including finally the House of Lords, held that the conference's conduct was not actionable on grounds of conspiracy and therefore not forbidden by law. The adverse publicity caused a short-term dissolution of the cartel, but soon thereafter it was reestablished and continued to exist throughout the twentieth century.[4]

The judges' various opinions in the *Mogul* litigation set out the British common-law policy toward restrictive agreements. Lord Justice Edward Fry observed matter of factly, regarding what in American would very likely have been criminally indictable, that the "scheme of the conference was by means of competition in the near future to prevent competition in the remote future." Judge Charles S. C. Bowen concluded that "competition, however severe and egotistical, if unattended by circumstances of dishonesty, intimidation, molestation, or such illegalities . . . give [*sic*] rise to no cause of action at common law. I myself should deem it to be a misfortune if courts attempted to prescribe to the business world how honest and peaceable trade was to be carried on, adopting some standard of judicial 'reasonableness,' or of 'normal' prices or 'fair freights' to which commercial adventures, otherwise innocent, were bound to conform" (61 L.T.R. 826, 827, 828, 829).

The *Mogul* case also raised the issue of enforceability. On the point of whether cartel agreements were enforceable between the conference members themselves, Lord Chancellor Halsbury pointed out that they were not. Some contracts in restraint of trade were void as contrary to "public policy," Halsbury said. And "contracts so tainted the law will not lend its aid to enforce. It treats them as if they had not been made at all," even though the "parties have agreed." Thus businessmen could form anticompetitive, restrictive combinations. But this very freedom also meant that they had little legal recourse against those in the combination who decided that continued cooperation was no longer in their interest. Thus the conference's victory in court did not prevent in the short-term the dissolution of the cartel itself (66 L.T.R. 4).

The other main precedent of the 1890s, the *Maxim Nordenfelt Guns* case, also involved the issue of enforceability, but with different results. In 1888 Swedish inventor and businessman Thorsten Nordenfelt sold for a considerable

---

4. *Mogul Steamship Co. v. McGregor, Gow and Co.,* 59 L.T.R. 514 (1888); *Mogul Steamship Co. v. McGregor, Gow and Co.,* 62 L.T.R. 820 (1889); *Mogul Steamship Co. v. McGregor, Gow and Co.,* 66 L.T.R. 1 (1892).

sum his arms-manufacturing business to a new British firm, the Maxim Nordenfelt Guns and Ammunition Company. In the sales contract Nordenfelt agreed not to manufacture anywhere in the world for twenty-five years various of the precision weapons he had developed, leaving that market to the new company. The contract also permitted him to remain with the firm as a senior partner. Within a short time, however, Nordenfelt resigned and reentered the armaments business in Belgium with the very weapons that the Maxim Company was selling. The firm sued in 1892, asking for an injunction to compel Nordenfelt to cease competing in accordance with his contract. He responded by arguing that the twenty-five-year proscription was an unreasonable restraint of trade. Although the trial court agreed, on appeal the House of Lords reversed in favor of Maxim.[5]

On one level the question was simple: should the court enforce the contract with an injunction, or not enforce it because it was an agreement in restraint of trade and therefore void? But on another level the issue was complicated because, as the *Mogul* decision showed, late-nineteenth-century British courts generally interpreted freedom of contract to mean that the *enforcement* of restrictive agreements was exceptional. Although this particular case required only a relatively minor adjustment in restraint-of-trade rules affecting contracts, it raised the issue of whether restraints deemed reasonable could be enforced. The "time for a new departure," to be "authoritatively decided" had risen, said Lord Morris (1894 A.C. 575), and Lord Mcnaghten provided a precise definition: "[R]estraints of trade and interference with individual liberty of action may be justified by the special circumstances of a particular case. It is a sufficient justification, and indeed it's the only justification if the restriction is reasonable—reasonable, that is, in reference to the interests of the parties concerned and reasonable in reference to the interests of the public" (1894 A.C. 565).

Mcnaghten's reasonableness standard facilitated the enforcement of restrictive agreements, especially in light of *Mogul.* Prior to *Nordenfelt,* British judges had at times, on the basis of particular facts and principles of a case, enforced trade restraints. Lacking a consistent standard, however, such enforcement was exceptional. As *Mogul* had shown, British courts were willing to allow what amounted to private enforcement mechanisms through cartel arrangements. But since no coherent legal enforcement standard existed, the courts' approach to enforcement issues was ultimately ad hoc. What Mcnaghten did was to create a formal legal principle—the rule of reasonableness—which through legal analysis of a case's facts and policy considerations enabled the judge to enforce restrictive agreements. In effect, Mcnaghten's rule strengthened *Mogul*'s sanction of cartel practices by establishing a legal analy-

5. *Maxim Nordenfelt Guns and Ammunition Co. v. Nordenfelt,* 67 L.T.R. 469 (1892); *Maxim Nordenfelt Guns and Ammunition Co. v. Nordenfelt,* 68 L.T.R. 833 (1892); *Nordenfelt v. Maxim Nordenfelt Guns,* 1894 A.C. 535.

sis for determining whether the courts would do what previously had been generally left to private self-regulation.

From the mid-1890s on, the British courts worked within the *Mogul* and *Nordenfelt* principles. In 1900 a case arose involving vertical price-fixing agreements between a manufacturer of embrocations for horses, cattle, and human use and wholesalers who sold it to retailers. The manufacturer, Elliman, Sons and Company, required a wholesaler purchasing the product to sign a contract agreeing he would not sell it below a fixed price. The agreement also bound the wholesaler to procure a similar contract from any retailer buying the embrocation. Carrington and Son conveyed Elliman's goods to a retailer but failed to make the required contract, whereupon the manufacturer sued Carrington in chancery, asking the court to enforce that provision of the price-fixing agreement. The court held that the agreement between the manufacturer and wholesaler was valid and enforceable (2 Ch. 275 [1901]).

The courts also considered vertical restraints derived from a patent to be within the limits of reasonableness and hence enforceable. The United Shoe Machinery Company (USMC) owned a patented technology used by many of the world's manufacturers of boots and shoes. The American-based company used its monopoly to impose upon those leasing the technology certain tying agreements that restricted or denied altogether the use of other equipment. According to one of these vertical clauses, the British manufacturer, Somervell Brothers, contracted to use only the USMC's machinery for twenty years. After three years, Somervell found elements of the technology uneconomical for the particular demands of its business and began using other machinery. In 1906 USMC sued for breach of contract and asked the chancery court to enforce it. Somervell responded that the tying agreement was a restraint of trade and contrary to public policy. The judge admitted that he was "rather startled" at the "very considerable time" for which the contract ran. But, he said, "there it is, and we have got to make the best of it as it stands." The ground "for discontinuing the machine—namely, reasons of economy—is wholly insufficient," the judge concluded, and so there was "a breach of the contract," which must be corrected by the court requiring enforcement.[6]

An appeal from Canada revealed that the House of Lords was also willing to enforce such tying agreements. In order to complete part of its manufacturing process, Brunet, a Quebec firm, began using equipment produced locally in violation of its lease with USMC. In 1905 the company sued, arguing that Brunet had violated the "tying clause" of the lease. A special jury of local Quebec businessmen decided in favor of Brunet's claim that the vertical constraint was a restraint of trade and therefore void. Canada's highest court upheld the verdict, whereupon in 1909 USMC appealed to the Judicial Commit-

---

6. *British United Shoe Machinery Co. Ltd. v. Somervell Bros.,* 95 L.T.R. (Ch.) 711, 713, 714 (1907). BUSM was a subsidiary of the American company. See *U.S. v. United Shoe Manufacturing Co.,* 258 U.S. 451 (1915).

tee. Unanimously following *Mogul,* the Lords' Judicial Committee overruled the Canadian courts' opinions.[7]

Even where the Australian legislature acted to outlaw self-regulating, anti-competitive agreements, the Lords found reasons to support them. In 1906 the new commonwealth's parliament passed a federal law not unlike the Sherman Antitrust Act. It declared illegal any contract or combination the intent of which was "to destroy or injure by means of unfair competition any Australian industry which is advantageous to the commonwealth. . . . [and] the interests of producers, workers, and consumers." Provincial coal companies formed a pool designed to fix prices, distribute output among members, and provide a fund supporting weak producers. The resulting stability enabled the colliers to establish a cartel agreement with several shipping companies to further control prices. The record showed that the agreements sought to ameliorate cut-throat competition, which had not only weakened the coal producers themselves but had also engendered labor strife because of low wages and unemployment. Nevertheless, in the *Adelaide Steamship* case the Australian government challenged the cartel as a violation of the nation's antitrust law. Australia's highest tribunal overruled the trial court's decision, which favored the government, whereupon, in 1913, the attorney general appealed to the Lords' Judicial Committee.[8]

The Lords interpreted the statute in light of the principles established in *Mogul* and *Nordenfelt.* They rejected the argument that the Australian parliament had intended all contracts in restraint of trade to be either void or unenforceable, because such a holding threatened the existence of "trade unions, the economic advantage of which has often been recognized in modern legislation." It also denied claims that U.S. decisions based on the Sherman Act were relevant, rejecting the Supreme Court's use of the rule of reason in the *Standard Oil* decision of 1911. More significantly, the Judicial Committee linked the price stability the cartel agreements facilitated to the colliers' ability to employ workers and pay satisfactory wages, an outcome "eminently reasonable and well calculated to prevent labor troubles." The court held that the cartel agreements raised no "legitimate inference that any of the parties concerned, whether colliery proprietors or shipping companies, acted otherwise than with a single view to their own advantage, or had any intention of raising prices or annihilating competition to the detriment of the public." Thus, the court declared that the cartel practices were permissible under the law (1913 A.C. 800, 801, 802, 810, 813).

By early 1914 the judiciary's willingness to enforce anticompetitive agreements was clear. Most of the salt manufacturers in western England formed a cartel known as the North Western Salt Company for the "purpose of

---

7. *USMC of Canada v. Brunet,* 1909 A.C. 330.
8. *Attorney-General of the Commonwealth of Australia v. the Adelaide Steamship Co. Ltd.,* 1913 A.C. 781, 782.

regulating supply and keeping up prices, and it had the practical control of the inland salt market." The Electrolytic Alkali Company, though not a cartel member, entered into a contract with North Western, limiting output and agreeing to sell to no one else for a period of four years. In return the cartel guaranteed the annual purchase of Alkali's production at a fixed price. Despite the agreement the company sold to a third party, whereupon North Western sued for breech of contract, asking the court to compel compliance. Alkali argued in defense that the contract was void as a restraint of trade and therefore not enforceable. Although the trial judge decided in favor of the cartel, the Court of Appeal reversed by a vote of two to one. For final review the case went to the House of Lords.[9]

The Lords reversed the appellate court's decision, thereby not only permitting but also enforcing the restrictive agreements. As was true of the Australian antitrust case decided the year before, the court linked social order and business necessity. All four lords wrote opinions, but Haldane's was representative. "Unquestionably," he conceded, the purpose of the cartel was to "regulate supply and keep up prices. But an ill-regulated supply and unremunerative prices may, in point of fact, be disadvantageous to the public. Such a state of things may, if it is not controlled, drive manufacturers out of business, or lower wages, and so cause unemployment and labor disturbance." Accordingly, it "must always be a question of circumstances whether a combination of manufacturers in a particular trade is an evil from a public point of view. The same thing is true of a supposed monopoly." Haldane concluded that the parties were the "best judges of what is reasonable as between themselves." As a result, the "detailed provisions" of the agreement at issue embodied primarily the "machinery for working out the bargain." The contract between the cartel and Alkali was therefore neither illegal nor contrary to the public interest, and Alkali was bound to honor it (1914, A.C. 469, 471).

6.3   Evolution of U.S. Laws

Although its legal phraseology was similar to Mcnaghten's *Nordenfelt* opinion, the rule of reason articulated by U.S. Supreme Court Justice Edward White in the *Standard Oil* and *American Tobacco* decisions had very different implications. Most significantly, the American version of the rule applied the reasonableness standard only to tight combinations—that is, combinations that took the form of mergers. In sharp contrast to British practice, the U.S. Supreme Court declared cartels to be illegal per se, regardless of their reasonableness.

The different implications of these rules of reason reflected the divergent trends in the way courts in the two nations had handled restraint-of-trade cases

9. *North Western Salt Co. Ltd. v. Electrolytic Alkali Co., Ltd.*, 3 K.B. 422 (1913); *North Western Salt Co. Ltd. v. Electrolytic Alkali Co.*, 1914 A.C. 46.

in the late nineteenth century. In the United States, for example, courts in the individual states generally disposed of private suits in a way unfavorable to cartels. An Alabama decision in 1900, *Tuscaloosa Ice Mgf. Co. v. Williams,* was typical. One of two ice manufacturers in Tuscaloosa contracted to sell his business to the other firm, which then possessed a monopoly. Wanting to re-enter business, the plaintiff (named in the report only as "Williams") sued the Tuscaloosa Ice Company, arguing that the contractual agreement under which he sold his business to his former competitor was void under common-law rules prohibiting contracts in restraint of trade. The plaintiff won at trial, whereupon the Tuscaloosa Ice Company appealed. The issue was whether a contract between the two ice manufacturers, in which one party granted the other a monopoly, was unlawful under the common law. The court found that the contract was a "vicious restraint of trade, and is therefore violative of the public policy of the state and void" (28 So. Rep. 669, 670 [Alabama, 1900]).

The circumstances of the case were similar to *Nordenfelt,* but the Alabama court did not apply the *Nordenfelt* principle of reasonableness to enforce the anticompetitive agreement. There was no doubt that the contract "tends to in-jure the public by stifling competition and creating a monopoly," the court said, giving one company the power "to arbitrarily fix prices," thereby creating a "partial ice famine, upon which [it] . . . could batten and fatten at its own sweet will." Resorting to colorful language, the court observed that any defense of such practices was "exceedingly nude and bald." Yet, though the unfettered manufacture of ice in and of itself was undoubtedly important to the small town of Tuscaloosa during the hot, humid summer months, when the case was decided, the court stressed further considerations it apparently regarded as equally compelling. Because of the contract to shut down one of two firms, the "public loses a wealth producing instrumentality. Labor is thrown out of employment." This in turn forced workers upon the public welfare or drove them to become criminals. Hence, profits from a contract that established a monopoly were not the "just reward" of "skill and energy and enterprise in building up a business," but "a mere bribery and seduction of . . . industry, and a pensioning of idleness." The "motives actuating such a transaction" were "always . . . sinister and baleful."[10]

Other cases similar to British precedents also yielded different results. The shipping conference at issue in *Mogul* was similar, for example, to the pipe manufacturers' cartel challenged in the federal government's famous *Addyston Pipe* suit, involving an attempt to control the manufacture and distribution of pipes throughout the Midwest and upper South. On their face the two cases seemed quite different. In *Mogul* the formal issue was whether the conference's predatory pricing was criminally culpable. The formal issue raised in *Addyston Pipe,* by contrast, was whether the cartel's allocation of market territory and determination of "fair" prices among its members violated the Sherman Anti-

---

10. 28 So. Rep. 672–73 (Alabama, 1900). Compare discussion of *Nordenfelt* above.

trust Act. Consistent with other cartel decisions, the courts held the pipe manufacturers' cartel to be criminally illegal. But the underlying issue common to
both cases was whether the courts would indirectly sanction self-regulatory
systems of private enforcement. The British courts, of course, did permit and
therefore indirectly approved such private self-regulation, which in turn paved
the way for judicial enforcement of restrictive agreements once Mcnaghten's
rule of reasonableness was established. In *Addyston Pipe* and other cartel
cases, however, the American judiciary consistently not only refused to enforce
private self-regulatory systems, but held them to be violations of the criminal
law. *Addyston Pipe* was thus indicative of an emerging per se rule against cartel practices.

In the United States private actions were more numerous and probably more
important than the suits initiated by the states' attorneys general. In the private
suits, like the public ones, a per se rule against cartel practices increasingly
emerged. From every jurisdiction for all the years up to the 1870s there were
perhaps no more than 130 recorded private suits challenging restrictive trade
practices. Between 1880 and 1914 however, the number rose from 70 to 200,
totaling 520 (May 1987, 503). Hans Thorelli concluded that this private litigation "was one of the prime factors preventing the lapse of American industry
into general cartelization of . . . the contemporary German type" (1955, 266).
The *Tuscaloosa Ice Co.* case was indicative of the states' refusal to enforce
restrictive agreements.

The law's repudiation of enforceability throughout the states in turn compelled commercial lawyers to look for tighter organizational structures permitting more centralized command and control. One important solution, devised
by Standard Oil's lawyer S. T. C. Dodd, was the trust device, whereby individuals surrendered their right of private enforcement to a central board, which
established its own policies. Under Dodd's trust, previously separate owners
of firms within Rockefeller's cartel structure turned over trust certificates to the
executive board; these certificates surrendered control because they were le-
gally enforceable, contractual obligations. The use of such certificates to
achieve greater centralized control was, however, new, so Dodd hoped the
courts might sanction them (Freyer 1992, 32, 84–88).

During the 1880s other corporate giants followed Standard Oil's lead and
replaced horizontal cartel arrangements, often with trusts and then eventually
a holding company. Between the mid-1880s and mid-1890s, however, the attorneys general of Louisiana, Illinois, Nebraska, California, New York, Ohio, and
other states won from their courts decrees dissolving trusts. They secured these
actions on the basis of new legislation and court decisions that made loose
corporate arrangements not only unenforceable, but also subject to civil and
criminal prosecution. Essentially, the states enacted legislation and state courts
employed interpretations formally removing from local law common-law principles of the sort that the *Tuscaloosa Ice Company* had used as a defense and
that the British courts relied upon to establish a rule of reason governing cartel

practices in *Nordenfelt* and other decisions. In altering their common law the states thus established a more stringent policy toward restrictive practices than that sanctioned by the reasonableness standard of *Nordenfelt*. Meanwhile, in 1889 New Jersey enacted a law permitting corporations to form holding companies, and soon other states followed suit. As a result, when Ohio finally dissolved the Standard Oil Trust, the company was able to avoid destruction by reconstituting itself as a holding company. The other trusts followed a similar strategy, until such giants as American Sugar, American Tobacco, the meatpacking industry, and even firms such as Du Pont and U.S. Steel, which had never been trusts, all adopted the holding company (May 1987; Thorelli 1955; McCurdy 1979).

In certain instances improved organizational efficiency enabled the more managerially centralized corporations to integrate vertically, taking over marketing and production operations that previously had been handled by independent operators. In other cases increased managerial centralization may have not resulted in the actual takeover of independents; enough organizational control nevertheless resulted so that corporate giants could use their market power to dominate middlemen and other small businesses. The competitors that the large firms absorbed through horizontal mergers also often were smaller businesses. During the great turn-of-the-century merger wave, which primarily involved horizontal combination, many smaller firms lost their independence, providing yet another source of discontent and demand for political action against the trusts.

The early stages of this conflict encouraged passage of the Sherman Antitrust Act; the persistence of struggle influenced the act's subsequent application. The act made illegal *every* trade restraint and monopoly, though the actual meaning of these words was left to the federal courts and for some years there was considerable disagreement. Interestingly, most of the lower federal tribunals construed the Sherman Act much as had the Lords' Judicial Committee in the Australian antitrust case—that is, quite narrowly. In most of these decisions federal judges displayed a preference for interpreting the act according to British rather than American precedents. An original purpose for creating the federal judiciary under the Constitution was to provide a forum capable of enforcing uniform rules amid diverse state laws. Accordingly, faced with the confusing pattern of state anticartel decisions, on the one hand, and liberal holding-company laws, on the other, it was not surprising that federal judges looked for guidance to the record of consistent precedents British courts provided. Once the Supreme Court began reviewing the lower courts and made its own construction of the Sherman Act, however, the adherence to British precedents generally ceased (see Letwin 1981, 148–49; Freyer 1979).

When the Supreme Court first construed the Sherman Act in the *Knight Sugar Trust* case of 1895, it interpreted the act's provisions as prohibiting only contracts and combinations in restraint of interstate trade. Upholding state control over corporations, which the holding-company law represented, the majority held that the act applied only to restrictive practices involved directly in interstate trade, not to horizontal agreements among manufacturers involved in production within a single state. The Sugar Trust was a holding company whose production was confined principally to one state, Pennsylvania. Because such corporations were traditionally subject to state regulation, the Court decided, with only Justice John M. Harlan dissenting, that the Sherman Act did not reach them. The *Knight* decision seemed to signal that tight combinations would not be broken up under the Sherman Act.[11]

In *U.S. v. Trans-Missouri Freight Association* (1897), the Court strengthened the businessman's preference for tight over loose corporate combinations. The issue was whether a cartel agreement among competing railroads to fix rates violated the Sherman Act. The lower federal court had applied the British reasonableness standard to sustain the agreement. The Supreme Court divided five to four, reversing the lower court. For the majority, Justice Rufus W. Peckham held that the cartel's rate-fixing practices violated the antitrust law. Peckham reasoned that the act should be read literally, without recourse to the ambiguities of the common law, including the *Mogul* and *Nordenfelt* decisions, a result that was consistent with the general course of anticartel decisions followed in the state courts. Justice White for the dissenters argued, however, that the more flexible rule of reasonableness established in the British cases and applied by the lower court should govern the application of the Sherman Act (166 U.S. 290 [1896]; Letwin 1981).

Peckham, of course, did not have the last word. By 1899 (the peak of the great merger wave) the Court suggested in several decisions, including most notably the sustaining of the result in Judge William H. Taft's *Addyston Pipe* opinion, that common-law principles could provide guidelines for applying the Sherman Act. Yet division among the justices persisted as to whether Peckham's literal reading (and the state anticartel decisions it paralleled) or White's rule of reason should govern the interpretation of the antitrust law.[12]

A turning point was the *Northern Securities* case of 1903. Two major railroads formed a holding company specifically in order to avoid competing in interstate commerce. The Court held for the first time that such a tight corporate combination was a violation of the Sherman Act. The five-to-four vote affirmed, however, the extent to which the justices remained divided. The majority supported Harlan's decision that the preservation of competition was a primary purpose of the Sherman Act. In so doing, the Court for the first time applied to a holding company the policy against restrictive practices underlying the state's anticartel decisions. As one of the four dissenters, White argued that the evidence as to the intent of the act's framers was too ambiguous to support Harlan's interpretation. He also claimed that neither Peckham's literal

---

11. *U.S. v. E. C. Knight Co.,* 156 U.S. 1 (1895); McCurdy 1979.
12. *Addyston Pipe and Steel Co. v. U.S.,* 175 U.S. 211 (1899); *U.S. v. Joint Traffic Association,* 171 U.S. 505 (1898); *Hopkins v. U.S.* 171 U.S. 578 (1898).

reading nor Harlan's emphasis upon a single policy favoring competition permitted the flexibility provided by the rule of reason. Given the uneven course of combined state and federal decisions since 1890, he asserted, flexibility was essential. By this point White was ready to apply a per se rule against cartels, but he remained adamant that a rule of reason should govern various forms of mergers. Moreover, in what became a famous dissent, Holmes categorically rejected Harlan's expressed preference for unrestrained competition. By favoring the values of self-regulating cooperation, Holmes revealed a sympathy for the theoretical approach and substantive results of British law (193 U.S. 197 [1903]).

White's point of view ultimately won out, and in the *Standard Oil* and *American Tobacco* cases his dissent in *Trans-Missouri Freight Association* became the basis for a fundamental principle of antitrust law. Both Standard Oil and American Tobacco were giant holding companies doing business throughout the United States and around the world. Both firms had entered into anticompetitive contracts involving discriminatory pricing and marketing practices, which they defended on grounds of efficiency. White relied upon a reading of British and American common law to decide whether these contracts were lawful; though consistent with the contrast noted above, his formulation had a different substantive content from that established in *Nordenfelt.* He acknowledged that "freedom of contract" was the "rule in English law," but that under the Sherman Act freedom to contract was the "essence of freedom from the undue restraint of the right to contract." Undue restraint arose, White said, from "pernicious conduct or acts" which "operated to the prejudice of the public interests by unduly restricting competition . . . or which, either because of their inherent nature or effect or because of the evident purpose of the acts . . . injuriously restrained trade." White's emphasis upon undesirable consequences resulting from pernicious conduct established a legal standard permitting considerable flexibility. If the Court discovered offensive behavior that produced restrictive results, it was contrary to the public interest and unlawful. Accordingly, in the *Standard Oil* case the Court found that the corporation had engaged in wrongful predatory pricing practices and therefore ordered the firm's dissolution. The American Tobacco Company suffered a similar fate.[13]

Yet White's decisions of 1911 also expressly acknowledged that in other cases the Court might find restraining conduct to be reasonable. In such cases, he said, the "words restraint of trade should be given a meaning which would not destroy the individual right to contract and render difficult if not impossible any movement of trade in the channels of interstate commerce—the free movement of which it was the purpose of the [Sherman] statute to protect." Essentially, White blended economic fears of market power with moralistic concerns, to hold that proof of predatory pricing practices, arbitrary allocation of market territories, and other conduct resulting from market domination were

---

13. *U.S. v. Standard Oil,* 221 U.S., 56 (1911); *U.S. v. American Tobacco,* 221 U.S. 106 (1911).

"unreasonable" and therefore violated the Sherman Act (221 U.S. 106, 179 [1911]; see also Sklar 1988).

The Court also strengthened further its opposition to cartels. In the same year the Court handed down the *Standard Oil* and *American Tobacco* opinions, the justices reaffirmed their opposition to cartel practices by declaring that vertical price-fixing agreements between manufacturers and their wholesalers or retailers were unlawful. The case, *Dr. Miles Medical Co. v. Park and Sons Co.,* did not involve the Sherman Act directly. The majority opinion noted in passing, however, that such practices were in principle contrary to the law (220 U.S. 373 [1911]).

Thus by 1911 the course of American antitrust law was apparent. Notwithstanding the early efforts of the lower federal courts and Justice White, the Supreme Court adopted and the federal government enforced the anticartel policy fostered by the state courts. Between 1890 and 1914 the number of suits rose steadily, and in about 80 percent of these cases the government won. Significantly, six out of seven of the government's prosecutions were of cartel agreements among comparatively small enterprises in the furniture, lumber, and apparel trades, both wholesale and retail. The government focused on these industries because it was easier to obtain testimony from customers and competitors providing unlawful conduct. Meanwhile, the court used the flexibility inherent in White's rule of reason generally to sanction large-scale corporations such as U.S. Steel, whose conduct was demonstrably neither morally culpable nor economically exploitive of competitors, while in exceptional cases where "unreasonable" conduct was provable the court broke up tight corporate structures (McCraw 1984, 144–46; Freyer 1992).

6.4 Legislative Influence on Managerially Centralized Companies

The contrast between the two nations in cartel law and in the construction of the rule of reason was paralleled by differences in the laws governing incorporation. Parliament had supported Britain's free trade spirit by enacting the "most liberal company law in Europe." The Joint Stock Companies Act of 1844 established the basic principles governing incorporation. The law defined the difference between private partnerships, which possessed no limited liability, and joint stock companies, which did operate under that principle. The act also required corporations to accept the light of publicity through registration. Amendments passed in 1855 and 1856 and modest reforms in 1888 permitted "incorporation with limited liability to be obtained with a freedom amounting almost to license." Increasingly after 1900, some major British firms formed holding companies in which a central or parent corporation owned the stock, rather than the actual properties, of the various constituent companies. Further changes in Britain's company law encouraged tighter corporate concentration through merger. In 1912 Parliament sanctioned the formation and registration of "a properly constituted limited liability company for the investment of all moneys received from the members," which approved investment decisions permitting the attainment of greater control of an executive board through merger. With control concentrated in a smaller group, it was easier to form a tighter merger, though most British firms did not do so (Freyer 1992, 80, 81, 178; see also Robson 1936).

British incorporation law thus offered firms an attractive alternative to cartels. Since cartels were not illegal, however, British firms continued to enter into various anticompetitive agreements in order to preserve those firms' formal independence. Nonetheless, firms in certain industries chose tighter forms of organization. In heavily capitalized industries such as iron and steel, for example, the tendency was toward a mixed industrial structure composed of "a comparatively few large units in each branch," which then combined into "a loose organization for the regulation of their trade" (Macrosty 1907, 82, 128–29). In other industries, such as textiles, the trend toward merger facilitated effective enough forward integration into marketing that the survival of wholesalers was threatened. Most middlemen did not suffer this fate, however, because a primary benefit offered by British law was greater organizational choice and most firms preferred some sort of cartel structure. But market realities clearly existed that led some firms to adopt the tighter corporate structure permitted under the holding-company act (Freyer 1992, 103).

Various factors influenced a firm's decision to surrender its independence through some form of tight combination. Still, in Britain these factors did not include concerns about potential legal challenges to the new corporate entity. British judges applied the reasonableness standard so narrowly that the legal advantages between cartel and holding company or holding company and tighter merger were limited. In America, however, the more complete the merger the greater was the likelihood that the firm would survive legal challenge and, thereby, attain improved organizational efficiency (Bonbright and Means 1932; Chandler 1977, 499, 500; 1990, 288, 296, 303, 311, 312, 320, 370, 379).

Similarly, in Britain only the parties to a restrictive contract could sue, whereas in America any third party, including the government, even though not a party to the contract, possessed a cause of action. Reinforcing this difference was the fact that in Britain there were no treble damages. In America, however, such damages were common in state cases and the norm in federal cases (Freyer 1992). Thus, as James C. Bonbright and Gardiner C. Means (1932) observed, American plaintiffs possessed incentives that did not exist in Britain to challenge restrictive practices.

The absence of an external threat meant that British firms could choose whether to organize their industry through cartels or holding companies. It also meant that, once a holding company had been formed, the decision whether to adopt a tighter form of organization was left to the formerly independent entities retaining influence within the new firm. In such holding companies, according to the London School of Economic's Henry W. Macrosty, the "interests inevitably clash and dire confusion results" (1907, 16–17). As a result, internal conflict prevented many British firms from adopting a more efficient managerially centralized structure through tighter merger (Freyer 1992, 39). As Hannah concluded, the British turn-of-the-century merger wave was an important economic innovation, but the "industrial partnership and the family-owned factory remained the typical unit in most branches of manufacturing." Legal forms such as the holding company, "which strengthened tendencies to large scale, had also given a new lease of life to smaller businesses. Partnerships and family firms adopted the new institutional form to their own purpose." As a result, the "separation and professionalization of management" associated with "modern corporations still had a long way to develop" (Hannah 1983, 23–24).

As Bonbright and Means noted, this was not the case in America. The law's coincident criminalization of cartel practices and tolerance of tighter forms of corporate consolidation encouraged greater managerial centralization within larger corporations. The emerging per se rule against cartels combined with the abolition of the trust and the enactment of holding company laws undoubtedly fostered adoption of the holding company during the merger wave. Similarly, the *Northern Securities* decision of 1903, in which the Supreme Court for the first time held that holding companies were subject to prosecution, spurred managers to resort to tighter forms of corporate consolidation in order to avoid such suits. Moreover, once the Court established the rule of reason in *Standard Oil* (1911), the principle was applied to favor tighter corporate structures over looser ones.

The rule of reason proved to be sufficiently flexible that a wide range of tight corporate structures could withstand legal challenge. According to Chief Justice White's formulation, the test of reasonableness was grounded on conduct. Thus the predatory pricing practices of Standard Oil and American Tobacco were found to be unreasonable and therefore illegal. U.S. Steel, however, although the world's largest corporation, did not use its market power "unreasonably," and therefore the Court held that it had not violated the antitrust laws (Freyer 1992; Chandler 1988, 363–64).

Unlike British law, therefore, American antitrust hedged the holding company within ambiguous but nonetheless real limits. The central consideration determining whether a court would resolve the ambiguity for or against the legitimacy of the holding company depended on whether it found the firm's conduct to be reasonable. At the threshold, however, the question arose whether a third party—the Justice Department, a state attorney general, or, in a private suit, some plaintiff business—had reason to challenge such conduct. As Bonbright and Means suggested, the facts of a particular case influenced both the initial decision to sue and the suit's eventual outcome. Nevertheless, the tighter the corporate structure, the greater was the likelihood that the defendant corporation would prevail.

Thus the question was, why were tighter corporate structures more immune to third-party challenge? Part of the answer went back to the principle that the corporation was entirely the creature of state law. Accordingly, in acquiring the assets of other firms through merger, the new entity possessed the legitimacy conferred by the state in the original charter. Under the rule of reason a cause of action existed against such a firm if a link between its internal operational character and pernicious conduct could be proven. Establishing such a link was difficult, however, because the states' corporate law gave management considerable legal freedom over the firm's operation. The more extensive was management's direct control of the operational parts of the firm, the harder it was to prove criminal culpability. Thus the *organizational* reason why a tighter merger increased the firm's protection from antitrust challenge was that such a structure resulted in more extensive managerial centralization.[14]

Yet managerial centralization was only part of the answer. If a third party could prove that management's decisions had led to "unreasonable" conduct, the firm had violated the antitrust laws. The broader benefit that such centralization of operational control brought was that it minimized incentives to resort to "unreasonable" conduct.[15] The problem with the holding company was that its level of managerial centralization was often inadequate to "coordinate the day-to-day activities of a large number of plants because the central office could not effectively regulate the flow of products. Indeed, single plants could adapt more easily to changes in supply and demand" (Fligstein 1990, 26; see also Lamoreaux 1985). As a result, firms such as Standard Oil and American Tobacco sought greater organizational control through tighter combination, integrating backward into production-related processes and forward into marketing. Even so, the uncertainty resulting first from the *Northern Securities* case and then the flexibility inherent in the rule of reason enmeshed antitrust enforcement in sufficient legal ambiguity that attaining tighter organizational structure sometimes did not remove internal exigencies resulting in what could be proven to be unreasonable conduct. The level of market domination that resulted from greater organizational concentration thus in some cases led to predatory pricing practices and divisions of market territories that aroused opposition from middlemen, and ultimately competitors, which in turn led to government prosecution. Once it became clear that the judiciary would apply the rule of reason against such practices, firms were encouraged to acquire greater managerial control over the process of production, leading to, as in the case of U.S. Steel, increased scale, but market and pricing strategies that nonetheless did not offend competitors and other participants in the industry.[16]

Of course, the formation of a tighter merger required the consent of stockholders. In Britain former owner-operators of firms who combined to form such large holding companies as Imperial Tobacco continued to exercise considerable influence within the corporation. These individuals, and the stock-

14. Chandler 1977, 333–34, 499, 500; Fligstein 1990, 24–26; Freyer 1992, 20–42; 1979.
15. Freyer 1992, 35–42, 132–41; Fligstein 1990, 24–26; Bonbright and Means 1932.
16. Chandler 1977, 333–34, 499, 500; Fligstein 1990, 24–26; Freyer 1992, 20–42; 1979; Lamoreaux 1985.

holders identified with them, formed a powerful interest capable of blocking greater managerial centralization attained through tighter merger. In America such groups undoubtedly existed. The difference, however, was that directors operated within a legal environment in which the tighter the corporate structure the greater was the possibility of avoiding an antitrust suit. Accordingly, directors could, as Bonbright and Means noted, use the threat or reality of legal prosecution to justify the need to choose the tighter merger and the increased managerial centralization it required.[17]

Finally, the interplay between law and small business influenced the movement toward tighter corporate forms in another way as well. In Britain the law governing cartels and the holding-company statute permitted small firms to survive and even thrive. Louis Brandeis and others predicted that the American judiciary's refusal to apply the rule of reason to cartel practices would foster corporate consolidation and the demise of small firms. If the Court reversed this policy and followed British doctrine allowing the enforcement of loose agreements, Brandeis argued, small businesses might enjoy scale and organizational economies and still preserve their independence. If the British example was any indication, this policy reversal would also have reduced the incentive for third-party suits in cases involving managerially centralized firms because it would have limited the sort of conduct that was held to be unreasonable and therefore illegal. In either case, enforcement of Brandeis's idea would generally have depoliticized small business and reduced the political and symbolic significance of antitrust. Ironically, however, the result might have been to impede the triumph of the managerial revolution that contributed to the dominance of the American economy throughout the twentieth century (Freyer 1992, 66–67).

6.5   Conclusion

The rise of big business thus engendered a divergent response from British and American lawmakers. Prior to the 1880s, neither nation's courts generally enforced the restrictive practices businessmen established. Yet by the early 1890s British and American courts were called upon to decide the legality of new business structures. In Britain, the *Mogul* case condoned but did not enforce a sophisticated system of self-regulating cartel practices. A few years later in *Nordenfelt* the House of Lords established "reasonableness" as the general rule governing the enforcement of restrictive practices arising from the changing economy. The self-restraint these and subsequent decisions represented provided a legal framework for the perpetuation of family enterprise. It also helped to explain the smaller (compared to the United States) turn-of-

17. Chandler 1977, 333–34, 499, 500; Fligstein 1990, 24–26; Freyer 1992, 26–42; 1979; Lamoreaux 1985; Bonbright and Means 1932; Chandler 1990, 288, 296, 303, 311, 312, 320, 370, 379; Payne 1988; Reader 1982; Saul 1962.

the-century merger wave and the corresponding underdevelopment of large, managerially centralized corporations.

The difference in American business and law was noteworthy. During the 1880s the inability to enforce cartel agreements encouraged businessmen to adopt Dodd's trust device. Most states responded by revising their laws to make restrictive trade agreements, including both cartels and trusts, not only unenforceable but also subject to prosecution as illegal. At the same time, however, New Jersey and other states permitted firms to adopt a tighter form of corporate structure, the holding company. In a series of decisions stretching from *Knight* and the anticartel cases of the 1890s to *Northern Securities* of 1903 and the cases establishing the rule of reason in 1911, the Supreme Court's construction of the Sherman Antitrust Act signaled that the tighter the form of organization, the less likely a combination was to be dissolved. Unlike their British counterparts, then, American businessmen during the turn of the century considered merger issues not solely in investment terms, but also as the safest means of avoiding government prosecution. Market factors undoubtedly influenced the great merger wave in both nations. But given the otherwise similar technological and industrial development of the two countries, a salient difference was the presence or lack of antitrust.

Comparing British and American business structures provides a basis for measuring the broader impact of antitrust. The principle of freedom of contract to which British courts adhered in applying their rule of reason reflected a preference for the invisible hand of the market, whereas the ambivalent interpretations of the Sherman Act, culminating in the Supreme Court's rule of reason, demonstrated American confidence in the visible hand of the lawmaker. These divergent views of government intervention in the economic order grew out of different social relations and political conflicts in the two nations. There may have been inconsistencies and failures in the American antitrust experience. Yet in the long run, antitrust benefited consumers by encouraging the more efficient production of goods managerial centralization made possible. Ironically, antitrust thus achieved consumer welfare by its failure to limit the spread of corporate bigness.

References

Bonbright, James C., and Gardiner C. Means. 1932. *The Holding Company, Its Public Significance, and Its Regulation.* New York: Scribners.

Chandler, Alfred D., Jr. 1977. *The Visible Hand: The Managerial Revolution in American Business.* Cambridge: Harvard University Press.

———. 1988. Reprint. The Development of Modern Management Structure in the US and UK. In *The Essential Alfred Chandler: Essays toward a Historical Theory of Big Business,* ed. Thomas K. McCraw, 355–81. Boston: Harvard Business School Press. Originally published 1976.

————. 1990. *Scale and Scope: The Dynamics of Industrial Capitalism.* Cambridge: Harvard University Press.

Cornish, William R. 1979. Legal Control over Cartels and Monopolization, 1880–1914: A Comparison. In *Law and the Formation of the Big Enterprises in the Nineteenth and Early Twentieth Century,* ed. N. Horn and J. Kocka, 281–303. Gottingen: Vandenhoeck and Ruprecht.

Dennison, Jeannie Anne Godfrey. 1980. *The Reaction to the Growth of Trusts and Industrial Combinations in Britain, 1888–1921.* Ph.D. thesis, University of London.

Fligstein, Neil. 1990. *The Transformation of Corporate Control.* Cambridge: Harvard University Press.

Freyer, Tony. 1979. *Forums of Order: The Federal Courts and Business in American History.* Greenwich, CT: JAI Press.

————. 1992. *Regulating Big Business: Antitrust in Great Britain and America, 1880–1990.* Cambridge: Cambridge University Press.

Hannah, Leslie. 1979. Mergers, Cartels, and Concentration: Legal Factors in the U.S. and European Experience. In *Law and Formation of the Big Enterprises in the Nineteenth and Early Twentieth Centuries,* ed. N. Horn and J. Kocka, 306–15. Göttingen: Vandenhoeck and Ruprecht.

————. 1980. Visible and Invisible Hands in Great Britain. In *Managerial Hierarchies: Comparative Perspectives on the Rise of the Modern Industrial Enterprise,* ed. Alfred D. Chandler, Jr., and Herman Daems, 41–76. Cambridge: Harvard University Press.

————. 1981. Mergers. In *Encyclopedia of American Economic History,* ed. Glenn Porter, 639–51. New York: Scribners.

————. 1983. *The Rise of the Corporate Economy.* London: Methuen.

Hovenkamp, Herbert. 1991. *Enterprise and American Law, 1836–1937.* Cambridge: Harvard University Press.

Lamoreaux, Naomi R. 1985. *The Great Merger Movement in American Business, 1895–1904.* New York: Cambridge University Press.

Letwin, William. 1981. *Law and Economic Policy in America: The Evolution of the Sherman Antitrust Act.* Chicago: University of Chicago Press.

McCraw, Thomas K. 1984. *Prophets of Regulation.* Cambridge: Harvard University Press.

McCurdy, Charles W. 1979. The Knight Sugar Decision of 1895 and the Modernization of American Corporation Law, 1869–1903. *Business History Review* 53:304–42.

Macrosty, Henry W. 1907. *The Trust Movement in British Industry: A Study of Business Organization.* London: Macmillan.

May, James. 1987. Antitrust Practice and Procedure in the Formative Era: The Constitutional and Conceptual Reach of State Antitrust Law, 1880–1918. *University of Pennsylvania Law Review* 135:495–593.

Payne, P. L. 1988. *British Entrepreneurship in the Nineteenth Century.* London: Macmillan.

Reader, William J. 1982. Versatility Unlimited: Reflections on the History and Nature of the Limited Liability Company. In *Limited Liability and the Corporation,* ed. Tony Orhnial, 191–204. London: Methuen.

Robson, T. B. 1936. *Holding Companies and Their Published Accounts.* London: Macmillan.

Saul, S. B. 1962. Motor Industry in Britain to 1914. *Business History* 5:1–17.

Sklar, Martin M. 1988. *The Corporate Reconstruction of American Capitalism.* Cambridge: Cambridge University Press.

Thorelli, Hans N. 1955. *The Federal Antitrust Policy: Organization of an American Tradition.* Baltimore: Johns Hopkins University Press.

Comment   Victor P. Goldberg

This paper presents, but does not satisfactorily resolve, a paradox. Alfred Chandler has argued that in the three or four decades around the turn of the century the United States and England developed different ways of organizing business and that these differences resulted largely from differences in the legal regimes. I think it is possible to make that argument, but it will not be easy.

The basic features of the American argument are well known. The antitrust laws were generally perceived to be hostile to restraints between firms—price fixing, market division, and so forth. At the same time, consolidations (which facilitated coordination within organizations) were viewed with more equanimity. The classic example is the legal fate of the Addyston Pipe conspirators. Their cartel behavior was treated as a per se violation of the Sherman Act, which subjected them to criminal penalties and treble damages; their merger while the criminal prosecution was proceeding, however, was not even challenged. The different legal response contributed, so it is argued, to the great merger wave at the turn of the century and to the emergence of the large managerially controlled firm as the dominant form of organization for American industry.

At the same time, the British policy toward restraints of trade was more lenient. When the restraints were not explicitly approved by the courts, they were held merely to be not legal rather than illegal. That is, price fixers would not be penalized; they just would not be able to rely on the courts to enforce their agreements. By treating cartels and consolidations in a more even-handed fashion, the legal regime did not tilt British industry toward merger and consolidation. The British merger wave was smaller, and the dominant form of organization was the holding company, which generally remained a loose confederation of formally independent family firms.

Thus, both countries began the period with an industrial structure dominated by small firms, but they responded differently to the changing technological constraints. England, relatively unconstrained by the law, chose the loose confederations; the United States, subjected to more binding legal constraints, chose consolidation. And herein lies the paradox. Why would the constrained choice (American) result in a more efficient outcome than the unconstrained choice (British)? One should think, *ceteris paribus,* that broadening the choice set would make it more likely that the most efficient regime would be chosen. If, as Freyer argues, the American organizational form was superior to the British, then why did more choice result in the survival of the unfittest?

There are a number of ways out. First, Chandler's starting point could be wrong. It might well turn out that the technological constraints in the two countries were sufficiently different so that the outcomes in both countries were

Victor P. Goldberg is the Thomas Macioce Professor of Law and codirector of the Center for Law and Economic Studies at Columbia University.

efficient—the legal constraints didn't much matter. I suspect that there's some truth to this. Second, Freyer might have been mistaken. The British solution might have been the most efficient—the legal constraints forced the Americans to adopt an inferior organizational technology. Doubtful. Third, it might be possible to tell some sort of "path dependence" story—what made sense at time t leads to an inferior outcome at time $t + 1$ and it is now too difficult to change. I think that there might be something to this, but some real work is necessary to make the argument fly.

Path dependence has been on somewhat shaky ground since the debunking of everybody's favorite example, the QWERTY keyboard (Liebowitz and Margolis 1990). I think that the American failure to adopt the metric system and the Japanese failure to adopt a more computer-friendly language suggest that some vitality remains. In the present context, it is plausible that reasonable businessmen circa 1900 could have opted for the loose cartel rather than consolidation. (Recall that a large proportion of the American mergers failed.) But why would the English stick with the inferior organizational technology? I suspect that a satisfactory answer would require most of the following: weak international competition (inefficient firms can survive); a thin supply of entrepreneurs willing to introduce new organizational forms; a thin supply of capitalists willing and able to finance the new forms; the emergence of supporting institutions (lawyers, accountants, banks) well suited to serving the loose cartels but not for supporting larger organizations (so the relative costs of the two organizational forms would evolve differently in America and Britain); and legal doctrines that enabled minority shareholders to make life more difficult for the majority (perhaps adopted at the behest of the loose cartels to impede the potential competitors). If we are to rescue Chandler's story and resolve the paradox, then the preceding laundry list suggests the appropriate research agenda.[1]

Freyer has, I believe, overstated the differences between the American and British case in two dimensions. First, while it is true that agreements that were acceptable in England were criminal violations in the United States, the threat of criminal prosecution in the United States in this era was remote.[2] It is hard to accept Freyer's implication that the criminalization of American antitrust mattered. Second, *Dr. Miles Medical Co. v. Park and Sons Co.* (220 U.S. 373

---

1. My colleague, Mark Roe, argues that the repeated fragmentation of American financial institutions influenced the evolution of the large American public corporation, giving managers considerably more control than they would have had otherwise. See, for example, Roe 1994. He suggests that efficiency effects might have been quite modest, partly because of other adaptations; now that the efficiency consequences seem to be more severe, we observe more efforts to reverse the evolutionary path. That is, while the form might display considerable path dependence, the consequences (in terms of efficiency) might be muted. This kind of efficiency spin on the path dependence story might carry over to Freyer's problem as well.

2. See Posner 1970. Of the six criminal prosecutions in 1890–1904, only one resulted in a conviction. Aside from labor cases, no one went to jail prior to 1930 (391).

[1911]) almost certainly had less impact on behavior than Freyer suggests. True, the vertical price restriction was technically unlawful. Still, the relationship between drug manufacturers, wholesalers, and retailers remained essentially unchanged in the quarter century following *Dr. Miles.* The changes that did finally come had little to do with changes in the legal regime; they had more to do with the diffusion of the automobile, radio, and television and the concomitant changes in retailing.

I want to make one more point about Freyer's paper. He has performed a useful function by reframing the questions about the origins of American antitrust policy. Too often, the debate is framed in terms of Robert Bork's claim that the goal of the Sherman Act is consumer welfare. But, as Freyer makes clear, whatever the motives of Senator Sherman and his supporters, the act itself is only a piece of the story. There is a mix of federal and state statutes and common-law doctrines dealing with questions that would now be labeled restraints of trade or antitrust, but also including matters that would now be included under the corporation-law rubric. This amalgam of rules reflected protectionist (especially from out-of-state competition) and populist responses to a changing world in which there were increased advantages from cooperation (both for achieving efficiency and for collecting monopoly rents). The paper gives us a sketch of what this more complex background looks like; it provides a nice advertisement for the book from which it is derived (Freyer 1992).

References

Freyer, Tony. 1992. *Regulating Big Business: Antitrust in Great Britain and America, 1880–1920.* Cambridge: Cambridge University Press.

Leibowitz, S. J., and Stephen E. Margolis. 1990. The Fable of the Keys. *Journal of Law and Economics* 33:1–25.

Posner, Richard A. 1970. A Statistical Study of Antitrust Enforcement. *Journal of Law and Economics* 13:365–419.

Roe, Mark J. 1994. *Strong Managers, Weak Owners: The Political Roots of American Corporate Finance.* Princeton: Princeton University Press.

III   Between Firms

7 The Evolution of Interregional Mortgage Lending Channels, 1870–1940: The Life Insurance–Mortgage Company Connection

Kenneth A. Snowden

The American mortgage market experienced a burst of financial innovation between 1870 and 1890 when several new types of intermediaries arose to facilitate the flow of mortgage credit from the Northeast and Europe to areas of settlement in the South and West.[1] But progress toward a fully integrated national mortgage market stalled when most of the new institutions failed during the mortgage crisis of the 1890s. The most important survivors were a few life insurance companies that had already become the nation's largest interregional lenders. Other large life insurance companies established interregional lending operations soon after 1900, and the industry remained the primary source of long-distance mortgage credit in the United States until the 1950s. This paper traces the historical process that brought life insurance companies to their position of dominance in the interregional mortgage market and explains why no other intermediary served the same function.

In order to lend interregionally, intermediaries had to employ loan agents who could make and enforce mortgage contracts in distant markets. But these agents also had to be monitored. A few insurance companies internalized the supervision of loan agents within elaborate branch office networks, but most contracted with other firms, called mortgage companies, to supervise loan agents for them. The life insurance–mortgage company connection dominated the interregional mortgage market in the United States because other interme-

Kenneth A. Snowden is associate professor of economics at the University of North Carolina at Greensboro.

The author thanks Naomi Lamoreaux for her encouragement, insight, and support throughout the preparation of this manuscript. He also gratefully acknowledges the comments of Charles Calomiris, Tim Guinnane, Lourdes Anllo-Vento, and the conference participants. Support for this research came from the Excellence Foundation of the University of North Carolina at Greensboro.

1. Lance Davis (1965) first articulated the connection between nineteenth-century American financial market integration and financial innovation.

diaries either did not incorporate loan agents into their lending structures or failed when they attempted to do so.

Local building associations, savings banks, and commercial banks did not use loan agents because they made mortgages only in their local markets. Many of these institutions were prohibited from lending out of state, but regulation cannot explain why they all shunned the national mortgage market. I argue in section 7.2 that local lending agencies restricted their mortgage operations to spatially concentrated markets because they were poorly designed to cope with the unique information imperfections associated with long-distance mortgage lending. To make the point I examine the notable exception: the "national" building associations of the 1880s. These intermediaries extended the cooperative mortgage lending structure popularized by local building associations to the interregional market, but nearly all of them had collapsed by 1900.

Western farm mortgage companies appeared in the 1870s specifically to make and enforce loans for eastern and European investors, first by simply brokering mortgages and later by issuing mortgage-backed securities. These companies grew rapidly in number for more than a decade, but nearly all of them failed in the 1890s. In sections 7.3 and 7.4 I examine the rise and fall of the farm mortgage companies to characterize the complex contractual arrangements that were used in the interregional market. These contracts linked borrowers to loan agents, loan agents to intermediaries, and intermediaries to investors. All three types of contracts can be rationalized as responses to the specific information asymmetries that arose in each of these bilateral relationships. A rapid increase in the supply of mortgage credit during the 1880s, however, led to a breakdown of the incentives built into the contracts and generated an episode of "overlending." So the fragility of interregional lending arrangements was responsible for the mortgage crisis of the 1890s and, as a result, the incomplete integration of the national mortgage market before 1900.

Unlike other interregional intermediaries, life insurance companies externalized their loan agent networks by establishing relationships with independent mortgage companies. This structure also proved to be fragile, however, and actually became the driving force behind the farm mortgage boom of the 1920s. In fact, the insurance companies came to dominate the national mortgage market not because they were able to avoid bouts of overlending, but because they were able to survive the subsequent mortgage crises. They did so by establishing internal monitoring structures to enforce outstanding mortgages and to manage foreclosed properties when their relationships with mortgage companies broke down. This complex inside-outside lending structure was ideally suited to withstand the instability that was an inherent characteristic of the interregional mortgage market before 1950. These themes are drawn out in sections 7.5 and 7.6, where I examine the development of the life insurance–mortgage company connection before 1900, its rapid expansion during the interwar period, and the collapse of this most durable interregional lending structure in the 1930s.

Insurance companies once again regained their dominance in the interre-

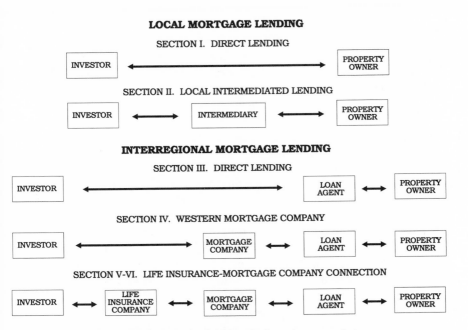

Fig. 7.1   Lending arrangements in the historical mortgage market

gional mortgage market after World War II by establishing connections with a new generation of mortgage companies. This time, however, they concentrated on federally insured and guaranteed loans. In the conclusion I argue that these government programs ameliorated the informational forces which had previously destabilized interregional lending structures, encouraged intermediaries other than insurance companies to lend over long distances, and led to an integration of the national mortgage market.

In section 7.1 I characterize the information imperfections that are associated with mortgage lending and discuss their influence on the costs of making and enforcing historical mortgage contracts. I also examine the role of "delegated monitors"—individuals or institutions who made and enforced contracts for other investors. I use these insights in the rest of the paper to explain why several types of lending arrangements were used in the historical mortgage market and why so many interregional structures failed. Some of these institutional arrangements may be unfamiliar to readers, so all of the contractual relationships that are discussed in the paper are outlined schematically in figure 7.1.

7.1   Negotiation and Enforcement of Historical Mortgage Contracts

Before 1930 American mortgage contracts differed from modern loans in several respects. They generally had maturities of only three to five years, were normally written for less than one-half of the property value, and required the borrower to pay only interest while the loan was outstanding. The entire principal was due at maturity, but it was common for the borrower to renew the mortgage several times before extinguishing the debt.[2] In this section I explain how mortgage debt was negotiated and enforced in the historical mortgage market and why investors sometimes used a third party to perform these services for them.

The owner of real estate realizes the returns from his investment by retaining ownership and earning a stream of income, or by selling the property for the present value of the income that it is expected to earn in the future. When the acquisition of property is externally financed, the outside investor must be paid from one or both of these sources. These arrangements are generally complicated by two types of information asymmetries. First, the owner directly observes information about the actual level of current returns, whereas the outside investor does not. Second, the owner can take unobserved actions that affect the level of current and future returns. "Hidden information" and "hidden action" problems have a profound influence on the contractual relationship between owner and investor and are the reasons that real estate investments are generally financed with mortgage debt.

To understand why, consider the problems of financing a real estate project with equity. Under this contract the owner might claim that the current return on the project was lower than its actual level and blame the poor performance on a bad "state of nature." Since the announcement might be true, the investor would have to accept a smaller payment than her share of the actual return. Moreover, the owner might choose to increase current returns by overworking the property and depreciating its value, opt to consume leisure rather than maintain the property's physical condition, or even sell off portable property improvements—all without the investor's knowledge. Any of these actions would lower the investor's payment below its promised level if the property were then sold. Under an equity contract, then, an uninformed investor can protect her interests only by directly observing the project's current return and the owner's actions. Contracts like these are very costly to enforce, however, because the investor must continuously monitor the property owner.

Mortgage—rather than equity—contracts have typically been used to finance real estate projects because they mitigate hidden information and action problems while generating relatively low expected enforcement costs.[3] Such contracts stipulate a fixed payment of principal and interest which is independent of the project's current return or of the property's value. Because the owner cannot affect the size of the payment made to the investor by under-

2. Snowden 1987 and 1988 provide detailed information about the lending terms that were used in the historical mortgage market.

3. Much of the discussion in this paragraph is based on Townsend's explanation (1979) of the optimality of debt when state verification is costly. Townsend's analysis is restricted to the hidden information problem, however. See also Gale and Hellwig 1985.

reporting the project's current return, he has no incentive to do so. In particular, the owner is discouraged from declaring a "false" default under a mortgage contract because the investor is then allowed to take possession of the property, sell it, and recover all principal, forgone interest, and expenses. Because the owner knows that a false default only delays full repayment and triggers a "penalty" as well (the costs of foreclosure proceedings), he is better off simply honoring the contract when he can. In addition, a mortgagor has incentives to make and maintain improvements to his property because he holds the residual claim if it is sold. So the mortgage contract is costlessly self-enforcing so long as the owner chooses to retain possession of the property and earns sufficiently high returns to make the stipulated payments.

If the owner defaults, however, the investor must actively enforce a mortgage, and the cost of doing so depends on the reasons for the delinquency. Sometimes the owner would like to make the payments stipulated by the contract, but is unable to do so because current returns are too low. In this situation the investor must first confirm that a temporary problem exists, and then normally seeks to reschedule the payments.[4] The investor incurs only modest enforcement costs during a "temporary" default, since she must only confirm that the owner continues to value his residual claim on the property. The problem is much more serious, and enforcement costs far greater, if the owner chooses to default because the market value of his property falls below the discounted value of the remaining mortgage payments. In this case the owner's residual claim on the property is worthless, and the investor already "owns" the entire project (less the foreclosure costs she must absorb to assume ownership). In these situations the hidden-information and -action problems also arise in full force because the owner has incentives to hide all of the project's return, to make no interest or property tax payments, and to sell off or depreciate all improvements. To protect her interests, therefore, the investor must monitor the property owner carefully and at great cost when foreclosure is imminent.

These elements of contract enforcement were clearly at work in the historical mortgage market. Despite Populists' claims to the contrary, investors consistently sought to accommodate mortgagors by rescheduling mortgage payments when they defaulted.[5] In fact, most states required mortgagees to exercise this type of forgiveness during the late nineteenth and early twentieth

---

4. Bagnoli and Snowden (1993) examine an environment in which the hidden-action problem becomes critical in the default state. They also provide historical evidence of the contingent nature of enforcement costs in the mortgage market during the late nineteenth and early twentieth centuries.

5. An interesting feature of the analysis in Bagnoli and Snowden 1993 is that the optimal secured debt contract calls for the investor to take all of the surplus under rescheduling, and leave the borrower at his reservation level of utility. The reason is that the original scheduled payment is minimized and, therefore, the expected cost of monitoring is lowest, when the investor's return is maximized whenever costly default occurs. This helps to explain why investors in the nineteenth century consistently claimed that "we seek interest, not land," while borrowers (and Populists) perceived that investors were trying to push them off the land during negotiations subsequent to default.

centuries. During statutory "redemption" periods of one or two years, a defaulter had the right to maintain possession of the land and to terminate the foreclosure proceeding at any time by paying all arrears (Skilton 1944). When all efforts to reschedule failed, however, the property owner was left to choose one of three actions (Bogue 1955; Woodruff 1937). Sometimes he simply abandoned the property and left the investor to initiate foreclosure proceedings. Alternatively, the owner deeded the land over to the lender for a nominal fee to avoid the costs and delays of foreclosure proceedings. The third response was worst from the investor's viewpoint; the owner could choose to remain on the land during the redemption period so that the investor had to monitor the borrower and inspect the property until foreclosure proceedings had been completed.

No matter how ownership changed hands, there were still greater costs ahead. The investor had to sell the property to liquidate her investment, and the outlays associated with this activity were substantial (Mehr 1944; Woodruff 1937). Taxes had to be paid so that ownership did not pass to the local government. If the property was not sold through the court (the procedure when foreclosure was contested), advertising and selling costs had to be borne. More important, the property had to be managed and maintained until it was sold. If the improvements had depreciated (during the redemption period, in anticipation of deeding the land, or as a result of abandonment), investments had to be made to bring the land back to salable condition. The investor would often lease the land to a tenant until a buyer could be found. While this approach yielded income, it also required intensive monitoring to collect rental payments and to make sure that the tenant did not depreciate property improvements. Therefore, the investor would break even on a foreclosure only if the sale of the property covered the original payments that she had been promised and the substantial expenses that were associated with seizing encumbered real estate and liquidating her investment.

The important point is that the enforcement costs associated with mortgage lending varied across contingencies: they were negligible so long as the project's current return was sufficient to cover interest charges and the property owner preferred to retain ownership; increased modestly if the borrower defaulted because of a transient shock to the return stream; but rose to much higher levels when foreclosure became imminent. So expected enforcement costs under a historical mortgage contract depended critically on the probability of default and foreclosure. Investors were compensated for these costs by a premium that was stipulated in the contract when the mortgage was negotiated. The investor absorbed all "enforcement risk," however, because she did not know whether any particular loan would involve low or high enforcement cost when it was made. We shall see below that the allocation of enforcement risk played a critical role in all interregional lending arrangements.

The theory of optimal contracting predicts that agents will choose the least-cost mechanism from the set of incentive-compatible contracts. So expected enforcement costs under mortgages should have been lower than those under other types of contracts that could have been used to finance real estate investments. In fact, to lower expected enforcement costs investors used a rule of thumb in the historical market that may appear conservative when compared to modern practice—"the principle of sound . . . mortgage [lending] is that the loan shall not exceed one-half the value of the land even though [the property] be abandoned, the improvements destroyed, and the land reduced practically to its primitive state" (Robins 1916, 124). The idea, of course, was to avoid foreclosure (and very high enforcement costs) by restricting total debt payments to a level well below the property's current value. A serious problem with this system, however, was that the risk of foreclosure was completely determined by the accuracy of the property appraisal which, in turn, depended heavily on the judgment, experience, and honesty of the person performing it (Hurd 1923, 197). The great danger was that the property might be overvalued during negotiation, in which case its owner would have been more likely to renege on the contract if property values declined during the life of the loan.

I have spoken as if investors perform all negotiation and enforcement themselves, and, in fact, most American mortgage loans were directly negotiated and enforced by investors until the early twentieth century. But I am interested here in explaining the development of more complex lending arrangements in which investors contracted with third parties to negotiate and enforce mortgages for them. Financial intermediaries normally take up the role of the third party in loan transactions, and by 1900 savings banks and building associations had become the nation's most important sources of intermediated mortgage debt. But these institutions operated only within local markets. All interregional loans, on the other hand, were made through loan agents who negotiated and enforced the mortgage for a distant investor. Sometimes these individual agents would contract directly with an investor, but most interregional mortgage credit passed through complex hierarchical arrangements in which one or more financial institutions intermediated the relationship between investor and loan agent. The goal of this paper is to explain why these complex forms of intermediation arose in the interregional market, and why so many of them failed.

To do so I appeal to a framework that has recently been used to show that intermediaries act as "delegated monitors" when they negotiate and enforce information-intensive loans.[6] The critical insight of this new understanding of financial intermediation is that a delegated monitor must have incentives to negotiate and enforce loans in the investor's best interest. This requirement, which I refer to as credibility, stems from the fact that the intermediary, rather than the investor, observes the private information of the borrower. Unless its behavior is constrained, there are several ways that the intermediary could use

---

6. Diamond 1984 and Williamson 1986 show why delegated monitors arise when loan contracts are subject only to hidden information.

this information advantage to raise its own payoffs at the expense of the investor: by negotiating loans carelessly; by selecting high-risk, high-interest loans without informing the investor; or by falsely reporting loan defaults. It can be costly, however, to provide an intermediary with incentives not to engage in these behaviors. So the intermediary qualifies as a cost-effective and credible delegated monitor only if the information asymmetry between it and the investor can be ameliorated without exhausting its relative cost advantage over investors in the negotiation and enforcement of loans.[7]

I argue below that the uneven and irregular development of the interregional mortgage market resulted from the difficulty of establishing lending structures within which loan agents could serve as delegated monitors. I will show that the primary determinant of mortgage negotiation and enforcement costs was proximity to the property owner—so loan agents clearly enjoyed a cost advantage over distant investors. The vexing problem was to establish the agents' credibility. In sections 7.2 and 7.3 I argue that locally focused intermediaries and most individual investors found it prohibitively costly to monitor distant loan agents, and so were shut out of the interregional market. Then I show that the intermediated lending structures that were specifically designed to incorporate loan agents were inherently unstable.

7.2   Intermediated Mortgage Lending within Local Markets

In this section I consider intermediaries that restricted their mortgage lending operations to local markets before 1900. The discussion provides historical evidence that proximity to the borrower was the critical determinant of the costs of mortgage negotiation and enforcement and that this constraint represented a particularly troublesome impediment to the development of interregional intermediaries. I also explain why intermediated structures that operated successfully in local markets did not enter the national mortgage market.

Two of these intermediaries, mutual savings banks and local building associations, rank among the most successful American financial innovations of the nineteenth century. Mutual savings banks were introduced in a few northeastern cities in the 1810s and 1820s to serve as a repository for the savings of the working poor. Building associations, on the other hand, were first established in Philadelphia during the 1830s so that members could cooperatively finance

---

7. In Diamond 1984, for example, the cost advantage of intermediation arises because individual investors must share loans in the absence of a delegated monitor because of a wealth constraint. No single investor can credibly promise to act as a faithful delegated monitor for the others, so each one must enforce the contract separately. He then uses the law of large numbers to show that the delegated monitor can charge borrowers an infinitesimal premium and drive to zero the probability that the return on the loan portfolio will fall below the deposit liability. Since it is nearly impossible for the delegated monitor to actually default, he cannot falsely declare that he has.

the purchase of homes. These institutions became so popular that by 1900 savings banks were operating in seventeen states and building associations had been organized in every state and more than two thousand cities (Lintner 1948, 49; Rotella and Snowden 1992). Both institutions specialized in raising funds from small investors who could not have made mortgage loans directly. In 1890, for example, the average deposit in a savings bank was $355, and the average shareholding in a building association was $303, while home mortgages ranged in average size from $900 in the North Central states to $1,600 in the Northeast (Lintner 1948, 49; Wright 1893, 15; U.S. Census Office 1895a, 75). But these modest investments added up. In 1890 these two intermediaries claimed more than five million depositors and members, and held 60 percent of the nation's intermediated mortgage debt.

With so many members dispersed so widely across space, these intermediaries could have become large in size and lent broadly within and across the nation's urban markets. By doing so they could have become large and highly diversified delegated monitors, and stimulated the flow of mortgage funds among regional markets. But mutuals and building associations chose to lend only within their local markets. Both lending structures relied on social, cultural, and economic relationships in their communities to make and enforce loans at lower cost than individual investors, and to establish their credibility as delegated monitors. Outside community boundaries, however, they were neither cost-effective nor credible.

Mutual savings banks were organized and run by local business leaders and entrepreneurs who already had accumulated knowledge about local real estate markets and lending conditions. They were less qualified, however, to make and enforce loans in more distant markets. Two early antebellum mutuals, for example, adopted "investment polic[ies] . . . marked by a considerable degree of provincialism. It is almost as if the managers refused to invest in any asset that they could not touch" (Davis and Payne 1958, 404). John Lintner (1948, 406–8) explained why mutuals continued to behave in the same way during the early twentieth century. He found that between 1918 and 1931 Massachusetts' savings banks experienced a 3.8 percent net loss rate on mortgages that were made close to the home office (in the same or adjoining cities), while the loss rate was 7.1 percent on loans made two or three cities distant, and 10 percent on those located four or more cities away from the bank. He concluded that "[t]he results clearly point up the greater hazard of lending outside the area with which the bank is most familiar and within which its lending facilities are most adequate" (Lintner 1948, 408).

Building associations relied on its members to make and enforce mortgages cooperatively, and had to restrict their activities to areas that were already well known to the membership and easy for them to observe. Members pledged to purchase association shares equal in value to the principal of the home mortgage loan for which they planned to apply in the future. The installment payments on these shares were collected at mandatory monthly meetings, and each member eventually received his loan as the share payments accumulated. Members jointly monitored the condition of the property that secured the others' loans, and the ability of other members to make share and interest payments as promised (Bodfish 1931; Clark and Chase 1925). Not surprisingly, building associations were often small, single-neighborhood organizations. In fact, in 1890 more than twenty-three hundred building associations operated in just the twenty-eight largest cities in the country. Each averaged only 314 members. The focus on community lending continued during the late nineteenth and early twentieth centuries even after elected officers and committees of members assumed the responsibility for the mortgage business of most associations. These individuals were drawn from the general membership and had no special knowledge of remote loan markets, much less experience in them (Bodfish 1931).

Besides the cost advantage, these two mutual organizations also used their local character to establish credibility. The general membership of these mutual organizations need not have been overly concerned that the trustees or member committees would exploit their informational advantage because none of these "insiders" held residual claims on their institutions' portfolios. The greater danger was that trustees or member committees, who served without pay, might neglect their duties or select and enforce mortgages carelessly. These individuals had strong incentives not to shirk their responsibilities, however, because to do so risked the loss of their reputations as well as the imposition of sanctions within their local community.

The trustees of mutual savings banks were self-proclaimed philanthropists who publicly committed themselves to help the poor by providing a safe outlet for the savings of the working class. The goal was to raise the material and spiritual welfare of the unfortunate and to relieve the "better-off" citizens from having to care for the destitute population. Whatever other motives trustees may have had, and there has been controversy on this score, there is little doubt that a failure of a savings bank would have resulted in substantial public embarrassment for its organizers (Olmstead 1976, 108–16). This may explain why "[f]or the country as a whole, the total losses to depositors over their entire 131 year history have been less than 1/4 of 1% of the deposit balances now outstanding" (Lintner 1948, 21). It seems unlikely that the trustees would have shown such care and diligence if they had been serving members located far away from their own communities. The officers of building associations, on the other hand, had incentives to perform their duties faithfully because their closest neighbors and friends relied on them to do so. Many associations served tightly knit ethnic and religious communities, so an irresponsible member or director could expect to suffer social sanctions as well as a loss of face.

The reader may worry that regulatory restrictions, rather than the cost and reputational advantages of localization, imposed a narrow geographic focus on these institutions. Mutual savings banks were prohibited from lending out of state until the 1950s, but we have already seen that they limited their activities to markets that were even more concentrated. The case is even clearer for the building associations. Most states did not even begin to regulate these organizations until the 1890s, but by then the members of some four thousand associations had already decided to restrict the lending operations of their cooperatives to their home counties (Rosenthal 1888, 103). Building associations were prohibited from lending out of state only after the "national" associations had unsuccessfully attempted to extend this lending structure to the interregional market in the 1880s and 1890s (Bodfish 1931, 113). It will be useful to briefly examine their story.

Beginning in the mid-1880s the "nationals" began to recruit members and make loans across and within broad regional markets (Bodfish 1931, chap. 7). These organizations attracted members by emphasizing the benefits that could be derived by extending the building-association form over a wider area: greater safety (because the loan portfolio was geographically diverse), higher earnings (because the association could penetrate markets with high mortgage rates), and lower expenses (because of efficiencies of large scale). The officers of the nationals could not cost-effectively make and enforce mortgages from headquarters, of course, and so local loan boards were established to perform these functions in markets hundreds of miles away. While these delegated monitors were knowledgeable about their home markets (many were real estate agents and developers), they were given no incentives to place the interests of an anonymous membership above their own. The directors of the nationals should have monitored loan agents of this type with great care. It would have been very costly to do so, however, and the nationals established no formal mechanisms to assure the reliability of their local boards. So it was no surprise when many mortgages went into default after 1893 and the nationals began to acquire substantial amounts of overvalued real estate. The end of the national movement is generally dated at 1896, after the failure of the largest national association in the country. A wave of closings followed, and only 6 out of 240 national associations survived the century.

The local associations believed that the failure of the nationals provided compelling evidence that long-distance cooperative mortgage lending structures were inherently unreliable. A more disinterested group, the Massachusetts Bank Commissioners, reached the same conclusion: "A co-operative bank is in all respects a local institution. Its members should be taken from the immediate vicinity where it is formed, and its loans made upon real estate in the same locality" (Eldredge 1893). Thus, a broad range of evidence, opinion, and experience all point to the same conclusion: intermediated structures that were successful in local mortgage markets could not lend over wider areas both credibly and at low cost.

Before considering the interregional market, it will be useful to provide a more precise picture of the significance of local intermediated lending channels. Table 7.1 reports the relative importance of these institutions by region

Table 7.1   Structure of Intermediated Mortgage Lending, 1890–93

			Held by Local Lenders[b]				Held by Interregional Lenders[b]			
			Banks (%)						Mortgage Companies	
				Savings		Local Building	Life Insurance	National Building		
Region[a]	Total Mortgage Debt (millions of $)	Held by Intermediaries (millions of $)	Commercial	Mutual	Stock	Associations	Companies (%)	Associations (%)	Bonds (%)	Passed-Through[e] (millions of $)
Northeast										
New England	519	328 (63%)	—	90	1	4	4	0.2	—	—(0%)
Mid-Atlantic	2,586	637 (25%)	1	53	—	22	24	0.7	—	— —
North Central										
East North Central	1,027	315 (31%)	4	3	5	49	35	3	—	—
West North Central	603	144 (24%)	2	—	18	10	41	7	23	67 (11%)
South										
South Atlantic	126	24 (19%)	3	1	6	61	5	25	—	3 (2%)
East South Central	173	39 (22%)	1	—	1	63	9	26	—	—
West South Central	658	149 (23%)	7	—	1	27	29	3	33	121 (18%)
West										
Pacific	324	158 (49%)	14	—	71	12	2	1	0.2	3 (1%)
U.S.	6,017	1,793 (30%)	3	36	9	24	22	3	5	194 (3%)

Sources: Mortgage debt outstanding: U.S. Census Office 1895b. Commercial and savings banks: U.S. Comptroller of Currency 1895b. Local and national building associations: Wright 1893. Life insurance companies: Pritchett 1977. Mortgage companies: Massachusetts 1890–95; New York 1891–97.

Notes: Debt for 1 January 1890, while debt held by intermediaries for as close to 1 January 1893 as possible. Debt allocated to region of intermediary's headquarters, except for the insurance companies.

[a]Regions are New England: CT, ME, MA, NH, RI, VT; Mid-Atlantic: DE, NJ, NY, PA, MD, DC; East North Central: IL, IN, MI, OH, WI; West North Central: IA, MN, NB, ND, SD, WY, MT; South Atlantic: VA, WV, FL, GA, NC, SC; East South Central: AL, KY, MS, TN, LA; West South Central: MO, AR, KS, TX, CO, NM; Pacific: AZ, ID, NV, UT, CA, OR, WA.

[b]The percentage shown in the table is the share of "Held by Intermediaries" in each region.

[c]Mortgages held by insurance companies are allocated to the region where they were originated.

[d]Debentures issued by mortgage companies backed by mortgage portfolios.

[e]"Passed-through" mortgages are originated by mortgage companies but held by individuals. In parentheses is the percentage of the total regional mortgage debt passed through.

and for the nation as a whole. The numbers in the table are rough: mortgage debt outstanding was measured by the Census Office as of 1 January 1890, whereas the amounts of debt held by intermediaries were taken from a variety of government reports prepared between 1890 and 1893. My aim is to provide a sense of relative magnitudes, however, and the estimates are reliable enough for this purpose.

As noted earlier, mutual savings banks and local building associations were the most important institutional mortgage lenders in the late nineteenth century and together held three-fifths of the nation's intermediated mortgage debt. When deposit and stock savings banks are included, the share supplied by strictly local lending agencies increases to three-quarters. In addition, we shall see later that many insurance companies were also lending close to home at this time. So the vast majority of all intermediated mortgage lending was local in character right before the turn of the century.

The rest of the paper focuses on the interregional market. I have already discussed the national associations which, for all of their notoriety, contributed only 3 percent of the intermediated lending flow in 1893 and disappeared altogether by 1900. Life insurance and mortgage companies were the only other institutional channels through which interregional mortgage lending took place in the early 1890s.

7.3 Loan Agents as Delegated Monitors

We have seen that mortgage lending was primarily a local activity before 1900. An accurate appraisal required a detailed inspection of the property and an intimate familiarity with the determinants of current and future property values in that market. Effective monitoring of a defaulter entailed continuous, "hands-on" contact and periodic reappraisals of the property as well. The requirement for local supervision and control became even greater if the lender acquired the land through deed or foreclosure. So an investor could lend interregionally only if she employed a representative located close to the property to make and enforce the mortgage contract. These loan agents were used by every intermediary or individual investor who participated in the national mortgage market. In this section I show how loan agents established themselves as low-cost and credible delegated monitors.

Because proximity to the borrower was the critical determinant of the cost of mortgage making, loan agents normally resided in the county in which they conducted business. To be an effective delegated monitor the agent also had to be familiar with local real estate conditions. We have seen that national building associations appointed real estate brokers and developers to their local loan boards. Allan Bogue (1955) has documented a similar pattern for the Davenports, a New York family that invested heavily in farm mortgages in Illinois, Iowa, Kansas, and Nebraska between 1870 and 1900. The family chose either lawyers, real estate promoters, or, most frequently, bankers to serve as their loan agents in all four states. Agents like these could observe information about individual owners and property values in their local markets at low cost.

There were individuals willing to serve eastern investors in most western towns, but a reliable loan agent first had to be selected and trained. Mortgage lending was a complex undertaking that required a thorough understanding of the investor's particular preferences and methods, and the ability to implement these with good judgment. The Davenports sent a son to live in Illinois for several years in the 1860s to establish the family's western mortgage loan business (Bogue 1955, 9–11). During this time he learned how to select borrowers, set loan terms, and maintain lending records. He also developed techniques for handling delinquencies, foreclosure proceedings, and land sales. Potential agents had general knowledge of these matters, but the Davenports corresponded extensively with new agents to instruct them about the family's particular procedures and methods. Furthermore, after training an agent, the investor still had to evaluate his competence and judgment. The Davenports typically made a few loans through a new loan agent and evaluated his performance on these before allowing him to make more loans (Bogue 1955, 62). Investors as large as the Davenports, who made $4 million of loans in thirty years, could spread the fixed costs of selecting and training a loan agent over many loans. For small investors, however, these costs were prohibitive.

A second, and greater, difficulty associated with interregional mortgage lending was that the loan agent had to be given incentives to negotiate and enforce loans faithfully. Like any delegated monitor, the loan agent observed hidden information about the borrower before and after the loan had been made. He had both opportunity and incentive, therefore, to increase his own well-being at the investor's expense by making high-risk loans, sharing "hidden returns" with the property owner, or supplying too little enforcement effort. In addition, the opportunities were greater and incentives stronger because agents had collateral interests in their local real estate markets.

So investors monitored loan agents to assure their performance. The Davenports, for example, corresponded frequently even with their most experienced agents and sent a family member west each year to evaluate their agents' work directly. Supervision of this type protected against gross negligence or fraud, but could not assure that the agent was diligent when negotiating or enforcing each loan. So a mechanism other than supervision was required to provide loan agents with incentives to be credible delegated monitors.

To explain the mechanism that was used I must be more precise about the structure of the contract between an investor and a loan agent. The agent agreed to search for prospective borrowers, take their applications, perform appraisals, and forward the papers for the investor's approval. If the investor accepted the loan, the agent was compensated with a commission. The commission was calculated as a percentage of the loan's principal and was normally paid by the borrower when the loan was closed. The agent then passed the mortgage to the investor and agreed to collect payments and to enforce the loan until it was repaid.

This contract had a peculiar feature. The uninformed investor bore all of the monetary risk, while the informed agent received a commission that was fixed and independent of the loan's outcome. We have seen earlier that the mortgage loan itself specifies a fixed payment for the uninformed party (the investor), and made the informed party (the property owner) the residual claimant. It appears, therefore, that the contract between investor and loan agent placed risk on the wrong party and exacerbated, rather than solved, the hidden-information and -action problems. Why would an agent select a safe mortgage or enforce a loan if he suffered no monetary loss when the borrower defaulted?

The contract can be rationalized on informational grounds when the agent's payoff and incentives are clearly understood. Under the contract, the agent faced the risk associated with searching for a mortgage loan. He might spend considerable time and effort taking applications and making appraisals before finding a loan that the investor would approve. If the investor did not approve, of course, the agent received no compensation. Had agents been compensated with a salary, on the other hand, they could have expended no effort, reported that no qualified borrowers were available, and still received compensation. The commission system placed the costs and risks of search on the agent so he had an incentive to discontinue negotiations with unqualified borrowers quickly and to pursue only high-quality applications that the investor was likely to approve.

The agent's incentives to enforce an outstanding mortgage under this contract are less obvious. Recall that intensive monitoring was required when the borrower defaulted or foreclosure became imminent. Under the contract, however, the agent received a commission when the loan was closed and no additional compensation if he had to enforce the loan later.[8] For this reason the agent's commission had to include a premium to compensate him for the effort he expected to apply if the loan went bad. Once the loan had been made, however, the agent assumed the enforcement risk of the loan while the investor remained exposed to monetary losses.

Note that this feature of the commission contract strengthened the agent's incentive to search for high-quality loans. If the investor had agreed instead to compensate enforcement effort only when a default actually occurred, the

8. One could argue that the enforcement problem would have disappeared if the commission was paid during the loan period, or after the debt had been extinguished. Commissions were sometimes taken as second mortgages. The costs to the agent of enforcing a defaulted loan were much greater than the commission, whenever it was paid. Recall that the commission compensated the agent for expected enforcement costs and that foreclosure was a low-probability event most of the time. Even if the entire commission was paid after the loan was repaid, the agent would still need some other inducement to not walk away. The commission was most frequently paid lump-sum when the loan was closed, as I discuss here.

agent could have created a demand for these services by making risky loans look safe. Under the commission system, however, the agent imposed costs and risk on himself by recommending a low-quality loan to the investor so long as he intended to enforce the mortgage if it went bad. The great danger with the commission system, in fact, was that the agent might simply walk away from a defaulted loan rather than apply the effort required to enforce it. Even worse, if the agent were not committed to enforcing a bad loan, he would have been far less concerned about its quality during negotiation.

The contract, therefore, had to provide the agent with incentives to enforce a delinquent mortgage even though he received no explicit payment for the substantial amounts of time and effort that were involved. To provide these incentives the agent had to expect to lose something of value if he walked away from a bad loan. Investors in the interregional mortgage market entered into long-term relationships with their agents and threatened to discontinue lending through them if they failed to enforce a loan. It was the promise of future commissions, therefore, that provided the loan agent with the incentive to enforce outstanding loans.

The effectiveness of this mechanism depended on several factors: the agent's prospects for employment with other investors, the credibility of the investor's threat to terminate the relationship, and the willingness of the investor to continue lending within the agent's market. For example, if the agent's reputation mattered—so that no other investor would hire him if he shirked on enforcement—then the mechanism worked well.[9] Later in the paper, however, I will emphasize situations when it did not. In particular, the mechanism broke down if there was an increase in the demand for the agent's services outside the relationship, or if the investor refused to approve applications for new loans while other mortgages remained outstanding. Moreover, the mechanism was weakened if the investor was reluctant or unable to bear the costs of selecting and training a new agent. We shall see that a combination of these factors arose periodically in the historical mortgage market and played an important role in the collapse of interregional lending structures.

For the enforcement mechanism to work at all, of course, the investor had to be large enough so that she could credibly promise a steady flow of future commissions. I emphasized earlier that large investors also enjoyed scale economies when they selected and trained new agents. For both reasons the small investor faced formidable obstacles if she attempted to hire a loan agent directly. During the late nineteenth century, however, mortgage rates in the West were high enough to attract many eastern investors who were not as wealthy as the Davenports. To mobilize this potential flow of mortgage credit, a new

9. Reputation effects in the investor–loan agent relationship were likely to have been weak in areas of recent settlement, which was the area where loan agents were used most frequently. A distant investor would find it difficult to observe the complete history of a prospective loan agent's relationship with all previous investors.

mechanism had to arise—one that could cost-effectively mediate the relationship between investors and loan agents.

7.4   Western Mortgage Companies as Monitors of Loan Agents

Farm mortgage companies first began to monitor loan agents for eastern investors during the 1850s.[10] Most were organized by successful loan agents who sought to expand the volume and geographic scope of their mortgage brokerage businesses. The industry grew rapidly during the 1870s and 1880s as the pace of settlement accelerated in the plains states, and by 1890 more than two hundred of these agencies were selling western farm loans in eastern and European markets (Herrick and Ingalls 1915, 8–16; Frederiksen 1894; see table 7.1). In this section I show how mortgage companies established their credibility as monitors of loan agents and explain why that mechanism broke down when the supply of interregional mortgage credit expanded rapidly during the 1880s. I argue that nearly all mortgage companies collapsed during the 1890s because they had "overlent" in response to competitive market pressures several years earlier.

The western mortgage companies used sophisticated methods to negotiate and broker loans. A network of field agents located borrowers, filled out standardized applications, appraised property, and passed the information along to the home office. The company reviewed these materials, along with the agent's confidential assessment of the quality of each loan, and determined whether the borrower was creditworthy. If so, the loan then had to be matched with an investor located thousands of miles away. Investors were solicited by advertisements in the eastern and European press, by sales trips of company representatives, and through offices set up in New York and other major financial centers (Bogue 1955). After receiving funds from the investor, the company forwarded a loan application to her for approval. If the investor approved, the company closed the loan and formally assigned it to the investor. At this point, the agent (and frequently the company) received a commission paid by the borrower. The company then collected interest payments and sent them to the investor minus a one-half to one percentage point servicing fee.

This system of negotiating and servicing loans offered several advantages over the methods used by investors who dealt directly with loan agents. Most important, the mortgage companies provided "hands on" monitoring of loan agents by full-time traveling supervisors who also evaluated lending conditions in established and potential loan markets. In this way the mortgage company provided much closer supervision of loan agents than individual investors even as large as the Davenports could undertake. The companies also reduced the

10. Mortgage companies went by a variety of names in the historical mortgage market—loan and trust, loan and debenture, and investment companies among them. I refer to all of these organizations as mortgage companies.

need to monitor the loan agent by centralizing many administrative functions, such as title search and interest collection, in the home office. Finally, the mortgage company solved one of the vexing problems faced by eastern investors in the West—large balances of idle funds. The Davenports constantly prodded their agents to locate good borrowers and "get our money working" as repayments on existing loans were received or after funds had been sent West to make new loans. Mortgage companies, on the other hand, generated continuous flows of loan applications and reduced balances awaiting investment by quickly matching investors and borrowers. The J. B. Watkins Company, for example, began to pay interest to investors two weeks after receiving their funds even if there were no loans immediately available for assignment.

Because of its cost advantages in making and administering loans, the western mortgage company attracted the funds of investors of modest means for whom the costs of directly selecting, training, and monitoring agents would have been prohibitive. The company also had to establish its credibility as a monitor of loan agents, however, because an information asymmetry arose between it and the investors. The return on each mortgage brokered by the companies was determined by three factors: the exogenous risk of the project being financed, the quality and intensity of the services provided by the loan agent, and the companies' own diligence in supervising the agent. The mortgage company observed information about all three influences, but the uninformed investor could not distinguish which factor had been responsible if a borrower defaulted. The mortgage company had both incentive and opportunity, therefore, to raise its own payoff by monitoring loan agents carelessly or by underreporting the loan payments made by borrowers.

Mortgage companies assured investors that they would not exploit their informational advantage by guaranteeing the loans they sold. One practitioner, Kingman Robins, showed a clear understanding that the guarantee served to establish credibility when he noted that a mortgage company "cannot allow [its] client to suffer the loss of a single dollar, for [s]he would make no allowances in case of loss—[s]he would lose confidence in [the company] and would wholly discontinue buying from [it]" (Robins 1916, 84). The mechanism worked informally in the 1870s. Investors were instructed to return delinquent mortgages to the company and were either repaid or given a replacement loan in return. Custom eventually became formalized in the 1880s when mortgage companies started to guarantee the principal and interest on the mortgages they brokered—the first use of mortgage loan insurance.

By guaranteeing its loans the mortgage company pledged to absorb all of the enforcement risk that investors faced in the interregional market. It could do so at low cost because of its scale and location. After a default, the loan agent monitored the borrower and rescheduled the loan if possible. If not, the loan was turned over to the legal department of the company, which conducted foreclosure actions from the home office. The farm then became the responsibility of a property manager who would rent the land until it could be advertised and sold. Establishing an in-house enforcement operation as sophisticated as this involved substantial fixed costs, but the mortgage company could spread these costs over many loans. The company also diversified away most enforcement risk by making loans over a relatively wide geographic area, and so could offer the guarantee to investors without demanding large risk premia.[11]

In the 1880s some mortgage companies adopted a second method of guaranteeing the investor's return. They incorporated, held individual mortgages in eastern trust accounts, and issued mortgage bonds backed by the loans.[12] Each bond series was secured by a different pool of mortgages, but all of the series were effectively secured by the company's total assets and so were referred to as debentures. The American mortgage bond market of the 1880s and 1890s never approached the size or depth of its European counterparts, but the volume of debentures expanded rapidly enough to alarm eastern regulators (Frederiksen 1894). By 1891 New York, Massachusetts, Connecticut, and several other northeastern states required annual financial reports from those "foreign" mortgage companies that sold loans within their borders. These reports were then published for the benefit of the public, but always with the warning that the regulators could not verify the quality of the loans that stood behind debentures because it was too costly for an outsider to inspect the properties that secured individual mortgages (New York 1891; Massachusetts 1890). Despite the warnings, eastern investors had purchased $93 million of mortgage debentures by 1893.[13]

Questions were being raised at the same time about the quality of the individual mortgages brokered by the newer and more aggressive companies. Edward Darrow (1892), the owner of a Minnesota mortgage company, wrote a guide to the western mortgage market in which he cautioned investors not to accept western loans too easily. He advised investors to demand that a photograph of the property be sent along with the loan application and appraisal, and then to examine these materials with their own lawyer and architect. Darrow also cautioned about difficulties that often arose when an investor attempted to exercise a loan guarantee—especially since some disreputable companies had no intention of honoring it.

Darrow was apprehensive that the rapid expansion of the western mortgage

---

11. The J. B. Watkins Company, for example, was one of the first companies to be established in Kansas and eventually extended its operations over five states and sold $20 million of mortgages between 1872 and 1893. See Bogue 1955 for an extensive discussion of its operations.

12. Mortgage bonds had first been introduced to the United States during the antebellum period (Sparks 1932). Brewer 1976 provides an excellent discussion of mortgage companies in the Northeast that issued mortgage-backed bonds in the early 1870s. Several of these companies were operating in the West at the same time as the western companies I discuss here. For a discussion of how the mortgage bond was imported from Europe to the United States during the nineteenth century, see Snowden 1993.

13. Table 7.1 reports the regional distribution of both passed-through mortgages and debentures bonds for this year.

business in the 1880s had created an intense competition for borrowers that threatened the reputation and credibility of all mortgage companies. In particular, Darrow believed that some of the newer companies were sending poorly secured loans to the East and were at risk of failure if the land boom abated. That process began in the late 1880s as droughts appeared in several areas. Most mortgage companies were able to survive these early pressures, but by the early 1890s the collapse had begun. Eastern regulators supervised 167 companies in 1893 but discontinued their published reports only four years later because so few companies remained in operation. In fact, only 14 survived to join the Farm Mortgage Banking Association twenty years later (Frederiksen 1894; Robins 1916).

To explain why western farm mortgage companies collapsed, I must describe an additional feature of the historical mortgage market. Borrowers in recently settled areas usually applied for their first mortgage after they had already acquired and partially improved their property. These loans were written for only three or five years and were normally renewed two or three times before the debt was extinguished. The appraisal was a particularly important negotiating point when dealing with borrowers who already owned their land, because their equity in the property represented their down payment. Mortgage companies did not make loans that exceeded one-half, or sometimes one-third, of the property's appraised value. Therefore, borrowers who already owned their land pressed for high valuations so they could qualify for larger loans or lower rates.

A reliable loan agent resisted pressures to inflate appraisals, but Darrow's observation suggests that the newer, aggressive companies used this practice to compete for borrowers. Other observers confirmed his fears. W. F. Mappin (1889, 440) argued that the increase in the supply of eastern credit during the 1880s created intense competition among mortgage companies, and that many were accepting loans that would have been rejected as poorly secured in normal times. Recalling this period, the secretary of one western mortgage company remarked, "I found drafts, money orders, and currency heaped on my desk every morning and could not loan the money as fast as it came in." This same company finally resorted to hiring inexperienced loan agents who made mortgages based on "absurd" appraisals (Harger 1906, 572).

The older, established companies should have maintained loan quality in the face of these pressures because they had been building reputations for safety and conservatism for more than a decade. But their agents in the field found that they could not compete for borrowers if they based loan terms on accurate appraisals. So even experienced and reliable loan agents began to recommend marginal applications for approval. In order to retain their agents the mortgage companies felt pressured to approve loans that they knew were poorly secured. Allan Bogue's incisive account of the Watkins Company's experience makes the point best.

During 1886 and 1887 the flow of eastern and foreign capital into the western mortgage business was at its flood. Companies competed strenuously for agents. Greater powers of discretion were placed in the hands of these men than ever before. Greater opportunities for lending unhealthily large sums of money on inadequate security were also present. Although the mortgage companies had inspectors who checked the work of these local agents, it was impossible for them to examine the security behind every loan. . . . If the traveling inspectors were too strict, the local representative could easily find other companies with funds to loan, and the original sponsor would see its flow of applications diminish. That Stanton and Sprankle [agent supervisors for the Watkins Company] endeavored to keep their agents in line is undoubted; that they unconsciously were stampeded into some of the excesses of their competitors is probable. Sprankle argued in February 1888, "One year ago sub-agents and borrowers run [*sic*] the loaning business in this state to suit themselves." (1955, 144)

The mortgage companies, like individual investors, established long-term relationships with their loan agents so that the threat of termination represented an effective incentive device. But the mechanism turned out to be a two-edged sword when the supply of mortgage funds and the demand for agents' services increased dramatically in the 1880s. By then the established companies had invested heavily in selecting and training their agents and relied on them to help enforce mortgages that were already outstanding. Had the companies refused to approve the marginal loans that their agents were sending forward, they would have had to discontinue lending operations and gone out of business. In order to retain their agents, therefore, even the largest and oldest companies began to pass through mortgages that they knew were of poor quality.

I refer to this behavior as overlending. Darrow, Watkins, and other insiders understood the implications of making loans on the basis of inflated appraisals, because the practice increased the average probability of foreclosure and introduced systematic enforcement risk to the western mortgage market. In this environment any reversal of land prices was certain to lead many borrowers to default at once, and to drive enforcement costs far above expected levels.

Thus, the collapse of the western mortgage companies in the 1890s was directly attributable to high rates of default and foreclosure on mortgages they had made in the late 1880s.[14] The newer companies failed first, either because they had made the poorest quality loans or because they did not have the resources to both honor their guarantee to investors and enforce the loans that had gone bad. As late as 1892 New York authorities continued to maintain that the crisis would affect only the most recently established firms. But older companies survived longer only by continuing to market low-quality loans, often on the same land they had acquired through foreclosure. By 1895 nearly

14. For an empirical examination of the failure of the Watkins Company, see Snowden and Abu Saba 1993.

all of the mortgage companies were in receivership and had left their investors with large amounts of unsalable land.

The transfer of land from mortgage company to investor created a powerful feedback effect that deepened and prolonged the mortgage crisis of the 1890s. Investors had neither the expertise nor the ability to manage, maintain, and sell foreclosed land, and had entrusted their funds to the mortgage company so that they would never have to perform these functions. So the land boom of the 1880s quickly turned to a land glut as eastern investors and the receivers of failed mortgage companies tried to liquidate their landholdings as quickly as possible. The sell-off reinforced the downward spiral in property values, caused more borrowers to default, and additional mortgage companies to fail. The lesson would not soon be forgotten, as individual investors never again entered the interregional mortgage market in the numbers or with the enthusiasm of the 1880s.

By 1900 the interregional mortgage market lay in institutional disarray. The most important institutional lenders, savings banks and building associations, were firmly committed to lending only within their local area. Meanwhile the two innovations designed specifically to facilitate an interregional flow of funds, national building associations and western mortgage companies, were both in ruins. Their failures had revealed the difficulties of establishing and maintaining incentive structures for distant loan agents. They also demonstrated that any investor who entered the interregional mortgage market faced the real possibility of one day having to enforce mortgages herself. By 1900 one type of investor had gained experience both in negotiating and enforcing mortgage loans interregionally: the life insurance company.

7.5 Interregional Lending by Life Insurance Companies before 1900: The Development of Links with Mortgage Companies

Before 1900 life insurance companies were the third-largest source of intermediated mortgage credit in the United States (see table 7.1). The majority of the industry's lending operations were local in character because most companies were permitted by law to lend only within the state where they were headquartered.[15] The notable exceptions were a few firms located in Connecticut and Wisconsin that had been granted broad lending powers right after the Civil War. For the next thirty years five of these companies—Aetna, Connecticut Mutual, Phoenix, Travelers', and Northwestern Mutual—dominated the interregional mortgage business of the life insurance industry. They made loans on commercial property and farms from Indiana to the western plains, and by 1890 together held 30 percent of the industry's mortgage portfolio. During the period this handful of companies settled upon three organizational principles

---

15. By 1870 New Jersey, Ohio, California, Iowa, Kansas, Kentucky, and, most notably, New York had prohibited companies headquartered in their states from lending out of state.

that would shape the industry's lending structures well into the twentieth century: (1) the separation of mortgage lending operations from insurance policy sales; (2) a reliance on independent mortgage companies to negotiate and service loans; and (3) the internalization of the property management component of mortgage enforcement. The activities of these five innovative firms represented the first phase in the development of "the life insurance–mortgage company connection." In this section I examine how and why these organizing principles were adopted.

It might interest the reader to learn that the first organizational principle enumerated above was in direct contrast to my expectations at the outset of this project. My original conjecture was that life insurance companies dominated the interregional mortgage market because of a technological complementarity between mortgage lending and insurance sales. Life insurance policies are subject to the same types of hidden-action and -information problems as mortgage contracts, and during the late nineteenth century most large companies began to market their insurance product throughout the nation. In doing so the companies had to manage geographically dispersed networks of policy sales agents and so faced an information problem similar to that of mortgage lenders who had to control distant loan agents. In particular, the insurance companies had to discourage their sales representatives from misrepresenting the quality of applicants simply to earn commissions, and to prevent these agents from shirking their responsibility to carefully investigate policy claims. To do so insurance companies appointed general agents to supervise sales agents in each regional market and also set up elaborate monitoring divisions at the home office to evaluate applications and claims sent in from the field. These mechanisms were strikingly similar to those implemented by the western mortgage companies. I thought it likely, therefore, that the insurance companies came to dominate the interregional mortgage market because they could both make loans and sell policies through a single agency network.

In fact, insurance companies separated mortgage lending activities from policy sales soon after the Civil War. Northwestern Mutual of Wisconsin confronted the issue in the early 1870s when the company's policy sales force was still permitted to solicit mortgage loan applications and send them to the home office for approval by the Investment Committee (Williamson and Smalley 1957, 63–67, 77–81). The investment group maintained an explicit policy of evaluating each loan application only on its merit, however, and did not consider whether it had been submitted by a policyholder. The sales agents pressed the company to adopt a new policy at this time so that the volume of mortgage lending in each state would be tied to the value of policies sold there and preference would be given to the loan applications of policyholders. The Executive Committee rejected this attempt to strengthen the connection between policy sales and mortgage lending. Its members noted that sales agents lacked the specialized knowledge of real estate markets that was required to accurately determine the quality of a mortgage. In addition, the committee was concerned that some sales agents would be induced to approve poor-quality mortgage loans simply to sell more policies and increase their commission income. A few insurance companies actually combined mortgage lending and policy sales during the 1870s, but these structures were quickly abandoned for the reasons cited by Northwestern's officials.[16] So policy sales and mortgage lending agency networks became completely separated within insurance companies even though they controlled similar informational asymmetries for the same intermediary.

After rejecting the sales agents' proposal, Northwestern established a more formal method of negotiating and enforcing its interregional mortgage portfolio. In 1877 the company hired several salaried "loan agents" and assigned each one to set up an office of the mortgage lending division in a different regional market. These branch offices operated as internal mortgage companies. They established contacts with independent loan agents and brokers, evaluated the loan applications submitted by these individuals, and then appraised the property that secured the loans. The application was then forwarded to the home office for final review. If approved there, the branch office closed and serviced the loan. The independent agent or broker was paid a commission by the borrower and normally helped the branch office enforce the loan without compensation in order to maintain a good reputation with the company.

Northwestern was a pioneer in the interregional mortgage business, but its reliance on a branch-office system turned out to be unusual. It was the Connecticut companies that developed the second general feature of the insurance industry's interregional mortgage lending system—the use of independent mortgage companies located in the West, Midwest, and South to negotiate and enforce loans for them. These mortgage companies were identical in structure and function, in some cases even in identity, to those that served individual eastern investors. Different Connecticut companies established different types of relationships with their mortgage company correspondents, however. Aetna chose to lend through only one mortgage company in each market and relied on the exclusivity of the relationship to strengthen that agency's incentive to perform faithfully. The company specialized in farm mortgages and made more than fifty thousand loans between 1870 and 1900 through a very small number of companies located in Indiana, Illinois, Iowa, and Minnesota. Travelers', on the other hand, used several companies in each state and made both urban and farm mortgages through them.[17]

---

16. Brewer (1976) discusses Equitable's unsuccessful attempt to establish its own independent mortgage company during the 1870s, and to use its policy sales force to make loans through it. Zartman (1906, 137) argues that the Life Association of St. Louis failed during the 1870s because it implemented a plan very similar to the one proposed by Northwestern's sales agents.

17. These generalizations about the number of mortgages made by the Aetna and Travelers' are drawn from an inspection of the companies' mortgage records, which are held at the American Heritage Center (Laramie, Wyoming).

Aetna's system worked well. The company suffered modest losses during the late 1870s when real estate holdings reached 5 percent of total mortgage investment, but it acquired very little additional property during the turbulent 1890s (Aetna 1947). In contrast, Travelers' had to foreclose on 650 of the 2,100 loans that it had made through just two companies during the 1890s and acquired $0.6 million in western farm property as a result. The company also saw nearly all of its western correspondents fail during the decade and so had to manage the liquidation of this property on its own (Travelers' 1890–95). Travelers' was much better equipped to assume the enforcement obligations of its western mortgage company correspondents, however, than the individual investors who had lent through the same firms. In fact, the life insurance–mortgage company connection became the dominant interregional mortgage lending structure precisely because of this third characteristic of their organizational structure—the insurance companies could conduct their own property management operations if became necessary for them to do so.

Insurance companies learned of the risks and costs associated with mortgage loan enforcement during the Depression of 1873, when eastern urban land values collapsed and seventy-one companies failed from mortgage-related problems (Zartman 1906, 133). When the collapse in real estate values spread to western markets in the mid-1870s, therefore, attention naturally shifted to the few eastern companies that had recently entered the interregional mortgage market. In 1876 the Connecticut legislature commissioned an independent audit of that state's companies, which found that Aetna, Connecticut Mutual, Phoenix, and Travelers' together held $46 million in mortgages on western properties and had acquired $8.1 million of real estate through foreclosure (Connecticut 1878). At the time of the audit most of the property was held by Connecticut Mutual, and by 1880 this one company had acquired $5 million of real estate in Chicago, $3 million in St. Louis, and $2 million in Detroit (Zartman 1906, 30). Despite these apparent difficulties the auditors declared all of the Connecticut companies sound because each of them, including the Connecticut Mutual, had disposed of foreclosed real estate without absorbing substantial losses. This was a remarkable accomplishment, given that the companies had to manage and sell substantial amounts of property so far away from headquarters.

During the 1880s and 1890s Northwestern also demonstrated that it could effectively manage foreclosed real estate across regional boundaries (Williamson and Smalley 1957, 77–78, 122–23). In the 1870s the company acquired $1.5 million of farm property through foreclosure, or some 15 percent of the value of its mortgage portfolio. Northwestern then came under considerable pressure to dispose of these farms quickly, even though the strategy would have generated substantial losses. State regulators threatened to intervene because the company's charter permitted it to own real estate only in an emergency. In addition, some company officials argued that the recent wave of foreclosures justified discontinuing farm mortgage lending altogether. But other insiders argued that the company would earn a high return on its farmland by postponing liquidation until property values recovered. A compromise position prevailed. To keep real estate holdings at acceptable levels, the company quickly sold off those properties that were unlikely to appreciate in value. At the same time it established a separate real estate division to manage the better-quality farms until they could be sold at a profit. During the 1880s Northwestern gradually sold off farms under this program, but it acquired even more land in the early 1890s before liquidation of the property that had been acquired earlier had been completed. The company finally disposed of all of its farm real estate between 1895 and 1904, and its property management operation earned between 8.4 and 11.6 percent in each of these years.

The property management operations of Northwestern and the Connecticut companies proved to be profitable, but the reader should recall that these activities involved the most costly and effort-intensive contingencies associated with mortgage enforcement. This was especially true when property has to be managed across regional boundaries. Lester Zartman (1906, 119) calculated the ratio of management expenses to property value for the twenty-nine largest life insurance companies between 1896 and 1904 and found that it was highest for the three interregional lenders discussed here: Travelers' (17 percent), Aetna (9 percent), and Northwestern (7 percent). No other company had a ratio greater than 5.2 percent, and the New York companies, which were still lending almost exclusively within local markets, all had ratios under 3 percent. Life insurance companies were uniquely suited to bear the costs of these operations because of the economies of scale that were related to their primary business—selling life insurance policies. Efficiency required them to write a large number of insurance policies in order to reduce the variability of claim payments and, thus, the share of assets they were required to hold in low-earning reserves. To accomplish this end, insurance companies had to grow very large in size and sell policies broadly across space. As a result, they were free to invest in very long term assets, such as property acquired through foreclosure, and had already made some of the fixed investments that were necessary for operating interregional property management divisions.

The unique combination of large size, a national market, and the long-term nature of their liabilities provided insurance companies with the resources and organizational flexibility to assume substantial investments in interregional property without jeopardizing their solvency. This was in marked contrast to national building associations and independent mortgage companies that were inadequately capitalized, given the short-term nature of their liabilities, to absorb the very high levels of enforcement costs that were generated during mortgage crises. Insurance companies came to dominate the interregional mortgage market because of their intrinsic ability to cope with contingent enforcement costs, therefore, and not because they had an advantage in negotiating and enforcing interregional mortgage loans under "normal" circumstances. In fact, eastern insurance companies found it efficient to make mortgage loans through external mortgage companies and to assume enforcement activities only when these correspondents failed. So the dominance of the life insurance–mortgage company connection was intimately associated with the instability of the national mortgage market.

Northwestern and the Connecticut companies demonstrated that interregional mortgage lending was both feasible and profitable for insurance companies, but the great bulk of the industry's mortgage lending was still local in character by the end of the nineteenth century. This pattern was largely the result of New York's restriction on out-of-state lending because companies headquartered there held such a large share of the industry's assets. Had the New York companies allocated their investments in the same manner as Connecticut firms, they would have held an $82 million portfolio of interregional loans in 1890—an amount equivalent to the total farm mortgage debt in Nebraska or twice the actual volume of interregional lending by the life insurance industry.[18] In fact, the New York regulation probably had a larger impact on the spatial allocation of nineteenth-century mortgage funds than the more notorious prohibition on mortgage lending by National Banks.

The New York companies lobbied for a relaxation of out-of-state lending restrictions throughout the 1870s and 1880s, and had good reasons to do so. The companies were aggressively expanding national policy sales networks at the time, and were concerned that some western and southern states might restrict their sales operations if they appeared to be "draining" savings from the rest of the country to finance mortgage investment back east. More importantly, they were aware that western and southern mortgages rates were much higher than those in eastern metropolitan areas, and that interregional mortgage loans were an attractive investment outlet. But the New York companies did not immediately enter the interregional mortgage business when they were finally granted broad lending powers in 1886. An executive of the Metropolitan explained that his company continued to lend close to home in the 1890s because the higher rates of return available in the West were more than offset by the extra costs and risks associated with interregional lending during these crisis years (Keller 1963, 135). But by then the stage was set for Metropolitan, and most of the large northeastern insurance companies, to follow Northwestern and the Connecticut companies into the national mortgage market.

7.6   The Expansion and Collapse of the Life Insurance–Mortgage Connection

Northwestern and the Connecticut companies had worked out the basic structure and methods of interregional mortgage lending by 1890. But by then

---

18. The Connecticut companies allocated 52 percent of all assets to mortgage lending in 1889, while those headquartered in New York allocated only 32 percent (U.S. Census Office 1890).

it was still unclear whether the life insurance–mortgage company connection would become widely used within the industry or just how important insurance companies would become to the interregional flow of mortgage credit. Events over the next decade did little to clarify the prospects. Northwestern and the Connecticut life insurance companies survived the western land crisis of the 1890s, but the disruption had a chilling effect on their mortgage lending operations. Between 1892 and 1902 mortgage loans decreased from 80 to 46 percent of total assets at Northwestern, from 60 to 37 percent at Travelers', and from 46 to 41 percent at Aetna (Williamson and Smalley 1957, 126). From this point life insurance companies increased mortgage lending activities through their mortgage company correspondents so rapidly that by the early 1920s the industry had become the most important source of farm mortgage credit in the country, and had begun to play a substantial role in the nation's residential mortgage market as well. During the expansion, however, this lending mechanism succumbed to pressures to overlend, and ultimately collapsed in the 1930s.

The second period of development of the life insurance–mortgage company connection was driven by an unprecedented expansion of farm mortgage debt between 1910 and 1920. During the decade farmers borrowed heavily to expand and improve their operations as farm prices and incomes trended upward before and during World War I. By 1920 outstanding farm mortgage debt in the United States exceeded $8 billion, and the most important institutional sources of mortgage credit were local commercial banks ($1.5 billion) and life insurance companies ($1 billion) (Wickens 1932).

Total farm mortgage debt grew at a much more modest pace during the 1920s, but the institutional structure of the market changed dramatically during the decade. Banks began to experience problems with their mortgage loans when farm prices and incomes fell violently during the recession of 1921, and by 1929 more than five thousand of them had been forced to close because of these difficulties (Johnson 1973). As bank holdings of farm mortgages decreased, insurance companies actually expanded their farm mortgage portfolios—by $0.5 billion in 1921 alone and by an additional $0.7 billion over the next five years (Mormon 1924, 42–47). As a result of these portfolio adjustments commercial banks held only 12 percent of the nation's farm mortgage debt in 1930, while the life insurance industry held 23 percent of the total. The recently created federal land banks and federally chartered mortgage banks also expanded their mortgage lending operations dramatically during the 1920s and held another 19 percent of the nation's farm mortgage debt by the end of that decade.[19] By the early 1920s, therefore, life insurance companies

19. The federal agencies concentrated on different areas of the country than the insurance companies did. Seventeen percent of the loan portfolios of both groups were made on land in the east North Central region. But the insurance companies had made only 22 percent of their loans in the Northeast, South Atlantic, South Central, Mountain, and Pacific regions, while the land and joint-stock banks had made 55 percent of their mortgages there. The big difference, therefore, was in the west North Central region. The federally sponsored banks held $500 million in mortgages in this area by 1929, while the insurance companies held $1.3 billion—60 percent of all loans made by the industry (Horton, Larsen, and Wall 1940, 222–24).

had become the most important source of interregional farm mortgage credit, and the most important farm mortgage lender of any kind.

The life insurance industry began to dominate the farm mortgage market because several large northeastern companies finally began to lend interregionally. Prudential of New Jersey established its farm mortgage lending operation in 1898, and the Equitable of New York followed in 1912 (May and Oursler 1950, 213; Skogvold 1956, 114). But Metropolitan of New York made the most dramatic entry into the interregional lending field (James 1947, 232–45). Before establishing its farm mortgage division in 1916, Metropolitan lent almost exclusively on commercial property in New York City. By 1918, however, its farm mortgage portfolio had swelled to $10 million and was spread over five states in the Midwest and the plains, and six states in the South. The expansion of the company's new line of business continued at this rapid pace for more than a decade, and by 1929 Metropolitan had become the second-largest farm mortgage lender in the country, with a portfolio of $196 million of farm loans spread over twenty-five different states (Woodruff 1937, 49).

Metropolitan's rise to prominence in the interregional farm mortgage business reflected a general trend within the insurance industry. Seven life insurance companies held more than $100 million of farm mortgages in 1929, and six of them were relative newcomers to the interregional market—Metropolitan, Equitable, and Mutual of New York; Prudential and Mutual Benefit of New Jersey; and John Hancock of Massachusetts (Temporary National Economic Committee 1940a, 161). Together these companies held $921 million of farm mortgage loans by the end of the 1920s, or 44 percent of the entire insurance industry's agricultural portfolio. On the other hand, the four Connecticut companies that had played such a prominent role in the western farm mortgage market before 1900 held a combined farm loan portfolio of only $165 million.

Of the firms that had pioneered the interregional business in the nineteenth century, only Northwestern maintained a leading position after 1900. In fact, its farm mortgage portfolio of $216 million was the largest in the industry in 1929. Northwestern was also unique because it continued to make interregional loans through a system of twenty-five branch offices that were staffed by company employees. In contrast, all of the large eastern companies relied on the same type of mortgage company connections that had been developed by the Connecticut insurance firms before 1900 (Woodruff 1937, 7–15). As before, these mortgage companies screened applications from local agents, made loans out of their own funds, and then sent the loans to the life insurance company for approval. Just like their nineteenth-century counterparts, moreover, these correspondents were paid by commission and a share of interest payments, and accepted the "effort risk" associated with enforcing outstanding loans.

Woodruff (1937, 9) attributes the widespread use of correspondents during the 1910s and 1920s to two refinements made to the system that the Connecticut companies had developed decades earlier. First, all of the eastern insurance firms chose to establish exclusive relationships with mortgage companies similar to those that Aetna had developed in the 1880s and 1890s. In fact, the life insurance–mortgage company connections of the 1920s were so strong that fully 88 percent of all the farm mortgages originated by mortgage companies were purchased by their insurance company partners. A second refinement was the "right of reinspection," which was a more limited version of the guarantee that mortgage companies had offered individual investors during the late nineteenth century. Under these agreements the insurance company could return a mortgage to the correspondent if it performed poorly during its first year. Once the year had passed, however, the company was obliged to retain nonperforming loans, even though the correspondent remained responsible for enforcing them.

The expansion of the life insurance–mortgage company connection succeeded in mobilizing substantial flows of interregional farm mortgage credit between 1910 and 1930. But the viability of a loan agency network, whether internal or external to an intermediary, continued to depend on a constant flow of new loans and commission income. So the insurance companies, just like the western mortgage companies in the late 1880s, came under pressure to approve loans that they knew were marginal. The development of the life insurance–mortgage company connection did not eliminate the pressure to overlend in interregional markets; therefore, it simply transferred the pressure through the mortgage companies to their exclusive partners.

Northwestern came under pressure to overlend even though it supervised loan agents through branch offices (Williamson and Smalley 1957, 179–81, 210–15). As early as 1912 its president became concerned about the quality of loans because farm property values had already doubled from 1900 levels. His proposal to discontinue farm-lending operations was overruled by the Finance Committee, however, because its members believed that outstanding loans could not be adequately serviced if the branch offices were closed and the company's relationships with loan agents disrupted. In the following year the volume of loan applications began to run far ahead of the company's mortgage portfolio requirements, and it was forced to institute quotas to spread commissions evenly among its loan agents. Pressure from the field then increased over lending terms as well as volume. Northwestern's agents had difficulty attracting borrowers because the company adhered to its strict policy of making loans for no more than 40 percent of conservatively valued farmland, while the representatives of other lenders offered lending terms based on more liberal appraisals. Northwestern chose to meet the competition by lowering its lending rates, but by 1923 the company was actually making small losses on new mortgages net of commissions and service charges. The company finally abandoned its new farm loan program in 1925.

Northwestern came under pressure to overlend because of the activities of its large eastern competitors. These companies relaxed lending standards to accommodate mortgage companies and loan agents and, thereby, to expand their farm loan operations. Metropolitan, for example, instructed its correspondents to lend no more than $62.50 per acre on Iowa farmland in 1917, but raised the loan ceiling to $75 in 1918, and to $100 in 1919 (James 1947, 236–37). In doing so, the company was forced to ratify a two-year permanent capital gain of 60 percent on farmland to maintain its burgeoning lending network in that state. Under these conditions it was hardly surprising that the volume of loan applications submitted to the company increased rapidly in 1919, or that the company's $20 million annual allotment for farm loans was exhausted by 9 April of the following year.

Metropolitan was not alone in its actions, for the pressure to overlend was felt industrywide and intensified over time. In Story County, Iowa, the debt per acre for all mortgages made by insurance companies increased from $38 to $84 between 1910 and 1920 (Murray 1938). The companies appear to have maintained loan quality, because the appraised value of an acre in this county increased from $130 to $289 during the same period. Despite maintaining the appearance of a constant 30 percent loan-to-value ratio, however, the companies were almost certainly aware that land appraisals were being systematically inflated by correspondents in the field.[20] After 1920 the evidence of overlending in Story is much clearer; land prices fell to $150 in 1925, while the debt per acre on mortgage loans fell only to $77. This sharp jump in the average loan-to-value ratio occurred just as the insurance companies expanded their Iowa mortgage portfolios by $183 million and replaced the commercial banking system as the most important source of farm mortgage credit in the state. Archibald Woodruff, whose father served as the chief of farm mortgage operations for Prudential, remains the authority on the lending practices of the life insurance companies during the period. His observations leave little doubt about the link between the aggressive expansion of the industry's interregional lending networks and "overlending": "More serious was the disposition of the correspondent to emphasize the quantity of new business at the expense of quality. The income of the correspondent was derived chiefly from commissions on new loans so that the desire of the correspondent was to get through as many loans as possible. . . . The life companies had no trouble with the class of loans the correspondents had sent in up to 1910, [but] they were too free in accepting some of the loans sent in after that year, particularly during 1920 and 1921" (1937, 13).

The evidence of overlending drawn from Iowa is particularly compelling because the life insurance–mortgage company connection had its greatest impact in this state. Between 1910 and 1920 total farm mortgage debt in Iowa increased by 176 percent and land values by 136 percent—magnitudes twice as large as in Ohio, Indiana, and Illinois over the same period. Jones and Dur-

---

20. I should point out that Murray (1938) argues that the reasons for the Iowa land boom during the 1920s was the use of second mortgages, and that the first mortgages made by life insurance companies were well secured because the loan-to-value ratio was stable until 1920.

and (1954, 81) were led to conclude that "the causes of the Iowa land boom are difficult to explain," but these authors failed to connect the episode to the prominent role that insurance companies and their agents played in the state. In fact, 25 percent of the farm mortgages made by all insurance companies between 1910 and 1920 were on Iowa land, and by 1930 the industry was supplying more than 40 percent of the state's total farm mortgage debt (Jones and Durand 1954, 41).[21] More than a decade later the Temporary National Economic Committee concluded that "[i]n Iowa . . . many [life insurance] companies lent amounts on farm properties in excess of their true values," and blamed the practice of using correspondents that were paid commissions (1940b, 349).[22]

Even though the life insurance–mortgage company connection of the 1920s proved to be susceptible to overlending during the 1910s and 1920s, it continued to dominate the interregional mortgage market well into the post–World War II era. The reason, of course, was that insurance companies were able to absorb the costs of enforcing outstanding mortgage contracts after the farm mortgage lending boom ended in the 1920s, and rates of delinquency and default soon reached very high levels. The insurance companies assumed these responsibilities as their correspondent networks began to break down in the early 1930s (Woodruff 1937, 78–79; Saulnier 1950, 31–31). At first, insurance companies released correspondents from the obligation to take over bad loans under the right of reinspection. With new lending at a standstill, however, mortgage companies and loan agents were receiving no commissions to compensate them for enforcing outstanding loans. The insurance companies remained reluctant to disband their lending networks even at this point and began to pay management fees to their correspondents. But under this arrangement there was little difference between a correspondent and a salaried employee of the company, so this stopgap measure was quickly abandoned and the correspondents discharged. By the mid-1930s all of the major insurance companies had been forced to internally manage their remaining farm mortgage portfolios as well as the real estate that had been acquired through foreclosure.

These enforcement activities grew to staggering proportions. The industry's farm mortgage portfolio decreased from its peak of $2.2 billion in 1929 to $0.9 billion in 1938, and by then the companies owned more than $0.6 billion of farmland (Temporary National Economic Commission 1940a, 174–84). All of the large companies established internal operations to enforce the terms of defaulted loans and to undertake the costly enforcement tasks that were enu-

21. Recall from note 19 above that the federal land banks and joint-stock mortgage banks were much less active in the west North Central regions than the life insurance companies were.

22. In Iowa, defaults reached epidemic proportions by 1930, and during the 1930s insurance companies initiated two-thirds of the foreclosures in the state although they held only 40 percent of the mortgage debt. The companies could not quickly liquidate so much property and as late as 1939 still owned 8 percent of the farmland in Iowa (Temporary National Economics Commission 1940b, 349).

merated in section 7.2; they worked with delinquents to reschedule loan payments and prevent foreclosure, supervised defaulters who chose to remain on the land as tenants, and made substantial investments to improve, rent, and sell abandoned farms.[23] The companies received some relief when 30 percent of their loans in Iowa, Kansas, South Dakota, and Tennessee were extinguished through an emergency mortgage program operated by the federal land bank commissioner. But even with this "bailout" of $0.3 billion the companies were forced to undertake mortgage enforcement activities on a monumental scale (Temporary National Economic Commission 1940b, 347).

Those companies that had expanded their lending activities most aggressively during the 1910s and 1920s were more seriously affected. Because Northwestern maintained stringent loan standards during the 1910s and suspended new farm lending completely in the early 1920s, it acquired property on only 14 percent of its farm mortgage portfolio (Williamson and Smalley 1957, 261–65). In contrast, 49 percent of Equitable's loans went into "serious default," and the company eventually acquired 5,035 farms and did not sell off the last of these properties until 1947. At its peak in 1938 the company's Farm Real Estate Division employed a force of four hundred men to make repairs on 2,800 farms at an average cost of $1,100 (Skogvold 1956, 114–19). Prudential established its Foreclosure and Property Section in 1928, and shortly thereafter one of the company's officers described the operation as the "stepchild who wandered in and couldn't find its way out" (May and Oursler 1950, 206). His comment was both incisive and prescient, as the company acquired 46,159 farms by 1939 and was still managing 2,000 of them in 1945. The largest enforcement task fell to Metropolitan's Department of Agriculture, however, which eventually managed 13,290 farms that represented the security on 58 percent of the loans it had held in its portfolio (James 1947, 294–305). By 1939 Metropolitan had become the largest private property owner in the United States because of these operations, as it held land equal in size to a farm one mile wide stretching from New York to Los Angeles.

Despite the nearly complete dissolution of the insurance industry's farm mortgage lending operations in the 1930s, the companies survived to dominate the interregional market for residential mortgage credit in the 1940s and 1950s. In fact, the life insurance industry had just begun to make inroads into this line of business before the onset of the Great Depression. Metropolitan was the innovator in the field and made its first loans in 1920 through a Kansas City banker who sought to finance a suburban housing development. Within three years Metropolitan's 66 residential mortgage loan correspondents were supervising 163 agents in 37 states (James 1947, 251). The impact on the company's portfolio was profound. In 1919 it had written four-fifths of its $272 million urban mortgage portfolio on New York property, and only one-third of that on

---

23. Woodruff 1937 and Mehr 1944 provide extensive discussions of the farm property operations of the life insurance companies during the 1930s.

residential real estate. Ten years later the company held $1.2 billion in urban mortgage loans, and more than 40 percent of the total had been written on single-family homes and apartments in out-of-state markets. The rest of the industry followed Metropolitan into the residential business during the late 1920s, and insurance companies held some $4.4 billion of residential debt by 1930, much of it made through loan correspondents.

There is little direct evidence that overlending affected the industry's residential mortgage business as it had its farm mortgage operations. Nonetheless, by 1935 the industry had acquired $1 billion of foreclosed urban property and faced an enforcement task equal in scale to its farm operation. At that point the Home Owners' Loan Corporation made nearly $3.1 billion of mortgages to refinance the debt of delinquent residential borrowers (Harriss 1951). It is likely that the share going to insurance companies was substantial, because by 1936 their residential mortgage portfolio had fallen to only $1.5 billion (Saulnier 1950, 2). Soon thereafter the insurance industry began to make interregional loans on residential real estate that were guaranteed by the new Federal Housing Administration (FHA). In fact, the expansion of federal mortgage insurance and guarantee programs in the postwar era provided the foundation for the revival of the life insurance–mortgage company connection in the 1950s.

7.7 Conclusion

Between 1870 and 1940 the cost of mortgage credit varied dramatically across regions of the United States. The mortgage rate gradient reflected severe imbalances in regional supplies and demands for mortgage finance and persisted because intermediaries were unable to move enough funds across space to equalize lending rates (Snowden 1987, 1988). Lance Davis (1965) argued that the national mortgage market remained regionally segmented because "information and transactions costs" inhibited the interregional flow of mortgage credit. The analysis presented here provides a more concrete picture of the informational forces that were at work. In particular, I have tried to explain how information imperfections destabilized most historical interregional lending structures in the late nineteenth century and why the life insurance–mortgage company connection emerged as the only viable mechanism to integrate the national mortgage market during the first half of the twentieth century.

Several types of lending structures arose in the interregional market before 1900, and I have interpreted all of them as hierarchical contractual arrangements that connected borrowers, loan agents, and investors. Each particular contract in these hierarchies was structured to provide the better-informed party in a bilateral relationship to faithfully perform certain obligations. Secured mortgage debt encouraged borrowers to fully repay loans, and commission payments induced loan agents to carefully negotiate and enforce mortgage contracts for interregional investors. Mortgage companies arose to supervise loan agents for investors and established their own credibility by promising to absorb all of the enforcement costs associated with mortgage lending. Each of these contracts makes sense when considered alone, but in combination they created pressures to issue debt under terms that some participants knew were unsafe, led to massive waves of delinquency and foreclosure, and generated such large enforcement costs that mortgage companies were forced to renege on their pledge to enforce loans. By 1900 life insurance companies had proven to be the only investors with sufficient resources and institutional flexibility to enforce mortgage loans when their mortgage company correspondents failed. This was the fundamental reason that the life insurance–mortgage company connection became the dominant interregional lending channel between 1900 and 1950.

The final phase in the development of this lending structure occurred during the 1950s and has already been explored in several treatments of the postwar mortgage market (Behrens 1952; Morton 1956; Klaman 1959, 1961; Colean 1962). Each of these studies concludes that the nation's residential mortgage market became fully integrated in the 1950s after the insurance industry reestablished its connections with a new generation of mortgage companies. All of them also emphasize that the basis of the restoration was the FHA mortgage insurance and Veterans Administration (VA) loan-guarantee programs. Mortgage companies, more than eight hundred in number by the early 1950s, became FHA- and VA-qualified lenders and originated nearly all of the mortgages that entered the interregional market. Life insurance firms became their most important clients and lent broadly enough across space through them to equalize regional residential mortgage rates. As a result, the national mortgage market finally became integrated after eight decades of nearly continuous innovation and experimentation.

Federal intervention integrated the mortgage market by eliminating mortgage crises and protecting investors from the major risk associated with interregional lending. To begin with, FHA and VA programs ended the practice of overlending. These agencies popularized the long-term, amortized loan and ended the widespread use of the short-term mortgage that had to be renewed several times. The change in contract duration eliminated most borrowers' preference for an overappraisal because modern mortgages are typically negotiated only when property is being purchased and the borrower derives little benefit from an overappraisal at that time. Moreover, loan agents cannot independently inflate the appraisal on a federally underwritten loan because an additional property evaluation must be performed by a disinterested, independent expert. The FHA made overlending even more difficult by implementing a system of loan-risk evaluation that considers characteristics of the borrower and property other than the loan-to-value ratio (Massey 1939, 2–4). With the incentive and opportunity to overlend eliminated, and the federal agencies prepared to step in if a mortgage company failed for any other reason, investors in the interregional mortgage market no longer faced the risks of having to enforce loans made thousands of miles away.

With the stabilization of the mortgage market, life insurance companies no longer enjoyed their intrinsic advantage in the interregional lending field that had led to their dominance in the first place. In fact, mutual savings banks finally entered the interregional mortgage market in 1950, but they were permitted to invest only in out-of-state mortgages that were government insured or guaranteed. Then, in 1970, all types of institutional investors gained access to the interregional market when federal agencies began to securitize pools of insured and guaranteed residential mortgage loans and sold them as mortgage-backed securities. So the historical development of the life insurance–mortgage company connection was intimately connected to the instability of the mortgage market. It dominated the interregional mortgage market between 1900 and 1950 because no other type of investor could survive mortgage crises. Since then it has come to play a more limited role because government intervention has eliminated the sources and impacts of these crises.

Besides identifying the forces that drove the integration of the national mortgage market, this history also demonstrates how informational considerations determine the boundaries of the financial firm. Financial innovation often occurs by the introduction of a single type of intermediary, and we have seen that the development of local mortgage lending structures fits this view of the unified financial firm quite well. But in other settings, such as the markets for interregional mortgages, commercial paper, or corporate securities, new financial services are produced by combinations of several intermediaries. These complex financial structures arise to deal in contracts that are negotiated and enforced under complex technological constraints that prevent any single intermediary from efficiently producing all of the required financial services.

In the case examined here independent loan agents negotiated and enforced mortgage loans efficiently because they enjoyed a locational advantage. The same spatial constraint that protected them from competitors outside of their local markets, however, prevented agents from expanding the size of their operations sufficiently to establish their credibility with investors. Mortgage companies arose, therefore, to monitor loan agents for distant investors. These firms performed quite well in normal times, but could not be profitably capitalized deeply enough to survive periodic mortgage crises. So life insurance companies, with no intrinsic advantage in interregional mortgage making, became the exclusive partners of mortgage companies because it was efficient for them to grow so large in their primary line of business that they were able to absorb substantial enforcement costs during a mortgage crisis. I conclude, therefore, that the historical development of complex multifirm financial structures like the life insurance–mortgage company connection can be understood only by clearly specifying the informational basis of financial contracts and the technologies that are used to negotiate and enforce them.

References

Aetna Life Insurance Company. 1862–99. Company Mortgage Ledgers. Hartford.
———. 1947. A Record of Mortgage Loan Experience. Hartford.
Bagnoli, Mark, and Kenneth Snowden. 1993. Secured Debt as an Optimal Contract. Mimeo.
Behrens, Carl. 1952. *Commercial Bank Activities in Urban Mortgage Financing.* New York: National Bureau of Economic Research.
Bodfish, Morton. 1931. *History of the Building and Loan in the United States.* Chicago: U.S. Building and Loan League.
Bogue, Allan. 1955. *Money at Interest.* Ithaca, NY: Cornell University Press.
Brewer, H. P. 1976. Eastern Money and Western Mortgages in the 1870s. *Business History Review* 50:356–80.
Clark, H., and F. Chase. 1925. *Elements of the Modern Building and Loan Associations.* New York: Macmillan.
Colean, Miles. 1962. *Mortgage Companies. Their Place in the Financial Structure.* Englewood Cliffs, NJ: Commission on Money and Credit, Prentice-Hall.
Connecticut. 1878. Report of the Special Commission on the Condition of the Life Insurance Companies. Hartford.
Darrow, Edward N. 1892. *A Treatise on Mortgage Investments.* Minneapolis: L. Kimball, Prt.
Davis, Lance. 1965. The Investment Market, 1870–1914: The Evolution of a National Market. *Journal of Economic History* 33:355–93.
Davis, Lance, and Peter Payne. 1958. From Benevolence to Business: The Story of Two Savings Banks. *Business History Review* 32:386–406.
Diamond, Douglas. 1984. Financial Intermediation and Delegated Monitoring. *Review of Economic Studies* 51:393–414.
Eldredge, D. 1893. *Massachusetts Cooperative Banks or Building Associations: A History of Their Growth from 1877 to 1893.* Boston: George H. Ellis.
Frederiksen, D. M. 1894. Mortgage Banking. *Journal of Political Economy* 2:210–21.
Gale, Douglas, and Martin Hellwig. 1985. Incentive-Compatible Debt Contracts: Part 1: The One-Period Problem. *Review of Economic Studies* 52:647–64.
Harger, Charles. 1906. The Farm Mortgage of Today. *Review of Reviews* 5:572–75.
Harriss, C. Lowell. 1951. *History and Policies of the Home Owners' Loan Corporation.* New York: National Bureau of Economic Research.
Herrick, Myron, and R. Ingalls. 1915. *How to Finance the Farmer: Private Enterprise—Not State Aid.* Cleveland: Ohio State Committee on Rural Credits.
Horton, Donald, H. Larsen, and N. Wall. 1940. *Farm Mortgage Credit Facilities in the United States.* Miscellaneous Publication 478. Washington, DC: U.S. Department of Agriculture.
Hurd, George. 1923. Margins on Mortgage Loans. In *Practical Real Estate Methods.* New York: Doubleday and Page.
James, Marquis. 1947. *The Metropolitan Life.* New York: Viking Press.
Johnson, Thomas. 1973. Postwar Optimism and the Rural Banking Crisis of the 1920s. *Explorations in Economic History* 11:173–92.
Jones, Lawrence, and David Durand. 1954. *Mortgage Lending Experience in Agriculture.* Princeton: Princeton University Press.
Keller, Morton. 1963. *The Life Insurance Enterprise, 1885–1910.* Cambridge: Harvard University Press.
Klaman, Saul. 1959. *The Postwar Rise of Mortgage Companies.* NBER Occasional Paper no. 60. New York: National Bureau of Economic Research.

————. 1961. *The Postwar Residential Mortgage Market.* Princeton: Princeton University Press.

Lintner, John. 1948. *Mutual Savings Banks in the Savings and Mortgage Markets.* Boston: Harvard University.

Mappin, W. F. 1889. Farm Mortgages and the Small Farmer. *Political Science Quarterly* 4:434–51.

Massachusetts, 1890–95. Annual Reports of the Commissioner of Foreign Mortgage Corporations. Boston.

Massey, Maurice. 1939. The Influence of FHA on Mortgage Lending. In *Michigan Business Papers* 4:1–8.

May, Earl, and Will Oursler. 1950. *The Prudential.* New York: Doubleday.

Mehr, Robert. 1944. *Mortgage Foreclosures and Property Management by Life Insurance Companies.* Philadelphia: University of Pennsylvania.

Mormon, James. 1924. *Farm Credits in the United States and Canada.* New York: Macmillan.

Morton, J. 1956. *Urban Mortgage Lending: Comparative Markets and Experience.* Princeton: Princeton University Press.

Murray, William. 1938. Land Booms and Second Mortgages. *Journal of Farm Economics* 20:230.

New York: 1891–97. Annual Report of the Superintendant of Banks relative to Foreign Mortgage, Loan, or Investment Companies. Albany.

Olmstead, Alan. 1976. *New York City Mutual Savings Banks, 1819–1861.* Chapel Hill: University of North Carolina.

Pritchett, Bruce. 1977. *A Study of Capital Mobilization: The Life Insurance Industry of the Nineteenth Century.* New York: Arno Press.

Robins, Kingman. 1916. *The Farm Mortgage Handbook.* New York: Doubleday.

Rosenthal, Henry. 1888. *Manual for Building Associations.* Cincinnati: Rosenthal and Company.

Rotella, Elyce, and Kenneth Snowden. 1992. The Building Association Movement of the Nineteenth Century. Mimeo.

Saulnier, Raymond. 1950. *Urban Mortgage Lending by Life Insurance Companies.* New York: National Bureau of Economic Research.

Skilton, Robert. 1944. *Government and the Mortgage Debtor.* Philadelphia: University of Pennsylvania.

Skogvold, F. J. 1956. Farm Loans and Farm Management by the Equitable Life Assurance Society of the United States. *Agricultural History* 30:114–19.

Snowden, Kenneth. 1987. Mortgage Rates and American Capital Market Development in the Late Nineteenth Century. *Journal of Economic History* 47:671–92.

————. 1988. Mortgage Lending and American Urbanization, 1880–1890. *Journal of Economic History.* 48:273–85.

————. 1993. Twentieth Century Mortgage Securitization in Historical Perspective. Mimeo.

Snowden, Kenneth, and Nidal Abu Saba. 1993. Why Did Late Nineteenth Century Mortgage Banking Fail? Mimeo.

Sparks, Earl. 1932. *History and Theory of Agricultural Credit in the U.S.* New York: Crowell Company.

Temporary National Economic Committee. 1940a. *Life Insurance: Operating Results and Investments of the Twenty-Six Largest Life Insurance Companies Domiciled in the United States.* Par 10-A. Washington, DC: GPO.

————. 1940b. *Study of the Legal Reserve Life Insurance Companies.* Monograph 28. Washington, DC: GPO.

Townsend, Robert. 1979. Optimal Contracts and Competitive Markets with Costly State Verification. *Journal of Economic Theory* 21:265–93.

Travelers' Life Insurance Company. 1887–1900. Complete History of Real Estate Loans. Hartford.

U.S. Census Office. 1890. *Report on Class A Insurance Companies.* Washington, DC: GPO.

———. 1895a. *The Report on Farm and Home Proprietorship and Indebtedness.* Vol. 13. Washington, DC: GPO.

———. 1895b. *The Report on Real Estate Mortgages in the United States.* Vol. 12. Washington, DC: GPO.

U.S. Comptroller of the Currency. 1890–1900. Annual Reports. Washington, DC.

Wickens, David. 1932. *Farm-Mortgage Credit.* USDA Technical Bulletin 288. Washington, DC: GPO.

Williamson, Harold, and Orange Smalley. 1957. *Northwestern Mutual Life: A Century of Trusteeship.* Evanston: Northwestern University Press.

Williamson, Steven. 1986. Costly Monitoring, Financial Intermediation, and Equilibrium Credit Rationing. *Journal of Monetary Economics* 18:159–79.

Woodruff, Archibald. 1937. *Farm Mortgage Loans of Life Insurance Companies.* New Haven: Yale University Press.

Wright, Carroll. 1893. *Ninth Annual Report of the Commissioner of Labor: Building and Loan Associations.* Washington, DC: GPO.

Zartman, Lester. 1906. *The Investments of Life Insurance Companies.* New York: Henry Holt.

Comment   Timothy W. Guinnane

One of the great themes in the economic history of the United States is the regional integration of markets for both products and factors of production. Market integration permitted the efficient exploitation of this country's great human and material resources. Lance Davis showed long ago, in a justly famous paper, that the nineteenth century witnessed substantial integration in the market for capital. Kenneth Snowden's admirable paper reminds us that underlying Davis's convergence of interest rates were some complicated institutional developments. Market integration required the creating and improvement of mechanisms through which lenders could acquire and use the information they needed to move capital to the place where it was best rewarded. Snowden uses a nice balance of economic intuition and knowledge of institutional details to explain why interregional mortgage lending evolved in fits and starts and why life insurance companies grew to become such important lenders in that market.

Snowden's explanation of the role of life insurance companies in this process is, in my view, correct. One task he did not tackle—for entirely understandable reasons, including page constraints—was to ask why other institutions were not tried, or if they were tried, why they were not successful. Life insurance companies *did* become important, but why didn't other institutions emerge to

Timothy W. Guinnane is assistant professor of economics at Yale University.

take the place they eventually filled? At several places in Snowden's account the reader may be reminded of institutions that dealt with similar information problems in quite different contexts, or may be led to ask why people did not adopt some alterations to their basic arrangements that would seem to provide a better incentive structure. My remarks seek to highlight certain features of Snowden's account by restating it in slightly different form, and then to consider why lenders and borrowers did not find other ways to contend with information problems in interregional mortgage markets. For brevity I will focus on his account of the development of the life insurance–mortgage company connection prior to World War I.

Information and Interregional Mortgage Lending

At first blush it seems odd to devote so much attention to information problems associated with *mortgage*-based loans. Textbook accounts of the role of asymmetric information in credit markets often refer to collateral as one way to *solve* many of the problems associated with asymmetric information. A borrower who is willing to pledge collateral shows that he intends to repay the loan. And once a loan is made, collateral reduces the borrower's incentive to shirk or to invest the loan in risky activities. Consider the loan-to-value ratio typical of the mortgages Snowden discusses. If the land's value is appraised accurately and if the loan is only for one-half (or even less) of the land's value, then a borrower has much to lose through foreclosure. Land, moreover, is usually an excellent form of collateral. A borrower cannot run away with land, unlike tools or personal property; land does not burn or die of disease, unlike buildings and livestock; land's condition can be monitored simply by walking by the property in question; and in most legal environments land cannot be alienated without a transfer of title that serves to impede fraudulent exchanges.

The reader (or author) of the textbook view of collateral then, might be somewhat surprised to learn that mortgage lending in the United States evolved in fits and starts and eventually prospered only with the backing of the federal government. Why? Snowden's story stems from two distinctive features of the U.S. economy at the time, the spatial distribution of population and economic activity and the boom-bust cycle of western real estate markets. The demand for capital for agriculture and new housing was concentrated most heavily in the Midwest and the West. Yet the people of these regions were unlikely to have funds to lend their neighbors. To match savers with the most lucrative outlets for their savings, mortgage lending in the United States in this period had to reach across great distances. And here arises the information problem central to Snowden's paper. Much of what makes land desirable as collateral— the land is fixed in place, so the borrower cannot run off in the night with his farm—means that to evaluate a property and to supervise a loan, a lender must either incur the cost of travel to the farm's location or employ an agent to do so on her behalf. In the nineteenth century the distances required for lenders to investigate and supervise loans personally were prohibitive. In addition, the booms and busts that characterized western real estate markets placed additional constraints on solutions to the information problem. Any individual or institution that would invest in these real estate markets had to be prepared to contend with the recurring general declines in prices. During such busts, many borrowers would default on their loans, forcing lenders either to sell the foreclosed property at depressed prices or to try to manage the property from a distance. To the extent lenders did not fully anticipate declines in real estate prices (and many did not), some institutional arrangements that functioned well in times of stable or even increasing land prices collapsed during price declines. The combination of information problems and fluctuating real estate prices meant that many conventional forms of financial intermediation could not facilitate interregional mortgage lending.

Thus, as Snowden shows, local mortgages in the nineteenth-century United States might have solved the textbook's information problem, but the need for *interregional* lending gave rise to a distinct set of information problems. Because it would be costly for lenders to contract directly with borrowers and for lenders to monitor the use of loans, lending had to occur through third parties. Interregional lending created principal-agent problems that concerned primarily the lenders and their intermediaries in addition to the textbook focus on lenders and their borrowers. The principals (the lenders) had less information about the characteristics of the loans than their agents (who arranged the loans). The problem faced by borrowers, loan agents, and lenders was to structure a set of institutions that could overcome those information barriers without incurring costs that would price credit out of the market.

The problems posed by long-distance lending are best appreciated by considering some of the most successful nineteenth-century institutions for financial intermediation. Many of these institutions have the common feature of restriction to small geographic areas in which members are likely to know each other and to encounter each other in their daily activities. This geographic restriction imposed costs on the institution, including correlation of the incomes of members, but also allowed the institution to maximize the cheap information that came from daily social interactions. Students of U.S. financial history are familiar with the image of the country banker who knew most of his customers and could inspect their fields during Sunday buggy rides. Snowden discusses the first building associations, institutions that voluntarily restricted themselves to operations within a single county. A more dramatic example of this principle is the rural credit cooperatives formed in Germany in the second half of the nineteenth century. Most of these cooperatives restricted their operations to single small villages. Because cooperative members had good information about one another and could impose some severe, noneconomic sanctions on defaulters, cooperatives could make loans other financial intermediaries would not, including loans without collateral. The obvious drawback to such arrangements, one that was in part responsible for the rise of "national" building associations in the United States, was that such arrangements could not satisfy the demand for loans in the presence of the spatial mismatch between the supply of and demand for credit that characterized the United States in the second half of the nineteenth century. Germany's agricultural credit cooperatives relied primarily on local savings and made only local loans. Clearly the basis upon which they were organized would have required substantial modification for them to succeed at interregional lending.[1]

Whatever the mechanism employed for making interregional loans, to be successful it must involve some way to structure the relationship between the lender and her agent such that the agent does not take advantage of his superior information. This problem is common to many situations involving long-distance economic transactions. Recently economic historians have argued that some institutional arrangements amount to systems whereby an agent or group of agents commits not to take advantage of an informational or power asymmetry. A commitment mechanism amounts to an arrangement that alters the agent's incentives: he can be trusted not to cheat because, once he is part of the commitment mechanism, it is not in his interest to do so.[2] This is not the only way to structure such an arrangement, nor is there universal agreement about the role of commitment mechanisms in economic history. Another way to solve the principal-agent problem would be for principals to rely exclusively on people they could trust, such as family members or members of the same ethnic or religious group. If the agent fears punishment by God if he takes advantage of his superior information to cheat the principal, then the principal can trust the agent even in the absence of any commitment structure. Family connections function in an analogous way; presumably most of us are less willing to cheat a family member because we fear alienation from family members more than alienation from others. Snowden focuses on why a satisfactory commitment mechanism did not emerge and survive in the United States. Agents found ways to effectively commit themselves not to cheat lenders, but these arrangements could not survive the booms and busts of the real estate market.

Agents, Mortgage Companies, and Life Insurance Companies

The first widespread interregional lending took the form of individual loan agents in the Midwest and West, acting on behalf of individual lenders elsewhere. Although working through a loan agent might have been preferable to trying to conduct all business in person, this structure gave the agent considerable latitude to exploit his superior information. The agent's income was a

---

1. Guinnane (1994) discusses the unsuccessful attempt to introduce the German model into Ireland in the 1890s, and contains details on the structure and organization of the German cooperatives. The German agricultural credit cooperatives did create a system of "Centrals," regional cooperative banks that accepted deposits from some cooperatives and made loans to others. But these institutions functioned primarily to smooth credit needs over agricultural cycles and over bad years; they did not exist to intermediate credit between regions with chronic excess deposits and regions with chronic excess demand.

2. Greif 1989, an analysis of medieval trading groups, is a recent example of this style of argument.

finder's fee, and all he really had to do was to convince the lender to accept the loan. What was there to deter the agent from misrepresenting properties and borrowers to arrange as many loans as possible? The only sanction an individual lender could apply to an uncooperative or dishonest agent was to refuse to do business with him in the future and to refuse to recommend his services to others. Neither sanction meant much so long as the market consisted of many individual lenders dealing with many individual agents. Given the volume of lending conducted by a single person and the difficulty of establishing an accurate reputation in the fluid societies in question, neither the threat of losing future business nor the potential damage to the agent's reputation was very costly. The only commitment the agent could make not to take advantage of his superior information would be to agree to take back any loan at any time, in essence saying that he had confidence in any loan he passed through to a lender. Given the small size of his own portfolio, however, he simply could not commit to hold the entire stock of outstanding loans he had arranged. If land prices fell too much, his portfolio would become worthless.

Mortgage companies had several advantages over individual loan agents. Snowden rightly emphasizes gains from volume and standardization of practices. For lenders, the great volume of loans meant that their funds were less likely to lay idle waiting for a borrower. More importantly, perhaps, mortgage companies could make commitments to lenders that individual agents could not. Their size and relative permanence meant that the sanctions of loss of future business and damage to reputation were effective deterrents to dishonest behavior. Mortgage companies, moreover, could attempt the more effective commitment mentioned above, to take back any loan. This policy worked for a while because mortgage companies were sufficiently large that a small number of bad loans would not overwhelm their portfolios. Yet when a general decline in land values occurred in the late 1880s and 1890s, this commitment could not be honored. Mortgage companies were simply incapable of holding all the bad loans in their portfolios.

Snowden argues that life insurance companies—which in most cases worked through mortgage companies of the sort that had failed in the 1880s and 1890s—succeeded in this market for two related reasons. First, insurance companies were large enough to develop specialized departments to manage property. The costs of enforcing a bad loan were thus lower, because the insurance company could hire and train its own staff to supervise the property it held. Second, the life insurance companies did not issue demand liabilities, and so had relatively small need for liquidity. Life insurance company portfolios were so large and diversified that they could afford to take over and manage properties that came their way via foreclosures, even in a general downturn in prices. Although convenient for a real estate investor in any situation, this trait was particularly valuable during general downturns in land prices because the insurance company could simply sit things out and wait to sell its property until prices had recovered.

Some Why Nots

Snowden's account is a convincing explanation of why life insurance companies came to play a dominant role in interregional lending in the United States in the nineteenth century. He places rather more stress on explaining why life insurance companies succeeded than on explaining why other possible arrangements did not succeed. This is a sensible approach; one can hardly consider and discard every possible institutional arrangement. Yet his account suggests several arrangements sometimes used in other circumstances, and it is useful to ask why they were not employed in the United States.

The first question concerns the contract between the individual agents and the individual lenders. (Much the same questions can be asked about the mortgage companies, as well.) Snowden notes that the agent was paid a finder's fee, giving the agent no incentive beyond concern for repeat business or his reputation to refrain from passing through bad loans or to provide any services to the lender in managing a foreclosed property. Why would lenders agree to this sort of scheme? One could imagine two modifications that would provide better incentives for the agent. First, lenders could offer a different way to pay the agent. One could imagine, for example, a system that paid the agent's fee *only* when a loan was successfully paid off. This system would require agents to forgo a certain finder's fee now in return for a more uncertain income later. But lenders and their agents might find it in their mutual interest to increase the fee to compensate the agent for waiting and for bearing some of the default risk. Second, lenders could use as their agents only individuals who had some other tie to a community and some other reputation to protect. Lawyers or bankers might seem natural candidates, especially since many could treat their mortgage-agent business as a natural adjunct to their main line of work. Snowden mentions that the Davenport family preferred to use lawyers as their agents, but does not pursue the point beyond that.

The success of the Davenport family raises another set of questions. Snowden notes that this family made some $4 million in loans in a thirty-year period, relying on a network of agents that the family selected and trained. The organization of economic activity through families is not uncommon and, as noted above, has particular advantages when long distances make information difficult to obtain and use. Yet the use of family members could not obviate *all* the difficulties Snowden identifies. Some additional detail on this family's operations could provide useful insights into the principal-agent problem more generally. For example, Snowden notes that, in the face of declining demand for loans, mortgage companies faced the choice of losing their trained agents or knowingly accepting low-quality loans. How did the Davenports keep their trained agents under these conditions? What did the Davenports do in the face of general downturns in land prices? Were their liquidity needs so slight that they could hold large numbers of foreclosed mortgages in their family portfolio? One also wonders why families such as the Davenports did not expand their lending activities beyond their *own* capital, drawing on their networks of trained agents to make loans for others. The Davenports and families like them, one would think, could easily increase their profits by using their eastern neighbors' funds and their own midwestern agents to achieve the economies of scale in investigation and monitoring that Snowden attributes to the mortgage companies. The Davenports could have dealt with the commitment problem by showing that their family fortune was invested in the activities in which they expected others to invest.

Snowden's account of the Davenports also raises questions about another form of interregional organization. Many of the people who needed capital in the West and Midwest must have had relatives themselves back east, relatives who could either lend the required money personally or function as intermediary for friends and neighbors who wanted to invest in western mortgages. These isolated, informal arrangements are of course quite difficult to track down in historical sources, but it would be interesting to know whether there is mention of them.

This brings us to a final option, and perhaps the most natural one to consider: full-fledged mortgage banks. Snowden notes that some mortgage companies began to issue bonds in the 1880s and 1890s, becoming, in a real sense, true financial intermediaries. By issuing bonds the mortgage companies came to resemble the mortgage banks common in Europe at the time. Following this suggestion and the logic of Snowden's own argument about the life insurance companies lead us to wonder just why the bond-issuing mortgage company would not be a *superior* interregional lender. Note first that a company that issues bonds to finance the mortgage loans it makes faces *no* principal-agent problem; it is both principal and agent.[3] Second, by issuing bonds of the right terms and maturity, the mortgage company could be just as happy holding property in its portfolio as the insurance company; liquidity problems are most severe for individuals and for institutions (such as banks) that issue demand liabilities. Finally, rather than setting up a separate unit to manage properties, the mortgage company could make property management a part of its more general business of gathering and using information on borrowers and their collateral.

The answer to my question may lie in regulatory restrictions on financial intermediaries. Clearly the institution we are imagining could run afoul of prohibitions on interstate banking, branch banking, or both, although one could imagine that those who stood to profit from organizing and running such an institution could lobby the Congress and state legislatures for appropriate changes in the law. More salient is the difficulty of issuing bonds with the right terms. Snowden identifies liquidity as the central shortcoming of both individual agents and the mortgage companies. To be successful our hypothetical mortgage bank would have to be able to hold nonperforming loans in its

---

3. Agency problems remain *within* the firm, of course, but both Snowden and I are ignoring those in this discussion.

portfolio long enough to ride out depressions in real estate markets. This in turn would entail the issuance of long-term liabilities. Could the mortgage bank in fact market long-term liabilities? Perhaps not. Short-term liabilities have long been a feature of banking institutions, even in circumstances where the assets had fairly long maturities and the mismatch between the two sets of maturities could lead to bank runs and other costly incidents. This mismatch is not an unfortunate product of custom. Calomiris and Kahn (1991) have shown that short-term liabilities function as an important policing device: because bank managers know more about the bank's portfolio than its depositors, one way for bank managers to commit not to capitalize on their superior information by absconding with the funds is to stand willing to refund deposits at any time. Lamoreaux (1991) refers to a similar principle in her study of New England banking in the nineteenth century. A mortgage banking institution might have found it very difficult to raise funds. European mortgage banks, in fact, usually borrowed money on public capital markets, but were based on governmental guarantees and often hefty government subsidies.

More compelling, however, is Snowden's argument that full-fledged mortgage banks would have been superfluous at the time of the life insurance company's dominance of the interregional mortgage market. By the end of the nineteenth century, when most states had removed their restrictions on insurance companies' investing out of state, the United States had in life insurance companies what amounted to *de facto* mortgage banks. Life insurance companies issued liabilities (insurance contracts) with long and actuarially predictable maturities and invested considerable portions of the funds raised this way in interregional mortgage lending. Because the life insurance companies did not need liquidity, they could ride out the recurring depressions in real estate prices. As Snowden emphasizes, the life insurance companies had their own difficulties in the interregional mortgage markets, including continuing problems with the mortgage companies. Yet for a period the life insurance companies were able to play a role that no previous financial intermediary had been able to play. Life insurance companies grew to play the role filled by mortgage banks in European countries, and so serve as yet another example of a distinctively American financial innovation that arose to overcome constraints put in place by our banking system.

References

Calomiris, Charles, and Charles M. Kahn. 1991. The Role of Demandable Debt in Structuring Optimal Banking Arrangements. *American Economic Review* 81 (3): 497–513.

Davis, Lance. 1965. The Investment Market, 1870–1914. The Evolution of a National Market. *Journal of Economic History* 33:355–93.

Greif, Avner. 1989. Reputation and Coalitions in Medieval Trade: Evidence on the Maghribi Traders. *Journal of Economic History* 49 (4): 857–82.

Guinnane, Timothy W. 1994. A Failed Institutional Transplant: Raiffeisen's Credit Co-operatives in Ireland, 1894–1914. *Explorations in Economic History* 31 (1): 38–61.

Lamoreaux, Naomi. 1991. Information Problems and Banks' Specialization in Short-Term Commercial Lending: New England in the Nineteenth Century. In *Inside the Business Enterprise: Historical Perspectives on the Use of Information,* ed. Peter Temin. Chicago: University of Chicago Press.

8 The Costs of Rejecting Universal Banking: American Finance in the German Mirror, 1870–1914

Charles W. Calomiris

8.1 Introduction

The American financial system has been an outlier internationally in virtually every important respect for the past century. It has been the most geographically fragmented and the most susceptible to financial crises (Calomiris and Gorton 1991; Calomiris 1993). It has been among the most restrictive of combinations of financial services within intermediaries, although in recent years some of these restrictions have begun to be relaxed (Kaufman and Mote 1989, 1990). The American system has also been the most persistently innovative financial system in the world. Often, important innovations have been induced by regulatory restrictions that raised the cost of finance under preexisting financial technology.

These observations are commonplace. Other unusual aspects of American financial history have received less attention, including the relative lack of bank involvement in industrial finance, the heavy reliance on corporate bonds as a means of finance, the high costs of securities underwriting, and the high cost of capital in American industry.

The main goal of this paper is to weave these peculiar features of the American system into a single interpretive tapestry. The central argument of the paper is that regulatory limitations on the scale and scope of banking in America

Charles W. Calomiris is associate professor of finance at the University of Illinois at Urbana-Champaign and a faculty research fellow of the National Bureau of Economic Research.

The author thanks Henning Bohn, Nancy Calomiris, Marco Da Rin, Barry Eichengreen, John James, Charles Kindleberger, Naomi Lamoreaux, Daniel Raff, Carlos Ramirez, Jay Ritter, Kenneth Snowden, Peter Temin, Richard Tilly, Lawrence White, seminar participants at Brandeis University, participants at the NBER Conference on Financial Institutions and Macroeconomic Stability, and participants at the NBER Conference on Microeconomic History for helpful suggestions. Jurgen Wiesmann, Susanne Hellmann, and Sandra Gerling provided invaluable assistance as translators.

hampered financial coordination and substantially increased the cost of capital for industrialization, particularly in the period of the growth of large-scale industrial enterprises prior to World War I. This may seem a strange claim in light of American growth and financial innovativeness. The claim is not that America failed to grow and prosper, but that large-scale industrial investment was stunted relative to its potential by a faulty financial system.

To gauge the costs of American banking regulation, I compare and contrast the American and German financial systems. Rapid industrial growth in new industries and the increasing importance of large-scale enterprises are common features of the German and American experience in the pre–World War I era. The second industrial revolution witnessed rapid growth in industries that exploited new technological breakthroughs and produced entirely new products. The scale of firms was much larger than during earlier episodes of industrial expansion. Large-scale production of new products using new technologies created unprecedented challenges for the financial system. Large-scale production implied greater reliance on external funding, and the novelty of the products and techniques made it especially difficult for uninformed "outsiders" with available funds to judge the merits of the various investment opportunities. The ability of the financial system to mobilize and direct large amounts of funds into new firms was a prerequisite to rapid industrialization.

The means of financing industrial expansion during this period in the United States and Germany were quite different. The German universal banks (*Kreditbanken*)—sometimes referred to as the joint-stock or credit banks—were large-scale, externally financed, limited-liability banks. These banks operated nationwide branching networks and provided an unrestricted range of services, including lending, underwriting, trust services, and deposit taking. They held and underwrote securities issued by clients and made conventional loans for industrial purposes. They maintained close ties with the firms they financed and exerted control over corporate decision making in their combined role as lenders, stockholders, trustees of stock portfolios, and members of boards of directors.

The American banking system, in contrast, was shaped by restrictions on branching and consolidation that protected unit (single-office) banks.[1] The fragmentation of commercial banking limited American banks' involvement in supplying credit to large-scale firms. Over the nineteenth century, as industrial firm size grew, the role of banks as suppliers of industrial credit waned, and commercial banks focused increasingly on financing commerce (Lamoreaux 1994). Private bankers operating partnerships (also known as investment bankers) filled the gap in American finance, but because they had limited resources, they relied on underwriting syndicates, funded in a decentralized way by an elaborate network of commercial banks, trust companies, and brokers,

1. Direct restrictions on the types of activities banks could finance—notably, attempts to confine bank lending to the financing of commerce, which is often referred to as the "real bills doctrine"— appear not to have been a binding constraint on bank lending activities (Lamoreaux 1994).

to raise funds for the firms they financed. Like universal bankers in Germany, investment bankers established methods for monitoring and controlling corporate management of the firms they financed.

Clearly, these are two very different ways of coordinating the flow of funds from savers to investors. But did these differences matter? In section 8.2, I review general theoretical and empirical perspectives that suggest why they may have mattered. Here the review is selective, and serves to introduce concepts that will be emphasized in section 8.3's detailed discussion of the German and American financial systems and economies. Section 8.3 compares and contrasts the German and American experiences, argues that the various differences between them are mutually consistent, and points to evidence of higher costs of industrial finance in the United States. That section closes with a brief historical review of the different evolution of financial regulations and institutions in the two countries.

Section 8.4 offers some conjectures on why inefficient restrictions on banking have persisted in the United States. Limitations on branching and restrictions on joint production of financial services did not disappear as their costs became apparent. Indeed, the Great Depression saw an increase in restrictions, most notably the separation of commercial and investment banking, many new restrictions on securities transactions, a reversal of direction in the regulatory trend toward branching and consolidation of the 1920s, and the subsidization of unit banking by the creation of federal deposit insurance. Political considerations, as well as endogenous changes in financial technology that lowered the costs of regulation, may help to explain persistently poor banking regulation in the United States.

8.2 General Perspectives on Universal Banking

This section provides an overview of general theoretical and empirical perspectives on universal banking, which will serve as a basis for the discussion of section 8.3. I begin with a discussion of the role of various intermediaries and contracting arrangements for mitigating financing costs. Second, I argue that the form of financial instrument and the intermediation arrangement chosen by a firm reflect its place in the financial "pecking order," which is largely determined by the stage it has reached in its financial "life cycle." Third, I examine the role played by universal banking in reducing firm financing costs. Universal banking is defined as a combination of activities performed by banks, including deposit taking, trust services, direct lending, equity holding, and underwriting. Informational economies account for economies of scope among the three forms of intermediary financing of firms (lending, equity holding, and underwriting). These economies of scope are driven by considerations of time consistency, the reusability of information over the firm's life cycle, and improvements in the quality of signals generated by underwriters. Fourth, I consider the effect of restrictions on bank branching on the efficiency of universal banking. The benefits of universal banking are enhanced in a system that allows banks to branch. Direct access to sources of funds through deposit and trust accounts reduces the costs of marketing securities by facilitating the flow of information and limiting the number of layers of securities transactions.

This four-part summary of the economics of universal banking places universal banking in the context of theoretical literature on the role of banks and the financing structure of corporations. The changing needs of corporations over time correspond to different financial products produced by the universal bank. The advantages of a long-term relationship between a firm and an intermediary are best achieved by allowing the intermediary to perform a variety of tasks. The advantages of universal banking are best achieved in the context of large-scale banking, where transactions and information costs of syndications are minimized.

The theoretical discussion closes by linking these arguments to others made in the existing literature, both for and against universal banking. My emphasis on benefits of universal banking from reductions in corporate finance costs is also related to the question of portfolio diversification benefits under universal banking. Much of the recent policy debate over universal banking in the United States has focused on potential advantages from diversification from allowing commercial banks broader powers. A weakness of some of these studies has been the implicit assumption that available market assets are invariant to the establishment of universal banking. Potential benefits from diversification depend on the effect universal banks have on the feasible set of externally financed investments. If universal banking reduces corporate finance costs, then it enlarges the set of investments available to "outsiders."

Common theoretical arguments against universal banking are considered in light of theory and history. These include destabilization of the financial system, conflicts of interest, and inefficiency from lack of competition in banking or in industry. Theory and history support the view that universal banking is a stabilizing influence on banking. Furthermore, potential problems of conflict of interest can be overcome if universal banks are allowed to hold or manage equity as well as to underwrite and lend. Finally, while bank concentration and long-term links between firms and their banks may encourage lack of competition among banks or firms, Germany's universal banking system had many observable advantages, and was not a necessary condition for the formation of industrial cartels.

8.2.1 The Roles of Financial Intermediaries

Financing investment is fundamentally a problem of coordination. Savers and investors need a low-cost means to transact. Of course, ultimate savers and investors virtually never meet. Rather, each deals with an intermediary, and often ultimate savers and investors do not use the same intermediary. In many transactions, complex hierarchies of intermediation may be employed. For example, many individuals own securities primarily through pension funds. Pension-fund managers might purchase securities through local bankers or dealers, who in turn may be marketing these securities for an investment banking syndicate formed and financed by a small group of banks, and managed by a lead investment bank who negotiates the deal with the issuing firm.

The links separating the individual saver and the firm issuing the security in this case are many, and involve substantial costs. These costs can be divided usefully into two categories: costs of information collection and transmittal—that is, costs of creating and enforcing mechanisms that lead to credible monitoring of firms and revelation of the true state of firm finances—and physical transactions costs—costs associated with legal and accounting paperwork, and with physically distributing securities to ultimate holders.

Recent contributions to the literature in banking and corporate finance have drawn attention to the ways various institutional arrangements can economize on such costs. For example, the costs to investment banking syndicates of collecting information about the proper pricing of new issues may be affected by the mechanism chosen for the initial marketing of the securities. Rationing of issues to a select group of securities purchasers who have repeated contact with the investment banking house may encourage truthful revelation of information about the value of the securities by those purchasers prior to the issue. Benveniste and Spindt (1989) argue that this beneficial revelation effect explains various otherwise puzzling features of the marketing and pricing of initial public offerings (IPOs). More generally, investment banks are valuable to the economy because they provide a low-cost means of generating and disseminating credible information about firms' characteristics, which benefits both securities issuers and purchasers in deciding on the form and price of the security used to finance an investment.

The recent literature on banking also views commercial banks as solving problems that arise from physical transactions costs and information asymmetry, and sees the form of intermediaries' contracts as a key determinant of the cost of finance. Banks economize on physical costs of transacting (clearing payments, liquidating insolvent firms), costs of generating information (monitoring firms' actions and outcomes), and costs of enforcing contractual compliance on the part of firms and bankers (disciplining borrowers and protecting against improper behavior by the banker at the expense of those funding the bank).

Models of banking stress the economies of concentrating funds in banks and appointing the banker as the "delegated monitor" of bank borrowers (Campbell and Kracaw 1980; Diamond 1984; Calomiris and Kahn 1991; Calomiris, Kahn, and Krasa 1992). Banking arrangements can avoid duplication in monitoring bank borrowers and thus reduce banking costs. Enforcement of contracts (monitoring and discipline) is also less costly if a single agent with proper incentives can specialize in the task.

Empirical evidence on the characteristics of firms choosing banks as financing sources confirms the view that banks specialize in performing ongoing monitoring and contractual enforcement for firms whose access to outside funding otherwise would be limited (Butters and Lintner 1945; Fazzari, Hubbard, and Petersen 1989; James and Wier 1988, 1990; Mackie-Mason 1990). Other firms—older, better-known firms—have access to securities markets on better terms and can avoid the costs of bank finance. These firms typically still use intermediaries (like investment banks) to assist them in determining what types of securities to issue and in credibly signaling the value of their securities (Benveniste and Spindt 1989; Ramakrishnan and Thakor 1984), but they avoid at least some of the ongoing costs of bank finance. Costs of bank finance include regulatory costs (like reserve requirements), monitoring costs, and rents the bank may extract from firms it finances by virtue of its possession of private information, as in Rajan 1992a.

Empirical studies of the effects of bank lending decisions on the prices of existing securities or bank borrowers also provide evidence of the role of banks as "insiders" with respect to information relevant for valuing claims on firms to which they lend. Announcing financing arrangements between banks and firms increases firms' stock prices (James 1987; James and Wier 1988). Bank participation in working out corporate distress increases the value of distressed firms' stock (Gilson, John, and Lang 1990), especially when banks are willing to take a junior position in the firm (Brown, James, and Mooradian 1991). Japanese firms with close, long-term banking relationships are better able to maintain investment levels than other firms during episodes of financial distress (Hoshi, Kashyap, and Scharfstein 1990a, 1990b).

8.2.2   The Financial "Pecking Order" and the "Life Cycle" of Firms

The growing theoretical literature in corporate finance focuses on how particular financing arrangements mitigate some costs at the expense of others. In some cases, using an investment bank may be desirable because it provides a low-cost means of signaling the value of securities. In other cases, bank loans may be the appropriate financing vehicle, possibly because of banks' low costs of managing financial distress or of monitoring managers' actions and enhancing corporate control.

The new "information-based" approach to corporate finance revolves around the financial "pecking order"—a continuum of financing instruments defined according to the elasticity of their cost with respect to problems of asymmetric information (Myers 1984; Myers and Majluf 1984; Diamond 1991). Firms progress up the pecking order of finance as they mature. Firms just starting out may be forced to rely exclusively on retained earnings and the wealth of insiders. After a successful beginning, the firm can rely on "inside debt" in the form of bank loans. The bank spends resources to monitor the firm, and protects itself against "lemons" problems by holding a debt claim on the firm.[2] As the firm matures and develops a track record, its financing will change. Informed intermediaries will be willing to take equity positions in the firm (as in the venture capital market), which will reduce the leverage of the firm and its exposure to financial distress, and provide a positive signal to outside investors. Outside finance through securities may initially take the form of senior instruments with protective covenants (e.g., bonds). Later, firms will graduate to issuing preferred and common stock on the open market to outsiders, using underwriters as a means for providing credible signals of the firm's value to outsiders.

The maturity of debt instruments chosen can reflect a tradeoff between the information and transactions costs of finance. Short-term debt mitigates incentive problems between banks and firms. As Jensen and Meckling (1976, 334–37) show, debt contracts create a potential agency problem known as the "asset substitution effect." Once debt contracts are entered into, managers with an equity interest in the firm may have an incentive to take on greater risk, because they are only concerned with expanding the upper tail of the asset returns distribution. Short-term debt can be useful as a means to restrict such risk taking. Firms that increase risk face the threat that their loans will not be rolled over, or will be rolled over only at a higher interest rate. If lenders keep debt short-term and monitor borrowers' actions, borrowers will find little benefit in increasing risk, so long as the threat of the bank's rollover response is credible (e.g., see Pennacchi 1983; Gorton and Kahn 1992). Similarly, bank-loan contracts typically allow acceleration of the maturity of debt when the firm's position deteriorates. This right of acceleration is particularly powerful in restricting borrower risk taking when combined with compensating balance requirements (which force firms to hold their checking accounts in the bank) and the option of deposit setoff (bank seizure of deposits), as Garber and Weisbrod (1991) argue.

Despite the advantages of short-term debt in protecting lenders and encouraging proper behavior by borrowers, short-term debt has higher transactions

---

2. Given the general predominance of debt finance, particularly in banking, recent contracting models try to explain the optimality of debt. Debt claims are often a desirable means of finance when claimants are relatively uninformed about firm opportunities or outcomes, or when outcomes are difficult to demonstrate to a third party. As Myers and Majluf (1984) show, in a world where firms' opportunities are unobservable ex ante, debt suffers less of a "lemons premium" than equity because the payoffs to debt depend less on the unobservable information. Townsend (1979), Diamond (1984), Gale and Hellwig (1985), Williamson (1986), and others have argued that costs of ex post monitoring and third-party verification favor the use of debt contracts. Lacker (1991) shows that debt is especially useful in these environments as a means to penalize firms by threatening to take collateralized assets that have special value to the firms' operators.

These arguments for the optimality of debt contracting may help explain the reliance by banks on deposits and banknotes as the primary means of "outsider" financing of bank activities historically (as argued above), and the use of debt as the primary means of "outsider" finance of many corporations. But these arguments do not suggest that bank financing of firms will always, or even mainly, occur in the form of debt. Indeed, the pecking-order theory of corporate finance—which emphasizes the role of debt as an optimal means of financing outsiders' contributions to the firm—suggests advantages from insiders' avoidance of debt, as argued below.

costs than long-term debt. The costs of renegotiation and rollover are especially large for *nonbank* debt, which must be physically redeemed and reissued to a widely dispersed group of creditors.[3] For example, the costs of issuing bonds (costs charged for paperwork and for fees to the investment banking syndicate marketing the bonds) averaged 6 percent of the size of the issue in the United States during 1925–29 (Securities and Exchange Commission 1940, 10–11). If the maturity of these bonds had been, say, one year rather than the actual fifteen-to-twenty-year average maturity (Hickman 1960, 152), this would have entailed a significant increase in the cost of funds. Thus, short-term debts of firms typically take the form of bank loans (with low rollover costs) or short-term trade credit.[4]

In summary, banks, investment banks, and other intermediaries can be seen as "optimal mechanisms" for connecting particular groups of savers and investors in a world of costly transactions and asymmetric information. Informational characteristics of firms (the availability of a track record, the costs to outsiders of monitoring and controlling activities of the firm) are important determinants of whether firms choose to finance themselves with securities issues or with bank lending, and of the form and maturity of the financing instrument. This approach emphasizes the importance of financing through banks in the early stages of the life cycle of the firm, and sees other forms of intermediation (investment banking) as depending on earlier information creation by the firm's track record with inside lenders. Choice variables for minimizing financing costs include the intermediation technology used, the forms of the claims issued (e.g., debt or equity) by firms and intermediaries, their maturity, covenants on behavior and options granted to holders or issuers of claims on firms or banks, liquidation rules, allocation of voting authority, agreements that ensure a long-term relationship between or among contracting parties (and thereby solve problems of time inconsistency), and the voluntary formation of coalitions (of banks, investment banks, or informed IPO purchasers), which regulate the behavior of members.[5]

---

3. Another reason why banks may be in a better position to offer short-term debt is suggested in recent work by Diamond (1992). He argues that short-term debt can be costly when held by uninformed lenders because they may be too quick to liquidate a solvent, but illiquid, firm. One could argue that, if banks are better informed about firms, they will be able to reap the disciplinary advantages of short-term debt without creating losses through excessive liquidations.

4. In addition to bank loans, the United States developed an important innovation in commercial and industrial finance, which became known as the commercial paper market. For reasons related to its fragmented banking system, bankers' acceptances and foreign bills of exchange never reached the level of importance in the United States that they did elsewhere (Calomiris 1993). The commercial paper market developed as a means for banks to transfer their lowest-risk customers to other intermediaries, to take advantage of lower costs of finance in other locations. The commercial paper market was a unique feature of the American financial system, which grew substantially in importance during the last quarter of the nineteenth century.

5. An important contributor to minimizing finance costs has been coalitions of banks, whose function includes cooperation in underwriting networks, interbank correspondent relations, cost-

8.2.3   The Advantages of Universal Banking

The pecking-order framework implies that financing arrangements that accelerate the process of seasoning a firm and economize on the costs of information production and corporate governance can stimulate investment by reducing the costs of external finance. In this light, the main advantage of universal banking is that it encourages a long-term relationship to develop between a firm and its intermediary by allowing the intermediary to vary the form of firm financing as the firm matures, in keeping with the optimal financing arrangement, which changes over the life cycle of the firm. Initially, the intermediary lends directly to the firm. Later, it will be best for the same intermediary to underwrite the firm's securities issues (either by itself or as a leader of a syndicate of universal banks). Underwriting will require that the bank be allowed to own (and act as trustee for) shares of the firm. Without the flexibility to vary the form of the bank-firm relationship, relationships between firms and banks are unlikely to persist over the firm's life cycle.

By "long-term" I mean that the firm and bank have a credible implicit contract to continue to do business in the future. The firm cannot switch banks costlessly. The advantage of a credible long-term relationship is that it encourages banks to lend to firms on favorable terms in anticipation of a continuing relationship. The costs of gathering information about a firm's credit risk is high for unseasoned firms, which pay for bank monitoring in the form of higher interest cost on loans. If banks can spread the cost of monitoring over many periods, this reduces the initial costs of borrowing and allows firms to pay less for credit during their early years when investment needs are high and cash flow is low. Despite the advantages of a long-term relationship for smoothing the cost of credit to firms, there is a potential "time-inconsistency" problem that makes it difficult for banks to postpone charging firms for high early monitoring costs. Firms receiving low-interest loans in their early years may opt out of the initial banking relationship once they become seasoned and have opportunities to borrow from other intermediaries. Competing intermediaries may be able to provide credit at lower cost in the later stage of the firm life cycle because the costs of monitoring the firm have fallen as the result of its observable credit history with the initial bank (James and Wier 1990). Thus, competing banks may be able to "free ride" on the initial bank's efforts.

In practice, long-term exclusivity can be enforced in two ways. First, to the extent that competing banks are unable to learn relevant information about the firm from the initial bank's lending decisions, the initial bank's investment in

---

effective payment clearings, and perhaps most important, coalitions for mutual protection. Such coalitions are more easily organized, managed, and self-regulated in a concentrated banking system. For discussions of several examples, see Gorton 1985, 1989; Gorton and Mullineaux 1987; Calomiris 1989, 1990, 1993; Calomiris and Kahn 1990, 1991; and Calomiris and Schweikart 1991.

information about the firm at an early stage reduces future costs of granting credit or underwriting only for the initial bank, so the firm and bank are naturally drawn to one another for repeat business.[6] Second, banks may prohibit "their" firms from doing business with other banks (Neuburger and Stokes 1974, 713). Presumably, such prohibitions would be enforced by cooperation among the banks to limit deviation from this rule. While finance historians have argued that banks in Germany and the United States were not successful in enforcing exclusivity once clients became large, well-known firms (Tilly 1992, 109), nevertheless, for a limited period of time such enforcement may have been important.

Given the benefits to borrowers from interest cost smoothing, such collusion among banks is not necessarily a bad thing. Although it may allow banks to extract rent from firms, without it the advantages of a long-term relationship may not be available to young, growing firms. Mayer (1988) cites post–World War II Japan as an example of successful elimination of information externalities among banks through credible long-term contracting, made feasible by limits on period-by-period competition among banks. Without a credible long-term relationship between firms and banks, banks may have been unwilling to pay fixed costs initially and bear risk during early stages of industrialization of infant industries.

Another important avenue for internalizing externalities for banks lending to young, growing firms is to allow banks to take equity positions in these firms. This allows banks to benefit fully from the positive signal they create when they finance firms. Also, by making banks junior claimants on the firm, equity holding provides a strong incentive for continuing diligence by the banker (Pozdena 1991).[7] Equity financing has other advantages as well. It re-

---

6. Given the evidence of disadvantages from not creating a long-term bank relationship, or of deciding to discontinue one (Hoshi, Kashyap, and Scharfstein 1990a, 1990b; De Long 1991; Ramirez 1992), it may seem puzzling that some firms did not opt for such a close, long-term relationship. A simple example will help to fix ideas, and help one to understand why some firms may choose not to borrow from universal banks, or to discontinue borrowing eventually. Suppose that the costs to a bank at time zero of starting a relationship with a firm consist of monitoring costs, which decline over time. To be concrete, assume the initial cost to the bank is X, and the costs for all subsequent periods is m per period. Furthermore, assume that, if the firm cannot borrow from a bank, it must rely only on retained earnings to finance investment, and that this entails a reduction in profitable investment (alternatively, one could assume the firm will borrow from nonbanks at a higher cost, reflecting a lemons premium on uninformed lending). For simplicity, assume the firm will need external funding for only 10 periods, after which its investment opportunities can be completely financed from its (larger) stream of retained earnings. The bank will charge a fee for the ten periods of z per period, which includes reimbursement for X and m costs, and possibly additional rents extracted by the bank (if the bank has an initial information advantage over its competitors). The firm compares the value of joining the bank (the present value of firm assets if it joins the bank minus the z fees), with the present value of firm assets if it does not join the bank. Firms that require a large X and m investment *relative to the advantages they would receive from rapid access to finance through a banking relationship* will prefer autarky.

7. By holding equity in the firm, the bank may also be able to exert influence over the firm's future choice of a bank to act as purchaser and underwriter of securities. Thus equity can help solve

duces financial distress costs for firms by reducing leverage, and by concentrating ownership stakes (which reduces bargaining and coordination costs among creditors during distress). Also, in distress states, firms may need their banker to credibly signal that the firm's prospects are good to other firm creditors. A bank's willingness to exchange debt for equity in the firm during distress can be a strong signal of the bank's confidence in the firm (Brown, James, and Mooradian 1991). Several recent studies of Japanese banking have emphasized the advantages of stock ownership by banks as a means of promoting monitoring and reducing costs of financial distress.[8] A final advantage of allowing equity finance is that this avoids potential conflicts of interest between the firm and its creditors. Reliance on debt can lead to an "underinvestment problem" (Myers 1977). Positive net present value (NPV) projects with relatively low risk may not be undertaken on the margin because undertaking the project generates a transfer of wealth from the firm's stockholders to its debtholders. Similarly, debt finance entices firms to substitute relatively high-risk assets for existing low-risk assets, since such substitution leads to a wealth transfer from creditors to stockholders.

These advantages from equity contracting may be offset by costs associated with equity finance. If the riskiness of firms is unobservable, those who finance firms must charge all firms the same cost of finance. For good firms, this entails a lemons premium on their cost of finance. The premium will be largest for junior securities, since their payoffs are the riskiest (Myers and Majluf 1984). Also, as Jensen and Meckling (1976) and others have stressed, if managerial effort depends on managers' stakes in the firm, or if management's objectives conflict with shareholders', then equity issues can reduce managerial incentives and encourage non-profit-maximizing behavior by management (by reducing the concentration of ownership in the firm, and hence the ability to discipline managers).

Mayer's (1988) time-inconsistency problem, in part, by allowing banks to control firm financing decisions in the future. As argued below, there is little evidence for this sort of monopoly control by banks in Germany or the United States, at least after the 1890s.

8. Sheard (1989) points out that a "main" bank's debt position in a firm often takes a junior position to other debt effectively, and is written down during financial distress to avoid bankruptcy. Thus Japanese banks' "equity" positions in firms are effectively larger than their balance-sheet statements would indicate. Kim (1992) finds that equity stakes by Japanese banks are higher for growing firms with high external finance ratios and high risk. In Japan, the incidence of bankruptcy is much lower, and the costs of bankruptcy when it does occur are also much lower, than in the U.S. Kim shows that these advantages in Japan depend on the ownership structure of firms—specifically, the concentration of ownership in the firm (or equivalently, the proportion of the firm owned by banks). Hoshi, Kashyap, and Scharfstein (1990b) find that firms with close ties to Japanese banks suffer much lower reduction in investment levels during periods of financial distress, but they do not find an effect from bank's equity interest on the costs of financial distress once one has controlled for other characteristics of the firms' financing sources. The upshot of their findings is that there are substitute means for achieving the desirable features of inside equity, which take the form of concentrating lending in the hands of few borrowers, or allowing banks to hold junior debt positions that have equitylike features. Further support for this interpretation comes from Prowse (1992) and Hoshi, Kashyap, and Loveman (1992).

Thus, reaping the advantages of equity depends on constructing mechanisms that provide adequate control over the firm's management to avoid prohibitive lemons premiums and managerial incentive problems. Bankers may sit on corporate boards of directors and exert direct control over managerial decisions. This entails large fixed costs to the bank, which may be prohibitive for small firms with uncertain prospects. Alternatively, firms could avoid equity issues and rely on debt. In this case, banks use debt covenants and short-term debt as a disciplinary device on management. Managers who behave improperly will find their credit lines discontinued by the bank, through either the "calling" of the bank's loan or the bank's decision not to rollover its debt. As discussed below, the history of German universal banking—in which both enforcement technologies were available to banks—suggests that banks began lending to firms via protected short-term debt. Once the firm had matured and the bank had become an informed insider, both parties benefited from a conversion of short-term debt into equity finance. The transition from debt to equity finance also entailed an increased role of the bank in controlling corporate decision making through the board of directors. The life cycle of "corporate governance" arrangements with intermediaries parallels the life cycle of the firm's financial structure.

Thus, the economies of scope from a single intermediary being able to lend, hold equity, exert corporate discipline, and underwrite securities for a firm may be entirely unrelated to conventional technological economies of scope (or transactions costs) in providing these services. Rather, the main advantages of allowing a single intermediary to perform all these activities revolve around information and control economies. First, in the context of the pecking-order approach outlined above, because lending to a firm precedes underwriting in the firm's life cycle, a bank that has lent to the firm in the past will have access to private information that will reduce the costs of underwriting. Second, consistent with Mayer's (1988) emphasis on time consistency, it may be important to allow the bank to hold equity and underwrite securities for the mature firm as an efficient means for the firm to pay for earlier bank investments in information with capital gains on stock and underwriting fees at later dates when the firm's cost of funds is lower. Third, when banks take long-term positions in a firm, by lending or holding the equity of the firm, their signals as underwriters may be more credible. This is particularly true if banks are allowed to hold equity; or alternatively, if the securities they underwrite are senior to preexisting claims on the firm.[9]

---

9. It is possible that universal banking can involve a conflict of interest. Banks with existing claims on a firm might use underwriting as a means of reducing losses on their existing claims on the firm by attracting outside investors, or, conversely, banks may discourage outside investors to keep a good-risk firm to themselves. These problems can be overcome if banks are allowed to have a stake in the securities they underwrite, or if the security being underwritten is senior to the bank's existing claim on the firm. For both of these reasons, it is important to allow banks to take equity positions in firms or manage equity holdings by bank trust customers.

8.2.4   Universal Banking and Bank Concentration

The recent literature on commercial banking has stressed advantages of allowing banks to be large. A concentrated banking system permits greater portfolio diversification of banks and allows banks to coordinate their response to crises by forming credible mutual-insurance arrangements, which would not be possible in a system of many geographically isolated banks. These theoretical propositions receive ample support from the comparative history of banking systems and their performance (see Calomiris 1993 for a review).

In the context of universal banking, there are further advantages to becoming a large bank operating a branching network. First, if industrial firms find it advantageous to operate large-scale enterprises over a wide geographic area (as Chandler 1977 argues), then monitoring the activities of the firm will be easier if a bank has similarly wide geographic scope. Second, large branching banks are better able to take advantage of long-term relationship economies of financing firms through a universal bank because of their access to both securities purchasers and depositors. Unit banking laws that prohibit the establishment of deposit-taking branches effectively limit banks' access to deposits on a large scale and, therefore, limit large-scale lending to firms.

Furthermore, given the overhead costs of setting up a bank office, restrictions on commercial bank branching limit branching in securities retailing, too, and this raises the costs of bringing securities to market.[10] Without access to a large number of securities purchasers, a bank may not be able to internalize all the benefits of collecting information about issuing firms' prospects and about the ultimate demand for firms' securities. The lack of retail branching also creates transactions and signaling costs associated with setting up networks of banks that collect and credibly transmit such information. Finally, branching reduces the physical cost of distributing securities.[11] Riesser (1911, 756–57) writes that the German banks are "able to find a wider and safer market for the sale of securities which [they] proposed to float. [They] can, therefore, acquire such securities on a larger scale and with greater confidence, knowing beforehand that such securities will go into good hands as permanent investments, and not be thrown back at once upon the market, to be taken up again by the bank." Riesser also argues that large-scale banking concentrates voting power (proxies from trust accounts), which can be useful for disciplining manage-

10. Implicit in this argument are the realistic assumptions that the depositors and holders of trust accounts required a branch to be located near them, and that depositors were not indifferent to holding claims on banks in nontransactable form; otherwise, unit banking laws would not have been a binding constraint.

11. White (1985) argues that economies of scale and scope in providing investment banking and trust activities, as well as the nonbank corporate merger wave, encouraged bank mergers in the 1920s. Peach (1941, 86) notes that affiliates often operated large branching networks, nationally or internationally. These networks no doubt reduced transactions costs of placing issues; however, they were not substitutes for full-fledged branch banking, which involves the taking of deposits, clearing of checks, management of trust accounts, and placing of securities within the same organization.

ment of firms banks finance. Jeidels (1905, 164–76) argues that industry-specific knowledge was important in evaluating the creditworthiness of German firms, and that economies of information gathering encouraged concentration and specialization by underwriters in particular industry niches.

Commentators on the emergence of some large-scale universal banking in the United States in the 1920s noted that one of the chief advantages of securities affiliates of commercial banks relative to investment banks was their larger size, which was due to their large branching networks. Chicago's growth as an investment-banking center in the 1920s was encouraged by the growth of regional correspondent relations centering in Chicago, which increased the deposit and securities accounts managed by Chicago commercial banks operating investment banking affiliates (Bureau of Business Research 1928, 40).

Preston and Finlay (1930a, 1154) argue that American investors were more confident of securities underwritten by a single bank, since concentration of underwriting "centers responsibility" for the issue in one bank. They also argue that research into the creditworthiness of a firm "must involve more than simply a study of statistics: it must include continuous contact with the management of companies whose equities are selected." These large fixed costs imply that stock offerings and underwriters' resources must be large.

Despite the advantages of concentration for universal banks, regulations limiting branch banking made large-scale universal banking impossible. Long before the 1914 Clayton Act restrictions on bank involvement on corporate boards or the 1933 Glass-Steagall restrictions on universal banking activities, branching restrictions hampered the development of long-term relationships between firms and banks and made large-scale underwritings by commercial banks very rare. In the United States, after Jay Cooke's bond campaign to finance the Union during the Civil War, underwriting syndicates relied on a complex hierarchy of banks and brokers to coordinate securities transactions. This network became an important vehicle for funding underwriting, defining securities holders' demand schedules (to set prices and determine types of securities underwritten), and distributing securities once they were underwritten (Carosso 1970). The network of interbank relationships established for this purpose was an important financial innovation of the post–Civil War era. Nevertheless, in the absence of regulations prohibiting branching and consolidation across states, such coordination of information could have been accomplished (as in Germany) within syndicates of a few nationwide banks, with far fewer transactions, and with stronger incentives to collect accurate information about firms' prospects and securities holders' demands. This system also would have enhanced control over the management of public firms by concentrating voting rights in the hands of a few agents.

8.2.5 Diversification and Universal Banking

My discussion of universal banking has focused on corporate-finance cost reductions that come from information and transactions cost savings under a universal banking system. Much of the current discussion of the economies of allowing universal banking has focused on a different issue. Empirical studies of the United States in the post–World War II era have examined primarily the potential benefits of diversification that would come from combining the activities of commercial and investment banks, as well as other intermediaries. Diversification lessens the chance of costly liquidation of intermediaries and reduces transactions costs of constructing diversified portfolios for wealth holders. Some of these studies examine the relative performance of firms with diverse activities (Meinster and Johnson 1979; Boyd and Graham 1986; Litan 1985; 1987, 105–11; Wall 1987; Brewer 1989), while others consider random combinations of firms actually pursuing separate activities (Boyd and Graham 1988; Litan 1987, 112–18; Boyd, Graham, and Hewitt 1988; Brewer, Fortier, and Pavel 1988). The results from this literature have been mixed, though on balance they indicate small benefits of diversification. Not only do these studies focus too narrowly on the issue of portfolio structure, but by design they are ill-suited to measure the portfolio-diversification advantages of universal banking.

The studies of random, counterfactual combinations of different activities suffer from the obvious problem that combining firms is not the same as combining balance sheets. The behavior of financial firms might change as the result of combining activities; indeed, this underlies the arguments of economies of scope outlined above. But even the studies that analyze the comparative performance of actual combinations of financial activities will understate the potential diversification advantages from universal banking for two reasons. First, the observed combinations have occurred in the existing regulatory environment, in which many potentially beneficial combinations are prohibited by law. Second, universal banking might enlarge the feasible set of traded assets in the economy in ways that cannot be observed under the current regulatory regime.

Obviously, a better measure of the diversification benefits from universal banking would examine diversification opportunities across regulatory regimes, and within regimes that permitted universal banking. In the latter category, White's (1986) findings for the United States in the 1920s are of interest. National banks with securities affiliates had lower risk of failure than other banks. This may reflect greater portfolio opportunities for banks that could establish credible long-term relationships with borrowers. White also found that securities affiliates reduced the overall risk to bank stockholders, since the incomes from affiliates and parent banks were uncorrelated.

In a series of interesting studies, Tilly (1980, 1984, 1986, 1992) analyzes the risk-return characteristics of the portfolios created by Germany's universal banks in the pre–World War I era, and compares them with a constructed "efficient" portfolio (the efficient frontier of risk-return tradeoffs available). He finds German universal banks' portfolios remarkably close to the efficient frontier of the economy, and interprets this as evidence against the suggestions of some (e.g., Neuburger and Stokes 1974; Gerschenkron 1962, 15) that German banks may have preferred some industries over others for reasons unrelated to efficient capital allocation.

Cross-regime comparisons for this period are also possible. Tilly (1984, 1986, 1992) and Kennedy and Britton (1985) compare British (nonuniversal) and German bank portfolios for the pre–World War I period. They argue that British portfolios were much more distant from the efficient frontier of the British economy and far inferior to Germany in the risk-return tradeoffs they achieved.

The results of the studies of Germany and Britain are controversial, since they rely on rather heroic assumptions to measure both the efficient portfolio frontier and the portfolio created by the banks. But they draw attention to the importance of a universal banking system's ability to produce, not merely to combine, investment opportunities. As Tilly (1986, 117; 1992) emphasizes, and as is too often ignored in the empirical studies of diversification from combining banking activities in the United States today, the banking system's achievement of an efficient portfolio in Germany did not merely reflect wise choices by passive money managers of the portfolio weights to attach to a set of exogenously given investment opportunities. The German banking system, with its ability to economize on a variety of costs, was essential to making investment opportunities available to the market, and hence to expanding the feasible portfolio frontier. Opportunities for efficient construction of portfolios through universal banking depended on the ability of the banks to mitigate information, control, and transaction costs (Tilly 1992, 110).

8.2.6 Criticisms of Universal Banking

Perspectives on universal banking have not always been favorable. Historically, in the United States, there has been substantial opposition to allowing both the concentration of banking and the combination of commercial lending, underwriting, and equity holding by financial intermediaries. Indeed, as will be discussed in section 8.3, for most of the period prior to the legal separation of commercial and investment banking in 1933, which forced the closing of state-chartered underwriting affiliates of commercial banks, lending and underwriting were performed mainly by different intermediaries. In particular, because banks typically were not allowed to branch or merge, they could not take advantage of the economies from internalizing the functions of the securities marketing network within a single intermediary. Changes in bank branching and consolidation permitted in the 1920s were an important precondition for the encroachments made by commercial banks into investment banking in the 1920s.

Thus, the time-honored tradition of American restrictions on the scale of banking effectively limited universal banking prior to Glass-Steagall in 1933. The outright prohibitions on investment banking affiliates of commercial banks in Glass-Steagall were justified by two accusations. First, banks were accused of taking advantage of conflicts of interest in securities dealings. Second, it was claimed that links between affiliates and parent banks contributed to the banking collapse of the Great Depression.

Scholars who have investigated these claims have found no supporting empirical evidence, and have disputed them on theoretical and empirical grounds (Carosso 1970; White 1986; Benston 1989; Kaufman and Mote 1989, 1990; Kroszner and Rajan 1994). On the question of whether affiliates weakened banks, White (1986) found that national banks with securities affiliates had lower failure propensities, and he linked these to diversification advantages. White also pointed out that, as documented in Peach 1941, affiliates were wholly owned by banks, and thus strategies to strengthen affiliates at the expense of parent banks would not have been chosen knowingly by management.

Benston (1989) argues that the presumed link between bank failures and securities activities of affiliates, on which much of the reasoning of the various banking committees relied, never received careful scrutiny in any of the many congressional "studies" of banking from 1931 to 1940. Nevertheless, this presumption underlay the drastic changes of the separation of investment and commercial banking in the Banking Act of 1933.

Conflicts of interest are unlikely to occur. In equilibrium, investment bankers—whether operating out of private investment banking houses or national bank affiliates—will not be able to attract customers if they cannot credibly signal the quality of securities they underwrite. If bank affiliates could not overcome potential investors' concerns over conflicts of interest (for example, by purchasing or managing some of the new issues, then they would lose business to private investment banks. The fact that affiliates were able to provide underwriting services on a large scale for many years in open competition with other underwriters indicates that conflicts of interest were not significant. Evidence against conflict of interest is provided by Kroszner and Rajan (1994). They analyze default costs for bonds issued by affiliates and their competitors prior to Glass-Steagall and conclude that the performance of affiliate-underwritten securities of a given ex ante class was at least as good as that of securities underwritten by their competitors.

Two other common criticisms of universal banking are that it increases inefficient bank rent extraction from firms, and encourages the development of industrial cartels. Coordination, of course, is not always efficient. In a concentrated banking system where firms have exclusive relationships with intermediaries, would collusion among banks in setting fees and interest rates increase the cost of finance in the economy? And would close corporate monitoring and control, along with long-term relationships between firms and universal banks, encourage the development of industrial cartels by providing a credible enforcement mechanism for collusive behavior within industries?

On the first point, it is doubtful that universal banking raises financing costs by allowing banks to extract greater rent from firms. As Rajan (1992a) shows, a banking relationship that involves the production of private information about firms may give banks access only to quasi rents (which are transferred back to the firm ex ante). The interesting question is whether universal banking will increase or decrease the distortions that come from asymmetric information. Here the point to emphasize is not the *extent* of quasi or true rents, but the way they are *extracted*. As argued above, universal banking may be beneficial for solving the time-inconsistency problem because it allows banks to reap long-term gains from large initial costs of investing in information. Thus, for example, banks will be able to "charge" for underwriting services partly by relying on long-term gains from their relationship with firms. In the absence of universal banking, banks may have to recover costs over a shorter horizon. This will require "front-loading" of financing costs, which will distort the firm's investment decision by making finance excessively costly in the near term. Thus, if universal banking allows banks to design compensation schemes that eliminate such distortions, then even if it increases the share of firms' rents that accrue to banks (as opposed to firms' entrepreneurs), this rent extraction may be relatively efficient. Empirical evidence (De Long 1991; Ramirez 1992) discussed below suggests that banking relationships added value to firms, and that investment bankers' fees reflected costs of providing information and transaction services, rather than simply rents.[12]

On the question whether investment banks promoted inefficient industrial cartels, two points are worth emphasizing. First, the development and enforcement of industrial cartels by intermediaries is not a weakness peculiar to concentrated universal banking systems. Indeed, such accusations were the hallmark of the Pujo committee hearings of 1912–13 in the United States (Carosso 1970, chap. 6). According to his critics, J. P. Morgan managed to exert as much control over "other people's money" in the context of the fragmented American banking system as would a universal bank in a concentrated banking industry. According to Louis Brandeis and Samuel Untermyer, Morgan oversaw a complex "money trust" involving corporate boards of directors dominated by investment bankers who effectively enforced collusion among firms, limited competition by commercial banks (which were controlled by the investment bankers as well), and extracted rents for investment banking firms. From this jaundiced perspective, bankers' corporate-control services were really just selling protection, Mafia-style (Brandeis 1914). With respect to the German experience, Riesser (1911) argues that bank involvement in firms was neither a necessary nor a sufficient condition for enforcing cartels. Riesser claims that the influence of the banks was "decisive in some cases, less so in others, and

12. A separate question is whether the universal bank's possibly higher share of its client firms' rents will discourage entrepreneurial investment. Universal bankers should vary the amount of rent, and the variables on which it depends, to ensure that the entrepreneur receives his reservation level of rent, and that the entrepreneur's incentives will be minimally distorted by rent extraction. In other words, a perfectly discriminating monopolistic banker with access to a "lump-sum tax" will not discourage entrepreneurial investment. Indeed, if universal banks are better able to gauge the total rents of the firm because of better information, then they will make fewer mistakes than other intermediaries in determining how much rent to extract from entrepreneurs.

hardly perceptible in some cases" (712). Notably, in the chemical industry, industrial cartels were enforced with great apparent success despite the absence of bank involvement (721–25). Jeidels (1905, 199–252) provides a much more detailed accounting of the role of German banks in industrial cartels. He argues that banks focused on individual customers and were not instigators in organizing cartels. Only after firms moved to establish cartels did banks assist in enforcing arrangements so made. Both German and American history shows that bank discipline was not a unique means of enforcing industrial cartels. Policies other than prohibitions on universal banking are likely to be superior for facilitating competition within industries.

Second, it is not clear that an important or primary function of German universal banks or the American "money trust" was the enforcement of inefficient industrial cartels.[13] There have been many recent challenges to the notion that the Morgan syndicate was exclusively or mainly a device for extracting rent. Carosso (1970) and Huertas and Cleveland (1987) dispute the "findings" of the Pujo committee, arguing that investment banking was a competitive, contestable business. Entry was not blocked, and firms in need of finance did not feel compelled to use the same investment banker repeatedly. There was active competition for business, and repeated contacts reflected economies of information. If these authors are right, it follows that attempts by banks to restrict competition within industries would have encouraged entry by intermediaries to finance competing industrial firms. With respect to Germany, even Alexander Gerschenkron, a staunch advocate of the notion that banks enforced industrial cartels during the period of early industrialization, argued that this was not possible after 1900 because of ease of entry into banking (1962, 15, 21, 88–89, 139). Jeidels (1905, 122–30), Whale (1930, 35), and Tilly (1992, 109) support this view, arguing that German banking was a competitive industry after 1890, particularly in financing large, mature industrial firms.

Quantitative studies have been helpful, but not conclusive, in resolving the question of whether industrial cartel enforcement was historically an important

---

13. To the extent cartels were inefficient in Germany, it was through monopolistic restriction of output. Another possible inefficiency associated with cartels—lack of innovation—does not seem to have been relevant in Germany. Indeed, Webb (1980) argues to the contrary that cartelization of the steel industry encouraged innovation. Furthermore, the ability to solve information problems efficiently is especially important to spurring innovation, as Schumpeter (1939), Butters and Lintner (1945), and many others have recognized. Here, too, German industry was at a distinct advantage, as the discussion in section 8.3 will show. Tilly (1982) also points out that acquisitions within industries by best-practice producers were frequent, and this too can be credited to financing elasticity. Financing new ideas quickly may have increased competition within industries and quickly driven out inefficient firms. One should exercise caution in interpreting comparisons of the rate of start-up of new firms in the United States and Germany as a measure of innovativeness (and costs of cartels). New firms may have been more necessary to innovation in the United States because of a lack of corporate discipline, exercised in part through intermediaries (Berle and Means 1932). As the record of post–World War II Japan shows, innovativeness can be a feature of relatively concentrated industries, particularly if the management of firms in those industries are "disciplined" (Japan Development Bank 1994).

function of intermediaries. De Long (1991) finds that the presence of a Morgan partner on a firm's board of directors increased the value of the firm's common stock by 30 percent. More importantly, he traces this increase in stock value to the superior earnings performance of Morgan companies: "The Morgan partnership and its peers saw themselves—and other participants saw them—as filling a crucial 'monitoring' and 'signaling' intermediary role between firms and investors in a world where information about firms' underlying values and the quality of their managers was scarce. . . . The presence of Morgan's men meant that when a firm got into trouble—whether because of 'excessive competition' or management mistakes—action would be taken to restore profitability" (1991, 209). De Long shows that investment banking firms were not simply vehicles for extracting rent, but he is not able to distinguish whether investment bankers increased the productivity of firms, or simply helped firms by eliminating their competition. "[T]he relative roles of monopoly and efficiency in the 'Morganization premium' cannot be determined in a fashion convincing enough to overcome prior beliefs" (224–25). Another recent study, by Ramirez (1992), connects Morgan involvement with increases in the elasticity of credit supply for firms. Ramirez finds similar advantages in reducing cash-flow sensitivity of investment for German firms with universal banking connections. While these studies show that at least some of Morgan's contribution, and those of German universal banks, involved a credit relationship with the firm, they do not refute the notion that banks helped their clients by limiting competition within industry. Indeed, by giving client firms "deep pockets," Morgan may have helped them effectively threaten competitors with potential price wars.

In sum, the role of intermediaries in developing and enforcing industrial cartels remains a murky area in economic history. But to the extent such accusations have been made, they apply more broadly to the problems of all forms of interbank coalitions (notably to the American "money trust") and are not a peculiar feature of a concentrated universal banking system. Clearly, eliminating industrial cartels requires more draconian measures than restrictions on universal banking. These would include limits on cooperation, communication, and oversight among firms, banks, and securities dealers. Some of these were adopted in the United States as early as the 1890s, culminating in the 1914 Clayton Act prohibitions on interlocking directorates, the 1933 separation of commercial and investment banking, and the new trend toward fragmentation of both investment banking and commercial banking under the restrictive regulations of the New Deal. To the extent that these changes undermined monitoring and control networks, such drastic action may have caused more problems than it solved, by increasing financing costs of firms and by allowing firms' managers to escape the discipline of their stockholders and the marketplace (Berle and Means 1932; De Long 1991; Calomiris and Hubbard 1994). The most important point for the purposes of the German-

American comparison in section 8.3 is that allowing a concentrated universal banking in the United States during the pre–World War I era would have had little *marginal* effect on industrial cartelization.

8.2.7 Summary

This review of general perspectives on universal banking has argued that there are significant advantages of allowing banks to combine lending, equity holding, underwriting, trust activities, and deposit taking in the same intermediary, and thus significant costs to restricting this combination of activities. The advantages of universal banking arise from a combination of three factors. First, the corporate financial life cycle (or pecking order) entails a progression in which a firm's external financing evolves from short-term debt directly held by banks to widely held equity finance underwritten by banks. The optimal form of corporate finance and governance changes as firms become seasoned. Initially, banks discipline firms and limit their exposure to risk by holding short-term senior debt. As firms become seasoned, they come to rely on junior claims for their financing needs, and intermediaries underwriting firms' stock issues protect their interests by exercising direct control over firms through boards of directors. Second, there are economies of establishing long-term relationships between firms and intermediaries that revolve around the reusability of information and the smoothing of costs of external finance over the firm's life cycle (which may only be possible within the context of a long-term relationship).

Together, firms' changing financial needs over the life cycle and the advantages of long-term relationships between firms and intermediaries imply benefits to allowing intermediaries to engage in both underwriting and lending. A universal bank's ability to provide funds to firms at low cost requires a third factor—that the bank be allowed to operate a network of branches for collecting deposits and placing and managing securities. Widespread branching allows banks to diversify when making large loans to customers. It also economizes on information and transactions costs of placing and managing securities. The costs of credibly communicating the condition of firms to outsiders, and of gauging the market demand for new securities issues, are particularly large for equity issues. Large-scale universal banking reduces these costs by placing a single intermediary between ultimate holders and securities issuers. True universal banking allows banks to combine underwriting, lending, trust activities, and deposit taking within a single branching intermediary. Thus, despite the fact that national banks operated investment banking and trust affiliates in the 1920s, true universal banking never was permitted in the United States because of limitations on branching that effectively limited a bank's direct access to funds, and hence its ability to finance large-scale industry.

The next section is devoted to measuring German-American differences in financial structure and costs and relating them to theoretical perspectives on the advantages of universal banking. I argue that the absence of universal banking in the United States, and its presence in Germany, resulted in different methods and higher costs of financing American industrialization in the pre–World War I period.

8.3 Banking and Finance in Germany and America, 1870–1914

By the outbreak of World War I, Germany and the United States had developed financial systems that bore little resemblance to one another. The role of banks in corporate finance and corporate control, the types of financial instruments that dominated the scene, the way financial instruments were underwritten and sold, the combinations of activities that banks performed, and the financial structure of industrial firms and banks differed sharply between the two countries. This section reviews these differences in detail along dimensions suggested in section 8.2, focusing on consequences for the cost of industrial finance. The evidence suggests substantially higher costs of industrial finance in the United States.

In light of these differences, I describe and attempt to explain the "inversion" that took place from 1850 to World War I in German and American financial institutions. American financial institutions circa 1850, like their German counterparts circa 1900, played a much greater role in industrial finance, especially in New England's early industrialization. In antebellum New England, a financial system flourished that bore much resemblance to the mature German system. The German financial system circa 1850 was more fragmented and less integrated than New England's, but rapidly progressed after 1870, and quickly developed a concentrated universal banking system. At the same time, New England's financial system moved away from its early structure, and from financing industrial activities of those closely involved with the banks. The "regressive" history of American banking from 1850 to 1920 reflected the increasing scale of industrial borrowers and their credit needs and the restrictions on bank branching and consolidation, which kept banks' size and geographical scope small while the size and scope of their customers grew. These restrictions on U.S. banks prevented them from reaping advantages of universal banking long before the separation of commercial and investment banking in 1933.

8.3.1   Relative Factor Intensity and Capital Scarcity in
U.S. and German Industrialization

The second industrial revolution, beginning in the mid–nineteenth century, saw rapid industrial expansion especially in the areas of railroads, steel, chemicals, and electricity. Germany and the United States were among the most impressive examples of industrial growth during this period, although Germany's heyday of industrial expansion began later than that of the United States. As table 8.1 shows, in the United States, nonagricultural output grew most rapidly

Table 8.1   Nonagricultural Growth in Germany and the United States

	Germany		United States		
	Nonagricultural NNP 1913 Prices (millions of marks)	Nonagricultural Labor (thousands)	Nonagricultural VA 1879 Prices (millions of $)	Nonagricultural NI 1869 Prices (millions of $)	Nonagricultural Labor (thousands)
1849			670		
1850	5,052				
1869			1,550	5,325	6,193
1870	8,431				
1871		8,796			
1889				7,543	12,540
1890	15,857	12,807			
1910–13				16,519	20,871
1913	37,210	20,267			

Sources: Real nonagricultural activity in the United States was calculated using value added in mining, manufacturing, and construction for 1849–69, from Gallman, as reported in U.S. Department of Commerce 1975, 239. For 1869–1913, I used Martin's data on current national income outside of agriculture (U.S. Department of Commerce 1975, 240), deflated by a nonagricultural output deflator. This deflator was constructed as follows. Romer's (1989, 22) GNP deflator is assumed to equal a weighted average of the nonagricultural deflator and the agricultural deflator (from Warren and Pearson for 1869–1890 and BLS for 1890 to 1910–13, as reported in U.S. Department of Commerce 1975, 200–201, using Martin's weights for agricultural and nonagricultural income. For Germany, nonagricultural net national product and labor are derived from Hoffmann 1965, 205, 454–55.

Notes: NNP = net national product; VA = value added; NI = national income.

from 1850 to 1870, while in Germany rapid growth was more concentrated in the period from 1870 to the First World War. In the United States, value added in manufacturing, mining, and construction more than doubled from 1849 to 1869. Nonagricultural income grew by less than half from 1869 to 1889 and doubled from 1890 to 1913. In Germany, nonagricultural net product increased by less than half from 1850 to 1870, then doubled from 1870 to 1890 and more than doubled from 1890 to 1913.

Despite the similarity in nonagricultural output growth rates in Germany and the United States from 1870 to 1913, the way growth was achieved was quite different. In the United States, employment in the nonagricultural sector grew by the same rate as output, while in Germany nonagricultural employment grew at half the rate of output. Relative to Germany, American industrialization relied more intensively on labor.

Goldsmith (1985) defines three capital-to-output ratios, using broad, intermediate, and narrow definitions of capital. The intermediate measure excludes land, and the narrow measure also excludes consumer durables and residential structures. A comparison for all three measures, for Germany and the United States at selected dates from 1850 to 1913, is provided in table 8.2. The German capital-to-output ratio is substantially higher than that of the United States regardless of which measure is chosen, but the proportionate difference between the United States and Germany is greatest for the narrow measure, which focuses on the reproducible capital of producers. On average, from 1850 to 1913, the U.S. narrow capital-to-output ratio is half that of Germany.[14]

Field (1983, 1987) and Wright (1990) have emphasized the reliance placed by the United States on substitutes for fixed capital in the production process, especially natural resources. As Cain and Paterson (1981) document, materials prices fell sharply in the United States after the Civil War. Continuing discoveries of new resources, especially metals and oil fields, kept resource costs low throughout the pre–World War I period. Wright (1990, 658) notes that U.S. exports had far higher resource content than imports and that the resource intensity of exports increased substantially during late-nineteenth-century industrialization. By 1928, resource intensity of exports was 50 percent higher than its 1879 level. Wright follows Piore and Sabel (1984) and Williamson (1980) in linking the American utilization of resources with the "high-throughput" system of manufacture emphasized by Chandler (1977), which Field (1987) points out is a means to economize on capital costs. Wright and others also emphasize that the reliance on resources in the United States was not exogenously determined. America's natural resource base is not among the richest in the world. Rather, the American reliance on natural resources, the develop-

---

14. The capital intensity of the German economy in 1850 cannot be attributed to universal banking, since universal banking under limited liability laws began in 1870. Centralized government subsidization and planning of railroads, built ahead of demand, may account for the large capital-to-output ratio in the pre-1870 period (Dunlavy forthcoming).

Table 8.2   **Ratios of Capital to GNP**

	Narrow Capital Measure		Intermediate Capital Measure		Broad Capital Measure	
	United States	Germany	United States	Germany	United States	Germany
1850	1.24	4.20	1.66	5.04	2.83	9.29
1875		3.29		4.26		7.12
1880	1.78		2.45		3.56	
1895		2.70		3.79		5.68
1900	1.81		2.91		4.56	
1912	1.71		2.69		4.17	
1913		3.42		4.82		6.58

Source: Goldsmith 1985, 39–42.

Notes: Narrow capital is nonresidential structures, equipment, inventories, and livestock. Intermediate capital is narrow measure plus residential structures and consumer durables. Broad capital is intermediate measure plus land.

Table 8.3   **Components of Tangible Reproducible Assets**

	Germany (1913) (%)	United States (1912) (%)
Dwellings	25	24
Other structures	31	35
Equipment	26	13
Inventories	10	10
Livestock	5	5
Consumer durables	3	13

Source: Goldsmith 1985, 111.

ment of production techniques that were resource intensive, and the emergence of high-throughput production and distribution processes were induced in part by the high cost of raising capital.

Goldsmith's (1985) breakdown of the components of the capital stock also provides interesting evidence about differences between the United States and Germany in the allocation of capital across different uses. Table 8.3 compares the shares of various components of tangible reproducible assets for Germany in 1913 and the United States in 1912. The shares of livestock, inventories, and structures are quite similar. The principal difference is the relative importance of equipment and consumer durables. In Germany, equipment is 26 percent of reproducible assets, while in the United States, it is half that percentage. Conversely, in the United States, consumer durables account for 13 percent of the total, while in Germany they make up only 3 percent. Comparisons for other years during the interval 1850 to 1900 lead to similar results, although in

Germany the relative importance of equipment in reproducible assets grew during the pre–World War I era.

While there are many possible interpretations of the different weights for equipment in Germany and the United States, two points warrant emphasis. First, the greater relative weight in Germany is unlikely to be the result of measurement error. Both countries' data are derived from the same individual's work—Goldsmith 1955–56, 1976; and Goldsmith, Lipsey, and Mendelson 1963. Thus, gross incomparabilities across categories or insensitivity to data source differences are unlikely to explain the differences. One problem worth worrying about is whether the German data on equipment include items that would have been excluded from consumer durables in Germany, but included in consumer durables in the United States. I examined the items included in U.S. consumer durables to see whether production equipment located at home might explain the observed differences. Goldsmith (1955–56, 1:680) reports nonfarm individuals' expenditures on the main categories of consumer durable goods. These categories include "furniture, household appliances, house furnishings, china etc., musical instruments, books, passenger cars, passenger car accessories, medical appliances, and miscellaneous." None of these sounds like production equipment. Even if "household appliances" or "miscellaneous" includes some producer durables, these constitute such a small share of total consumer durables (16 percent in 1913) that they could not account for the difference between German and American equipment shares.

The second point to emphasize, in anticipation of the discussion that follows, is that the greater reliance on equipment in Germany is consistent with a lower cost of financing industrial expansion, particularly in the form of large-scale factory production.[15] Equipment-intensive production is more capital intensive because of its lower "throughput" rate (Field 1987). Also, equipment is less liquid than materials, which makes it harder to collateralize and finance.

8.3.2   Interregional and Intersectoral Capital Allocation in the United States

The cost of capital was not uniform within the United States across locations, sectors, or time. Interregional and intersectoral differences in rates of return on capital in the United States (a measure of inefficiency in capital allocation) were largest during the mid– to late nineteenth century. But even as late as the 1920s, Federal Reserve surveys show that interest rates on like bank loans in provincial U.S. cities could be 4 or 5 percent higher than rates in eastern financial centers (Riefler 1930, 79). Breckenridge (1899, 5) contrasted the enormous interregional variation in low-risk U.S. interest rates with those of European countries, including Germany. For Germany, he cites evidence that the interest rates in 260 provincial towns were identical to those charged

---

15. It is also interesting to note that the production of producer durables is relatively capital intensive. Creamer and Borenstein (1960, 52) show that the capital-output ratios of capital-equipment industries were 1.05 in 1900, compared to 0.68 for consumption-goods industries.

in Berlin for loans of a standard quality. As Bodenhorn (1992) shows, the antebellum United States did not suffer from large interregional differences in costs of funds. The integration of capital markets seems to have worsened during the geographical expansion and industrialization of the postbellum era. In their study of the profitability of American enterprises from 1850 to 1880, Atack and Bateman (1992) find that interregional profit-rate differentials in the United States were largest in the industrial sector, that industrial profit rates were far above profit rates in other sectors, and that convergence in profit rates for manufacturing was most protracted. They attribute this to capital immobility across regions and across sectors that kept the capital stock of manufacturing enterprises low.

8.3.3   The Different Roles of Banks in Industrial Finance

Qualitative discussions of the importance of German banks to industrial progress date from Jeidels 1905, Riesser 1911, Schumpeter 1939, and Gerschenkron 1962. Goldsmith (1985) provides detailed comparative analyses of many countries, and quantitative measures of important features of German finance from an international comparative perspective. Goldsmith (1958) and Goldsmith, Lipsey, and Mendelson (1963) analyze the funding sources of American industrialization in detail.

Goldsmith (1985, 135) defines the "financial intermediation ratio" as a rough, general measure of the economy's reliance on intermediation for the creation of wealth. The financial intermediation ratio for Germany rose from 20.3 in 1850 to 30.1 in 1913. Over this same period, the U.S. ratio rose from 12.5 to 21.3. By this measure, the United States was fifth from the lowest in a field of thirteen, while Germany was near the top. Seven nations had ratios in excess of 29 for 1913, and the average ratio for twelve nations (excluding the outlier, India, with a ratio of 8) was 27.

If one focuses on the specific links between bank lending and industrialization, the contrast between the roles of banks in Germany and the United States is greater. In Germany, the universal banks were responsible for providing a large share of industrial finance. The financing of industrial credit involved some four hundred joint-stock banks operating more than one thousand branches nationwide by 1913. Eleven large incorporated banks accounted for more than one-third of the capital and assets of the system. Banks lent directly to firms through very short-term overdraft accounts (with average maturities of less than one month), held and managed stocks and bonds of firms, and acted as investment bankers for firms' securities issues. The importance of universal banking in German industrial finance was especially pronounced after the 1890s' consolidation movement in banking, which Jeidels (1905, 83–107) argues largely reflected the increasingly large-scale financing needs of industry.

Consistent with section 8.2's discussion of the changing role of universal banks over the life cycle of the firm, new projects were often financed directly through short-term bank loans. Later, financing was transformed to long-term securities, placed by the bank that had originally made the loan (Jeidels 1905, 109–22; Riesser 1911, 364–69; Whale 1930, 37–38; Eistert 1970, 91). Jeidels (1905) provides a detailed accounting of the involvement of banks over the life cycle of firms. The first stage of the firm-bank relationship saw keen competition among banks in the loan market for overdraft credit accounts (Jeidels 1905, 122). Interest costs for overdraft credit were typically set at the interbank lending rate plus 1 percent (Whale 1930, 37–38). In the early stages of the firm life cycle, the bank's main lever of influence over the firm was the threat of revoking the line of credit. Jeidels (126) cites as an example of bank discipline a 1901 letter the Dresdner Bank wrote to one of its customers, threatening cancellation of credit if an upcoming vote by the board of directors went the wrong way. As the firm-bank relationship matured, equity took the place of overdraft credit and the bank's role in corporate governance changed from threatening the board of directors to becoming part of the board of directors (Jeidels 1905, 128). On occasion, when bank positions were challenged by other members of boards of directors, banks resorted to massive purchases of company stock to secure controlling interest (Jeidels 1905, 111). Still later in the firm's life cycle, the influence of its principal banker typically waned, and other banks competed for its underwriting business (Jeidels 1905, 128–30).

With respect to the quantity of bank holdings of claims on firms, table 8.4 reports Eistert's year-end estimates of the amount of direct overdraft financing of industry (a component of overdrafts, or *Kontokorrentkredite,* from which Eistert excludes overdraft lending for securities transactions and bankers acceptances for financing trade). Table 8.4 also reports the amount of "permanent" participations of the banks (typically confined to bank shares in subsidiary financial institutions: Whale 1930, 47–48, 150), banks' other securities holdings (including underwriting inventories), and the amount of bankers acceptances financing commerce. The table also displays each of these asset categories as a fraction of total bank assets. While banks played an important role as holders of claims, just as important was their role in helping firms graduate (apparently rapidly) to find ultimate sources of funds outside the banking system. Thus, the banks used their special position as "delegated monitors" to "lever" their clients' finances—allowing their clients to reach a broad market for external finance by providing direct lending at early stages of projects, and later underwriting equity as a signal of their clients' quality possibly and as a vehicle for sharing in capital gains (as argued in section 8.2's discussion of time consistency).

Jeidels (1905, 106) and Eistert (1970, 142) interpret the rising importance of *Kontokorrentkredite* after 1890 as evidence of increasing bank involvement in financing new industrial projects after the 1890s, which they see as significant evidence of the role of banks in priming the pumps of industrial finance during this crucial period of German industrial growth. The bank acted as a monitor of the firm's conduct, a source of discipline over management (through

Table 8.4 Selected Assets of the German Credit Banks, Levels and Percentage of Total Assets

	Industrial Credit (millions of marks)	%	Acceptances (millions of marks)	%	"Permanent" Participations (millions of marks)	%	Other Securities (millions of marks)	%
1888	329.1	12	448.3	16	32.4	1	338.4	12
1893	416.5	12	631.5	18	67.9	2	351.9	10
1898	902.1	14	984.4	15	183.4	3	728.0	11
1903	1,334.2	15	1,301.2	15	236.1	3	956.5	11
1907	2,336.6	18	1,890.7	15	439.4	3	1,289.6	10
1913	2,930.3	18	2,450.6	15	—	—	—	—

Sources: Industrial credit and acceptances derived from Eistert 1970, 92. Data for permanent participations and other securities are from National Monetary Commission 1910, table 15, except for total assets for 1913. Total assets for 1913 is taken from Deutsche Bundesbank 1976, 56.

Notes: Some asset categories are omitted from this table, including cash assets, collaterlized loans, and lending for securities purchases. Industrial credit is defined as *Kontokorrentkredite* (overdraft account credit) for industrial purposes. Acceptances are bankers' acceptances used primarily to finance goods in transit. Permanent participations are long-term securities holdings of banks, which are mainly stock held in other (essentially subsidiary) financial institutions. Other securities pertains to all other securities held, which mainly reflects ongoing underwriting activities.

directorates and voting of clients' shares), and a source of advice on financial and business organization.

Specific evidence from industry case studies on the role of German banks in industrial finance is abundant. Jeidels (1905) and Riesser (1911) provide lengthy discussions of the evolution of the major German industries and the roles played by banks. For example, Riesser (1911, 713–21) argues that assistance by informed bank lenders was crucial to the development of the electrical industry. He discusses the coevolution of firms and banks and describes how the role banks played changed with the industrial organization of the industry. Initially, banks promoted widespread entry by a multitude of firms, and funding of firms' needs was accomplished through direct lending, followed later by placements of securities. As the industry developed, consolidation of firms raised the scale of financing needs, which in turn, increased the need for interbank cooperation through financing syndicates. Banks reinforced the trend toward industrial concentration by helping to coordinate decision making among firms. The history of the electrical industry illustrates how banks encouraged technological innovativeness at the crucial early stage of industrial development and made efficient large-scale operations feasible. The Germans developed a larger and more interregional electrical utility system than that of Britain or the United States during this period (Hughes 1983). Carlson (1991) argues that the greater fragmentation of the U.S. electrical system reflected financing constraints. On the demand side, utility customers were financed by electrical manufacturers rather than banks. According to Carlson, this hampered the ability of manufacturers to expand and integrate their operations, and led to a less standardized range of products in the United States.

Links between industrial firms and banks were much weaker in the United States. This reflected in large part the small size of incorporated banks relative to the large needs of industrial borrowers. More than twenty-six thousand banks were operating in 1914, and the overwhelming majority of these were not permitted to operate branches, even within their home state. Even the limited operation of universal banking through securities affiliates did not begin in earnest until after World War I. The first three investment affiliates of national banks were organized between 1908 and 1917, and served as models for the growth of affiliates in the 1920s (Peach 1941, 18–20, 61–64).

Much of bank financing of firms occurred without any direct (much less ongoing) relationship between the bank and the firms it financed. Intermediaries' claims on firms primarily took the form of corporate bond holdings placed through syndicates. According to Goldsmith (1958, 222), for the period 1901–12, bonds held by all intermediaries accounted for 18 percent of funds supplied by external sources (that is, excluding retained earnings) to nonfinancial firms. Commercial banks accounted for two-thirds of corporate bond holdings by intermediaries in 1912.[16] Based on flow-of-funds accounting, bank loans (for

---

16. Goldsmith (1958, 335) gives total intermediaries holdings of bonds. He provides data on commercial banks' bond holdings, decomposed according to type of issuer (339–40).

all purposes) accounted for 12 percent of externally supplied funds for 1901–12. Using balance-sheet data of nonfinancial corporations for 1900 and 1912, Goldsmith, Lipsey, and Mendelson (1963, 2:146) calculate that bank loans amounted to roughly 10 percent of firms' debts, and less than 5 percent of firms' assets. Bonds and notes accounted for roughly half of firms' debts, and trade debt made up 15 percent. The use of short-term bank lending to finance industrial operations, as distinct from commerce, cannot be quantified (see Goldsmith 1958, 344).

Reliance on bank loans was relatively high for small firms. Large manufacturing firms relied more on bond issues as a means of indirect bank finance (Goldsmith 1958, 217–18) and less on loans from banks as a source of financing, especially prior to the 1940s. Of course, under a unit banking system, large-scale firms operating throughout the country would have had to borrow from many small unit banks simultaneously. Bond market syndications facilitated this transaction by providing a means for banks to share risk and coordinate capital allocations. The commercial paper market (a unique innovation of the American financial system) performed a similar role for short-term borrowing needs of large, high-quality borrowers. From humble beginnings in the 1870s, the commercial paper market reached its pre–World War II peak in 1920 at $1.3 billion, consisting of the debts of over four thousand borrowers (Selden 1963, 8).

Dobrovolsky and Bernstein (1960, 141–42) report funding sources for a sample of fourteen large manufacturing firms from 1900 to 1910, based on accounting records of sources of net inflows of funds. For the period 1900–1910, these firms reported a total financial inflow of $1.2 billion, of which $357 million came from external finance. Of this, only $29 million was in the form of short-term debt. Some bank loans during this period also took the form of long-term debt, but judging from Goldsmith (1958, 335, 339), long-term loans from commercial banks were uncommon around the turn of the century.

While small firms relied more on banks, it does not follow that banks contributed to the financing of industrial capital expansion by small firms any more than they did to that of large firms. Two detailed studies of the sources of capital in manufacturing provide a glimpse of the contribution of banks to industrial expansion in Illinois (Marquardt 1960) and California (Trusk 1960) in the mid– to late nineteenth century. In the case of California, thirty-three of seventy-one manufacturing firms studies over the period 1859–1880 financed their investment entirely from internal sources. The others incorporated, took in partners, and supplemented these sources with earnings of existing partners from other sources, sale of stock or real estate, "eastern capital" (in three cases), and loans from a *private* banker (the same banker in both instances). Clearly, commercial banks had no role in the expansion of manufacturing capital in California prior to 1880.

Illinois's experience was similar, but the role of banks in financing industrial expansion may have been greater. The rapid expansion of manufacturing in Illinois began in the 1860s. From 1860 to 1870, manufacturing production and capital each increased sevenfold, and employment increased sixfold. From 1870 to 1880, manufacturing production doubled. Marquardt (1960) examined the personal and business histories of fifty entrepreneurs. She found that these firms were financed initially from accumulated savings of would-be manufacturing entrepreneurs, or by entrepreneurs taking on a partner with savings. Subsequent funding typically was provided by retained earnings. Occasionally, this was supplemented by the sale of entrepreneurial assets, the expansion of the partnership, or incorporation. In twenty-six out of fifty cases, manufacturing entrepreneurs of relatively mature firms used profits to invest in an interest in a bank, which "marked the beginning of more rapid success for them. They owned in part or had access to, funds, either large or small, which would enable them to grow and to progress." This was especially important in the 1860s because manufacturing was moving rapidly toward mechanization and opportunities for expansion outpaced accumulated profits (507). In short, firms progressed up the pecking order as they matured. Entrepreneurs secured access to external funds by investing in banks, on which they could rely for funds. While Marquardt's study does indicate a role for banks in industrial finance, it says as much about the limits of that role as it does about banks' potential importance. Access to bank funds was extremely limited, and bank stockholders were given preference as bank borrowers. Such a system had worked well to provide the needs of business in New England in the antebellum period (Lamoreaux 1994), but by the 1870s, this system was insufficient. Restrictions on insider lending, combined with the rising scale of manufacturing and the limited size of unit banks, meant that access to a unit bank's deposit base could not keep pace with the needs of bank insiders. Thus, while banks may have played a role in financing industrial expansion in Illinois and elsewhere, the importance of this role was limited to the "adolescent" stage of the firm's life cycle—after the firm had become mature enough to invest in becoming a bank insider, but before the firm had become too large to rely on a unit bank for its funding needs. Even this role of banks in industrial finance is apparent only in the histories of some firms (roughly half of those chosen for case studies by Marquardt).

To summarize, unlike German industrialists, American industrialists could not depend on a single banking relationship to guide them through their growing and changing financial needs over the years. They relied less on banks for credit, especially to finance large-scale projects. At each stage in their financial life cycle, firms had to change their financial relationships as they moved to new financial instruments and new funding sources for their investments. The small size of banks limited bank lending to large-scale firms. Even relatively large banks in major cities considering lending to industrial firms would have foreseen limited future relationships with borrowers, making some lending prohibitively expensive (Mayer 1988). Finally, given the reduced role of intermediaries in direct lending, bank finance of industry was limited mainly to holding securities placed through syndicates. The form of these financial instruments and their costs are subjects to which I now turn.

8.3.4   Financial Instruments and the Financial Structure of Industrial Firms

Section 8.2 highlighted some important disadvantages of long-term debt financing compared to a combination of short-term debt and equity. Relative to short-term debt, long-term debt can be costly because of incentive problems (the firm's incentive to add risk increases in the absence of a rollover option). Relative to equity, all forms of debt increase the probability of financial distress by raising leverage. Finally, when a firm's debt takes the form of dispersed debt holdings, rather than concentrated lending from intermediaries, the costs of managing financial distress (coordinating workouts) is increased (see Riesser 1911, 365–66, on German banks' roles in managing reorganizations). For all these reasons, long-term debt is a costly form of finance. If, however, firms are constrained to finance themselves through syndication networks rather than through intermediaries, then the transactions costs of rollover of short-term debt can be prohibitive. And equity may not be a feasible alternative to debt, either because the costs of resolving asymmetric information between firms and ultimate sources of funds are large (because the "lemons discount" for equity will be larger than that for debt, as in Myers and Majluf 1984), or because the equity holder is unable to exert control over corporate management (Jensen and Meckling 1976). Baskin (1988) argues that asymmetric information explains the dearth of equity issues historically in the United States. Thus, despite its high costs, long-term debt may be the best means for firms to raise funds in the absence of large-scale, universal banking. Of course, in light of incentive problems of issuing long-term debt, risky firms may be denied access to this market as well, leaving them to rely on retained earnings alone as a source of finance.[17]

According to this interpretation of long-term debt as a "last resort" in the absence of alternatives—albeit one not available to all firms—one would expect the structure of German firms' balance sheets to rely far less on long-term debt than do American firms. Table 8.5 confirms this prediction. Private domestic corporate bond issues are a much smaller fraction of total securities issues in Germany than in the United States over the pre–World War I period, and represent a relatively small fraction of outstanding corporate claims. Moreover, the German data on bond issues are for gross issues, while the U.S. data are for net issues; thus, the difference reported in table 8.5 in the relative amount of stock and bond issues understates the true difference. In Germany,

---

17. Indeed, access to bond markets has sometimes been very selective. Calomiris and Hubbard (1994) found that very few firms in their sample of publicly traded firms in the mid-1930s had access to the bond market. Only a quarter of all firms issued bonds, and 10 percent of firms accounted for 90 percent of bond issues. Bond-issuing firms were three time as large as non-bond-issuing firms. Interestingly, while firms with higher measured costs of finance had higher debt ratios, they were less likely to have outstanding debt in the form of bonds. These data lend support to the view that incentive problems of long-term debt may have limited its use. An alternative explanation for the Calomiris-Hubbard sample would argue that access to the bond market was substantially limited by regulatory change in 1935. Prior to the Banking Act of 1935, banks were allowed to sell low-grade bonds to their customers. After 1935, this was prohibited (Haven 1940, 7).

Table 8.5   **Corporate Finance in Germany and the United States prior to World War I**

Balance-Sheet Data for Nonfinancial Corporations

	United States, 1900 (millions of $)	United States, 1912 (millions of $)	Germany, 1900 (millions of marks)	Germany, 1912 (millions of marks)
Equity	19,960	33,108	19,210	31,157
Total liability	15,038	33,246		
Trade debt	3,066	4,355		
Bank loans	1,420	3,780		
Mortgages	778	1,674		
Bonds and notes	7,072	18,096	1,883	3,560

Securities Issues Data

	U.S. Manufacturing and Mining		U.S. Industrials		German Nonfinancial Domestic Corporations	
	Net Bond Issues (millions of $)	Net Stock Issues (millions of $)	Gross Bond Issues, Annual Average (millions of $)	Gross Stock Issues, Annual Average (millions of $)	Gross Bond Issues (millions of marks)	Gross Stock Issues (millions of marks)
1896					177	324
1897					172	381
1898					303	677
1899					329	911
1900	37	128			276	562
1901	557	256			339	276
1902	151	141			263	362
1903	252	119			188	299
1904	74	103			187	398
1905	122	118			339	540
1906	113	165			245	1,251
1907	125	168			272	637
1908	107	136			473	651
1909	139	183			419	682
1910	124	178			221	573
1911	206	203			422	505
1912	50	288			509	984
1913	−10	185			460	811
1900–13	2,047	2,371				
1901–12			110	150		
1896–1913					5,594	10,824

Sources: Balance sheets of U.S. nonfinancial corporations are from Goldsmith, Lipsey, and Mendelson 1963, 2:146. German data on equity and bonds are from Deutsche Bundesbank 1976, 290, 294. The German data on bonds seem to be face values (which are essentially the same as market values).

Table 8.5 (continued)

To calculate the market value of German equity, I combined the book-value estimate (290) with the market-to-book-value index for corporate stocks (294). For example, German equity book-value in 1900 was 10,384 million marks and the index was 1.85. Data on securities issues of U.S. manufacturing and mining corporations are from Dobrovolsky and Bernstein 1960, 333. Data on securities issues of industrials are from Friend 1967, 68. Data on German securities issues are from Eistert 1970, 105.

firms made a relatively rapid transition from *Kontokorrentkredite* into the equity market, and relied relatively little on bond finance. In the United States, industrial finance through outside equity was more limited. Indeed, as Carosso (1970, 81–82) points out, for many industrial and retail establishments prior to World War I, outside equity issues were not a possibility. As Doyle (1991) points out in his detailed analysis of sugar-refining and meat-packing industries, equity issues of American firms during this period typically were associated with "strategic" restructuring of the firm's preexisting liabilities, and not with the financing of industrial expansion.

8.3.5 The Financial Structure of Banks

Sources of finance for banks also were very different in Germany and the United States, with German banks relying to a much greater extent on equity rather than deposits as a source of funds. Of course, unlike national banks, the German credit banks did not issue currency, so one might expect them to show larger equity ratios than American banks for this reason. But this does not explain the difference. State-chartered banks in the United States lacked note-issuing authority, but had similar capital ratios to national banks. As table 8.6 shows, the difference between German banks' and U.S. national banks' capital-to-asset ratios is larger than can be explained by the presence of notes on national bank balance sheets.

The high German capital ratios are especially puzzling when one considers the large size of German banks compared to U.S. banks. Within the United States, larger banks tended to have lower capital ratios than small banks. For example, Calomiris (1993) shows that branching banks in California had half the capital ratios of other U.S. banks. Similarly, adjusting for differences in portfolio risk, large nationwide (nonuniversal) commercial banks in Canada had lower capital ratios than their American counterparts. Calomiris (1992) argues that lower capital ratios for large commercial banks reflected risk reductions brought about by large size. As banks became large, they were able to satisfy depositors' concerns about risk with smaller capital ratios. Banks wanted to conserve on capital because it was a relatively expensive form of finance. The limitation on banks' access to capital is illustrated by the fact that the demand for bank stock was confined mainly to investors located near the bank. A study by the Comptroller of the Currency of stock ownership in national banks in 1897 revealed that the largest out-of-state holdings were for the

Table 8.6   Sources of Bank Financing, Germany and the United States, 1904

	German Credit Banks (millions of marks)	U.S. National Banks (millions of $)
Net worth (book)	2,873	1,341
Liabilities	6,518	5,364
Deposit accounts	1,897	
Credit accounts	3,301	
Acceptances	1,320	
Currency issued	0	433
Net worth/liabilities	0.44	0.25

Sources: National bank balance-sheet data are derived from state-level data reported in Board of Governors of the Federal Reserve System 1959. National banknotes are from Board of Governors of the Federal Reserve System 1976, 408. German data are from National Monetary Commission 1910, table 15.

western and Pacific regions, which had out-of-state holdings of less than 12 percent (Breckenridge 1899, 10). Thus a possible explanation of the higher capital ratios of German universal banks could be the higher demand for bank stock by "outsiders."

What would explain higher demand by outsiders for universal banks' stock? First, given the potential for German nonfinancial firms to issue large amounts of equity, "thick-market" externalities may have favored similar financing by banks. Second, if German banks were better able to communicate information about their portfolio risks to their stockholders, then lemons discounts would be mitigated, allowing them to reap the advantages of equity finance. Thus, the efficiency of capital markets in Germany due to universal banking may have helped finance banks, too. Third, the confidence of outsiders in bank stock may have been enhanced by a reputational effect. If outsiders were aware that banks had long-term reputational capital worth preserving, then they should have been less concerned about short-term cheating by banks. Thus, the disciplinary role of demandable debt (stressed by Calomiris and Kahn 1991, and Calomiris, Kahn, and Krasa 1992) would be less relevant for German banks. From this perspective, German banks may have been able to finance themselves more through outside equity than American banks because of long-run benefits they could expect to realize through their relationships with firms. These long-run benefits increased the reputational consequences of cheating and helped to support the credibility of bankers.

It may never be possible to distinguish among these explanations for the higher equity ratios of German banks. But this decomposition is relatively unimportant. The important common feature of all these explanations is their dependence on universal banking as a precondition to permitting banks to rely on outside equity as an important source of finance.

8.3.6   Investment Banking Spread as a Measure of Financing Efficiency

An important dimension of cost savings stressed in section 8.2's discussion of the benefits of universal banking is the reduction in the cost to firms of underwriting and distributing securities. The investment banker's "spread" is defined as the difference between the market value of securities issued and the value received for these issues by the issuing firm. Data on spreads are useful for three purposes. First, average issue costs provide an overall comparison of the costs of issuing securities in the United States and Germany. Second, variation in spreads across securities and firms of different types can be used to gauge cross-country differences in the relative costs of issuing particular kinds of securities. For example, one would expect equity issues to be especially costly in the United States relative to Germany because of the greater costs of placing junior securities in a nonuniversal banking system. Finally, firm-level data on the factors that raise or lower costs of securities issues offer evidence on the sources of the costs of issuing bonds and stocks. For example, one can examine whether bankers' spreads primarily reflect information costs, physical transactions costs, taxes, or economic rents of the investment banker.

American investment bankers have guarded the details of their financial arrangements carefully, and data on investment bankers' spreads are notoriously hard to come by. For the United States, detailed data are known only for a few cases prior to the 1920s, and only after 1936 are data available for the whole population of securities issuers. For Germany, I have been able to locate some data on individual spreads for the pre–World War I period from *Saling's Borsen Jahrbuch* (the German equivalent of *Moody's Industrial Manual*). For many firms (roughly half), *Saling's* reports details of the underwriting costs of equity issues and/or the total amount of funds received by firms through equity issues. A minor problem with the data is that it is not always clear whether reported numbers include fees other than bankers' commissions. Equity issues entailed local and national taxes, as well as physical costs (printing, etc.). From examples where the breakdown of such costs are known, the total costs of taxes and physical expenses seem in the range of 2–3 percent. For example, Harpener Bergbau A. G., a large Dortmund mining company, issued 9 million marks of stock in 1909. The spread was 436,000 marks, or 4.84 percent of the issue. Of this cost, 176,000 marks (40 percent of the total cost) reflected the national government tax on equity issues.[18] Thus, in the absence of the government's securities tax, the bankers' spread would have been 2.9 percent. While reported data on commissions may overstate true commissions (because bankers sometimes paid these fees for firms), and reported data on total costs may understate total costs (because measured costs may not always include federal or local taxes), errors from these sources cannot be large, and data from firms that reported both measures indicate that reported total costs generally in-

---

18. I thank Richard Tilly for providing this example.

Table 8.7   **Bankers' Commissions (Spreads) and Total Issuing Costs for German Common Stock Issues, 1893–1913 (%)**

	Mean Bank Spread	25th Percentile Bank Spread	75th Percentile Bank Spread	Mean Total Cost	25th Percentile Total Cost	75th Percentile Total Cost
All Issues						
Electrical	3.67	2.57	4.55	5.08	3.61	7.00
# firms	13	—	—	12	—	—
# observations	21	—	—	20	—	—
Manufacturing	3.90	2.94	4.35	5.30	2.78	7.60
# firms	19	—	—	15	—	—
# observations	30	—	—	20	—	—
Issues Less Than 1 Million						
Electrical	3.94	3.49	4.26	5.24	4.00	6.72
# firms	4	—	—	3	—	—
# observations	7	—	—	3	—	—
Manufacturing	3.45	2.78	3.86	5.29	3.33	6.92
# firms	10	—	—	10	—	—
# observations	18	—	—	15	—	—
Firms with 1913 Capital Less Than 2 Million						
Manufacturing	4.11	3.57	4.80	5.93	3.33	8.80
# firms	3	—	—	5	—	—
# observations	6	—	—	5	—	—

Source: Saling's Borsen Jahrbuch 1913.

Notes: Percentages of bankers' commissions (spreads) is the difference between the amount paid for an issue by purchasers and the amount paid by the bankers to the issuing firm divided by the total amount paid for the issue. Percentage of total costs is the net funds raised by the firm (net of all expenses, including taxes, printing costs, and commissions) divided by the amount paid for the issue. Data are for firms that reported such information in *Saling's Borsen Jahrbuch* in the electrical industry (electrical equipment producers and power plant operators) and the metal manufacturers industry. The sample includes all reporting firms in the electrical industry and all reporting firms whose names begin with A through K for the metals manufacturing industry.

cluded all costs and that reported commissions generally did not include fees other than commissions.

Data on commissions for common stock issues earned by German banks from 1893 to 1913 are provided in table 8.7. The sample of firms for which data were collected include all reporting firms in the electrical industry (which includes manufacturers of electrical equipment and operating power plants) and firms in the metal manufacturing industry whose names begin with the letters A through K. Both of these industries are important producers of new products, and both are central to the second industrial revolution. The metal manufacturing industry includes many small firms, while the electrical industry is dominated by large firms, so together these two industries can provide some evidence on the role of firm size and issue size in determining bankers' commissions. For both industries, I divide the sample into small and large issues (less than or greater than 1 million marks, which equals $220,000). For metals, I also report data for firms with small total capital in 1913 (less than 2 million marks). The difference between average spreads and average total costs is 1.41 percent for the electrical industry and 1.40 percent for metal manufacturing, which suggests that taxes and physical costs were generally included in total costs and not in commissions. Bankers' commissions averaged 3.67 percent for the electrical industry and 3.90 percent for metal manufacturing. Commissions on small and large issues are essentially the same. Although small metals issues show lower average costs, the difference is not statistically significant for this small sample. Metals firms with low total capital had average commissions of 4.11 percent, compared to 3.90 percent for the industry as a whole. Again, this difference is small and not statistically significant. Overall, these data support the view that commissions on common stock were roughly 3–5 percent, and that they did not vary much by industry, firm size, or size of issue.

For the United States, firm-level data on bankers' commissions are not generally available for the pre–World War I period. Indeed, the dearth of equity issues in the United States historically made it difficult for the Securities and Exchange Commission to locate data on common stock spreads prior to 1936. Even with respect to bonds and preferred stock, the SEC's retrospective study begins only in the 1920s. Despite this problem, it is possible to gauge roughly the range of commission charges during the pre–World War I period using data from the later period and a few observations on individual transactions from the pre–World War I period. Data on bankers' spreads for bonds and preferred stocks during the 1920s and common stock spreads for the 1930s reported in table 8.8 are a reasonable, and possibly a conservative, measure of their pre–World War I values. There is little evidence of change in preferred stock or bond spreads from the 1920s to the mid-1930s, so there is little reason to believe that spreads were influenced by the Glass-Steagall separation of commercial and investment banking.[19] As argued above, the fundamental restrictions on universal banking were regulations that fragmented the banking system, and these were in place long before Glass-Steagall. Moreover, there is some discussion of spreads for the pre–World War I period that confirms this view. Brandeis (1914, 94–99) discusses bankers' spreads at length in his attack on the money trust. He notes that Morgan's spread exceeded 20 percent for the organization of U.S. Steel, and was 25 percent for underwriting the "Tube Trust." More generally, Brandeis writes: "Nor were monster commissions limited to trust promotions. More recently, bankers' syndicates have, in many instances, received for floating preferred stocks of recapitalized industrial concerns, one-third of all common stock issued, besides a considerable sum in cash. And for the sale of preferred stock of well established manufacturing

---

19. Calomiris and Raff (1993) report data on common stock spreads from the Lehman Brothers deal books and argue, based on these data, that common stock spreads were essentially the same in the 1920s and 1930s.

Table 8.8   Bankers' Spreads in the United States before World War II

	1925–29 (% of issue)			1930s (% of issue)		
	Common	Preferred	Bonds	Common	Preferred	Bonds
Issues < $5 million				(1935–38)	(1935–38)	(1935–38)
Total costs	NA	8	6	18	10	5
Compensation	NA	7	5	16	9	4
Other expenses	NA	1	1	2	1	1
# of issues	NA	96	423	241	206	210
All to public, IBs[a]				(1938)	(1938)	(1940)
Total costs				22	12	3
Compensation				20	11	2
Other expenses				2	1	1
# of issues				68	37	76
All to public, IBs[a]				(1938)	(1938)	(1940)
Total cost, underwritten issues				23	4	3
# of issues				16	9	31
Total cost, best efforts[b]				21	14	16
# of issues				52	28	1

Source: Securities and Exchange Comimssion 1940, 1941.

[a]All issues of securities to the public transacted through investment bankers.

[b]Best-effort issues are placed by investment bankers without price guarantees.

concerns, cash commissions (or profits) of from 7 1/2 to 10 percent of the cash raised are often exacted. On bonds of high-class industrial concerns, bankers' commissions (or profits) of from 5 to 10 points have been common" (95). These figures are similar to the numbers for the 1920s and mid-1930s reported in table 8.8.

Interestingly, the spreads for common stock far exceed those for preferred stock, which in turn far exceed those for bonds. This is what one would expect if the spreads largely represent compensation for information costs incurred in arranging the issues. The underwriting (insurance) aspect of the investment bankers' services do not explain the differences in the spreads for different types of securities. In fact, best-effort flotations, on which there is no underwriting risk, show *larger* commissions on average than underwritten flotations. This typically is explained by the fact that best-effort flotations involve riskier firms (Friend 1967, 39) and therefore entail greater due diligence and marketing costs.

It is worth emphasizing how large these spreads are. A 20 percent spread indicates that a firm only receives 80 cents for every dollar of claims it issues. This places a substantial cost on investments, especially by young, unseasoned firms. An investment opportunity must be able to generate enough income to pay interest or dividends to claimants *and* compensate existing shareholders by an amount (in present value) in excess of 20 percent of the project's cost.

There is corroborating evidence that external finance costs placed wedges of this magnitude between the social and private benefits of pursuing investment projects. Calomiris and Hubbard (1994) find that in the mid-1930s roughly a quarter of publicly traded firms in the United States had a cost differential between internally and externally generated funds in excess of 20 percent. They used a firm's dividend-payout reaction to the undistributed profits tax of 1936–37 to measure this shadow price differential. In a study of nineteenth-century profits, Atack and Bateman (1992) find large and widening differences in profit rates between small and large manufacturing firms in the United States of a similar order of magnitude, which suggest barriers to entry and geographic immobility of capital for financing small and medium-sized firms in manufacturing.[20]

The data reported in tables 8.7 and 8.8 indicate a substantially lower average cost of bringing equities to market in Germany, which helps to explain the relative dearth of equity issues in the United States shown in table 8.5. German bankers' spreads on equity were less than one-fourth those in the United States. Small German firms were able to issue equity for less than the cost large American corporations paid for issuing bonds. Interestingly, in Germany, spreads did not vary by size as they did in the United States. This is consistent with viewing universal banking networks (which permit internal marketing of new issues) as economizing on fixed costs of marketing stock issues.

One possible explanation for this difference is that German banks earned large anticipated capital gains on underwritings in addition to spreads. While a detailed examination of this proposition must await further research on firm-level data, an analysis of aggregate data suggests capital gains were small. Riesser (1911, 466) cites data on income earned from the sum of commissions and capital gains on securities transactions in 1903 published in the *Kölnische Zeitung* (see also Whale 1930, 26). A rough measure of capital gains earned by banks on securities holdings can be derived by combining this estimate with Eistert's (1970) estimates of total securities issued to derive a measure of total income from spreads and capital gains as a ratio of total issues. These data are reported in table 8.9. Using additional data on the composition of securities issues from Eistert (1970, 103), and the estimates of bankers' commissions, one can place some bounds on the rate of capital gains. To do so requires an assumption about banks' relative earnings from underwriting government bonds, corporate bonds, and equity. I assume that the banks' earnings from commissions and capital gains on equities are double those for corporate bonds, and that earnings on government bonds are 1 percent. Under these as-

20. Average manufacturing profit rates of firms rose form 18 percent in 1850 to 34 percent in 1880, while profit rates weighted by capital fell from 16 percent to 15 percent. In the South in 1880, unweighted profit rates were 43 percent, compared to 30 percent in the North. Clearly, for large numbers of small and medium-sized firms, profit rates did not converge over time within or across regions during this period. Differences of 20 or 30 percent in profit rates across firms were common throughout the period 1850–80.

Table 8.9   Estimate of German Banks' Capital Gains Rate from Securities
                   Underwritten in 1903

Gross profits from commissions and capital gains	55.7 million marks
Total securities placed	1,285.1 million marks
Average spread	0.043
German government bonds placed	343.3 million marks
Bonds placed (excluding German government)	597.1 million marks
Stocks placed	344.7 million marks
Assumed ratio of profit rates from stocks and corporate bonds	2
Assumed profit rate for government bonds	0.01
Implied average profit rate for corporate bonds	0.040
Implied average profit rate for stocks	0.080
Implied capital gain rate for stocks given 4.0% commission	0.040

Sources: Securities placed are from Eistert 1970, 103. Gross profits are from *Kölnische Zeitung,* as cited in Riesser 1911, 466.

sumptions, the total income earned from commissions plus capital gains on equity issues in 1903 was 8 percent of the amount issued. Given the estimate of 4 percent for equity commissions, this implies a 4 percent capital gain on equity issues. Thus, it seems that one cannot explain the difference between U.S. and German commissions on equity by appeal to offsetting capital gains by German underwriters.

The U.S.-German underwriting-spread comparison illustrates more than the high cost of capital in the United States. It also indicates that rent extraction is an unlikely explanation of high underwriting costs in the United States. German banking was at least as concentrated and powerful an industry as the purported money trust of the United States. Yet their spreads were quite small. Thus, higher average U.S. spreads likely reflected higher underlying costs of bringing issues to market in the United States. The fact that spreads for small firms and small issues in Germany were the same as for large firms is also significant. In the United States, smaller firms suffered significantly larger spreads, as shown in table 8.10, and firm size has also proven important in cross-sectional regression analysis of spreads (Mendelson 1967). Thus, the lower cost of equity issues in Germany relative to the United States affected the financing cost of small firms even more than shown by comparisons of average commissions. This lends credence to the view that "time-consistency" advantages and lower information costs (which are most relevant for small, growing firms) are an important part of the explanation for why German commissions were lower.

Additional evidence from time-series and cross-sectional analysis of bankers' spreads in the United States also suggests that spreads were more a function of information cost than of rent. First, the fact that spreads were larger for preferred stock than for bonds, and largest for common stock, is consistent with the information-cost interpretation of the spreads, and not with the rent-extraction interpretation. As Miller (1967, 157) shows, concentration in Amer-

Table 8.10   **Costs of Flotation of Primary Common Stock Issues Offered through Dealers, Post–World War II**

Dates	Size of Issue	Number of Issues	Average Cost as % Proceeds
1935–38	Issue < $5 million	241	18
1945–49	Issue < $5 million	208	15
1951–55	Issue < $5 million	178	15
1963–65	Issue < $5 million	369	12
1940	Issue > $5 million	11	12
1945–49	Issue > $5 million	49	8
1951–55	Issue > $5 million	52	6
1963–65	Issue > $5 million	107	7

Sources: Securities and Exchange Commission 1940, 1941, 1970.

ican investment banking has always been highest in bond underwriting, yet bonds have always enjoyed the lowest spreads. Second, as table 8.10 shows, common stock spreads fell most dramatically from the 1930s to the early 1960s, but this was not associated with increased competition. Miller (1967, 163) finds that the only reduction in concentration of investment banking over this period occurred in the bond market, in which spreads fell least. Third, cross-sectional studies of stock and bond spreads (Cohan 1961; Mendelson 1967) find substantial evidence linking variation in spreads to "quality" or information-related variables. For example, bond spreads increase with bond yields. Stock spreads are higher for issues that include "extra inducements," and for issues with lower-quality underwriters, which Miller (1967) and Mendelson (1967, 445, 474) associate with lower-quality firms. The most plausible explanation for the technological change that lowered spreads over time was the increase in bulk sales to institutional investors, which reduced the signaling and marketing costs of appealing to a widely dispersed group of investors (Haven 1940; Mendelson 1967, 413–19). The rise of direct placements after World War II also provided an alternative to syndication. These innovations were a partial substitute for a universal banking system, in which the universal bank would have directly linked issuers and holders.

8.3.7   Financial Returns and Access to Securities Markets

Arguments about the effects of higher information and control costs in industrial finance in the United States relative to Germany do not have clear empirical implications for expected returns on financial instruments. On the one hand, if universal banking in Germany were superior as a mechanism for limiting ex ante lemons discounts on securities, for disciplining firms, and for managing corporate distress in default states, then more high-risk firms would be admitted to securities markets, and more financial claims would be held in the form of riskier junior instruments like stocks. On the other hand, if banks are very good at reducing lemons problems, disciplining firms, and organizing workouts, then to the extent that these risks are *systematic,* overall risk on traded assets could be lower for Germany.[21] Thus, depending on which of these two effects dominates, returns on financial assets could be higher or lower under universal banking.

Comparisons of interest rate and yield "spreads"—returns in excess of the riskless interest-rate benchmark within each country—provide more information than comparisons of nominal returns across countries. There are problems in making inferences from comparisons of returns on financial assets across countries. Imperfect international capital market integration for riskless assets, and different expectations of commodity price movements across countries make direct comparison of nominal yields and returns problematic measures of the banking system's effect on real costs of industrial finance. The spreads between riskless public bonds and private securities returns in both countries remove elements of difference attributable to the relative supply of savings.

A problem in relating differences in returns spreads to structural differences across countries is the need to infer average ex ante returns on equity from average ex post returns. Under the assumption that expected and actual returns were roughly equal on average, ex post returns can serve as a gauge of expected stock returns. The shorter the sample period, the more dubious this assumption becomes. Furthermore, it is not clear whether, under a specie standard, nominal or real stock returns provide a better measure of expected returns. If commodity prices under a specie standard follow a random walk (possibly with long-run mean reversion, as suggested by Klein 1975, Rockoff 1984, and Barsky 1987), nominal averages of returns may provide a superior measure of expected real returns. For this reason, and because of the availability of such data, I report nominal spreads.

Table 8.11 reports data on spreads between government bond yields and private securities returns (bond yields and stock returns) for Germany and the

---

21. According to the capital asset pricing model, the average return on the market portfolio will compensate for systematic (nondiversifiable) risk. If the absence of universal banking increases overall systematic risk for stocks, then it should increase expected stock returns, *ceteris paribus.* Increased systematic risk could result, in theory, from at least three causes. First, under asymmetric information, the stock value of firms subject to borrowing constraints will vary with the shadow cost of external finance, which in turn will increase in times of low cash flow (Myers and Majluf 1984; Gale and Hellwig 1985; Brock and LeBaron 1990). Since firms' cash flows are correlated over the business cycle, this will induce greater correlation in stock returns among firms in an economy without universal banking. Second, expected costs of financial distress also increase firm risk. Again, the probability of financial distress varies systematically for all firms over the business cycle. If universal banking reduces distress costs, then it will decrease systematic risk in the portfolio of stocks. Third, managerial discipline may be more important during certain phases of the business cycle, since managers' incentives to cheat vary with the state of the economy. For example, under limited liability, managers who hold stock in their firm may chose to take on excessive risk in bad times (Jensen and Meckling 1976; Myers 1977; Calomiris and Kahn 1991). As in the other examples, this will induce greater systematic risk for the stock portfolio.

Table 8.11   **Yields and Spreads on Financial Portfolios, Germany and the United States**

	(1) Government Bond Yield	(2) Corporate Bond Yield	(3) Stock Return	(4) Private-Public Bond Spread (2)−(1)	(5) Stock Spread (3)−(1)	(6) Private Portfolio Returns	(7) Portfolio Spread (6)−(1)
Germany							
1883–1912	3.29	3.65	8.30	0.36	5.01	7.84	4.55
United States							
1880–99	2.68	4.65	5.39	1.97	3.24	5.02	2.52
1900–1913	2.32	5.00	6.80	2.68	4.48	5.90	3.57

Sources: Data on stock returns is derived from Snowden 1990, 414–15. U.S. corporate bond yields for 1880–99 are Macaulay's (1938) unadjusted railroad series, as reported in U.S. Department of Commerce 1975, 1003. Hickman's (1958, 81) data on bond yields for 1900–1909 are used for the later period. U.S. government bond yields are from Homer and Sylla 1991, 316,343. German bond yields and nominal stock returns are from Tilly 1992, 103. German government bond yields are taken from Homer and Sylla 1991, 260–61, 504.

Notes: For the United States, equal weights are given to stock and bond holdings in the portfolio, consistent with the evidence in table 8.5. In comparing realized returns on portfolios with yields, it is assumed that ex post stock returns on average were close to ex ante returns, which cannot be measured.

United States in two forms: simple spreads between government bonds and private stocks and bonds, and weighted spreads (using the proportion of stocks and bonds as weights) between private securities and government bonds. The weighted spread is useful as a measure of the total return on corporate assets (to control for differences in bond or stock spreads resulting from different corporate leverage in the United States and Germany).

These data come from a variety of sources. U.S. stock returns for a market basket of stocks are reported in Snowden 1990, 387. Bond yields for U.S. government bonds are from Homer and Sylla 1991, 316, 343. Private bond yields prior to 1900 are the unadjusted railroad bond series from Macaulay 1938. For the period after 1900, by which time other corporate bonds had become important in capital markets, I use Hickman's (1958, 81) data on average ex ante corporate bond yields for 1900–1909 as the measure of private bond yields.[22] For German portfolio returns, I use Tilly's (1992, 103) data on industrial bond yields and returns on industrial stocks. German government bond yields are taken from Homer and Sylla 1991, 260–61, 504.

The differences between American and German returns spreads in table 8.11 suggest larger financial portfolio risk associated with German financial assets, which mainly reflects the larger share of equity in German finance, but also

22. During this period, government bonds had a "circulation privilege," meaning that they could be used as backing for national banknotes issued by national banks. Some researchers have avoided using these bond yields as measures of nominal riskless returns because of a possible liquidity premium making their yields artificially low. Calomiris (1988, 726 n. 9) argues against this view on theoretical grounds, and Snowden (1990, 388 n. 10) argues against it on empirical grounds.

the higher returns on equity in Germany. As noted at the outset, such a finding may indicate information-cost advantages that brought higher-risk firms into the market for traded securities under universal banking. The facts that the government-corporate bond yield spread is larger in the United States and that the stock and portfolio spreads are larger in Germany are consistent with German firms achieving rapid access to equity markets. By themselves, however, the data on spreads do not prove universal banking was advantageous, since an alternative interpretation of high stock returns in Germany is higher economywide risk in Germany. One way to sort out whether high financial asset returns reflected well on Germany's financial system is to compare traded portfolio risks and underlying total economic risks in the United States and Germany. If universal banking allowed riskier securities to enter financial markets (the sanguine view of universal banking), then risk differences in traded assets between the two countries should exceed underlying economic risk differences for all assets.

One measure of economywide asset risk is the rate of business failure. Using the Black-Scholes model of option pricing, bankruptcy risk is a function of underlying asset risk (sigma) and the ratio of debt to the value of assets. Holding the debt-to-asset ratio constant, a higher risk of bankruptcy indicates a higher asset risk. In fact, debt-to-asset ratios were similar in the two countries overall, despite the higher equity-to-debt ratio in German traded securities. In the United States, debt was 30 percent of total assets in 1990 (Goldsmith 1985, 324–25), while in Germany debt was 32 percent in 1913.[23] Thus failure-rate differences are a good proxy for differences in asset risk between the two economies. Table 8.12 reports data on liabilities of failed businesses in dollars and marks for 1900–1908 (the years for which I was able to locate German data on liabilities of failed businesses), and the ratio of the average annual level of these to national assets in 1912/13. Because Dun and Bradstreet's data on liabilities of U.S. commercial and industrial failures exclude railroads and banks, I have added estimates of those numbers from other sources. This comparison of liabilities of failures relative to national assets gives some sense of the relative magnitude of overall risk in the two economies. The all-inclusive ratio for Germany is slightly lower than that of the United States, and when bank failures are omitted from the U.S. series, the two ratios are identical. This lends support to the view that universal banking lowered the threshold for admission into securities markets, and stock markets in particular. The risk on traded assets in Germany was much higher than in the United States, even though the underlying economywide risk was essentially the same in the two economies. This is consistent with the proposition that lower information and control costs under universal banking allowed greater participation of high-risk firms in securities markets.

23. The German debt-to-asset ratio is calculated using definitions from Goldsmith's U.S. calculations for Germany (1985, 225, 324–25).

Table 8.12   **Risk of Failure in Germany and the United States**
                      (liabilities of failures/national assets)

Liabilities of Failed Businesses

	Germany (millions of marks)	United States (millions of $)		
		Dun and Bradstreet	Railroads	Banks (assets)
1900	188	138	0	19
1901	224	113	27	15
1902	392	117	13	8
1903	319	155	0	9
1904	398	144	7	32
1905	499	103	31	21
1906	346	119	15	9
1907	302	197	27	18
1908	311	222	74	208
1901–8	2,979	1,308	194	339 (275 = liabilities)

National Assets

1912		301,500		
1913	639,300			

Average Liabilities of Failures, 1900–08/National Assets, 1912 or 1913

	0.00052	0.00065		
		0.00055 (omitting bank failures)		

Sources: Dun and Bradstreet's series on liabilities of failed businesses (U.S. Department of Commerce 1975, 912) for the United States excludes railroads and banks. Railroad bonds in default (Hickman 1960, 250) is a lower bound of omitted railroad liabilities. Bremer (1935, 27) reports assets of all failed banks. Calomiris (1993, table 4) reports the liability-to-asset ratio of all U.S. banks in 1904 (0.81), which is assumed to hold for failed banks for 1900–08. German liabilities of all failed firms is reported in *Viertel Jahreshefte zur Statistik des deutschen Reiches,* sec. 4, various issues. Goldsmith (1985, 226, 301) provides data on national assets for both countries.

8.3.8   Summary

Germany and the United States both achieved substantial industrial growth from 1870 to 1913. Comparisons of financial system performance suggest that German industrial growth was helped, and American growth was hindered, by their respective financial systems. Relatively high German ratios of financial assets and physical capital to GNP, and the high proportion of equipment in the German capital stock, are at least partly explained by lower costs of finance for industrial firms. These lower costs of finance are reflected in greater access to equity markets in Germany for risky industrial firms and their bankers, and lower costs of bringing securities to market. The low cost of floating equity issues in Germany, particularly for small firms, is especially revealing. Overall, the statistical comparison of German and American financial systems confirms qualitative historical and theoretical analysis that has linked universal banking to low costs of industrial finance. Unfortunately, much of the analysis that has been undertaken here has been restricted to aggregate comparisons. Comparative industry- and firm-level studies of finance costs are the obvious next step, and an important step before reaching definitive conclusions about the size of the contribution of German superiority in industrial finance to industrial performance.

8.3.9   The Inverted Histories of German and American Industrial Finance

Perhaps surprisingly, the United States enjoyed a universal banking system of a sort long before universal banking was established in Germany. As Davis (1957, 1960) and Lamoreaux (1991b) emphasize, New England's antebellum banks were a primary source of funding for New England industrialists. Just as in Germany, the links between industry and banking were very close. The banks were chartered to provide credit to their industrialist founders. In many cases, the officers and directors of the banks were their principal borrowers. New England bank stock was widely held by outsiders, and banks had much higher ratios of equity to assets than banks in other regions. In the mid-1850s, Massachusetts banks' capital and surplus relative to assets was roughly double that of New York and Pennsylvania (Calomiris, 1991a, 198).[24] As Calomiris and Kahn (1990) show, stock returns were relatively low in New England compared to other regions. New England banks may have been able to attract large numbers of outside stockholders and pay lower returns on equity than other banks because their institutional arrangements mitigated information problems. Each bank's borrower-insiders had incentives to monitor each other, and interbank relationships ensured monitoring among members of the Suffolk system (the New England payments clearing system run by Boston banks) and among commercial banks and savings banks (which financed much of commercial banks' activities).[25]

Lamoreaux (1991b, 1994) documents the demise of this system. By 1900, New England's banks had identical capital ratios to other regions' banks (Calomiris 1991a) and had changed toward financing more commercial undertakings and toward lending to bank outsiders. Calomiris (1993) interprets these changes as reflecting the growing mismatch between ever-larger scaled firms, and inherently small unit banks. As firms became larger, small banks found it

24. In Calomiris 1991a, I argued that Boston and Providence banks were mainly responsible for the difference in capital ratios between New England and other states. While it is true that Providence had unusually high capital ratios, even for New England, I overstated the difference between city and country banks in New England. My claim that "the capital of Massachusetts banks falls from 51 percent to 33 percent" (199) when one removes Boston banks from the sample was based on a calculation error. In fact, city and country banks in Massachusetts had nearly identical capital ratios.

25. It is interesting to note the many similarities to the German system, including the close relationships between banks and firms, and the use of savings institutions as investors in industrial banks. Savings cooperatives (*kreditgenossenschaften*) were large depositors in the German credit banks (Riesser 1911, 198–202).

increasingly difficult to satisfy the investment-financing needs of customers, given the desirability of maintaining a diversified loan portfolio. As Lamoreaux (1991a) shows, many New England banks wanted to respond to the growing scale of firms, and the economies of scope and scale from universal banking, by merging. When banks were able to merge, their profits increased substantially. Ultimately, however, national and state banking laws stood in the way of bank mergers or branching, as unit bankers blocked attempts to liberalize branching laws and prevented attempted mergers.

Over this same period (1850–1900), a German financial system dominated by private bankers transformed into the premier universal banking system of the world. Early examples of success in chartering limited-liability industrial banks elsewhere in Europe (notably the Credit Mobilier) and legal changes in Germany allowing limited-liability banking on a national scale paved the way for financial innovations that spread rapidly after 1870 (Tilly 1966, 1992; Kindleberger 1984). In contrast to the United States, where banking powers were limited compared to the growing powers of industrial corporations during the Progressive Era, Germany was relatively liberal in its treatment of banking powers and restrictive of nonfinancial firms (Tilly 1982, 653).

8.4   The Persistence of Inefficient Regulation

Thus far I have argued from comparisons of German and American financial systems that differences in banking regulation inhibited the development of an optimal mechanism for corporate finance in the United States. Restrictions on branching and consolidation restricted the size of banks. These became important constraints on the development of universal banking during the late nineteenth century as the size of firms and their borrowing needs expanded. The Clayton Act of 1914 may have further hampered America's ability to develop universal banking, by limiting bankers' influence over client firms through interlocking boards of directors. Thus, universal banking of the German type was never possible in the United States, even before Glass-Steagall restrictions on underwriting by affiliates of commercial banks.[26]

Nevertheless, during the 1920s, the U.S. financial system began to "converge" to a system of larger banks operating branches and performing combinations of commercial banking, investment banking, and trust activities like

---

26. Kroszner and Rajan (1994), in their study of differences between the bond-underwriting activities of investment banks and investment banking affiliates of commercial banks, find little evidence for greater efficiency of affiliates. The experience of the 1920s in the United States indicates little, however, about the advantages of universal banking. Removing Glass-Steagall prohibitions along with repealing the Clayton Act and removing branching restrictions on banks (which would permit U.S. banks to operate true universal banks) would likely have a much larger positive effect. Furthermore, investment banking affiliates in the 1920s were very new enterprises. Given more time and experience, their performance might have improved.

Table 8.13   Progressive Developments in U.S. Banking and Corporate Finance, 1920s

Banking Trends

	# Banks in Securities	Bank Mergers	# of Banks Absorbed	Branching Banks (Branches)	Bank Short-Term Loans to Nonfinancial Corporations (millions of $)
1910		127	128	292 (548)	
1911		119	119		
1912		128	128		3,902
1913		118	118		
1914		142	143		
1915		154	154	397 (785)	
1916		134	134		
1917		123	123		
1918		119	125		
1919		178	178		
1920		181	183	530 (1,281)	
1921		281	292	547 (1,455)	
1922	277	337	340	610 (1,801)	8,834
1923	314	325	325	671 (2,054)	
1924	372	350	352	706 (2,297)	
1925	413	352	356	720 (2,525)	
1926	464	429	429	744 (2,703)	
1927	493	543	544	740 (2,914)	
1928	561	501	507	775 (3,138)	
1929	591	571	575	764 (3,353)	10,699

Gross Sales of Corporate Securities Issues, Annual Averages (billions of $)

	Stock	Industrial Stocks	Corporate Bonds	Industrial Bonds
1901–12	0.5	0.15	0.9	0.11
1913–22	0.7	0.40	1.3	0.35
1923–27	1.6	0.64	3.6	0.78
1928–29	6.5	2.70	3.4	0.68

Sources: Corporate finance data are from Friend 1967, 68. Data on banks operating securities affiliates are from Peach 1941, 83. Bank merger data are from Chapman 1934, 56. Bank branching data are from Board of Governors of the Federal Reserve System 1976, 297. Bank lending to nonfinancial firms is from Goldsmith 1958, 339.

German universal banks. As shown in table 8.13, the progressive trend in the United States in the 1920s is visible in many measures, including bank branching and consolidation, bank financing of industry, the development of long-term lending from banks to industrial enterprises, and the growing proportion of equity finance relative to debt. Consistent with the argument that economies of scope in universal banking are enhanced by large-scale banking, the dramatic increase in bank involvement in securities markets in the 1920s coincided with a dramatic increase in consolidation and branching by banks. Investment banking affiliates of national banks played an important part in these progressive trends. They operated on a larger scale than their investment bank competitors, performed a greater variety of functions, and often charged lower commissions to customers in securities transactions (Preston and Finlay 1930a, 1930b). While investment banking affiliates did not lead to universal banking of the German kind (branching restrictions still applied in many states and branching was not allowed across state lines), the relaxation of branching restrictions in the 1920s was associated with a trend toward greater bank involvement in underwriting. Even in nonbranching states like Illinois, concentration of deposit and trust activities in large Chicago banks encouraged bank underwriting (Bureau of Business Research 1928).

In the wake of the Great Depression of the 1930s, however, the United States chose to limit the scope of banking with the restrictive Banking Acts of 1933 and 1935, to discourage bank consolidation through mergers, and to eschew the relaxation of branching laws in favor of deposit insurance as a means to insulate small banks and their depositors from the threat of bank failure and systemic panic. This reversal in direction in the 1930s is hard to understand on efficiency grounds and seems best viewed as the last and most successful in a long series of attacks by populist forces on large-scale banking. It also suggests that, with respect to financial regulation, the United States is singularly incapable of learning from the past.

Explanations for the change in direction that occurred in the wake of the Great Depression have been suggested by Calomiris and White (1994). They argue that politicking by powerful unit bankers (Stigler 1971) does not explain the change in direction in banking regulation. The power of unit bankers was at an all-time low in 1930 due to the many failures of small banks. Furthermore, deposit-insurance legislation won by unit bankers from 1908 to 1920 in eight states was responsible for financial devastation in the states that had passed such legislation (Calomiris 1989, 1990, 1991b). Calomiris and White (1994) argue that despite these facts the credibility of large bankers, and of large banks operating securities affiliates, was undermined by the accusations of the Pecora hearings and by the political campaigning of Steagall and others who managed to portray big banking, and links between securities markets and banks, as the cause of the Great Depression. Furthermore, unprecedented depositor losses galvanized support for deposit insurance. Once the Great Depression legislation was passed, it resuscitated unit banks as a powerful special interest resisting reform or repeal of Great Depression protections.

Since the Great Depression, other factors may have worked against repeal of Depression-era regulations. Endogenous technological changes induced by inefficient regulations may have helped to perpetuate regulations by reducing their costs. For example, technological changes that produced declines in underwriting costs in the United States in the 1960s, notably the increased role of private placements and of securities purchases in bulk by institutional investors, may have lessened the pressure to repeal the separation between commercial and investment banking. Another example is the rise of finance companies and the modern commercial paper market, beginning in the 1960s, and the development of the relatively unregulated bank CD market, which kept Regulation Q restrictions from significantly increasing industrial finance costs. Today, the effects on financing costs from increased capital requirements and other regulatory costs on banking are mitigated by the growth of loan sales markets and asset securitization.

Of course, the past is not always a perfect guide to the future. Perhaps pressure from globalization of finance has lowered the tolerance for poor regulation in the United States. There is much discussion about expanding bank powers to branch and provide a wide array of products, and some limited progress has been made on both fronts. New entrants from abroad have encouraged these trends. From this perspective, recent international coordination in bank regulation (the Basle capital standards) is a particularly interesting development. It may signal the erosion of domestic autonomy in bank regulation and greater international competition, or it may be a harbinger of agreements among governments to limit international competition and protect regulatory autonomy. Time will tell.

References

Atack, Jeremy, and Fred Bateman. 1992. Did the United States Industrialize Too Slowly? Working paper, Vanderbilt University.

Barsky, Robert B. 1987. The Fisher Hypothesis and the Forecastability and Persistence of Inflation. *Journal of Monetary Economics* 19 (January): 3–24.

Baskin, J. 1988. The Development of Corporate Financial Markets in Britain and the United States, 1600–1914: Overcoming Asymmetric Information. *Business History Review* 62:199–237.

Benston, George J. 1989. *The Separation of Commercial and Investment Banking: The Glass-Steagall Act Revisited and Reconsidered.* Norwell, MA: Kluwer Academic.

Benveniste, Lawrence M., and Paul A. Spindt. 1989. How Investment Bankers Determine the Offer Price and Allocation of New Issues. *Journal of Financial Economics* 24 (October): 343–61.

Berle, Adolph, and Gardiner Means. 1932. *The Modern Corporation and Private Property.* New York: Macmillan.

Board of Governors of the Federal Reserve System. 1959. *All Bank Statistics.* Washington, D.C.: Board of Governors.

———. 1976. *Banking and Monetary Statistics, 1914–1941.* Washington, D.C.: Board of Governors.

Bodenhorn, Howard. 1992. Capital Mobility and Financial Integration in Antebellum America. *Journal of Economic History* 52 (September): 585–610.

Boyd, John H., and Stanley L. Graham. 1986. Risk, Regulation, and Bank Holding Company Expansion into Nonbanking. *Federal Reserve Bank of Minneapolis Quarterly Review* 10 (spring): 2–17.

————. 1988. The Profitability and Risk Effects of Allowing Bank Holding Companies to Merge with Other Financial Firms: A Simulation Study. In *The Financial Services Industry in the Year 2000: Risk and Efficiency,* Proceedings of a conference on bank structure and competition, Chicago: Federal Reserve Bank of Chicago. 476–514.

Boyd, John H., Stanley L. Graham, and R. Shawn Hewitt. 1988. Bank Holding Company Mergers with Nonbank Financial Firms: Their Effects on the Risk of Failure. Federal Reserve Bank of Minneapolis Working Paper no. 417.

Brandeis, Louis D. 1914. *Other People's Money and How the Bankers Use It.* New York: Frederick A. Stokes.

Breckenridge, Roeliff M. 1899. Branch Banking and Discount Rates. *Sound Currency* 6 (January): 1–14.

Bremer, C. D. 1935. *American Bank Failures.* New York: Columbia University Press.

Brewer, Elijah. 1989. Relationship between Bank Holding Company Risk and Nonbank Activity. *Journal of Economics and Business* 41:337–53.

Brewer, Elijah, Diana Fortier, and Christine Pavel. 1988. Bank Risk from Nonbank Activities. *Federal Reserve Bank of Chicago Economic Perspectives* (July–August): 14–26.

Brock, William A., and Blake LeBaron. 1990. Liquidity Constraints in Production-Based Asset-Pricing Models. In *Asymmetric Information, Corporate Finance, and Investment,* ed. R. Glenn Hubbard, 231–56. Chicago: University of Chicago Press.

Brown, David T., Christopher James, and Robert M. Mooradian. 1991. The Information Content of Exchange Offers Made by Distressed Firms. Working paper, University of Florida, Gainesville.

Bureau of Business Research. 1928. Chicago as a Money Market. Bulletin 17, University of Illinois, Urbana.

Butters, J. Keith, and John Lintner. 1945. *Effect of Federal Taxes on Growing Enterprises.* Boston: Harvard University Press.

Cain, Louis P., and Donald G. Paterson. 1981. Factory Biases and Technical Change in Manufacturing: The American System, 1850–1919. *Journal of Economic History* 41 (June): 341–60.

Calomiris, Charles W. 1988. Price and Exchange Rate Determination during the Greenback Suspension. *Oxford Economic Papers* 40 (December): 719–50.

————. 1989. Deposit Insurance: Lessons from the Record. *Federal Reserve Bank of Chicago Economic Perspectives* (May–June): 10–30.

————. 1990. Is Deposit Insurance Necessary? A Historical Perspective. *Journal of Economic History* 50 (June): 283–95.

————. 1991a. Comment on "Information Problems and Banks' Specialization in Short-Term Commercial Lending: New England in the Nineteenth Century." In *Inside the Business Enterprise: Historical Perspectives on the Use of Information,* ed. Peter Temin, 195–203. Chicago: University of Chicago Press.

————. 1991b. Do Vulnerable Economies Need Deposit Insurance? Lessons from U.S. Agriculture in the 1920s. In *If Texas Were Chile: A Primer on Bank Regulation,* ed. Philip L. Brock, 237–349, 450–58 (Washington, D.C.: Sequoia Institute).

————. 1993. Regulation, Industrial Structure, and Instability in U.S. Banking: An Historical Perspective. In *Structural Change in Banking,* ed. Michael Klausner and Lawrence J. White, 19–116. Homewood, IL: Business One–Irwin.

Calomiris, Charles W., and Gary Gorton. 1991. The Origins of Banking Panics: Models, Facts, and Bank Regulation. In *Financial Markets and Financial Crises,* ed. R. Glenn Hubbard, 33–68. Chicago: University of Chicago Press.

Calomiris, Charles W., and R. Glenn Hubbard. 1994. Internal Finance and Investment: Evidence from the Undistributed Profits Tax of 1936–1937. Working paper, University of Illinois, Urbana-Champaign.

Calomiris, Charles W., and Charles M. Kahn. 1990. The Efficiency of Cooperative Interbank Relations: The Suffolk System. Working paper, University of Illinois, Urbana-Champaign.

———. 1991. The Role of Demandable Debt in Structuring Optimal Banking Arrangements. *American Economic Review* 81 (June): 497–513.

Calomiris, Charles W., Charles M. Kahn, and Stefan Krasa. 1992. Optimal Contingent Bank Liquidation under Moral Hazard. Working paper, University of Illinois, Urbana-Champaign.

Calomiris, Charles W., and Daniel M. G. Raff. 1993. The Evolution of Market Structure, Information, and Spreads in American Investment Banking. Working paper, University of Illinois, Urbana-Champaign.

Calomiris, Charles W., and Larry Schweikart. 1991. The Panic of 1857: Origins, Transmission, and Containment. *Journal of Economic History* 51 (December): 807–34.

Calomiris, Charles W., and Eugene N. White. 1994. The Origins of Federal Deposit Insurance. In *The Regulated Economy: A Historical Approach to Political Economy,* ed. Claudia Goldin and Gary Libecap, 145–88. Chicago: University of Chicago Press.

Campbell, Tim, and William Kracaw. 1980. Information Production, Market Signalling, and the Theory of Financial Intermediation. *Journal of Finance* 35 (September): 863–81.

Carlson, W. Bernard. 1991. *Innovation as a Social Process: Elihu Thomson and the Rise of General Electric, 1870–1900.* Cambridge: Cambridge University Press.

Carosso, Vincent P. 1970. *Investment Banking in America.* Cambridge: Harvard University Press.

Chandler, Alfred D., Jr. 1977. *The Visible Hand: The Managerial Revolution in American Business.* Cambridge: Harvard University Press.

Chapman, John M. 1934. *Concentration of Banking: The Changing Structure and Control of Banking in the United States.* New York: Columbia University Press.

Cohan, Avery B. 1961. Cost of Flotation of Long-Term Corporate Debt since 1935. Research Paper 6, School of Business Administration, University of North Carolina.

Creamer, Daniel, and Israel Borenstein. 1960. Capital and Output Trends in Manufacturing and Mining. In *Capital in Manufacturing and Mining: Its Formation and Financing,* ed. Daniel Creamer, Sergei P. Dobrovolsky, and Israel Borenstein, 3–108. Princeton: Princeton University Press.

Davis, Lance E. 1957. Sources of Industrial Finance: The American Textile Industry: A Case Study. *Explorations in Entrepreneurial History* 9:190–203.

———. 1960. The New England Textile Mills and the Capital Markets: A Study of Industrial Borrowing, 1840–1860. *Journal of Economic History* 20:1–30.

De Long, J. Bradford. 1991. Did Morgan's Men Add Value? In *Inside the Business Enterprise: Historical Perspectives on the Use of Information,* ed. Peter Temin, 205–36. Chicago: University of Chicago Press.

Deutsche Bundesbank. 1976. *Deutsches Geld- und Bankwesen in Zahlen, 1876–1975.* Frankfurt: Deutsche Bundesbank.

Diamond, Douglas. 1984. Financial Intermediation and Delegated Monitoring. *Review of Economic Studies* 51 (July): 393–414.

———. 1991. Monitoring and Reputation: The Choice between Bank Loans and Directly Placed Debt. *Journal of Political Economy* 99 (August): 689–721.

———. 1992. Bank Loan Maturity and Priority When Borrowers Can Refinance. Working paper, Graduate School of Business, University of Chicago.

Dobrovolsky, Sergei P., and Martin Bernstein. 1960. Long-Term Trends in Capital Financing. In *Capital in Manufacturing and Mining: Its Formation and Financing,* ed. Daniel Creamer, Sergei P. Dobrovolsky, and Israel Borenstein, 109–340. Princeton: Princeton University Press.

Doyle, William M. 1991. The Evolution of Financial Practices and Financial Structures among American Manufacturers, 1875–1905: Case Studies of the Sugar Refining and Meat Packing Industries. Ph.D. diss., University of Tennessee, Knoxville.

Dunlavy, Colleen. Forthcoming. *Politics and Industrialization in Early Railroads in the United States and Prussia.* Princeton: Princeton University Press.

Eistert, Ekkehard. 1970. *Die Beeinflussung des Wirtschaftswachstums in Deutschland von 1883 bis 1913 durch das Bankensystem.* Berlin: Duncker und Humblot.

Fazzari, Steven, R. Glenn Hubbard, and Bruce C. Petersen. 1989. Financing Constraints and Corporate Investment. *Brookings Papers on Economic Activity,* 114–95.

Field, Alexander. 1983. Land Abundance, Interest/Profit Rates, and Nineteenth-Century American and British Technology. *Journal of Economic History* 42 (June): 405–31.

———. 1987. Modern Business Enterprise as a Capital-Saving Innovation. *Journal of Economic History* 46 (June): 473–85.

Friend, Irwin. 1967. Over-All View of Investment Banking and the New Issues Market. In *Investment Banking and the New Issues Market,* ed. Irwin Friend, James R. Longstreet, Morris Mendelson, Ervin Miller, and Arleigh P. Hess, Jr., 1–79. New York: World Publishing Company.

Gale, Douglas, and Martin Hellwig. 1985. Incentive-Compatible Debt Contracts: The One-Period Problem. *Review of Economic Studies* 52 (October): 647–63.

Garber, Peter, and S. Weisbrod. 1991. *The Economics of Money, Liquidity, and Banking.* New York: D. C. Heath.

Gerschenkron, Alexander. 1962. *Economic Backwardness in Historical Perspective: A Book of Essays.* Cambridge: Harvard University Press.

Gilson, Stuart C., Kose John, and Larry H. P. Lang. 1990. Troubled Debt Restructurings. *Journal of Financial Economics* 27:315–53.

Goldsmith, Raymond W. 1955–56. *A Study of Saving in the United States.* Princeton: Princeton University Press.

———. 1958. *Financial Intermediaries in the American Economy since 1900.* Princeton: Princeton University Press.

———. 1976. The National Balance Sheet of Germany, 1850–1972. *Konjunkturpolitik* 22:153–72.

———. 1985. *Comparative National Balance Sheets: A Study of Twenty Countries, 1688–1978.* Chicago: University of Chicago Press.

Goldsmith, Raymond W., Robert E. Lipsey, and Morris Mendelson. 1963. *Studies in the National Balance Sheet of the United States.* Princeton: Princeton University Press.

Gorton, Gary. 1985. Clearing Houses and the Origin of Central Banking in the U.S. *Journal of Economic History* 45 (June): 277–83.

———. 1989. Self-Regulating Bank Coalitions. Working paper, University of Pennsylvania, Philadelphia.

Gorton, Gary, and James Kahn. 1992. The Design of Bank Loan Contracts, Collateral, and Renegotiation. Rochester Center for Economic Research Discussion Paper no. 327.

Gorton, Gary, and Donald Mullineaux. 1987. The Joint Production of Confidence: Endogenous Regulation and Nineteenth-Century Commercial Bank Clearinghouses. *Journal of Money, Credit, and Banking* 19 (November): 458–68.

Haven, T. Kenneth. 1940. *Investment Banking under the Securities and Exchange Commission.* Ann Arbor: University of Michigan Bureau of Business Research.

Hickman, W. Braddock. 1958. *Corporate Bond Quality and Investor Experience.* Princeton: Princeton University Press.

———. 1960. *Statistical Measures of Corporate Bond Financing since 1900.* Princeton: Princeton University Press.

Hoffmann, Walther G. 1965. *Das Wachstum der Deutschen Wirtschaft seit der Mitte des 19. Jahrhunderts.* Berlin: Springer-Verlag.

Homer, Sidney, and Richard Sylla. 1991. *A History of Interest Rates.* 3d ed. New Brunswick: Rutgers University Press.

Hoshi, Takeo, Anil Kashyap, and Gary Loveman. 1992. Lessons from the Japanese Main Bank System for Financial Reform in Poland. Working paper, Graduate School of Business, University of Chicago.

Hoshi, Takeo, Anil Kashyap, and David Scharfstein. 1990a. Bank Monitoring and Investment: Evidence from the Changing Structure of Japanese Corporate Banking Relationships. In *Asymmetric Information, Corporate Finance, and Investment,* ed. R. Glenn Hubbard, 105–26. Chicago: University of Chicago Press.

———. 1990b. The Role of Banks in Reducing the Costs of Financial Distress. *Journal of Financial Economics* 27 (September): 67–88.

Huertas, Thomas, and Harold Cleveland. 1987. *Citibank.* Cambridge: Harvard University Press.

Hughes, Thomas P. 1983. *Networks of Power: Electrification in Western Society, 1880–1930.* Baltimore: Johns Hopkins University Press.

James, Christopher. 1987. Some Evidence on the Uniqueness of Bank Loans. *Journal of Financial Economics* 19:217–35.

James, Christopher, and Peggy Wier. 1988. Are Bank Loans Different? Some Evidence from the Stock Market. *Journal of Applied Corporate Finance.* 1:46–54.

———. 1990. Borrowing Relationships, Intermediation, and the Cost of Issuing Public Securities. *Journal of Financial Economics* 28:149–71.

Japan Development Bank. 1994. Policy-Based Finance. World Bank Discussion Paper no. 221.

Jeidels, Otto. 1905. *Das Verhältnis der deutschen Grossbanken zur Industrie, mit besonderer Berucksichtung der Eisenindustrie.* Berlin: Schmollers Forschungen.

Jensen, Michael C., and William H. Meckling. 1976. Theory of the Firm: Managerial Behavior, Agency Costs, and Ownership Structure. *Journal of Financial Economics* 3:305–60.

Kaufman, George G., and Larry Mote. 1989. Securities Activities of Commercial Banks: The Current Economic and Legal Environment. Working paper, Federal Reserve Bank of Chicago.

———. 1990. Glass-Steagall: Repeal by Regulatory and Judicial Reinterpretation. *Banking Law Journal* (September–October): 388–421.

Kennedy, William, and Rachel Britton. 1985. Portfolioverhalten und wirtschaftliche Entwicklung im späten 19. Jahrhundert: Ein Vergleich zwischen Grosbritannien und Deutschland: Hypothesen und Spekulationen. In *Beitrage zu quantitativen und vergleichenden Unternehmensgeschichte,* ed. Richard H. Tilly. Stuttgart.

Kim, Sun Bae. 1992. Agency Costs and the Firm's Ownership Structure: The Japanese Evidence. Working paper, Board of Governors of the Federal Reserve System.

Kindleberger, Charles P. 1984. *A Financial History of Western Europe.* London: Allen and Unwin.

Klein, Benjamin. 1975. Our New Monetary Standard: The Measurement and Effects of Price Uncertainty. *Economic Inquiry* 13 (December): 461–84.

Kroszner, Randall S., and Raghuram G. Rajan. 1994. Is the Glass-Steagall Act Justified? A Study of the U.S. Experience with Universal Banking before 1933. *American Economic Review* 84 (September): 810–32.

Lacker, Jeffrey. 1991. Collateralized Debt as the Optimal Contract. Working paper, Federal Reserve Bank of Richmond.

Lamoreaux, Naomi R. 1991a. Bank Mergers in Late Nineteenth-Century New England: The Contingent Nature of Structural Change. *Journal of Economic History* 51 (September): 537–58.

———. 1991b. Information Problems and Banks' Specialization in Short-Term Commercial Lending: New England in the Nineteenth Century. In *Inside the Business Enterprise: Historical Perspectives on the Use of Information,* ed. Peter Temin, 154–95. Chicago: University of Chicago Press.

———. 1994. *Insider Lending: Banks, Personal Connections, and Economic Development in Industrial New England, 1784–1912.* Cambridge: Cambridge University Press.

Litan, Robert E. 1985. Evaluating and Controlling the Risks of Financial Product Deregulation. *Yale Journal on Regulation* 3 (fall): 1–52.

———. 1987. *What Should Banks Do?* Washington, D.C.: Brookings Institution.

Macaulay, Frederick R. 1938. *Some Theoretical Problems Suggested by the Movements of Interest Rates, Bond Yields, and Stock Prices in the United States since 1856.* Cambridge: National Bureau of Economic Research.

Mackie-Mason, Jeffrey K. 1990. Do Firms Care Who Provides Their Financing? In *Asymmetric Information, Corporate Finance, and Investment,* ed. R. Glenn Hubbard, 63–104. Chicago: University of Chicago Press.

Marquardt, Mary O. 1960. Sources of Capital of Early Illinois Manufacturers, 1840–1880. Ph.D. diss., University of Illinois, Urbana-Champaign.

Mayer, Colin. 1988. New Issues in Corporate Finance. *European Economic Review* 32 (June): 1167–89.

Meinster, David R., and Rodney D. Johnson. 1979. Bank Holding Company Diversification and the Risk of Capital Impairment. *Bell Journal of Economics* 10 (autumn): 683–94.

Mendelson, Morris. 1967. Underwriting Compensation. In *Investment Banking and the New Issues Market,* ed. Irwin Friend, James R. Longstreet, Morris Mendelson, Ervin Miller, and Arleigh P. Hess, Jr., 394–479. New York: World Publishing Company.

Miller, Ervin. 1967. Background and Structure of the Industry. In *Investment Banking and the New Issues Market,* ed. Irwin Friend, James R. Longstreet, Morris Mendelson, Ervin Miller, and Arleigh P. Hess, Jr., 80–175. New York: World Publishing Company.

Myers, Stewart C. 1977. Determinants of Corporate Borrowing. *Journal of Financial Economics* 5:147–75.

———. 1984. The Capital Structure Puzzle. *Journal of Finance* 39:575–92.

Myers, Stewart C., and Nicholas Majluf. 1984. Corporate Financing and Investment Decisions When Firms Have Information That Investors Do Not Have. *Journal of Financial Economics* 13:187–221.

National Monetary Commission. 1910. *Statistics for Great Britain, Germany, and France, 1867–1909.* Washington, D.C.: GPO.

Neuburger, Hugh, and Houston H. Stokes. 1974. German Banks and German Growth, 1883–1913: An Empirical View. *Journal of Economic History* 34 (September): 710–32.

Peach, W. Nelson. 1941. *The Security Affiliates of National Banks.* Baltimore: Johns Hopkins University Press.

Pennacchi, George. 1983. Maturity Structure in a Model of Unregulated Banking. Working paper, University of Illinois, Urbana-Champaign.

Piore, Michael, and Charles F. Sabel. 1984. *The Second Industrial Divide.* New York: Basic Books.

Pozdena, Randall J. 1991. Is Banking Really Prone to Panics? *Federal Reserve Bank of San Francisco Weekly Letter* 91–35, 11 October.

Preston, H. H., and Allan R. Finlay. 1930a. Era Favors Investment Affiliates. *Journal of the American Bankers Association* 22 (June): 1153–54, 1191–92.

———. 1930b. Investment Affiliates Thrive. *Journal of the American Bankers Association* 22 (May): 1027–28. 1075.

Prowse, Stephen D. 1992. The Structure of Corporate Ownership in Japan. Working paper, Board of Governors of the Federal Reserve System.

Rajan, Raghuram. 1992. Insiders and Outsiders: The Choice between Relationship and Arm's-Length Debt. *Journal of Finance* 47 (September): 1367–1400.

Ramakrishnan, R. T. S., and Anjan Thakor. 1984. The Valuation of Assets under Moral Hazard. *Journal of Finance* 39 (1): 229–38.

Ramirez, Carlos D. 1992. Financial Capitalism in the United States and Germany at the Turn of the Twentieth Century. Working paper, Harvard University.

Riefler, Winfield W. 1930. *Money Rates and Money Markets in the United States.* New York: Harper and Brothers.

Riesser, Jacob. 1911. *The Great German Banks and Their Concentration, in Connection with the Economic Development of Germany.* Translation of 3d ed. Washington, D.C.: GPO.

Rockoff, Hugh. 1984. Some Evidence on the Real Price of Gold, Its Cost of Production, and Commodity Prices. In *A Retrospective on the Classical Gold Standard, 1821–1931,* ed. Michael D. Bordo and Anna J. Schwartz, 613–50. Chicago: University of Chicago Press.

Romer, Christina D. 1989. The Prewar Business Cycle Reconsidered: New Estimates of Gross National Product, 1869–1908. *Journal of Political Economy* 97 (February): 1–37.

Schumpeter, Joseph A. 1939. *Business Cycles: A Theoretical, Historical, and Statistical Analysis of the Capitalist Process.* New York: McGraw-Hill.

Securities and Exchange Commission. 1940. Cost of Flotation for Small Issues, 1925–1929 and 1935–1938. Washington, D.C.: Securities and Exchange Commission.

———. 1941. Statistical Series Release no. 572, June.

———. 1970. Cost of Flotation of Registered Equity Issues, 1963–1965. Washington, D.C.: Securities and Exchange Commission.

Selden, Richard T. 1963. Trends and Cycles in the Commercial Paper Market. NBER Occasional Paper no. 85. New York: National Bureau of Economic Research.

Sheard, Paul. 1989. The Main Bank System and Corporate Monitoring and Control in Japan. *Journal of Economic Behavior and Organization* 11:399–422.

Snowden, Kenneth A. 1990. Historical Returns and Security Market Development, 1872–1925. *Explorations in Economic History* 27 (October): 381–420.

Stigler, George J. 1971. The Theory of Economic Regulation. *Bell Journal of Economics and Management Science* 2 (spring): 1–21.

Tilly, Richard H. 1966. *Financial Institutions and Industrialization in the Rhineland, 1815–1870.* Madison: University of Wisconsin Press.

———. 1980. Banken und Industrialisierung in Deutschland: Quantifizierungsversuche. In *Entwicklung und Aufgaben von Versicherungen und Banken in der Industrialisierung,* ed. F. W. Henning, 165–93. Berlin: Duncker und Humblot.

———. 1982. Mergers, External Growth, and Finance in the Development of Large-Scale Enterprise in Germany, 1880–1913. *Journal of Economic History* 42 (September): 629–58.

———. 1984. Zur Finanzierung des Wirtschaftswachstums in Deutschland und Grosbritannien, 1880–1913. In *Die Bedingungen des Wirtschaftswachstums in Vergangenheit und Zukunft,* ed. E. Helmstadter, 263–86. Tubingen.

———. 1986. German Banking, 1850–1914: Development Assistance for the Strong. *Journal of European Economic History* 15:113–52.

———. 1992. An Overview of the Role of the Large German Banks up to 1914. In *Finance and Financiers in European History, 1880–1960,* ed. Youssef Cassis, 92–112 (Cambridge: Cambridge University Press).

Townsend, Robert. 1979. Optimal Contracts and Competitive Markets with Costly State Verification. *Journal of Economic Theory* 21 (October): 265–93.

Trusk, Robert J. 1960. Sources of Capital of Early California Manufacturers, 1850 to 1880. Ph.D. diss., University of Illinois, Urbana-Champaign.

U.S. Department of Commerce. 1975. *Historical Statistics of the United States: Colonial Times to 1970.* Washington, D.C.: GPO.

Wall, Larry D. 1987. Has Bank Holding Companies' Diversification Affected Their Risk of Failure? *Journal of Economics and Business* 39 (November): 313–26.

Webb, Steven B. 1980. Tariffs, Cartels, Technology, and Growth in the German Steel Industry, 1879–1914. *Journal of Economic History* 40 (June): 309–30.

Whale, P. Barrett. 1930. *Joint Stock Banking in Germany.* London: Macmillan.

White, Eugene N. 1985. The Merger Movement in Banking, 1919–1933. *Journal of Economic History* 45 (June): 285–91.

———. 1986. Before the Glass-Steagall Act: An Analysis of the Investment Banking Activities of National Banks. *Explorations in Economic History* 23 (January): 33–55.

Williamson, Oliver. 1980. Emergence of the Visible Hand. In *Managerial Hierarchies,* ed. Alfred D. Chandler and Herman Daems. Cambridge: Harvard University Press.

Williamson, Stephen D. 1986. Costly Monitoring, Financial Intermediation, and Equilibrium Credit Rationing. *Journal of Monetary Economics* 18 (September): 159–80.

Wright, Gavin. 1990. The Origins of American Industrial Success, 1879–1940. *American Economic Review* 80 (September): 651–68.

Comment   Peter Temin

This is a good, ambitious paper. It is a good paper for this conference and volume because Calomiris has undertaken to analyze an important economic organization. It is ambitious because it argues that institutional arrangements are very, very important. The structure of the banking system, Calomiris asserts, affects the rate of economic growth, the composition of the capital stock, and—implicitly—the rate of productivity change in the economy as a whole.

Before I comment on how Calomiris gets to these conclusions and on the support he musters for them, I would like to place this paper in the context of this conference and its predecessor. That conference, which was reported in *Inside the Business Enterprise: Historical Perspectives on the Use of Information* (Chicago, 1991), dealt primarily with flows of information inside business organizations—through accounting, production reports, standardized information, and so forth. This conference has extended the concern with information to include the coordination of activity both within and between firms.

Calomiris emphasizes the importance of information flows in his paper. He argues that one of the primary roles of economic organizations is to control the flow of information. On the assumption that information flows more easily

Peter Temin is professor of economics at the Massachusetts Institute of Technology and a research associate of the National Bureau of Economic Research.

within organizations than between them, Calomiris applauds the role of some large organizations, that is, universal banks. He does not assert that institutions all work equally efficiently or even that there is a tendency for the institutional control of information to become more efficient over time. He closes his paper with some thoughts on the political evolution of information-handling institutions.

Economists have paid increasing attention to the importance of information in recent years. Courses in advanced economic theory routinely spend much of their time detailing and analyzing the flow of information in different models. This research, expressed in the formal, mathematical terms beloved of economic theorists, is not very accessible to business historians. This clash of cultures gives rise to a problem of information flows in our disciplines that mirrors the problems we analyze.

Economic theorists express great interest in the work of business historians. They say that they are looking for examples of information flows to model in their theories. But these theories often do not feed back into business histories because they are hard to read and to apply. The historians assert that they deal with information flows all the time, that information is a critical part of management. But their expositions are not read much by economic theorists because they are not directed toward the questions posed by the theorists.

These conferences and volumes are designed to lessen the distance between these two groups. If business historians can learn how economists approach questions, they can present their narratives in ways that illuminate these problems. And if economic theorists learn more business history, they will find ample material to model.

Calomiris addresses this communication gap in his paper. He precedes his historical evidence with a description of the theoretical literature on the importance of information in banking. He provides a fine readers' guide to this literature for the interested business historian. This does not overcome the difficulty of reading abstract mathematical papers, but it is a start. In addition, Calomiris's history stays close to the questions raised in his theoretical overview, raising questions for economists interested in extending the theory.

While this explicit focus on information would be enough to make Calomiris's paper a fitting capstone for this volume, there is another connection to the preceding conference as well. The previous volume closes with two papers on banking. Lamoreaux argued that American commercial banks in the early nineteenth century provided investment funds, albeit primarily to the banks' directors. But as investments became geographically dispersed, making information about them costly, commercial banks gradually specialized in providing short-term trade credit. Commercial banks as we know them appeared only in the late nineteenth century. De Long analyzed the most famous of the private bankers who took over the role of providing industrial finance as the commercial banks abandoned this activity. He argued that the House of Morgan provided a real economic benefit to the firms doing business with it. Morgan firms were worth more than similar firms without the Morgan connection.

Calomiris extends these papers by comparing the financial system described by Lamoreaux and De Long to that in Germany. While those two authors asked how the American banking system functioned at the turn of the twentieth century, Calomiris evaluates the turn-of-the-century banking system by comparing it with a structure that evolved quite differently. The intellectual links among these three papers are evident from Calomiris's frequent citations of the two earlier contributions. Taken together, the three papers on banking constitute a model of the kind of intellectual inquiry that these conferences and volumes are designed to foster.

Like Gaul, Calomiris's paper is divided into three parts. He opens with the theoretical discussion just noted. This is followed by a description of the American and German banking systems as seen through this theoretical lens. Finally Calomiris argues that the different banking structures in the two countries led to a variety of different experiences. He suggests that universal banks had effects that stretched from the composition of aggregate German investment to the way in which individual German firms were financed.

Calomiris centers his theoretical discussion on what he calls the "pecking order" of corporate finance. The term suggests a normative hierarchy, but the order seems rather to describe the stages that companies actually go through as they age. More precisely, Calomiris's pecking order describes the stages of growth that American companies generally experience; he argues that the order is not a general one. One function of business history is to reveal whether such patterns are universal or dependent on specific institutional arrangements. (The theoretical literature may emphasize the American experience because it is largely American.)

In this story, a nascent firm first gets capital from retained earnings and rich uncles. As the enterprise grows, it begins to compile a track record. This information allows it to borrow from banks. That is, the firm generates enough information to attract short-term, fixed-yield investments by local institutions. A bit farther down the path, the enterprise can obtain equity investment from knowledgeable people or specialized institutions. The reach of the information is not necessarily any wider, but the longer record encourages investors to provide capital on longer terms and without fixed repayment schedules. Investors cross the line between loans and equity investment.

If the enterprise continues to prosper and grow, it reaches a size where information about it becomes publicly available. The company then can sell bonds on a public market. There is enough information generally available for a variety of people and institutions to perform the lending function first undertaken by banks. With continued growth, the public at large becomes willing to cross the line between bonds and stocks, just as knowledgeable specialized investors were with the younger, smaller firm. The mature enterprise then has available to it the choice of raising capital by issuing publicly available bonds or stocks.

This pecking order describes how a business firm interfaces with financial institutions at various stages of its growth. The implied order of preference comes from the fact that the large, mature enterprise has a choice of funding sources because information about it is prevalent. The mature enterprise chooses the least costly form of finance—which we consider the most desirable.

This five-step process is presented as a logical exercise. It is the result of the expanding size of an enterprise in need of capital and the growing circle of people and organizations with enough information to consider supplying the company's needs. But this pecking order is hardly the only way for the capital needs of growing companies to be supplied. The second part of Calomiris's exposition is a description of how this pecking order emerged in the United States and how an alternative banking structure arose in Germany.

Instead of going through five distinct steps, German companies went through only two or three. Calomiris does not discuss the first step of insider financing very much, and we can leave it aside. Bank financing for small companies was present in both countries. In America, it was supplanted by equity funding, then bonds, then publicly traded stocks. In Germany, by contrast, bank lending continued throughout the life of the firm, obviating the middle steps in the pecking order. A capital-hungry enterprise went directly from bank credit to public stock.

Calomiris argues that the simpler German system economized on resources used to gather information. Fewer steps meant fewer people and institutions that needed to be informed. Continuity in the source of capital further meant that new organizations did not have to gather information each time a firm moved to the next stage.

Several questions arise about this argument. First, did less articulation necessarily reduce costs? Could it also have led to mismatches between supplying and demanding banks and firms, say, for intermediate-sized enterprises? Is it possible that German firms were starved for capital at some stage in their growth? Second, even if the American system was more costly, is part of the extra cost attributable to the larger size of the United States rather than to the American institutions? Phrased differently, would the concentrated German banking system have worked as well in the vast United States as it did in Germany? Third, did the concentration of German capital supplies in a few institutions encourage market power either in the financial or product markets? (Calomiris discusses the last question and says no.)

One of the important contributions of this paper is Calomiris's clear statement of the problem and the theory underlying it. The other is the extensive information he compiled to demonstrate the effects of the different banking systems. The third part of the paper contains a collection of empirical demonstrations. The variety of these "tests" is both a strength and a weakness: a strength because Calomiris has marshalled an impressive array of disparate data; a weakness because there is no indication that any single test is critical.

Calomiris opens his demonstration with aggregate data about Germany and the United States. He argues that the capital-output ratio in late-nineteenth-century Germany, the share of equipment in the capital stock, and the growth of labor productivity were all higher in Germany.

These observations are consistent in the sense that a single view of German capital deepening can include them all. But it is not clear that the structure of the banking system can explain the per capita rate of capital accumulation. Demonstration of this point requires consideration of savings behavior as well of investment funds. Japan today appears to have both integrated banks and a high saving rate, but it is not usual to assert that the former is the cause of the latter. This is not to say it is not, only that the kind of data presented in Calomiris's paper cannot be used to test this hypothesis.

The key evidence in this paper to my mind is in tables 8.7 and 8.8. There Calomiris presents estimates of the cost of issuing common stock in Germany and the United States. Unfortunately, only the German data refer to the period before World War I that is the focus of the paper; the American data are from the interwar period. Calomiris argues that American bankers' spreads in the issuance of stock were not rising over time and that the later data can be seen as a lower bound for the (unobserved) earlier figures. This implies that the banking restrictions of the 1930s did not raise financing costs. More work is needed to evaluate this implicit contention.

Calomiris argues that what he labels "mean bank spread" is a better indication of the organizational and informational costs of issuing stock in Germany than "mean total cost," which includes taxes and physical costs like printing. The "mean bank spreads" are less than 4 percent of the issue for most firms. These German costs are contrasted with the American data from the 1930s in table 8.8. The cost of issuing common stock in the United States was about 20 percent—or five times as high as the German cost!

This is a dramatic result. I have pointed out some potential problems with the data, but these caveats only serve to show how difficult it is to find the relevant information. Calomiris is to be congratulated for finding as much as he did and encouraged to follow this general paper with a more focused exploration of these costs.

If the data are even approximately correct, they indicate that the theoretical arguments surveyed by Calomiris in the early parts of the paper are very important indeed. Capital was much cheaper for enterprises at the last stage of the pecking order in Germany. The German *Grossbanken* clearly were able to place common stocks with far less trouble than the syndicates led by investment banks in the United States.

This conclusion raises a theoretical question about Calomiris's pecking order. He has exposed the costs of moving from step to step. But it is not clear from the theory that companies at the top of the pecking order should have had high costs. Firms at this level were larger and well known; why was information about them so scarce in the 1930s? Are we sure this scarcity was a result of the banking structure? Could it have been a reflection of conditions in the Depression or of other aspects of the economy?

The data imply that the German banks were not exercising market power in their commissions, despite their concentration. By contrast, the data do not indicate whether the large American spreads are the results of the information costs described by Calomiris or the market power alleged by many contemporary observers. They also do not say how large financing costs were at other stages of the pecking order. Calomiris suggests that the costs at the top of the order should be a lower bound to costs along the way, but a test of this proposition would enhance his argument.

Although this is the most important evidence that Calomiris marshals, his other evidence also will repay study. He provides several different approaches—examining corporate balance sheets, national balance sheets, and a variety of estimated costs of financing—to bolster his contention that financing costs were far cheaper in Germany than in the United States in the early years of the twentieth century. It is a tour de force.

It may be fitting to close with a statement of issues we need to keep in mind as we continue this exploration of the common ground between economic theory and business history.

This paper, in common with most essays in business history, has a large-organization bias. Historians write about groups that leave records; business historians, about enterprises that succeed. This natural tendency shades into an implicit presumption that bigger is better. Alfred Chandler may be credited with providing intellectual justification for this presumption in manufacturing; Calomiris's theory does the same for banking. All these arguments may be correct, but their current popularity should make us always ask for proof.

In addition, this is a paper for the nineties. The American economy has its problems, and it is natural to find their roots in deep-seated malfunctions. A banking system that appears to have gotten steadily worse for a century or more is made to order for the current mood.

The explicit message of Calomiris's paper is that integration is needed when markets fail. The market failure in business financing comes from the high cost of information; an integrated bank that conserves information is the cure. The implicit message is even stronger: integration generally is better than the market. We must make very sure that we are not falling into a common attitude instead of examining each case on its merits.

Finally, this paper—like others in this volume—analyzes activities at the boundaries of business organizations. Too often we assume that activities internal to a firm are totally different from external processes, that there is a sharp break in information and other costs at the boundaries of corporations. These papers remind us that the boundaries themselves may be endogenous and that any discontinuity in the continuum of information costs at a company boundary may be specific to an industry. Calomiris argues forcefully in this paper that the discontinuity in banking is both large and important for the functioning of the entire economy.

Contributors

Charles W. Calomiris
Department of Finance
University of Illinois
340 Commerce West Building
Champaign, IL 61820

W. Bernard Carlson
A220 Thornton Hall
Division of Technology, Culture, and
    Communication
University of Virginia
Charlottesville, VA 22903

Michael J. Enright
Morgan Hall
Harvard Business School
Soldiers Field
Boston, MA 02163

Tony Freyer
University of Alabama School of Law
Box 870382
Tuscaloosa, AL 35487

Victor P. Goldberg
School of Law
Columbia University
435 West 116th Street
New York, NY 10027

Timothy W. Guinnane
Department of Economics
Yale University
New Haven, CT 06520

Naomi R. Lamoreaux
Department of History
Brown University
142 Angell Street
Providence, RI 02912

Walter Licht
Department of History
University of Pennsylvania
Philadelphia, PA 19104

Joel Mokyr
Department of Economics
Northwestern University
2003 Sheridan Road
Evanston, IL 60208

David C. Mowery
School of Business
350 Barrows Hall
University of California-Berkeley
Berkeley, CA 94720

Daniel Nelson
Department of History
University of Akron
Akron, OH 44325

Michael J. Piore
Department of Economics
Room E52–271C
Massachusetts Institute of Technology
Cambridge, MA 02139

Daniel M. G. Raff
Department of Management
Wharton School
University of Pennsylvania
Philadelphia, PA 19104

Kenneth A. Snowden
Department of Economics
University of North Carolina
Greensboro, NC 27412

Kenneth L. Sokoloff
Department of Economics
University of California-Los Angeles
405 Hilgard Avenue
Los Angeles, CA 90024

John Sutton
Department of Economics
London School of Economics
Houghton Street
Aldwych
London WC2A 2AE Great Britain

Peter Temin
Department of Economics
Room E52–280A
Massachusetts Institute of Technology
50 Memorial Drive
Cambridge, MA 02139

Name Index

Subject Index

Accounting systems' introduction, 36

Addyston Pipe case. *See United States v. Addyston Pipe & Steel Co.* (1899)

Adelaide Steamship case. *See Attorney-General of the Commonwealth of Australia v. the Adelaide Steamship Co. Ltd.* (1913)

American Tobacco case. *See United States v. American Tobacco Co.* (1911)

Antitrust law, United States, 195–96; corporate structure protection against, 198–200; influence of enforcement on motion picture industry, 113–14, 117, 138–39. *See also* Clayton Act (1914); Sherman Act (1890)

Antitrust policy: Australia, 189, 193; Britain, 157; United States: effect on business, 201; influence on firm structural change, 156–58; influence on high-technology start-up firms, 165; influence on industrial research, 155–58, 162–63. *See also* Cartels; Common law; Freedom of contract principle; Freedom of trade principle; Mergers; Monopoly; Per se rule; Price fixing; Pricing, predatory; Reasonableness standard of enforcement; Self-regulation; Trade practices; Trusts; Tying agreements

Associations, Swiss watch companies: change in contemporary, 135–36; control of industry, 131; organization of, 130

Attorney-General of the Commonwealth of Australia v. the Adelaide Steamship Co. Ltd. (1913), 189

Banking, universal: advantages, 260, 265, 277; criticisms, 272–77; defined, 259; Germany, 258, 278; Glass-Steagall restrictions on, 272–73; industrial finance supplied in Germany (1849–1913), 283; pre-1914 limitations in United States, 270, 272, 278, 305; savings under system of, 270

Banking Act (1933). *See* Glass-Steagall Act (1933)

Banking Act (1935), 307

Banking system: Germany: role in corporate finance and control, 278, 283–88; sources of capital, 291–92; Switzerland, 133–34; United States: branch banking regulation, 270; costs of regulation, 258; role in industrial finance, 283–88; shaped by restrictions, 258; sources of capital, 291–92. *See also* Mutual savings banks, U.S.; Savings banks, U.S.

Bedaux system of industrial engineering, 42–43, 45–46

British United Shoe Machinery Co. Ltd. v. Somervell Bros. (1907), 188

Building associations: as local mortgage loan intermediaries (pre-1900), 215–21; national, 219, 221–22, 230

Capital: capital-to-output ratio: Germany and United States (1850–1913), 280–82; sources for Thomson-Houston Electric Company, 65; United States: allocation in nineteenth century, 282–83

Cartels: legal basis for participation, 158–59;